For all those involved in
child protection and welfare work

Child Protection and Welfare: Innovations and Interventions

HELEN BUCKLEY

IPA
INSTITUTE OF PUBLIC
ADMINISTRATION

First published 2002
Institute of Public Administration
57-61 Lansdowne Road
Dublin 4
Ireland

Reprinted 2003

ISBN 1 902448 73 1

British Library Cataloguing-in-Publication Data
A catalogue record for this book is available from the British Library

Cover design by Creative Inputs, Dublin
Typeset by Phototype-Set Ltd, Dublin
Printed by Modus Media International, Dublin

Contents

Foreword

Child protection and welfare remains one of the highest priorities for the Government, the professions in the field and our whole community. The title of this publication *Child Protection and Welfare: Innovations and Interventions* by Helen Buckley from the Department of Social Studies, Trinity College Dublin reflects our common concern to be ever vigilant and to be constantly up-dating our procedures and skills so that they reflect best practice. Maintaining progress has been our constant aim. The *Children First* guidelines, which were published in late 1999, are now being implemented nationwide while the passing of the Children Act in 2001 is the most recent major initiative to improve and protect the welfare of some of our most vulnerable children.

These initiatives are part of a wider programme of measures designed to ensure a more pro-active and coherent approach to children's issues in general. The National Children's Strategy which provides a blueprint for future actions has been launched. New structures, including the Cabinet Committee on Children, the National Children's Office and the National Children's Advisory Council, have been put in place to deliver the Strategy. A Bill to establish the Office of Ombudsman for children will shortly be published. One of the goals of the strategy is to promote research into children's lives and encourage its dissemination so that services will be more effective. I am, therefore, very pleased to be associated with the publication of this book which will allow the work of students of the Postgraduate Diploma in Child Protection and Welfare, in Trinity College Dublin, to be shared by a wider audience. We now have a framework and strategic goals to support the coherent development of the most modern and comprehensive services for children based on their full participation.

Finally, well trained staff are at the core of a quality service. This book is a testimony to the quality of staff working with children and their commitment to improving their skills for the benefit of the children they work with.

Mary Hanafin, TD
Minister for Children
March 2002

Acknowledgements

This book owes its existence to the contributions of a great number of people. The studies on which the book is principally based were conducted between 1990 and 2000 by students undertaking the Postgraduate Diploma in Child Protection and Welfare in the Department of Social Studies, Trinity College Dublin. The Department of Health and Children and the country's ten health boards have funded the Diploma course since it was established in 1990. Their foresight in supporting such an important opportunity for learning will, I hope, be affirmed by the dissemination of the large body of research which has emerged from it. Particular credit is due to Professor Robbie Gilligan of TCD who, together with Paul Barron, Donal Devitt and Augusta McCabe of the Department of Health and Children, originally negotiated the development of the Postgraduate Diploma in Child Protection and Welfare.

Thanks are also due to the health boards, voluntary child care organisations, the Departments of Justice, Equality and Law Reform, the Department of Education and Science and An Garda Síochána for providing financial support and time to members of their staff who undertook the Diploma course over the past twelve years. The hard work and dedication of the students must be acknowledged, along with the co-operation of their colleagues and managers and the many service users who willingly and actively participated in the individual projects. Each of the students was supervised and assisted in his/her research by academic tutors in TCD who included, over the years, Robbie Gilligan, Harry Ferguson, Ruth Torode, Helen Buckley, Shane Butler, Trish Walsh, Michele Clarke, Marie Faughey, Pat Dolan, Margy Dyas, Eoin O'Sullivan and Stephanie Holt.

A number of former students whose work is included in this book read and commented on draft chapters at various points during its gestation, for which I am very grateful. These include Samantha Ronan, Marguerite O'Neill, Breda Dunne, Patricia Flynn, Karl Heller, Carol Ann Coolican, John Edwards, Stephanie Holt, Pauline Underwood, Liz Kennedy and Sue Kane.

As anyone who has undertaken the challenge of starting a substantial piece of work will agree, the likelihood of its completion is greatly enhanced by support and enthusiasm of colleagues, friends and family. I am deeply appreciative of the interest, encouragement and help that was offered to me during what seemed like an endless period of writing by Robbie Gilligan, Shane Butler, Marguerite Woods, Eoin O'Sullivan, Conor Power, Ger

Crowley, John Collins, Karl Heller, Tom Dixon, Ger Hughes, Samantha Ronan, Richard Barker and Rosemary Sheehan, all of whose faith in the value of this work kept me going. Catherine O'Brien gave me an enormous amount of practical help throughout the entire process. My partner, Terry Odlum and my son, Shane T. Odlum, as always, provided much needed support, technical and otherwise.

Finally, sincere thanks are due to the National Children's Office, the Health Board Executive Agency and the health boards for financing the publication of this book and to Tony McNamara, Hannah Ryan and Eleanor Ashe of the IPA for their editorial expertise.

Helen Buckley
March 2002

1

Recent developments in Child Protection and Welfare

Introduction

Over the past decade in Ireland, an unprecedented shift has occurred in the public and political understandings of child abuse and child protection. Ten years ago the child welfare system was still regarded as fairly underdeveloped, with child care legislation enacted, but only nominally so, and preventive services at a minimal level of operation. Multi-disciplinary responsibility, social support, children's rights and consumer participation, some of the most significant elements of current child protection dogma, barely figured in the early 1990s. Nor was policy or practice based on any serious or in-depth study of the child protection system in this country as the knowledge base, with few exceptions, was virtually devoid of Irish research findings and dependent on the importation of studies from other English-speaking countries.

Development in the 1990s took place against a backdrop of legislative and policy reform. The Child Care Act, 1991 was enacted in 1991 and had been fully implemented by the end of 1996. In addition, two separate Children Bills were published (1996 and a revised version in 1999, culminating in the enactment of the Children Act, 2001). Other relevant legislation passed during this period included the Domestic Violence Act, 1996 and the Protections for Persons Reporting Child Abuse Act, 1998. In recognition of the necessity to integrate health, justice and education policies affecting children, a junior ministry was specially created in 1994. In 1997 the name of the Department of Health was extended to include the word 'children'. Having ratified the UN Convention on the Rights of the Child, the Government pledged its intention to appoint an Ombudsman for Children along with the continued development of the child care services, culminating in the publication in 1999 of new guidelines for the protection and welfare of children (Department of Health and Children, 1996a; 1999). In addition, the Social Services Inspectorate and the National Children's Strategy were both established in 1999 and produced their first reports in 2000. Finally, to signal its commitment to acknowledge and take seriously the damage done by previous shortcomings in its responsibility to children, the Government set up the Commission to Inquire into Childhood Abuse in 2000.

However commendable, this rush of progress in the Irish child protection and welfare system had been long overdue and its development could be said

1

to derive more from political reaction to single events than from any linear and considered passage towards a particular set of beliefs, values, policies and practices (Buckley, Skehill and O'Sullivan, 1997; Skehill, 1999). The triggers for advancement in the 1990s have undoubtedly been the child abuse inquiries and high-profile scandals that have challenged two of Ireland's strongest institutions, the family and the Catholic Church. The media have played an enormous role in both raising and reflecting public concern and much of the impetus for change emerged from publicity given to the criminal trials of perpetrators as well as some hard-hitting television documentaries about abuse in residential care. Starting with the 'X' case in 1992,[1] what now seems in hindsight to have been almost like a cultural and political indifference to maltreatment of children has been radically reformed to the point where child abuse and child protection have moved to a central position in the social milieu. The system is now characterised by a vastly expanded network of services, structures and increased accountability. These have together contributed to the new paradigm of child protection that has developed alongside a growing realisation of the value of family support, prevention, co-operation and inclusiveness. In the meantime, reports of suspected child abuse have increased by 150 per cent, bringing increased challenges to the system (Ferguson and O'Reilly, 2001).

On the one hand, heightened awareness and what sometimes seems like an inflated prevalence of child abuse and neglect can be understood in positive terms as a movement towards greater protectiveness and concern. The down side of course is a huge increase in pressure and high expectations of the services that have now been set up to respond to and intervene with the problem, along with what can be described as a naïve optimism about professional competence and ability to eliminate childhood adversity through the application of rational measures (Doherty, 1996; Buckley, 1999). The cost of this is visible in terms of the unfilled social work posts in the health boards and what is sometimes perceived to be a more defensive and narrow type of practice (Mid-Western Health Board 1998; Eastern Health Board/Impact 1997; Buckley, Skehill and O'Sullivan, 1997).

While both the implementation of the Child Care Act, 1991 and the increased focus on the safety and welfare of children have been unequivocally welcomed, some of the concurrent effects have been viewed less positively. For example, the tendency for case law to be a determinant of social policy

---

[1] The X case involved a fourteen-year-old rape victim who came to public attention when a court injunction by the Attorney General prevented her from travelling to England for an abortion. This ruling was later overturned by the Supreme Court and precipitated three national referenda on the subject of abortion and provoked major political controversy (McGrath, 1996).

has meant that disproportionate amounts of public money are being spent on specific areas that have attracted significant attention in the courts, to the detriment of preventive services (O'Sullivan, 1996). Research has also indicated that a greater proportion of resources are invested and expended in responding to suspicions of child abuse rather than in the sort of support services that may prevent abuse from occurring (Eastern Health Board/Impact, 1997). There is evidence too that even though child neglect continues to be the most widely identified and reported category of maltreatment, child sexual abuse still tends to be the most dominant and symbolically powerful form of child abuse in terms of its propensity to attract a multi-disciplinary response (Buckley, Skehill and O'Sullivan, 1997). There is no room for complacency, therefore, and it is clear that some sort of equilibrium between protective and preventive services needs to be reached before the system can be considered adequate.

Research on child protection and welfare
Section 11 of the Child Care Act, 1991 confers on the Minister for Health and the health boards the power to conduct research into any matter relating to the protection and welfare of children. Following this, a welcome and complementary development in the 1990s has been the commissioning by health boards of research and evaluation of practices. While useful studies had been conducted in the 1980s in relation to child sexual abuse (Cooney and Torode, 1989; McKeown and Gilligan, 1991) there had been a dearth of research on the practices of professionals in the child protection and welfare network. Most health boards commissioned research during the 1990s, e.g. the Western Health Board (Department of Social Studies TCD, 1993), the South Eastern Health Board (Buckley, Skehill and O'Sullivan, 1997), the Southern Health Board (Gilligan and Chapman, 1997), the Eastern Health Board (Ehb/Impact, 1997) and the Mid-Western Health Board (Ferguson and O'Reilly, 2001). The conduct of research is a crucial element of the current movement towards encouraging the sort of 'evidence-based' practice that challenges over-reliance on intuition and encourages critical reflection.

Research in an area like child protection can be problematic in certain key respects. Firstly, in relation to statistics. In theory, much can be inferred from numerical trends, for example in relation to children admitted to care on a statutory or voluntary basis, or referrals of suspected child abuse from various sources. However, the Department of Health and Children has acknowledged that Irish child protection and welfare statistics are inconsistent and therefore not completely reliable. One of the main deficits has been the lack of uniformity between health boards in terms of definitions, systems and the recording of statistical data. As a result it is difficult to make comparisons between data collected in different years, and even efforts to infer meaning from increased rates of referral for suspected child abuse must be exercised with caution. Following the implementation of new national guidelines, health boards are putting in place a system that will allow for the collection of a set of national data in the area of child protection and will ensure more accurate comparative material. However, definitional differences will always present challenges. It follows that inferences derived from national statistics must be complemented by a body of sound qualitative data that provide an explanatory context.

Secondly, evaluation of programmes and practices is an important component in guarding against what Everitt and Hardiker (1996) term 'self-justifying' activities and should ensure that the value of particular practices and interventions are made explicit, open and accountable while informing judgements with evidence. However, technical/rational approaches to evaluation that rely on description at the cost of explanation can ignore the less visible processes involved in the 'sense-making' employed by practitioners and can sometimes simply uphold poorly functioning systems. Measuring outputs, as Trinder (1996) points out, disembodies practitioners and clients and denies the social context of their lives. Most researchers in the field of child protection and welfare would now emphasise the importance of genuine and participatory dialogue in the research process, allowing the voices of consumers and practitioners to be heard from the 'bottom up'. Such methods, as Dullea and Mullender (1999) argue, are 'democratising' in intent and stress the fact that some action or change should flow from research and evaluation into policy and practice.

The third difficulty with research in child protection and welfare is that of dissemination. Part of the problem, according to Pinkerton (1998) is the number of influential social, technical, economic and political inputs that contribute to the final policy or practice output. Some of these influences have been alluded to and include child abuse inquiries and high-profile cases, as well as the effects of economic recession during the 1980s. The lack of published Irish research in this area up to the last decade has meant that government departments and agencies are unaccustomed to having a relevant body of up-to-date information from which to inform policies and practices.

However, the dearth of published research on child protection and welfare practice in Ireland gives the false impression that few studies have actually been carried out. The purpose of this book is to challenge that perception by bringing into the public domain a considerable body of practitioner research and evaluation which has been conducted in different agencies over the past ten years. The studies reported here have been completed by students of the Postgraduate Diploma in Child Protection and Welfare, a multi-disciplinary postgraduate course that was developed in the Department of Social Studies in Trinity College, Dublin in 1990. It has been sponsored by the Department of Health and Children and the country's health boards since that time. The course was initiated to assist the implementation of the Child Care Act, 1991 and one of its main components has been the Demonstration Practice Project, an agency-based practice initiative comprising a piece of action or evaluative research. Every student who has received the Diploma has produced a project that has satisfied the academic standards of the university and has addressed an issue or question relevant to child protection and welfare practice and policy in the students' own agencies.

The studies are largely qualitative in nature and have thus provided opportunities for participatory dialogue between researchers, policy makers, practitioners and consumers of the different services. Practitioner research is especially appropriate in the field of child protection and welfare. It assists workers to develop 'research mindedness' and a critical ability to accept or challenge the claims that emerge from studies or evaluations. In addition, it offers insight into the complexities and interacting dynamics that impact on professional practice, facilitates reflectiveness and also promotes understanding of the legal and policy framework within which child protection and welfare work is conducted. Importantly, the conduct of research that involves managers, practitioners and consumers of a service promotes ownership of any resulting changes. While practitioners conducting research in their own agencies must necessarily address certain ethical issues, they have the distinct advantage of 'street credibility' that often buys them the trust and co-operation of colleague participants in the different projects.

Most practitioners who undertake research in their own organisations select their topics with the expectation that the research will make a useful contribution not only to the individual organisations but also towards the knowledge base in the subject area. While the studies reported in this book have undoubtedly made a difference at a local level and raised awareness about particular aspects of policy and practice within individual organisations, their outcomes have not always penetrated beyond the borders of the individual health boards or organisations. Though the individual pieces of work are small in scale and may appear to be regional in their orientation, it is important to acknowledge that very few practice contexts are absolutely unique. Child protection and welfare practices are carried out within the framework provided by the Child Care Act, 1991 and national child abuse guidelines. Professionals are generally trained to standards set by national accreditation boards so that some claims to consistency in practices can be made. It follows therefore that all practitioners and policy makers in organisations providing services to children will derive considerable benefit from the findings of research carried out not only in their own areas, but in others as well. Many of the practitioners who completed the projects discussed in this volume have given oral presentations on their findings, and others have published papers in journals, but this book represents a unique opportunity to present a substantial body of work on contemporary topics. The fact that several projects have been carried out on similar subjects in up to three or four different health board regions and frequently have similar outcomes adds validity to the findings and considerable weight to the recommendations emerging from them. Equally, the pluralistic perspective offered by research carried out in a multi-disciplinary setting, together with the participation of a large body of service users, guarantees that the voices of all constituent groups in the child protection network are represented.

The chapters in the rest of this volume each cover a different aspect of child protection and welfare practice or policy. Current published research in each area is considered in addition to the research carried out by TCD students. For the sake of clarity and in order to differentiate between the different research sources, the studies carried out by the TCD students will be referred to as 'projects' albeit that this title may not fully reflect the depth or quality of each individual piece of work. The projects have been considered within different categories, not necessarily in chronological order but in a fashion that reflects the process of child protection and welfare work. The next chapter describes and evaluates family support and promotional programmes, including pre-school services. Chapter Three concentrates on the identification of risk or abuse, and Chapter Four goes on to describe strategies that have been put in place to facilitate referral and response. Chapters Five and Six deal with the complex area of inter-professional and inter-agency co-operation and Chapter Seven moves on to deal with interventions into cases of family violence. Chapter Eight examines the process of child protection conferences. Chapters Nine, Ten and Eleven deal with issues in out-of-home residential and foster care. Chapter Twelve explores how far parents can be involved in the child protection and care systems. Chapter Thirteen deals with the areas of supervision, support and case management in child protection and welfare work, Chapter Fourteen deals with certain aspects of the Child Care Act, 1991, and finally, Chapter Fifteen considers the main messages and implications emanating from the research. Each chapter will contain an introductory section outlining current international research and theory in the areas covered by the individual projects.

2

Prevention and Family Support

Introduction

The legal definition of child care and family support under the Child Care Act, 1991 encompasses such services as child health, speech and language therapy and dental care as well as child protection, fostering and adoption (Ward, 1997). However, as the studies to be discussed in this section will demonstrate, family support in Ireland is more usually defined in a practical sense as direct work that is carried out with vulnerable families in their communities and homes, in order to enhance their well-being and reduce stress and the risk of children either being harmed or separated from their parents.

Children First, the most recent national child protection guidance, has emphasised the importance of providing family support when children exhibit vulnerabilities or evoke concerns rather than confining interventions to situations where abuse is manifestly present. To date, as other chapters in this volume will illustrate, there has been a prevailing sense of frustration, particularly amongst health board social workers, that work with children and families is polarised between child protection and child welfare, with the latter being 'squeezed out' by the former (see Chapter Three). The objective of family support, however, is to empower rather than police families and children by reinforcing existing protective factors and compensating for those that are temporarily or permanently absent. This requires a broad and comprehensive view of needs, underpinned by knowledge, skills and resources. Research and policy documents published over the last decade in Ireland have pointed to the cost efficiency that would be achieved by concentrating resources at a primary level, not only in terms of money but also in relation to quality of life and welfare for children and families (Department of Health, 1993, 1997a; Buckley, Skehill and O'Sullivan, 1997; Eastern Health Board/ Impact, 1997). Yet, as experience in the UK illustrates, refocusing of services can be a challenging process and when public tolerance of error is high it is difficult to change from a reactive to a proactive position (Parton, 1997). However, despite the perceived slow development and under-resourcing of child welfare and family support programmes in Ireland, this chapter will demonstrate not only the extent, but also the efficacy of initiatives that have been operating over the past decade. It will begin with an overview of current literature in the area.

The nature of family support

Pinkerton (2000, p.207) cautions against the perception of family support as a 'warm and fuzzy' concept which, by being all-inclusive, means nothing. Despite its diverse nature, he argues, it can be conceived of as an invaluable synthesising term that challenges traditional welfare policies and accommodates the changing nature of families and their needs.

In order to take family support seriously, it must be grounded within an established theoretical paradigm. It is useful to consider what was first conceived of by Bronfenbrenner (1979) as an 'ecological' perspective, based on the premise that the development and behaviours of individuals can be fully understood only in the context in which they live. Within this framework, a child and family's environment is depicted in terms of concentric circles, with the child's micro system in the centre, surrounded by *meso*, *exo* and *macro* systems, representing family, community, culture and society all interacting with and impacting upon each other. This perspective makes visible the full range of factors that either support or undermine human functioning. It also allows us to see the interactions between each system, and the way that they change over time. It is, therefore, an ideal approach from which to develop social and familial supports. Jack (2000), using an ecological approach to outline key areas for assessment of children and families' needs, suggests four areas for attention:

- family history and functioning, including family composition, the effect of life events, relationships and parental strengths and difficulties
- wider family and social support, including the degree of integration into the community, friendships, peer groups and social networks
- social integration, housing and community supports, including the 'social capital' of interactions between families, friends, neighbours, work colleagues, community groups, schools and professional services that can be undermined by poverty, inequality and social exclusion
- income and employment, including a family's ability to meet basic needs, the effect of poverty and work patterns.

As Jack points out, awareness of the cumulative effects of adverse family circumstances and the potential for their negative impact on children's development through early and middle childhood to adulthood can be observed through this approach, allowing agencies to allocate their resources accordingly.

Gilligan (2000a) categorises family support in terms of informal sources that include family, kin, neighbourhood and friends, and more formal supports offered by health, social service or educational systems. He outlines three levels of support. The first level is what he terms 'developmental family support', This seeks to strengthen the social supports of children and adults in the context of their families and neighbourhoods, including personal and educational development, youth programmes and recreational projects; such supports should be universally available and not specifically problem focused. The second level is defined by Gilligan as 'compensatory family support' and would encompass services for disadvantaged families and children including early years programmes and projects directed at young people at risk of early school leaving or crime. The third level would be 'protective family support' aimed at children and families where risks have been identified, for example day care for children of drug-abusing parents, or home-based workers assisting in household and child care tasks.

An important feature of family support is its facility to focus on strengths rather than problems. A large body of work has emerged in the last two decades concerning the capacity of some children and adults to cope successfully in what are normally considered to be very stressful circumstances. Research shows that this ability, normally termed resilience, can protect from risk and disadvantage particularly when fostered and developed by the provision of material and emotional supports (Quinton and Rutter, 1988; Daniel, Wassell and Gilligan, 2000). Family support taps into the resilience of children and parents and finds ways of maintaining and developing it.

Boushel, Fawcett and Selwyn (2000) identify the key players in the provision of child and family welfare services as the family, local community, voluntary organisations, private charities and the state. They describe the approach adopted in the UK over the past decade in an effort to achieve 'joined-up' services focusing on needs and outcomes through strategic national planning within a framework of national priorities, goals and standards with designated lead agencies. This aim has been endorsed by the 'Quality Protects' programme launched in Britain in 1998 which sets out eight national objectives for social services departments. It was also influenced by the publication of a Home Office Consultation Paper entitled 'Supporting Families' which led to the development of Sure Start, an initiative designed to enhance the physical, psycho-social and educational development of children under four years of age living in disadvantaged communities.

It must be acknowledged that the development of family support services in Ireland is not as strategically integrated as the system operating in the UK appears to be, and has a lower profile than child protection work. Yet, there has been a long tradition of social services involvement with families at a primary level. Some programmes are well established, though limited to particular geographical areas. The Community Mothers scheme, in which locally recruited volunteers visit and share their parenting skills with vulnerable parents, has been running in the Dublin area for almost two decades (Johnson, Howell and Molloy, 1993) along with Homestart, a voluntary visiting and support scheme for isolated parents (Gilligan, 2000a). An initiative launched in 1998, known as the 'Springboard Project', probably represents the most concerted effort by central government to provide services of this nature, though it is as yet confined to a limited number of designated disadvantaged areas. The results of an interim evaluation carried out on the first five months of the project in operation indicate a small but positive impact on the lives of children and parents in the one hundred and twelve families who have received services (McKeown, 2000).

One of the reasons why the existence of family support programmes in Ireland has been perceived to be either inadequate or overshadowed by child protection services is their lack of visibility and the disparate nature and spread of services, rather than their absence. It is also due to the fact that they operate on a low-key, non-clinical and local basis and are thus more integrated in the communities in which they operate. This chapter will now illustrate the extent of family support programmes that have been operating and expanding in Ireland since the early 1990s, and will demonstrate their effectiveness through a number of locally and regionally conducted evaluations. It will begin by looking at family support at primary level, examining projects related to health promotion, teenage pregnancy, infant welfare and services for parents and young babies. It will then go on to discuss and analyse the impact of community and home based projects conducted at secondary and tertiary levels.

Health promotion and primary support for parents and young children
The subject of education on adolescent sexuality and pregnancy was studied in 1992 by Margaret Acton, at the time a public health nurse in the Eastern Health Board. She was keen to develop the potential for health promotion and sought a way in which it could be delivered to her clients in a relevant and manageable fashion. The high proportion of teenage lone mothers in the area also raised the need for attention to the health and welfare issues pertinent to this group. Acton was aware from both her experience and from research literature that many young girls coped very well with motherhood. However, she was also conscious of the problems caused by their being thrust into the role of parent without either maturity or training and observed a need to target this group for education and consciousness raising with regard to the demands and responsibilities inherent in parenthood. Her study was informed by the large body of literature that existed on the subject. Research had shown the association between teen parenthood and poor nutrition, low levels of general health, poverty, social isolation, educational deprivation and

psychological difficulties such as depression and low self-esteem (Barth and Schinke, 1983; Roberts and Endres, 1988). Studies also highlighted predisposing factors linked with teenage pregnancy including dissatisfaction at school, desire for adult status, need for affection and wish to keep a boyfriend (Hudson and Inchiechen, 1991). In addition, there was evidence to show that some teenage parents are less aware than older parents of their children's emotional and psychological needs (Johnson, Loxterkamp and Albanses, 1982; Landy, Cleland and Schubert, 1984).

Acton decided to target groups of fourteen and fifteen year olds in secondary schools in her area. She was working on the assumption that schools did not normally provide the opportunity for students to explore teenage parenthood and may in fact regard this topic as sensitive because of its link with sexuality. She speculated further that teenagers would respond positively to a health promotion exercise such as this, with the possibility that girls might react in a different manner than boys. Acton sought the necessary approval and organised four one-hour sessions in three schools, two of which were in working class areas and one in a middle class area. All together, sixty-six third year students took part in the project. One of the groups was mixed, with an almost equal number of boys and girls, and the others were all girls. In the middle class school, only five pupils took part, while in the working class schools, an average of twenty pupils participated in each session.

Each session consisted of an introduction and short talk about the issues involved in teenage pregnancy and parenthood. Acton showed a video illustrating relevant points and then introduced an eighteen-year-old single mother to the classes to talk about her own experiences. A discussion followed and the students were then asked to complete a questionnaire and carry out a two-part 'parenting project' over the next few days. The first part of the project consisted of spending time with and observing the activities of a teenage parent of their acquaintance. The second part involved spending four consecutive hours 'caring for' an imaginary baby, represented by an object such as an egg or a bag of potatoes, and taking note of all the demands and tasks involved. The participants then completed a questionnaire giving details of their experience. Finally, all the teachers concerned completed a questionnaire on their impressions of the project.

Students responded with interest to the sessions in school and looked for additional information on teenage pregnancy, abortion, contraception, sex education, parenting, relationships, drugs, budgeting, diet and AIDS. The comments of all participants suggested that they had not previously considered the difficulties associated with teenage parenthood, including tiredness, lack of money, and poor job prospects. All agreed that the classroom discussion encouraged them to give more thought to the subject.

The parenting projects were completed by forty-one of the students. Their reported observations demonstrated their surprise at the amount of time spent by parents on tasks like feeding and nappy changing and the difficulty in getting babysitters. The happiness and excitement associated with pregnancy and birth were acknowledged by the students but they also commented on the feelings of worry, uncertainty and tiredness experienced by the young parents. The baby-minding exercise was considered worthwhile, interesting and educational by the students, who noted how restrictive and demanding child care could be. Most concluded that they themselves would not be ready for such a challenge.

Data collected from the teachers indicated that the project was of more interest to girls than boys, who found it less relevant. In general, all the teachers judged the exercise to have been worthwhile, taking the 'glamour' out of teenage parenthood and raising the awareness of the pupils about the reality of the less attractive aspects. Teachers in the working class schools suggested that a similar programme should be incorporated into the school curriculum. In the middle class school, however, the teacher felt it had limited relevance and that the subjects of biology and religion were sufficient to meet the needs of the pupils.

Acton concluded that the project had been successful in enabling the students to reflect on the reality of teenage parenthood, and noted their need for more information and the gaps in their understanding about certain areas. She observed the difference in the reactions of teachers in the working class and middle class schools, linking the lesser degree of concern about teenage parenthood with the brighter and more affluent futures anticipated by children in more comfortable social environments.

Action recommended the development and expansion of her project to all schools in the area. She noted the need to devise methods of promoting the topic to make it more engaging for boys, and the requirement to update the video material and make it more relevant. Through the programme, she expected that teenagers would be better equipped to make decisions and widen their options beyond early parenthood.

Staying on the theme of teenage pregnancy, a project conducted in 1996 by Claire Barry, at the time a worker in a family centre based in North Dublin city, examined the provision of ante-natal services for this group. Like Acton, she was aware of research data that highlighted the extra vulnerability of teenage mothers and their babies and also drew attention to their tendency to attend ante-natal care late and often reluctantly (Simms and Smith, 1986). From her experience of working with parents in the family centre, Barry was familiar with the stresses associated with child rearing and her aim was to explore the need for intervention at a primary preventive level. She was aware that special clinics were operated for pregnant teenagers in the Coombe

Hospital in Dublin and that special parenting courses for young people were run in different areas. However, she argued that, in the absence of evaluation, the efficacy and value of these services was unproven. She sought to find out firstly, if a special service was desirable and relevant and secondly, if her own centre might be an appropriate location for such a service.

While Barry would have preferred to conduct her study through focus groups with pregnant adolescents, the feasibility of this approach was curtailed by the fact that, because of the unpredictable pattern of clinic attendance by teenagers, the hospital she contacted was unable to give her a list of potential interviewees. As an alternative method, Barry opted for a discussion group with seven public health nurses and a questionnaire survey of thirty-nine professionals (public health nurses, hospital staff, family support workers and social workers) of whom twenty-nine responded. She administered a suitably amended version of the questionnaire to five mothers who had given birth in their teens and were now attending her family centre. She was conscious of the limitations imposed on her research by her failure to ascertain the views of service users during pregnancy and by not involving the fathers of the children whose mothers she interviewed. The latter deficit was largely due to time restrictions, but she also noted that more than half of the fathers were no longer in contact with either the mothers or children and considered that this issue warranted a more extensive study.

The principal findings in Barry's study related to two areas. Firstly, the need to provide specific services for teenagers. There was an interesting conflict of opinion in relation to this, where a professional from the maternity hospital in the area offered the view that specialist services were unnecessary as, in her view, teenagers coped adequately in mixed groups. This contrasted with the views of the mothers interviewed, who unanimously agreed that specific services would have been more acceptable and appropriate in their cases. Professionals in the community also agreed that the provision of a special service was necessary. The public health nurses suggested that problems may not manifest themselves for several months or years and early intervention to deal with immaturity, loss of freedom and isolation could pre-empt or lessen the negative effects of some difficulties. There was less agreement between mothers and professionals on the nature of services to be provided, the professionals prioritising parenting skills and emotional support, and the mothers favouring the provision of crèches and practical advice, including areas like cooking and housekeeping.

The second major issue highlighted by Barry's research was the difficulty in engaging teenagers in any type of ante-natal service. The mothers identified the reasons for reluctance to attend services as shyness, nervousness, fear of going alone, fear of their babies being taken into care, and in one case, fear that a partner would be charged with statutory rape as the mother had been under seventeen.[2] Professionals identified similar reasons and suggested that mothers were often unaware of the importance of planned ante-natal care. Professionals also linked low uptake with shortcomings in the service as well as poor co-ordination between agencies. The public health nurses suggested that key factors in encouraging uptake of ante-natal care would be an improvement in its image and the involvement of mothers' extended family members in a supportive manner.

These findings affirmed Barry's original hypothesis that a service for teenage pregnant girls was necessary and could be provided by the centre in which she was employed. Considering the sometimes differing views expressed in the study regarding the nature and content of such a service, she emphasised the necessity to involve consumers in the design of programmes. She made the following recommendations:

- further research, to ascertain the views of teenagers during pregnancy
- joint input into the design of services, to include the views of consumers, community-based personnel and staff of maternity hospitals
- consultation at a local level between professionals and An Garda Síochána to find a way of dealing with underage pregnancy in a non-threatening way
- efforts made to engage extended family and mothers' partners
- appropriate advertising of the service.

On the basis of her findings, Barry recommended that her own service establish a pilot pre-natal group, to be evaluated from the perspective of participants.

Like Acton (1992) and later, Barry (1996), Ann O'Sullivan, at the time a social worker in a health board adoption service in the Southern Health Board, was concerned about the vulnerability of adolescent mothers to health and social problems and the consequent effects of these difficulties on their babies. O'Sullivan carried out a study in 1994 with the dual aims of exploring the experiences of a group of unmarried adolescent mothers and identifying the services most likely to enhance their welfare and that of their children.

O'Sullivan located her study in an area in North Cork that conforms with national indicators of social disadvantage, having a high rate of unemployment, early school leaving and children entering state care. It also has a higher than average rate of lone parents. O'Sullivan noted that in

---

[2] *Children First* has attempted to address this dilemma by devising a strategy for joint consultation between An Garda Síochána and the health boards in such cases. However, the current legislation continues to pose difficulties for professionals who believe that the law impedes young girls from seeking ante-natal care.

common with the UK, Ireland's rate of teenage pregnancy is actually falling in relation to pregnancy in older women, but still represents a significant figure. In common with Acton (1992) and Barry (1996), O'Sullivan cited international research findings to the effect that the health risks to teenage mothers and their children are higher than is the case with older mothers. She also quoted evidence that the children of adolescent mothers receive less psychological and emotional care and, as a group, experience developmental delays in comparison with the children of older mothers (Rothenberg, and Varga, 1981; Butler et al, 1981; Fry, 1985). However, as O'Sullivan argued, there is research evidence to show that when studies are controlled for social disadvantage, the relevance of the age of the mother is considerably reduced. She also illustrated the manner in which disadvantage perpetuates itself, e.g. the fact that early school drop-out is associated with pregnancy, and the way that further education can be curtailed or impeded by the demands of child care.

In order to try and identify the type of services most needed by teenage parents, O'Sullivan carried out in-depth interviews with ten mothers between the ages of seventeen and nineteen years, all of whom were caring for babies aged between six weeks and seven months. She asked them about their housing and financial situations, their educational attainment, the level of social and emotional support available to them and their general health and diet. She also sought to observe their attitudes to their babies and the level of stimulation they offered them and while she considered her own judgements in this area to be severely limited by their subjective nature, she considered them a useful complementary source of data. In order to fulfil the second aim of identifying relevant services, O'Sullivan held a seminar with a range of professionals working in the area of family support and ascertained their views.

O'Sullivan found that finance was a major issue for the mothers, the majority of whom were still living at home with their own parents for economic reasons in addition to their wish for support. Two had returned home after trying independent living, but wanted to leave again. Nine out of the ten mothers, including those living at home, were finding it very hard to manage on their social welfare payments. The tenth mother was working and was managing reasonably satisfactorily. Only three of the mothers had ongoing relationships with their babies' fathers who included the only two fathers out of the sample who were employed. Most of the mothers had not completed any state exams. A considerable number had completed FÁS courses and the majority of them had left work because of their pregnancies; only two had any intention of returning to work.

Although O'Sullivan felt that the research tool, the General Health Questionnaire (GHQ) used to measure the general health of the participants was not entirely appropriate (it was designed for adults with mental health problems), she found indications that seven of the young mothers suffered from psychological problems including unhappiness, isolation and depression. She found that none of them had used contraception prior to pregnancy and was left with the impression that their awareness and knowledge about sexuality and pregnancy was very limited. The study also indicated that most of the mothers had unsuitable and unbalanced diets, though their babies were adequately fed, mainly on formula food. However, none of the babies had been breast-fed.

The babies had all suffered various ailments including chest infections and gastro-enteritis, but at the time of the study were in good health. Although all the mothers said they had friends and confidantes and had received practical support from family and friends, O'Sullivan considered their social networks to be very confined and identified a need for some means of linking them to the wider community. O'Sullivan considered the parent-child interaction to be good in all cases and noted that the mothers all responded to their babies in her presence by talking to them, comforting them and playing with them. She did not use a research tool to measure these factors and acknowledged the limited nature of her personal observations but nonetheless considered them to provide useful complementary data.

One of O'Sullivan's most significant findings was that while the mothers all identified service needs, such as parenting groups, information services and befriending schemes, they had shown little interest in attending a family centre. Most of them valued their contact with public health nurses, but none of them was prepared to approach social workers about their child rearing difficulties, expressing fear and distrust of them.

Overall, while she considered all the babies well cared for at that point in time, O'Sullivan pointed out that the mothers' socio-economic circumstances, general physical and mental health, diet, and social and emotional support were areas that required attention.

When the findings were presented to a multi-disciplinary group of twenty-five professionals providing services to families and children, the need for outreach and consumer-led services was endorsed. The need to try and redress the negative image of social workers and family centres was acknowledged, as was the necessity of providing sex education for adolescent mothers. O'Sullivan concluded by recommending the development of the Community Mothers Scheme in the area, sex education at different levels including the education system but also for groups of young mothers, and the development of a breast-feeding programme targeted at young age groups. Finally she recommended a forum for channelling the views of young mothers in order to improve the uptake of services in the community.

It is a well-established fact that child care and maternal health are best promoted through interventions that encourage, amongst other practices, breast-feeding. Its benefits are known to be not only nutritional, but strongly associated with the development of healthy attachment between mothers and infants, thus promoting effective protective factors. The strategy adopted by the Department of Health in 1994, *Shaping a Healthier Future*, identifies an increase in the rate of breast-feeding as one of its targets, and in line with this, Teresa Keegan, at the time a public health nurse in the Eastern Health Board, carried out a study in 1994 with the dual aims of identifying the reasons underlying expectant mothers' choices of infant feeding options, and exploring ways of offering support and encouragement to breast-feeding mothers.

At the time of her study, Keegan was seconded by the health board as a Family Development Nurse in the Community Mothers Programme and carried out her research with the assistance of some other personnel engaged in it. She distributed questionnaires to a group of twenty-five pregnant women between the ages of eighteen and twenty-six from her area which she had defined as socially disadvantaged. The questionnaires were completed in either the women's local health centre or at the ante-natal clinic in a large maternity hospital. Fifteen of the women were without marital partners, but the findings did not indicate whether or not they were in long-term or cohabiting relationships. Keegan invited the women to indicate their choice of feeding method, the reason for it, the nature and source of information they received about breast-feeding and the point at which they had received the information. She also asked them for their perceptions regarding the benefits or otherwise of breast-feeding. The findings indicated that half of the expectant mothers had made up their mind about the method of feeding in advance of the baby's birth, with only 20 per cent choosing to breast feed. When asked for their reasons, the most commonly offered one was embarrassment, followed by the demands it would make upon their time. While half of the women indicated that they had reached their decision without being influenced by anyone else, only just under half of those had actually received information about breast-feeding during their pregnancy and some had received what they perceived as conflicting advice. Only one third had attended ante-natal classes, and almost two thirds believed that there was no difference between breast and bottle.

In addition to her survey, Keegan set up a support group, to meet on a pilot basis for four sessions at the health centre. The participants in the group were either breast-feeding mothers or women who were still pregnant and had opted for breast-feeding. She also arranged for a period of intensive home visiting of breast-feeding mothers by public health nurses and Community Mothers. While the number of women attending the breast-feeding support group was small and their attendance was not consistent (an average of three attending each of four sessions) the participants said that they found the meetings useful. The aims were to improve mothers' self confidence in their capacity to breast-feed, to prevent isolation and to address the problems and topics that arose in the groups. The first meeting addressed the benefits of breast-feeding, preparation for breast-feeding, diet, and stages of pregnancy. The second discussed birth and delivery, the mechanics of breast-feeding and coping with sleep patterns and negative attitudes. The third session covered growth, colic, expressing and storing milk and coping with older children, and the fourth covered feeding in public, going back to work, introducing bottles, and diet. Overall, it appeared to Keegan that mothers attended the group when they had a problem or needed information. She concluded that while the group meetings were useful, some mothers might require the additional support of home visiting.

Notwithstanding the presence of a number of complex social factors already cited in the literature, Keegan concluded that a strong link existed between the low rate of breast-feeding and lack of information and support. She was careful to distinguish between strategies of simply passing on information in the form of leaflets and those which provided opportunities for the women to react to it and participate in further discussion. She pointed out that while written health education material is useful and relevant, it is geared towards middle class and literate consumers and may need to be adapted for clients with different backgrounds and skills. Like Barry (1996) she found that one of the impediments to the dissemination of information was the low uptake by expectant mothers of ante-natal classes, suggesting the need for some review of their content and accessibility. While Keegan emphasised the importance of respecting clients' wishes and views, she suggested that greater effort should be put into gaining their interest and confidence, which may lead to their openness to different and ultimately more beneficial feeding options for their infants.

Keegan recommended early education about breast-feeding, starting in schools, along with the presentation of breast-feeding as normal and natural. She suggested the tailoring of ante-natal care to meet the needs of target groups and to include the promotion of breast-feeding. Finally, she recommended the dissemination of accurate and timely information.

Pre-school and early years services

Good quality child care in early or pre-school years has long been regarded as important to children's development and the quality of their later life (Hayes, 1999; Boushel, Fawcett and Selwyn, 2000). As well as having an obvious social function, child care in Ireland has recently become politicised by the combination of mothers wishing to return to the workplace and a serious labour shortage, both of which have highlighted the shortage of facilities

(National Child Care Strategy Report, 1999). In the light of this additional pressure, it is all the more important to ensure that child care arrangements are conducive to the enhancement of children's welfare and are of the highest quality possible.

Part VII of the Child Care Act, 1991, implemented in 1996, obliges health boards to inspect pre-school services in their areas. This legislative measure represents an important step in ensuring a minimum level of quality and safety in child care. From a child protection perspective, pre-school services have also been the focus of attention in a number of ways. For example, partial or full day care for young children has become recognised as a useful tool redressing the imbalance often later experienced by children from disadvantaged situations (Hayes, 1999). Nurseries, pre-schools, child-minders and play-groups are in a position to offer help to families and children who experience stress and disadvantage, and are well placed to minimise or even prevent difficulties from developing into abuse and neglect. While Irish statistics are not available, it has been established in the UK that the age range most at risk of child abuse is 0-4, highlighting the vulnerability of pre-school children (Corby, 2000). Early interventions into cases of child abuse and the provision of support to families have been shown to have a considerable impact on future outcomes in terms of an enhancement in welfare, reduction in harmful or neglectful episodes and a decline in the likelihood of separation of children from their parents (Gilligan, 2000a; Stevenson, 1998).

A project to assess the needs of children attending play-groups and evaluate the quality of services available in Co. Clare was carried out in 1994 by Geraldine Neylon, a playgroup organiser for a voluntary organisation known as Clarecare. This project was completed prior to the implementation of Part VII of the Child Care Act, 1991, but provides a useful and complementary framework for assessing the quality of care provided in pre-school settings.

Neylon set out to try and establish the percentage of pre-school children attending playgroups in order to ascertain if the service was reaching the client group for which it was intended. In addition, she attempted to evaluate the standards operating in the group in relation to training of staff and the nature of playgroup activities together with location and safety issues. One of her concerns was the fact that, given low state support for early years services, the pay and conditions offered by playgroups were unlikely to attract trained staff, thus affecting the overall quality of experience for children.

Neylon selected nine playgroups out of a possible twenty-four in the county for participation in the study. These groups were catering for a total of two hundred and eight children. Extrapolating from the census of population and the figures she obtained from the Irish Pre-School Playgroups Association and the National Montessori Association, Neylon estimated that only one in five children in Clare between the ages of three and four were attending playschool. She speculated that lack of transport in rural areas, and the tendency to send children to school early to boost pupil numbers, were partly responsible for the low attendance rate.

In order to measure the prevalence of behavioural problems in playgroups, and thereby establish where and in what context extra supports and specially trained staff might be required, Neylon applied an established behaviour screening instrument (McGuire and Richman, 1986) to her sample. The instrument consisted of a questionnaire with a range of pre-scored responses to be completed by the playgroup leader in relation to a child's concentration, speech and language, interaction, habits and the degree to which the child's behaviour was a cause for concern. The results indicated that 12 per cent of the children overall exhibited difficulties over the threshold for acceptable behaviour. There was a definite pattern whereby 15 per cent of children from urban areas manifested behavioural problems as against 7 per cent from rural parts, with similar results for boys and girls. The highest cluster of those over the threshold was in a playgroup for Traveller children, with 31 per cent exhibiting problem behaviour, all of whom were girls. These findings, in Neylon's view, could provide assistance to policy makers in their attempts to assess the needs of children from different environments. They also illustrated the necessity for services to be equipped to meet specific challenges.

To evaluate the overall quality of the groups, Neylon devised a system for scoring the ability of playgroups to provide for the developmental needs of pre-school children. She measured them in terms of the training of leaders, variety of play provided, provision of messy play, and room layout and safety. She found, as she suspected, that training and qualifications differed considerably. Some of this she attributed to the fact that playgroup leaders are poorly paid and are often trained to a very basic level. Three out of the nine leaders did not reach a satisfactory standard in terms of their qualifications. However, as Neylon cautioned, this finding has to be judged in relation to the other scores, as she found that one leader who was highly trained did not perform well in relation to the other areas examined. Over two thirds of playgroups (seven out of nine) reached the satisfactory score in relation to the range of play provided, and eight out of nine were judged satisfactory in relation to the provision of messy play. One third of groups were judged to have unsatisfactory facilities in terms of room layout and safety, some sharing their space with other community groups in the same building. In Neylon's view, such a lack restricted their ability to provide appropriate activities and this was confirmed by the fact that the one group that did not provide adequate messy play came into this category.

Neylon recommended the provision of an established training programme for playgroup leaders, capital investment in premises, the establishment of a data base of pre-school services and comprehensive provision of a range of day care including childminders and crèches. While the implementation of Part VII of the Child Care Act, 1991 has, in the meantime, addressed some of these needs, Neylon's project provides a useful model for the evaluation of current services. Additionally, it covered areas such as the quality of care and educational experience not necessarily addressed by the legislation.

Another project examining pre-school services in a rural setting was carried out in 2000 by Brenda Conway, a pre-school services officer in the South Eastern Health Board. Unlike Neylon's project, Conway's study was completed after the implementation of Part VII of the Child Care Act, 1991 and had the benefit of a legal framework from which to judge the quality of the service. In light of the statutory obligation imposed on the health boards to promote the welfare of children, Conway's study set out to explore pre-school services as a means of family support and to examine the options available to the SEHB for supporting and developing pre-school provisions. She also aimed, by means of her project, to empower local women to establish and operate their own pre-school.

The principal element of the project was the setting up of a community playgroup in a rural town which was bereft of any accessible pre-school services. In stages, Conway met with health board colleagues and recruited interested volunteers from the local community. Together, they located potential premises and agreed a strategy. Conway accessed funding for the playgroup from the SEHB and other voluntary organisations in the county and the premises was refurbished with appropriate and safe fittings and equipment. As a next step, training was provided for interested volunteers in two-hour sessions over eleven evenings by a multi-disciplinary group of health board professionals. Eleven women from the area participated in and completed the training. The community playgroup was advertised locally and commenced for three mornings a week with ten children, with a plan to expand and admit fifteen children for five mornings a week.

In order to introduce an evaluative element into her project, Conway conducted a focus group discussion with nine of the community volunteers who had participated in the training programme. She sought information on how the women had heard about the proposed playgroup, the factors that had motivated them to become involved and their views on the usefulness of the training. In the discussion, the very positive attitude of the community was expressed in relation to the provision of pre-school services, both to suit their own children and to fulfil their wishes to contribute to the well-being of the community through working with children. Most had heard about the proposed plan from their public health nurses, through word of mouth, or in the local parish newsletter. The training was considered useful, 'down to earth' and relevant. While they found the sessions on child protection very challenging, they learned a lot about managing children's behaviour and about the value of play and the need to consider children's feelings. They felt that it had benefited the community in terms of raised self-confidence and a sense of achievement. In terms of the long-term value of the playgroup, the women generally agreed that the children attending it had gained and that both they and the children had new and welcome opportunities to socialise. They expressed a wish for ongoing training and support to enable them to deal with issues as they arose and emphasised the need for a protocol on the age limits to be applied.

Conway noted the importance of engaging key community 'figures' such as the parish priest or the school principal in a positive way, given their power to influence the development of a project such as this. She had found that health board involvement in the development of the project had an image-enhancing effect and promoted co-operation between the community and the board. She suggested that the already proposed establishment of a County Child Care Committee by the Department of Justice, Equality and Law Reform would provide an opportunity for co-operation with the health boards with a view to delivering training on a joint basis. She also proposed that the role of the pre-schools services officer should be developed to provide ongoing advice and support to community projects.

Family support services provided to children, young people and families at a secondary or compensatory level
Family support services at a secondary or compensatory level are intended to meet the needs of children where some level of vulnerability or risk has been recognised and brought to the attention of a child welfare professional or agency. Many of the services are run by non-statutory organisations, and referrals tend to be channelled through social workers, An Garda Síochána, public health nurses and other professionals who have had previous involvement with the child and family. Admission is then usually determined by the fit between the child's needs and the facilities offered by the service and is often assessed by an inter-agency team comprised of representatives of the health board as well as the agency providing the service. Children are admitted for various reasons including delayed development, parental illness or addiction, domestic violence, behavioural or educational problems, truancy or involvement in juvenile crime.

Barnardo's have a long tradition of providing support services for children and families who are considered to be vulnerable. Their programmes are based in the community, the most popular and well established one in Ireland being the day nursery service for pre-school children. Two projects reported here focus on aspects of the day nursery service, one in relation to a specific activity and the other in terms of an overall assessment.

In 1992 Andrew Logue, at the time a senior manager in Barnardo's, carried out an examination of the recording practices in a day nursery. He considered the accurate and consistent recording of information to be essential to the ability of staff to complete certain tasks, including assessing the suitability of children for admission, measuring the progress of children in the centre, judging the degree to which their difficulties at referral were being addressed and involving parents in their day-to-day activities and tasks. He was aware that a good level of informal communication already existed in the nursery, and sought to explore the degree to which this was reflected in records.

Logue conducted his research by examining files and observing the interactions of staff together and with parents. He looked at the files relating to fifty children including current attenders and some who had left during the previous year and found a dearth of information in these records which consisted mainly of referral forms and notes, with child care plans in only about half of them. He also noted a fairly significant difference between the problems that were mentioned in the referral forms and those that were later noted by staff. This, in his view, reflected a gap in perception that could have been addressed earlier if recording practices had been more accurate and consistent. Interestingly, he noted that child care plans devised prior to 1991 were confined to addressing children's development and behaviour in the nursery, whereas later records contained more discussion of issues pertaining to their home environment and involving their parents. This, Logue asserted, reflected the growing confidence of staff and their awareness of the importance of the child's wider social network.

Logue's participant observation in the nursery setting demonstrated that a lot of important information concerning the children was exchanged freely among staff members during coffee and lunch breaks, but not recorded in writing. He also observed that much communication took place between staff and parents at the beginning and end of each nursery day which, again, was not recorded.

Reflecting upon his findings, Logue observed that already busy staff were unlikely to respond positively to the additional task of file-keeping, nor were they trained in the technique of recording family problems to the same extent as other professional staff. He therefore extracted from a British policy document, *Working Together* (Department of Health, UK, 1991), some examples of genograms, ecomaps and flow-charts which he believed would adequately reflect a lot of the everyday information that required to be recorded. Their use was discussed at a staff group meeting, and an example given of the economical yet relevant means of recording that they provided.

In addition to the implementation of these recording tools, Logue made additional recommendations including:

- an examination of recording practices throughout the organisation
- guidelines for staff regarding the status of information
- the adoption of recording techniques suitable for court.

Logue concluded that the implementation of improved working practices, as well as assisting the assessment of progress, would enhance the potential for parental involvement through information sharing.

Staying with Barnardo's day nurseries, Brian Kenny, at the time a senior manager in the organisation, conducted a study in 1995 to assess the level of satisfaction with the services and consider any necessary changes or improvements. He sought the views of parents of children in the nurseries, staff members, referring professionals and their managers, by means of group interview with the first three sets of respondents and individual interviews with the latter. In all, twenty-two persons participated in the study. Kenny was aware of the possibility that his position as a senior manager might influence the responses of participants, so he viewed his project as an exploration of the level of general satisfaction with the service rather than a formal evaluation of its effectiveness.

Kenny focused on two day-nursery services in two specific areas of Dublin, both associated with high levels of poverty, lone parenthood and unemployment. He was aware from his experience and from the literature of the need to provide integrated services that fitted in with all of the child and family's needs and contexts and of the importance of parental participation in the nursery work.

Assertions in the literature about the value of early childhood services were confirmed by the interview data. From their different perspectives, respondents commented on the positive impact that attendance at the nursery had on the children, from improvements in challenging behaviour to progress in speech and language skills and preparation for school. Public health nurses commented on the way that the nurseries offered a stimulating experience to the children while providing respite for parents. Referring social workers saw the service as enabling parents to seek help in a non-threatening environment while at the same time providing the workers with an opportunity to monitor the children's safety and welfare.

Respondents also commented that liaison and relationships between themselves and Barnardo's were good. There was positive feedback about the current level of involvement with parents and enthusiasm for more. The need for extra provision of places and continued flexibility about accepting referrals was highlighted. A number of improvements were suggested, including the development of more services directed at parents and specifically for fathers.

Given the very positive response to his assessment, Kenny acknowledged that change was needed to improve rather than radically transform existing programmes, particularly in relation to the issues of planning, parental involvement and provision of varied and flexible services. While parental involvement was already satisfactory, he acknowledged that its maintenance and development would depend on the physical accessibility of services, a factor that has implications for the location of a nursery. In his view, the day nursery service did not always form part of an overall planned approach to meeting the child or family's needs. A more integrated approach, he suggested, would focus on the reasons why children were offered places, review their progress and identify what other services they would need as they leave the nursery. Like Barry (1996) he identified the need to have parents involved in the planning process, in order to ensure that their needs were being targeted. Likewise, he considered that the integration of services would mean, in certain cases, the provision of complementary outreach work or liaison with children at home and continual assessment of the need for new and more varied programmes.

Kenny concluded that the implementation of his proposed changes would require the following:

- written agreement at admission regarding the reason for referral
- agreement with parents around mutual expectations
- initial liaison between individual, group and referring workers
- formal reviews involving parents and referring workers
- after-school programmes for 'nursery graduates' who require extra attention, with support for parents
- provision of 'aftercare' for parents and children leaving the nursery, by making links on their behalf with other relevant services or establishing some self-help activities
- increased parental participation through staff training and ensuring accessibility of services
- appropriate help to meet parents' personal needs
- establishment of parents' advisory groups
- publication of available services each September
- afternoon work with nursery attendees where appropriate
- alternatives to nursery such as home-based work
- availability of emergency places.

Finally, Kenny recommended that Barnardo's, as part of an overall effort to promote family support services, should endeavour to highlight its day nursery and early childhood work as an effective strategy.

Neighbourhood Youth Projects
Neighbourhood Youth Projects (NYPs) could also be described as providing

family support at a compensatory level. However, their informal and open method of connecting with consumers and their community base makes them more accessible than some projects where eligibility tends to be determined by defined need. As a consequence, they have the opportunity to make early interventions into families before difficulties become clearly visible. Two separate NYPs, one in Cork and one in Galway, were the subjects of projects. The first was undertaken in 1993 by Pat Dolan, at the time a manager in an NYP managed by the Western Health Board in Galway. His action-based project was specifically geared towards promoting parental participation and partnership.

For the purposes of his study, Dolan designed and conducted a course for a group of parents of the 40-60 young people attending the NYP. He based it on three principles: firstly, that successful preventive work with children implies intervention with their parents who can reinforce progress achieved within the project; secondly, that the more positive the image that parents hold of themselves and the better the relationship they hold with their children, the more they can act as emotional resources to them; thirdly, that parents need a basic support network in order to parent effectively.

Dolan enlisted the assistance of a health board social worker, another project worker, a home-school liaison teacher and a psychologist to run and evaluate the course. Its core objectives were:

- to increase the involvement of parents in their own right in the NYP
- to provide parents with an opportunity to share child care concerns
- to provide parents with an experience that would raise their self esteem
- to contribute to the process of integrating the NYP with the community.

Parents of all children attending the project were circulated with information, invited to attend a meeting and visited at home by project staff. Ultimately, eight parents 'signed on' for the course, consisting of seven mothers and one father. All of them had experienced difficulties with their children dropping out of school, exhibiting challenging, anxious or depressed behaviour including suicide attempts and running away. Most of them acknowledged that their relationships with their children were poor. Administration and measurement of the General Health Questionnaire (GHQ) rating scale indicated that the majority of them suffered from significant levels of stress and psychological difficulties.

The course consisted of six sessions devised in advance and adapted during the process to meet identified needs. The first session was aimed mainly at making the parents comfortable and allowing them to get to know each other. The next two were about parenting – identifying positive qualities in their children, looking at styles of parenting, locating their principal supports and building up their self worth as parents. The fourth session was geared specifically towards raising the parents' self-esteem through art therapy, the fifth was about anger management and discipline, and the final session was aimed at reviewing and integrating their learning from the entire process. Project staff made home visits to the parents during the course to encourage their continued attendance and help them deal with matters that had arisen during sessions.

Attendance throughout the course was 80 per cent, with all absences accounted for in advance. The first three sessions evoked powerful reactions from the parents, many of whom were desperately worried about their children and welcomed the opportunity to discuss their various difficulties. The art session proved successful in giving individual members the opportunity to produce something of their own, and the session on anger management and discipline elicited a lively interest and debate. Discussion in the final session indicated that each member had gained considerably in terms of knowledge and confidence.

The programme was evaluated by means of attendance records, evaluation sheets, re-administration of the GHQ instrument, and analysis of feedback at the last session. All these measures indicated that the course had been successful, with the GHQ indicating a significant improvement in the mental health of participants in terms of lowered anxiety, depression, social dysfunction and somatic symptoms. In the final session, the parents gave examples of their increased ability to listen to their children, to communicate better, to trust and praise their children, and to feel confident as parents.

Acknowledging the success of the project, Dolan analysed the key factors that helped it to achieve its aims. He considered the supportive home visiting to be crucial in maintaining attendance. In relation to the group process, the less directive and more facilitative approach taken with the parents was considered essential to building their confidence. Treating parents with respect, reinforcing their strengths, and focusing on their own needs to care for themselves as well as providing pleasant and relaxing experiences for them was, in Dolan's view, a significant factor in raising their self-esteem. An important element of the project's success was the ability of the project staff to work as a team. This was achieved by meeting together after each session and applying the same principles that were applied to parents, that is, honesty and respect for each other. Such practices meant that at times the team members needed to challenge one another but ultimately facilitated them to overcome disagreements and continue to work together successfully.

Dolan was satisfied that all the course objectives had been met. He noted that an additional positive outcome of the parents' participation in the course was an increase in the rate at which they visited the project, rising from four visits per week prior to the course to ten visits afterwards. By the time the course had concluded, project staff had agreed to run similar courses and interest in co-participation had been expressed by two other agencies. Dolan made the following recommendations:

- that the NYP make working with parents a policy objective
- that parental involvement should not deflect from the principal task of working with young people but should be part of it
- that future courses should be run on an inter-agency basis and a parent counselling facility should be developed with other agencies
- that evaluation methods should be considered for work with young people as well as with parents
- that parents who have successfully dealt with child care issues could themselves be trained as group leaders
- that the use of parenting courses be explored by NYPs on a national basis.

The second NYP-based project was carried out in 1996 by Pat O'Connell, at the time a worker in the Mayfield NYP in Cork. While Dolan's project had concentrated on including parents, O'Connell's focused on the young people participating in the project and sought to explore their views on various aspects of the service it offered. He conducted a focus group with three boys and three girls aged between 11 and 12, and individual interviews with six girls and six boys aged between 13 and 15 years. All of the respondents had experience of at least two of the methods of work carried out in the project. The questions were aimed at eliciting the views of the young people in relation to their first impressions of the project, the operation of the project, the different methods of work carried out, and their ideas in relation to how the service might be improved. The principal methods of work operating in the project were 'open house' (youth club), individual work, group work and family work.

The data from interviews clearly showed the positive image of the project held by the young people; they appeared to find it a friendly, busy place that they enjoyed attending. Though one of the respondents considered it to be a place for children 'in trouble', the remainder of the interviewees saw it in non-stigmatised and positive terms as a child-centred organisation.

The children had been asked if they were aware of any bullying or name calling and over two-thirds claimed that both behaviours prevailed in the centre. However, as O'Connell observed, their claims that they would report any such behaviour to the staff conflicted somewhat with actual practice where in fact very few reports were made. At the same time, the young people demonstrated a lot of trust in the leaders whom they seemed to hold in high esteem. When asked what they would miss most if the centre closed, the majority identified the games and the leaders.

While the older children expressed a preference for group activities, the younger ones tended to favour individual work. The 'open house' activities appeared to be very popular, though the girls would have preferred if more of their female peers attended it and suggested that more could be done to attract girls. As O'Connell pointed out, most of the youth leaders were male and suggested that this might be a cause of the gender balance in attendance. An interesting finding was the fact that while most the young people thought that family work was valuable, they thought that sessions should take place in their own homes rather than the centre, because home was more private. Some respondents, however, showed a preference for sorting out their problems without the involvement of their parents, a factor which O'Connell considered to be associated with their need for independent identities and one which endorsed their child-centred approach. On the basis of his findings, he recommended that staff should encourage the young people to take more of an active role in family work and be involved in a way that made them feel more like partners.

Home-based family support services

A model of family support that has become increasingly popular and has been adopted by a number of health boards since the early 1990s is the provision of intensive home-based services, an adaptation of the traditional model of homemaker designed to meet specific needs that have been identified in family situations where children are considered vulnerable. This model provides secondary and tertiary levels of family support to prevent the occurrence or reoccurrence of child abuse and to maintain family unity and stability, thus obviating the need for children to enter the care system. The work can be varied, from the provision of emotional support, to help and guidance in relation to practical household and child care tasks including counselling and behaviour management. However, as the following section will show, family support must be focused, purposeful and based on a comprehensive assessment of each family's needs if it is to be successful.

Four projects were conducted between 1995 and 1998 to evaluate the models operating in different health board areas: the Eastern Health Board, the Midland Health Board, the Mid-Western Health Board and the Southern Health Board. The geographical spread and contemporaneous nature of these studies provide not only a comprehensive picture of the type of services operating but a consistent profile of the challenges inherent in this type of work and the type of infrastructure that is essential to its success.

In 1997, Liz Donaghue, at the time a family support co-ordinator in the Eastern Health Board, based in Kildare, carried out a study to explore current family support provision in her area with a view to identifying the type of families targeted and the perceived effectiveness of the current service together with means of enhancing it. The service had been operating in Kildare since 1991 and had been initiated as a response to the increasing rate of child abuse referrals in the area. Donaghue administered questionnaires to social workers currently working with the twenty-five families in receipt of the family support service. On the basis of the data obtained through this process, she constructed a profile of family support service users. She then selected four families for closer study, and conducted in-depth interviews with the two social workers and two family support workers involved with them. Finally, she facilitated a group discussion with her colleagues in order to highlight issues for further development.

Donaghue's findings indicated that 68 per cent of the families in receipt of the service were headed by a single parent, including two fathers. The concerns that led to referral to the service were mainly related to neglect, poor parenting capacity and an identified need for support in broad terms. Most were receiving between four and seven hours family support from the health board each week. The family support workers and social workers reported a range of aims for the service, most of which were underpinned by the ideal of enabling families in a positive, creative and non-judgemental fashion that included supporting them in whatever decisions and plans they made themselves as long as the safety and welfare of the children was assured. It was thus defined as an empowering rather than a directive service, though the workers fully acknowledged that a degree of coercion may be necessary at times in order to reach a working agreement. The social workers and family support workers were clear about their separate roles, the family support worker being more supportive and the social worker being primarily protective. The necessity for family support workers and social workers to work together, support each other and review progress regularly was emphasised.

The social work responses to the questionnaire interview identified the positive effects of the service on the families in terms of a reduction in reports of neglect, improved parent-child bonding and insight into children's developmental needs, development of good child care routines, rise in parental self-esteem and confidence and improved communication between families and services such as general practitioners and schools. When asked to use De Shazer et al's (1986) progress rating scale of one to ten (one being the situation when the family was referred, ten being the situation if a miracle occurred) two families got a rating of five, one of six and one of eight.

In order to identify firstly, the key factors in the success of the current model and secondly, ways in which this success could be enhanced, Donaghue probed the views of the workers. Several critical factors were cited, the principal ones being the need for clarity of objectives, recognition of the demands of the tasks and the often limited capacity of families under stress. It was considered that unless realistic goals were identified, the intervention could be set up to fail at an early stage. The personal skills of family support workers in engaging with families in an empathetic fashion and persisting until they found 'the root of the problem' were seen to be vital.

The infrastructure within which family support workers were employed was considered important, including the appointment of a full-time co-ordinator to set objectives and review progress. It was felt strongly that the value of the service should be reflected in the way family support workers were treated in terms of conditions like training, supervision, status, pay and mileage, and resources such as materials and room to work with children.

Importantly, it was felt that child protection teams needed to move away from 'general case conference recommendations' to more specific and realistic objectives for family support work. The need to develop allied services to complement the work done at home, for example after-schools programmes and youth activities, was identified.

Several other important themes emerged from Donaghue's study. She was interested in finding out if the social workers and family support workers felt that work should be time-limited and task centred. Respondents suggested that both these models of work could be highly appropriate in certain situations, but that in general there was a need for flexibility. It was pointed out that some families took a long time to engage with and respond to the service, and therefore needed longer interventions. The view was also expressed that concentration on specific tasks often masked underlying difficulties and hence could be counter-productive. The greatest challenge, in their view and in the view of Donaghue's social work colleagues, was dealing with the ambivalence often manifested by families in difficulty. Once this barrier was removed, the potential for working in partnership was greatly enhanced. A suggested method of dealing with ambivalence was the presentation of services as attractive. This would have the dual function of enticing participation and reducing stigma through universal acceptance.

Donaghue recommended that conditions of employment for family support workers should be improved by the provision of supervision and training. She suggested that the Kildare Family Support Service should make itself available to a range of families, not exclusively those targeted as 'at risk'. She also recommended the development of a two-strand approach, i.e. short term and long term, in order to meet the complex and varying needs of families.

A project which looked in particular depth at the work of family support workers was conducted in 1998 by Gildas Gordon, at the time a senior social worker in the Mid-Western Health Board. He began by conducting a survey with family support workers on the eighty-one cases receiving family support services in the Limerick community care area. By this means, he established that the prime objectives of the workers were similar to those in Donaghue's (1997) project, including direct work to support families and individuals, building relationships within families, working to develop parenting skills, self-esteem and communication, and guiding families towards problem solving. The primary duties of the workers were home visits to carry out direct work, facilitating access visits, administrative work, attending case conferences and reviews, and liaison with other agencies. The family support workers identified the need for training, evaluation of the existing structure, improved communication and links with colleagues and other services, along with regular team meetings. However, Gordon considered these data to be limited given the impersonal manner of data collection, in comparison to the nature of information he later ascertained from in-depth interviews with one family support worker and two social workers involved in three cases.

In general, Gordon found that the family support inputs in the three cases were very successful. Each of them involved lone mothers. There had been, at referral, a combination of concerns involving domestic violence, mental health problems, child neglect and coping capacity. In each case, the option of removing the children to care had been considered prior to the involvement of the family support worker.

Though two of the mothers in the cases had initially resisted engagement, it was perceived that their self-esteem and confidence had increased through contact with the family support service. Improvements in the quality of their child care and home management were also noted. Confiding relationships had been established between the worker and mother in all situations. In each case the parents eventually managed to achieve certain tasks that had previously appeared too challenging, such as dealing with a school with regard to a bullying incident, reporting sexual abuse that had occurred many years earlier, and dealing with a troubling legal matter. In all three cases where support had been minimal beforehand, members of the extended family had now become involved in a helpful way. All mothers had become more adept at linking in with other services. Concerns about removing the children into care had abated in each case at the time the study was conducted.

When he analysed the key factors underlying the success of the service, Gordon found the following elements to be of significance:

- the three-way meeting at the start of involvement, between the family, family support worker and social worker
- the regularity of family support worker contact
- the support provided to the family support worker by health board colleagues, particularly social workers
- flexibility of family support worker to respond to unique circumstances as they arose

- availability of family support worker to do in-depth work over a long period, including the development of trust and openness with parents
- the practical and non-threatening approach of the family support worker
- the home-based nature of the work
- the efforts made to promote parental co-operation and partnership.

The case examples highlighted a number of issues about preventive work. Gordon noted that the families who had been offered the family support service by the health board had certain characteristics in common, principally isolation, lack of a supportive extended family or community network, along with personal stresses. Likewise, he pointed out that many of them had previously been in contact with a number of agencies, but that service provision from these had been uncoordinated. He was aware that family support services act as secondary interventions and are generally only offered to families who have come into contact with the health board. Often this contact is the result of a concern about the children, precipitated by a crisis and frequently associated with consideration about removing children to care. Gordon questioned whether the crises might have been averted altogether if community and family supports had been stronger, thus making a case for more work to be carried out at a primary level.

Like Donaghue (1997) Gordon highlighted the delicate balance between voluntary acceptance of a family support service and the sort of motivation created by the threat of having children removed into care. He emphasised the importance of parental co-operation, without which the family support process would not succeed. He noted that despite the difficult and fraught circumstances in the case examples, efforts to promote partnership were clearly beneficial and worth the effort. Gordon also acknowledged the tension between child protection and family support, noting the imbalance in service provision between the low ratio of family support workers to social workers and the fact that such important work is done by unqualified, temporary, low-paid workers on a part-time basis.

In conclusion, like Donaghue (1997), Gordon recommended that attention be paid to the employment conditions and level of support available to family support workers, and training between family support workers and social workers to enhance co-operation. He highlighted the need for further study in relation to the broader effects of family support work and the efficacy of the service in terms of keeping children out of care. In particular, he recommended that further research should reflect the views of users.

Two other projects, carried out in 1995 by Ria Opgenhaffen, at the time a social worker in the Midland Health Board (MHB) and in 1997 by Anne Beechinor, at the time a social work team leader in the Southern Health Board (SHB), succeeded in reflecting the views of service users. Their studies

provide a useful basis for comparison insofar as the services they examined
were set up quite differently and reflect some interesting issues. Both projects
sought to evaluate the effectiveness of family support services in their areas.
The service in the MHB had been set up in 1992, and the service in the SHB
somewhat later, in 1995.

In the area where Opgenhaffen conducted her study, the ratio of family
support workers to social workers was five to nine. Unlike the areas studied by
Gordon (1998) and Donaghue (1997), the MHB offered their family support
workers full-time, permanent employment, travel expenses, annual and sick
leave and provision for time-in-lieu. As in the other areas, the workers were
accountable to the social work manager and liaised closely with the social
workers on the team. The day-to-day co-ordination of the service was
assigned to an area social worker who conducted weekly supervision sessions
with the family support workers.

In common with the other projects considered here, Opgenhaffen aimed to
identify the family support needs of vulnerable families and investigate the
effectiveness of the family support system as it operated. She interviewed
seven social workers, five family support workers and five families availing of
the service. She added an extra dimension by interviewing five families who
had declined to avail of the service.

Opgenhaffen noted that thirty-four families in her community care area
were in receipt of the family support service at the time of the study. Four-
fifths of them were lone parent families where the parent was not working
outside the home. During the same year, fifteen families had been offered, but
declined, the service. These, she noted, were mostly married families where at
least one parent was employed outside the home. While it is not specified in
the study, it is implied that the families' refusal of the service did not result in
compulsory measures. Presumably it is possible to infer that the level of risk
and vulnerability was lower because of the supports and material resources
available to them.[3]

The professionals interviewed by Opgenhaffen expressed similar views to
those in other studies in relation to the purpose of the service, seeing it as the
provision of support to vulnerable families at a practical level with a view to
empowering them to cope on their own. The families receiving the service
also saw it as practical and supportive. They appreciated the companionship,
the advice on how to deal with children's behaviour, and the boost it gave to
their self-confidence.

[3] An alternate perspective to this, offered by Thorpe (1994), would suggest that the
child protection system targets unorthodox or marginalised families, particularly those
headed by one parent, paying less attention to those who conform to the societal norm
of respectability.

Addressing the problem of the reluctance of some families to accept the service, social workers who were interviewed by Opgenhaffen speculated that suspicion, lack of trust, and a sense of threat and fear of being undermined were the root causes. However, family support workers regarded the challenge of engaging families as simply part of the job and found that while it might take time, it was generally achievable. Both social workers and family support workers expressed views similar to those reported in Donaghue's (1997) and Gordon's (1998) later projects, stressing the importance of parental motivation and suggesting that a key factor in attaining it was the ability of workers to 'sell' the service well. The responses of the parents who declined the service affirmed the views of the social workers, claiming that the lack of privacy and fear of their weaknesses being exposed were the main reasons for their refusal to accept it. All parents, including those who did not avail of the service, expressed the importance of joint agreement and ownership of family support plans, clearly emphasising the importance of openness and respect for their own views.

It was the norm in Opgenhaffen's area for the social worker, family support worker and family to draw up a written agreement, which was approved and reviewed by the co-ordinating social worker. While family support workers found this to be a valuable tool, social workers pointed out that some families may be less literate or less able to fully grasp the meaning of the agreement than others and, in some cases, the family support worker's role was not always clear from the outset. The families who were interviewed were generally in favour of the agreement, believing it to represent the shared nature of the decision to work together.

While the need for more training and resources was identified, in general all the participants in Opgenhaffen's study were satisfied with the level of service provision. This project usefully highlights the benefits of a well-structured service that is freed from everyday stresses and enabled to get to grips with the tasks of engagement with and empowerment of clients. On the basis of her findings, Opgenhaffen emphasises the importance of partnership, signified by the written agreement and the flexibility of workers to respond to the needs of families as they arise. She concluded with the following recommendations:

- the development of ongoing training for family support workers and social workers in the area of family support
- the provision of resources to enhance the work of family support workers
- the expansion and broadening of the service to include support groups for parents and children
- dissemination of information about the family support service by the health board.

The Southern Health Board, the location of Beechinor's (1997) study, developed its family support service in 1995 with the creation of child care worker posts in each team. Beechinor set out to examine the service being provided by one of the teams and to make recommendations for future development. She was very conscious of the challenges involved in providing a preventive service in the context of increasing referrals of child abuse cases and aimed to examine the feasibility of providing a two-strand service of family support and child protection, from the one department. As a pre-cursor to her study, Beechinor interviewed child care professionals from three other health boards in order to hear their experiences of providing family support services. She noted the trend in other health boards towards the development of what she described as 'purpose built' family support services with an ethos of prevention, flexibility and 'working with' rather than 'doing for' people. She also became aware of the specific qualities and training of the workers and the budgetary arrangements along with the fact that in other health board areas, the role of child care worker was regarded as distinctly different from family support worker. Armed with this information, Beechinor sought to explore whether the current structure in her board should be modified in order to make a stronger distinction between the family support service and the child protection service.

Beechinor interviewed the four part-time (family support) child care workers, a full-time child care worker also assigned to family support work, two other full-time child care workers not assigned to family support work, four area social workers and four parents in receipt of the family support service.

Data from the interviews with practitioners revealed some discrepancies in their perceptions of the roles of child care worker and 'family support worker', despite the fact that tasks were effectively carried out by the one group. While all had a clear idea of the nature of family support work required, there appeared to be some ambiguity about where responsibility for it rested, or whether the workers should be child or family focused in their work. The child care workers acknowledged that the lack of guidelines and a clear job description resulted in differing perceptions about their aims, and caused confusion in the minds of other professionals. It also caused them to feel unconfident about the worth and meaning of their professional roles.

When parents were interviewed, however, the value of family support was endorsed by them. The profile of service users was very similar to the other health board areas discussed in this section. Three-quarters of the families in receipt of the family support service were headed by a lone parent and experienced a sense of isolation. Three out of the four interviewed by Beechinor had been positive about receiving the service from the beginning, with one having expressed initial reluctance. As in the other health board areas, the families found the service helpful, identifying particular elements such as having someone to talk to, share problems with, 'put order into a chaotic house', advise with behaviour management, and encourage children to help in the house and share some responsibilities.

Beechinor concluded that while the family support work currently being undertaken in her area was useful and effective, its potential was impeded by the lack of a clear structure for both the employment of staff and clarification of the aims of the service. She argued that a satisfactory balance between child protection and family support work required an input of necessary supports and resources, and the development of a specific service building on the experience and knowledge of those already engaged in the task. She also advocated further research on a larger scale to measure the impact of family support work.

Provision of a post-adoption service
From the early 1990s onwards, a group of children with particular needs became visible in Ireland. These were the infants and young children adopted under inter-country adoption legislation, many of whom had spent the first part of their lifetimes in institutions. There is considerable research evidence to indicate that while children adopted from institutional care may attain a high level of physical and psychological 'catch-up' when they are securely placed, they have a higher than normal potential to experience developmental delay and emotional, behavioural, educational and health problems (Rutter, 1998, 1999; Johnson, 1999). It follows that families who adopt children from sending countries where the level of care is very basic should receive compensatory and supportive post-adoption services in order to address existing problems and pre-empt the development of later difficulties. While it is fair to say that many families continue to receive support from the health board social workers who carry out their assessments, none of the health boards, up to the year 2000, was providing support in the form of a formal post-adoption service. A project on this subject was carried out in 2000 by Marie Symonds, a social worker specialising in inter-country adoption, based in the North Eastern Health Board. She carried out interviews with the parents of ten children who had been adopted from Eastern Europe. Her aim was to explore any difficulties that the children might be experiencing, the services used by the families and the parents' perceptions of the effectiveness of the services and supports available to them. She selected ten children who had been institutionalised prior to adoption and had been with their adoptive families for more than one year and where certain problems requiring services had been identified. In order to avoid any potential conflict of interest or compromise, she excluded families who were

intending to apply for further adoptions. Three of the families were from her own health board region and the remaining seven were from other areas.

The children in the selected families ranged in age from two and a half years to eleven years. Eight had been adopted from Romania and the two remaining had been adopted from Russia. All had been in orphanages. As all the families had visited the institutions from which they had adopted their children, they were in a good position to comment on the conditions therein.

Data from the interviews illustrated that most of the children had been small for their age on adoption, though they had caught up in the meantime. Six of the ten had needed speech and language therapy, all but one had exhibited attachment problems at some stage, and eight of the ten had educational difficulties. Between them, the families had availed of thirty-six different services for children, including psychotherapy, speech and language therapy, child guidance, play therapy, psychology and a range of medical services. In the interviews, seven of the ten sets of parents expressed dissatisfaction with the services they used. The three sets of parents who were reasonably satisfied had adopted their children relatively recently and were still in contact with the social workers that were completing the post-adoption interviews as part of the assessment requirement. In Symonds' view, the support they gained through that contact might have enabled them to access services more confidently.

The difficulties identified in relation to the services provided to the children included the length of time waiting, for example for psychology and for speech and language therapy. Two of the parents pointed out that it seemed to take a crisis to eventually link them with the services. Some families were critical of the inappropriate nature of some of the services that did not necessarily meet their children's needs. They acknowledged that the children's needs were often complex but felt that the professionals they encountered just did not have the necessary skills or knowledge to either correctly diagnose their child's difficulty or provide an appropriate intervention. For example, some suggested that public health nurses who visited them were unaware of the conditions their children had experienced in the orphanages. In Symonds' view, the parents were not unrealistic in their expectations of treatment where their children were concerned. Most, she claimed, were very aware of the effect of early trauma and were anxious to reduce their children's level of suffering or distress and enable them to reach their full potential. They appeared to be highly sensitive to some negative attitudes they had encountered from professionals and from the general public, including the assumption that had 'imported problems' or that they might not love their children because they were adopted. Most of the parents interviewed had found that other adoptive parents provided them with the most valuable support. They were also positive about neuro-psychology, psychotherapy and sensory integration therapy.

Symonds identified a particular difficulty for parents who have adopted children from other countries: their anxiety about being judged as inadequate if they are seen to be experiencing parenting difficulties. As she pointed out, this can be a particularly sensitive issue in a climate where views about inter-country adoption can vary from those which consider adopters to be humanitarian to those which consider them to be racist and exploitative. She also commented that as adoptive parents have the same rights as birth parents, they could not be compelled to accept help. However, on the basis of her findings, Symonds argued that children adopted from institutions in Romania and Russia should be regarded as having special needs and given every support and opportunity to grow and develop in as healthy and normal a way as possible. She asserted that post-adoption services should be made available to all adoptive families who share many concerns about culture, identity and telling children about their adoption.

On the basis of her findings, Symonds recommended that her health board adopt a formal policy on post-adoption services. She also suggested the development of some measures to connect adoptive families, such as newsletters and local support groups. Importantly, she emphasised the need for the health board to take a lead role in informing and educating their own staff about the issues involved in adoption of post institutionalised children. Finally, she advocated the availability of a social worker to help families access services if they are experiencing difficulties and suggested that social workers facilitate groups for adopted children.

The provision of a pastoral service in schools
Children of school-going age can find the experience of loss and change in their family circumstances to be very challenging. For example, adolescents whose parents divorce may have difficulty dealing with the conflicting loyalties and sense of fear and insecurity that might result and can often display regressed behaviour and under-achievement (Wallerstein and Kelly, 1980; Burgoyne, Ormonde and Richards, 1987). Children who lose a parent through death can experience anxiety, fear, reluctance to leave their surviving parent, anger, sleep disturbance and poor concentration (Wagner, 1995). Unchecked, many of these negative outcomes can severely impact on a child's developmental progress and general well-being. Aware that loss can be a significant issue amongst school-going children, Teresa Bradshaw, a secondary school teacher in a girls' school, undertook a project in 1998 to explore how a school might best support their students through this difficult period by implementing a specific curriculum.

Bradshaw employed a multi-method research approach. Firstly, she surveyed class tutors to ascertain the number of students who had experienced death or separation in their immediate families and subsequently checked the returned questionnaires against school records to confirm the results. She then examined the case studies of six students whom she knew were presenting challenging behaviour and all of whom had recently experienced loss of a parent either through death or separation. She obtained data for this exercise through school records and discussion with school colleagues as well as her personal knowledge of the students concerned. At the same time, she planned, designed and taught a module on the theme of loss to junior students with an average age of fourteen years. Finally, she evaluated the module by means of questionnaires completed by the students.

Bradshaw's initial survey results indicated that over 20 per cent of the 700 students in her school had experienced varying degrees of loss of a parent or sibling. This, in her view, was evidence that schools ought to provide some kind of structured response in order to provide assistance to the affected children and create a supportive atmosphere in the school. The six case studies illustrated common themes of depression, behaviour disturbance, erratic attendance, deterioration in academic performance and concerns about the general well-being of the children involved. These findings again confirmed the need for teachers to have some skills and knowledge in the areas of bereavement and loss, yet Bradshaw was aware from her discussions with colleagues that these were subjects about which many of them felt distinctly uncomfortable. An existing programme called 'Rainbows' which is run on an extra-curricular basis was operating in some schools in the area, but when Bradshaw surveyed a sample of the schools involved she found that the separateness of the programme from normal school activities acted against its success and attractiveness. She concluded that a classroom-based approach would be more suitable, and designed her module accordingly.

Bradshaw piloted her module, called 'Coping with Change', with a group of fourteen-year-old pupils. She was careful to address the ethical issues that arose by ensuring that she was in close contact with students at all times during the classes and in a position to monitor their responses. She also ensured that options were available so that the students did not feel pressurised to participate in aspects of the programme that they might find too stressful and that support was available for anyone that needed it. The module consisted of five lessons that dealt with the feelings that present when loss occurs, the images used to portray loss, the students' own experiences of loss, the typical problems associated with it and the best means of supporting friends and colleagues who had experienced loss and grief. The final session included an evaluation of the module by the students. In general, they indicated that the sessions were worthwhile, interesting and helpful in enabling them to understand both their own and other people's feelings and emotions. They appeared to have welcomed the opportunity to voice their thoughts and opinions. Bradshaw noted that no students expressed the need to approach the school counsellor after working on the theme of loss and bereavement and that no parental concerns were voiced to either herself or school management.

Analysing the outcomes of her project, Bradshaw concluded that it was absolutely vital for schools to respond to loss issues amongst students and to employ a clear and decisive policy in order to prepare staff and students to respond to the impact of death and separation on individual young persons. While she was aware of the limitations of her project, she recommended the implementation by schools of a similar module into their pastoral care system. This, she concluded, would facilitate them in providing a more nurturing environment.

Conclusion
These studies have illustrated the breadth of family support work already operating in Ireland under the Child Care Act, 1991 and have highlighted some key issues. The projects on health promotion illustrate the social, economic and psychological difficulties experienced by some teenage mothers and, by inference, their developing children. One of the most concerning factors indicated was the need to find a way not simply of providing services, but of making them attractive and accessible to service users. The gaps in information and education about sexuality, pregnancy, contraception and nutrition show that despite the provision of programmes, significant topics still remain to be addressed with some potentially vulnerable groups. The other issue that permeated all the studies on pregnancy and early infancy is the lack of engagement by young men, firstly in education about sexuality and related matters, and later in fatherhood. This is clearly an area requiring extensive study, but in the meantime is worth noting and pursuing by practitioners and policy makers.

The need to establish quality standards in early years settings to cater for different groups of children was elucidated, along with the necessity to integrate day services with other community services. Most of the studies highlighted the importance of involving service users in the planning and delivery of programmes, a practice which should assist the delicate and essential process of relationship building between professionals and families. Importantly, the research highlighted the requirement for health boards to invest in adequately resourced and structured services that reflect the value and essential nature of the work.

While the tension between child protection and family support will not be easily resolved, there are hopeful signs that preventive services are gaining recognition and currency. *Children First* has signalled their importance by including a chapter offering guidance on their nature and delivery (Department of Health and Children, 1999). The development and ongoing evaluation of the Springboard Projects (McKeown, 2000) has given a much needed impetus to the formalising of family support services and drawn attention to the potential for preventive work to make a real difference.

To achieve an integrated level of service provision will ultimately require the resolve of policy makers, managers, administrators and practitioners right across government departments, organisations and community and voluntary agencies. Tunstill and Aldgate (2000) have argued, in relation to practices in the UK, that the nature of statutory responsibility is frequently misunderstood by social services departments and has been seen as synonymous with child protection investigation. The studies discussed in this volume could imply that similar norms operate in Ireland, yet there is evidence that in many health board areas, original and creative work is being carried out with the intention of promoting the welfare of children and families. It is essential that the profile of family support is given as important a position in the official discourse of child protection as investigation and assessment. This will require the adoption of a mind-set which affirms the notion that prevention and social support are the building blocks upon which children's ultimate safety and welfare depend. Preventive services should, as Pinkerton (2000, p.223) argues, represent 'an instance of the state's relationship to civil society' and reflect a commitment to ensure social capital for all citizens, particularly those most at risk.

3

Identifying Children at Risk: Policies, Procedures and Practices

Introduction

The Child Care Act, 1991 compels health boards to identify children in their area who are not receiving adequate care and protection. The operationalisation of this responsibility requires professionals who work with children and families to understand the causes, signs and effects of child abuse and neglect. It also obliges them to have the skills and knowledge necessary to identify a child who may be at risk or may have already suffered abuse. This chapter discusses a number of projects undertaken to enable professionals and organisations to recognise and intervene early with suspected child abuse and either prevent its reoccurrence or take decisive action to protect a child from further harm.

Deficits in children's welfare manifest themselves in a range of different situations during early, middle and late childhood and are potentially visible to a range of practitioners. These include child minders, child care workers, residential workers, teachers, youth and community workers, family support workers, public health nurses, medical staff and social workers in different organisations. Health board social workers are generally regarded as central to the process of co-ordinating assessments and responding to suspected child abuse. However, as a professional group their workload is organisationally defined to the extent that concerns are normally identified, not by themselves, but by other practitioners or members of the public. For this reason are they usually one of the last links in a chain of professional recognition of child abuse and neglect.

On the other hand, those who work with what might be described as 'universal' populations of children, for example as carers, nurses or teachers, are generally accustomed to a wide continuum of standards in child care, from excellent to satisfactory, good enough, not quite good enough, to poor or dangerous. This experience means that they are not only knowledgeable about and experienced in child welfare and child development, but are well placed to observe a child who is troubled, hurt or neglected. For this reason, they have an essential role to play in the recognition and assessment of children's protection and welfare needs. However, as child abuse inquiries in Ireland and the UK have shown, many disciplines and agencies lack information, procedures and structures for piecing together information and

43

referring concerns to statutory agencies. These deficits have at times resulted in a failure to intervene and protect children (Department of Health, 1993; Western Health Board, 1996; Reder, Duncan and Gray, 1993).

While the matter of inter-agency co-operation and communication in child protection work is dealt with elsewhere in this volume, this chapter looks at methods of identifying, recognising and intervening early with children who are deemed to be abused, at risk of abuse, or vulnerable in some respect. A number of projects carried out by practitioners in recent years have sought to evaluate policies and design guidelines for practice within voluntary organisations providing services to children and train staff to recognise and act on their child abuse concerns. The organisations concerned include a regional pre-school inspection service, a co-ordinating and developmental agency for early childhood services, an agency for children with learning difficulties, a youth service and three residential units providing court referred assessments and/or ongoing care for children who have been in trouble with the law. The order in which the projects are discussed here reflects progress through different stages in the child protection process rather than the order in which the studies themselves were conducted. The first four projects to be considered were specifically concerned with the role of public health nurses in child protection work, the first two concerned with training and the latter two dealing with the identification of vulnerable children and families.

Training programmes for public health nurses on the identification of suspected or actual child abuse

The Report of the Kilkenny Incest Investigation (Department of Health, 1993) was one of the first official documents to recommend training in child protection for all professionals, including public health nurses. The need for training, however, had been identified by public health nurses in response to the implementation of the Child Care Act, 1991 which drew them, as health board employees, into the network of professionals with statutory responsibility for the safety and protection of children. In response to this, a number of training initiatives was undertaken during the early 1990s with the objective of enabling public health nurses to understand and carry out their new responsibilities.

The first of these was conducted in 1992 by Deirdre O'Rourke Higgins who was at the time a public health nurse in the Mid-Western Health Board area. She undertook two half-day training sessions with thirteen participants in each, with the objectives of providing public health nurses with a forum to discuss child protection and welfare issues, understand their roles, explore their work practices and share information and knowledge. She engaged the assistance of an experienced group worker in her area to advise her on the conduct of the training seminars and to assist in facilitating some of the sessions.

O'Rourke Higgins carried out an informal training needs survey through separate informal discussions with fourteen public health nurse colleagues. She ascertained that the public health nurses were interested in increasing their knowledge of child protection and child abuse including risk factors and child sexual abuse validation, case conferences, the roles of other professionals in the network, existing resources, procedures, and guidance on how to advise parents of suspicions. She noted that they had particular concerns about the role of the key-worker and particular aspects of child care law.

The seminars, as well as covering the above issues, included brainstorming exercises in which the participants were invited to identify questions about the various topics and then asked to work out ways of addressing them. Overall, the post-seminar evaluation sheets completed by the participants, together with feedback during the seminars themselves, indicated that the training had been worthwhile, though too short. A minority were uncomfortable with the group format. Some had been uneasy at the presence of senior management in their own profession at the seminars. Contrary to O'Rourke Higgin's expectations, only one of the group favoured the idea of inter-professional training. In her view, this inferred a need for further debate in order to enable the public health nurses to clarify their own roles.

O'Rourke Higgins observed and analysed the key issues that emerged from the various exercises, discussions and general feedback. These reflected the principal concerns experienced by public health nurses in relation to their child protection and welfare responsibilities and offered useful pointers for consideration. An important point discussed was the limited extent of public health nurses' flexibility in practice, explained by their heavy and varied caseloads and the structure within which they were employed. The fact that their work was weighted on a quantitative rather than a qualitative basis was also cited as a reason. Some debate had taken place on the question of public health nurses adopting a key worker role in child protection cases, with some expressing the view that they might jeopardise their role as a 'trusted confidential advisor' by doing so. However, O'Rourke Higgins' view was that a child's safety was more important than a professional's 'friendly' image and she argued that the reluctance displayed by the public health nurses should be challenged. While some of the participants had expressed a lack of worth in their child protection skills, particularly in relation to parents' rights, others suggested that they were all sufficiently qualified and experienced to carry out the key-worker role. The issue of client confidentiality and the best way to handle anonymous referrals was also the subject of some discussion. The public health nurses were, in O'Rourke Higgins' view, 'overwhelmed' at the implications for them contained in the Child Care Act, 1991 and expressed a need for more intense and specific training in relation to it (see the discussion on Kingston's [2000] project in Chapter Thirteen of this volume for a more specific discussion on legal training for public health nurses).

O'Rourke Higgins made several recommendations on the basis of her analysis. These included further training on the specific areas identified, including child care law, confidentiality, and the role of the key-worker. She concluded that public health nurses should take a pro-active role in changing work practices rather than reacting to current needs and that future training should be extended to include other professionals and agencies.

Another project on training for public health nurses was conducted in 1994 by Dorothy Meehan, a public health nurse in the NWHB, based in Donegal. Having reviewed the literature on the increasingly important role of her own profession in child protection work and being aware of the level of stress involved, she highlighted the absence of both supervision and specific training for nurses in the area, reflecting a situation common in most health boards during the early 1990s.

Meehan designed, conducted and evaluated a training day for twenty public health nurses in the region. The topics covered included the implications of the Child Care Act, 1991, bonding and attachment between parents and children, social indicators of risk, medical signs of child abuse, the statutory responsibilities of the public health nurse, and children with abnormal behavioural problems. The programme included inputs from the superintendent public health nurse, the director of community care, a psychologist, a social worker, the health board's legal advisor, a paediatrician and a child psychiatrist. Evaluation of the training day was conducted through post-training questionnaires.

The one-day training programme was, as Meehan later observed, somewhat over-ambitious in its aims. This is a common occurrence and usually a result of enthusiasm and a desire to hurriedly address an accumulation of perceived deficiencies all at once. Meehan estimated, from both her observations and the post-training evaluation, that at least two days would have been required in order to satisfactorily address the topics and provide adequate time for discussion. Nevertheless, the public health nurses' evaluations of the event indicated that it had been worthwhile, with the majority claiming to have gained both knowledge and reassurance from their participation in it. The evaluation also illustrated that while most public health nurses felt they lacked confidence and support in child protection work, the training event met only the needs of a minority in this regard, indicating the necessity for a broader strategy to address these deficits. Inter-agency issues that arose included lack of feedback from social workers following referral, and frustration at the lack of response to certain types of child protection referral, including neglect.

Having reviewed the evaluation and discussion, and acknowledging the limitations of the event itself, Meehan advocated the development of ongoing single and multi-disciplinary training as well as the implementation of a support structure, particularly as those working in rural areas often had little contact with colleagues. She also recommended a system for liaison and communication between public health nurses and other professionals.

Identification of vulnerable children and families

If public health nurses are to support and broker services for vulnerable families in their areas, it is important to establish what exactly is meant by 'vulnerability'. This was the subject of a project undertaken in 1997 by Anna Madden, at the time a public health nurse in the North Western Health Board, based in Donegal. From her review of existing research, Madden was aware that while public health nurses were now, under the Child Care Act, 1991, charged with greater responsibility for the protection of children, the criteria they employed for assessing child welfare and safety tended to be based very much on their professional experience and intuition. Although she recognised these as important and fundamental elements of the assessment process, she acknowledged the need for a more structured and holistic approach to ensure consistency and thoroughness.

In order to formulate an effective framework for assessment, Madden sought to establish the measures most commonly used by public health nurses when judging the adequacy or otherwise of children's care and any risks associated with their family environments. She chose a sample of ten public health nurses, four of whom had worked in the UK as health visitors. She administered a short questionnaire to establish the length of each nurse's professional experience along with a profile of their areas and then conducted a focus group with seven of the sample group.

Madden found that while the public health nurses appeared to apply consistent criteria when assessing the vulnerability of families, they found it very difficult to define the concept itself. This, she claimed, reflected the multi-faceted and interacting nature of parenting capacities that could change over time and according to circumstances. Interestingly, she noted in the focus group discussions that the nurses perceived a reduction in the level of vulnerability in families as the period of their own involvement with them lengthened, though they were not able to express this in an evidential fashion or link it directly to their own input. Madden inferred from this that the main change took place in relation to the nurses' own confidence in dealing with the individual cases whereby the longer they worked with families the more they were able to identify compensatory strengths as well as weaknesses. While some public health nurses rejected the notion that they had a policing or surveillance role with families, there was no obvious connection between this and the number of cases they passed on to social workers for child protection assessment. It became clear from the focus group that public health nurses were managing cases of neglect and emotional abuse that had received no attention from social workers who, they believed, 'made more of an issue' about child sexual abuse than anything else. This finding replicated the views of public health nurses in Meehan's (1994) study.

Madden found that the public health nurses used a number of skills in assessing vulnerability, including:

- relationship building
- information gathering
- observing relationships between parents
- observing parent/child relationships
- assessing physical aspects of the home (though taking care not to impose their own standards)
- assessing parental ability to perform child care tasks
- using 'gut feelings' and life experience.

While the focus group participants acknowledged that they did not routinely use checklists, they expressed an interest in them. However, some indicated caution about the potential for them to stigmatise families and produce a high rate of false positive results. There was also an expressed wish for more management support and further training.

Madden identified a need to support the public health nurses' assessment capabilities by providing an inter-agency forum where the unmet parents' and children's needs that they identified could be brought to the attention of other professionals, particularly social workers. She argued that such a forum would have the additional benefit of providing support to public health nurses in carrying out their child protection roles. Like Meehan (1994), she recommended further training in child protection and the introduction of review and supervision systems to ensure best practice and balanced distribution of their case loads. Primarily, Madden recommended that the key elements of the assessment process which she had highlighted should be formally developed into a model for practice for universal use, thus providing a framework that would be more valid and credible than the use of checklists.

While checklists cannot be relied upon to predict child abuse, the identification of risk factors can enable public health nurses to focus purposively on vulnerable families. It was for this reason that Rachel Devlin, then a senior public health nurse in the Eastern Health Board, developed a five-stage process for the identification of children at risk of abuse or neglect in 1993. As a manager, she was conscious of the need to establish the true extent of high-risk families on the caseloads of public health nurses and to find a means of guiding and supporting staff in making decisions about them. While she was aware of the usefulness of scales such as the Mary Sheridan developmental progress chart,[4] she acknowledged its limitations in relation to observing parent/child relationships and the impact of local and environmental factors. She therefore sought to find some way of rating vulnerability that incorporated a broader range of factors, and would provide a list of children at risk in the area which would inform the targeting of resources and interventions.

In the first stage, Devlin asked all the nurses in the area to return a list of families whom they considered, using their own criteria, to be at high, medium or low risk. On the basis of the data provided by the public health nurses, 5 per cent of children in the area were considered to be at risk of potential child abuse or neglect. The vulnerabilities identified ranged from inadequate care to inability of parents to meet either their own needs or those of their children, as well as a lack of resources in the area to help parents under pressure. The most common vulnerability factors were linked with concerns like maternal depression, marital disharmony, or crime, not directly related to parenting. Poor parent/child interaction also featured, along with smaller incidences of health, behavioural and developmental problems experienced by the children. For the second stage, Devlin asked four public health nurses from each health centre to identify the social factors common to the children and parents in each 'at risk' family. These consisted principally of poverty, debt, unemployment, mothers aged under 20, absence of a partner and poor co-ordination of services. As a third stage, the same nurses were asked to select a 'high' and 'low' risk case for what was described as a monitoring analysis. The analysis was conducted by discussing the cases in a group situation to identify ways in which support and guidance might be provided by management. The fourth stage consisted of a group discussion on optional interventions, and the final stage consisted of an evaluation of the entire process.

The discussion that took place within the groups, which concentrated on the supports and resources considered important by the public health nurse, indicated that they needed access to more information about clients, more multi-disciplinary consultation and collaboration, and the opportunity to discuss a case with a senior colleague. Delays in the transfer of records, a narrow focus on health and developmental screening, and lack of access to information already held by the health board were identified as obstacles to

[4] The Mary Sheridan scale charts the development of children in relation to the regulation of feelings, the development of attachments, the development of a sense of self, the formation of peer relationships and adaptation to school.

effective work. Further discussions on the cases resulted in a pooling of knowledge and experience that ultimately combined to produce a range of new options for working with the families in the selected cases.

When the public health nurses were asked to re-assess their cases following the group discussion, the numbers in the 'moderate' risk category declined and the numbers in the 'high' risk category increased by 13 per cent. Devlin inferred from this that the discussion had enabled some of them to identify risk factors that may have been overlooked, and to focus on aspects of a case that had not been considered before. In her view, it underlined the requirement to review cases other than those already categorised as 'high risk', as well as emphasising the obvious need for a forum to discuss vulnerable families. The evaluation sheets completed by the participants reflected their satisfaction with the group process.

While Devlin acknowledged the limitations of her study because of its scale and the amount of subjective judgement involved, she considered it a valuable step in the identification of at-risk families as well as of appropriate strategies of intervention with them. This project, when considered with Meehan's (1994) and Madden's (1997), adds considerable emphasis to the need for a system of supervision and support for public health nurses. (For further discussion on this topic, see Chapter Thirteen.)

Child protection policies and procedures in early years settings
In 1997, the Department of Health and Children published a policy document entitled *Putting Children First: Promoting and Protecting the Rights of Children*. In it, the government outlined the responsibility of voluntary child care organisations to implement their own child protection policies and procedures, cautioning that failure to do so could result in a withdrawal of funds. The same year, Part VII of the Child Care Act, 1991 came into operation. This legislated for the registration and inspection of pre-school services in order to ensure that services were safe and conformed to established standards. Within this context, pre-school services were now expected to operate policies and practices that promoted the protection and welfare of children. Concern about child abuse in nursery settings has been raised in the US and the UK (Finkelhor, 1988; Hunt, 1994) and while no major incidents had been reported in an Irish setting, it is now clearly seen as an area warranting attention.

One of the largest child care organisations, the Irish Pre-School Playgroups Association (IPPA), had provided its members in 1994 with an information pack which contained child protection guidelines. By 1998 this was deemed to be in need of review, and a project to evaluate the organisation's child protection policies was carried out by Hilary Kenny, the Director of Services for the IPPA. To inform her work, Kenny studied child protection procedures produced by a number of similar organisations in Ireland and elsewhere. She used questionnaires, focus group meetings and semi-structured interviews to identify the child protection issues considered most important by the principal stake holders in the early childhood sector, including tutors and advisors within the IPPA and senior managers of health board child care services. Her ultimate aims were to make recommendations for policy revision and raise the profile of child protection within the organisation.

Kenny sent questionnaires to eleven advisory field staff, of which nine were completed. Fifteen of the sixteen senior tutors in the organisation also participated in the focus group and five health board managers were interviewed. The questionnaires and focus group discussion concentrated on staff's perceptions of child protection policies, procedures and practices within the organisation, and their own experience of child protection issues. The interviews with health board managers focused on the fit between the health board perspective and that of the IPPA in relation to child protection.

The principal issues that emerged from the questionnaire survey and the focus groups were:

- the uncertainties and anxieties of IPPA staff, even though a child protection policy was operative
- the need to address these by training at a single and multi agency level
- the different levels of training and experience that existed within the organisation and, by implication, the voluntary child care sector generally
- the conflict for child care staff between their desire to work in a supportive way with children and families and their professional obligation to report suspicions of child abuse.

Issues arising from the interviews with health board managers revealed:

- the need for a consistent approach between voluntary and statutory agencies
- the importance of voluntary groups and agencies taking their child protection roles and responsibilities beyond the 'glossy brochure' to the point where they became part of the culture of each organisation.
- the perceived benefits of consultation between the two organisations in relation to the development of policies, guidelines and training.

On the positive side, Kenny found that the health board managers were familiar with and positive about the IPPA policies, and that the work carried out by the IPPA advisory staff in local communities had opened communication channels between the organisation and the health board with the subsequent development of good working relationships. The implementation of a child protection task force had already been recommended to the IPPA following a management consultants' study. Kenny further endorsed, on the basis of her own findings, the immediate development of the task force and the prioritising of its tasks with reference to the findings from her study. In particular, she suggested that:

- all levels of experience and expertise in the organisation should be represented on the task force
- priority should be given to updating policies and procedures, and disseminating them
- collaborative relationships with all health boards should be fostered, particularly through forums of mutual interest like child care advisory committees and area child protection committees
- joint child protection training at all levels should be initiated.

While Kenny's project indicated that the child protection policy of the IPPA required revision to bring them into line with current knowledge and legislation, its existence did at least confirm that a system was in place to ensure, as far as possible, safe child care practices. However, not all child care providers are affiliated to a development agency, nor do the pre-school regulations under the Child Care Act, 1991 oblige them to employ staff with any particular training or qualifications. There is no guarantee, therefore, that satisfactory or uniform child protection practices operate in private child care settings, even if they are registered with the health board. The recruitment, selection and induction methods and child protection policies operated by pre-school service providers was the subject of a project conducted in 2000 by Maureen Joyce, a Pre-Schools Services Inspector employed by the North Eastern Health Board, in Co. Meath.

The pre-schools inspection service was activated following the implementation of Part VII of the Child Care Act, 1991 and the enforcement of the Child Care (Pre-School Services) Regulations, both of which took place in 1996. Health boards now have an inspectorial function in relation to ensuring that services observe the minimum standards required by the regulations. However, as Joyce pointed out, the concentration of the regulations tends to be on 'quantitative' factors such as space, ratios and toilets, rather than the 'qualitative' elements of relationships and interactions between adults and children and the potential for play and educational activities to benefit children's development.

Joyce was aware that recruitment standards have suffered as a result of labour shortage in the child care area, but having surveyed the literature, she was concerned about the necessity for services to try and eliminate, as far as possible, the risk of any service employing a potential child abuser. The minimum standards to be applied included, in her view, widespread advertising of vacancies, a clear understanding of both the job to be filled and the necessary qualities in a potential employee, the collection and validation of references, police and medical checks where possible, and the provision of induction training.

Joyce used a structured questionnaire to survey all twelve full day-care providers in her area, and explored the extent to which they conformed to the standards just outlined. She was initially apprehensive that her role as Inspector might influence the nature of replies, but what she described as the 'starkness' of some responses assured her that the service providers were being quite frank.

Joyce found that less than half of the providers advertised for staff, the remainder preferring to rely on word of mouth or personal knowledge. She pointed out that this type of practice conflicts with advice given in guidance and reduces the choice of potential staff (Warner, 1992). Similar practices appeared to operate in relation to references – while they had been sought by two-thirds of the providers, one-third either did not collect them or relied on the commendations of friends. Although central Garda clearance was not currently available for staff in private child care services, local Garda clearance could have been obtained with the applicant's permission. However, this had not been sought by any employers surveyed and, as Joyce argued, even though criminal records reveal only a small number of child abusers, their existence may act as a deterrent to potential abusers seeking positions. In addition, as she claimed, they may also eliminate candidates with other patterns of offending behaviour such as repeated drink driving, assault or theft. Medical reports had not been requested by the service providers in relation to any applicants and, as Joyce pointed out, information regarding the health of an employee could have been a protective factor not only for children, but also for the staff themselves who might have been vulnerable to certain types of illness or infection that may have been carried by the children in their care. Overall, just under half of the service providers operated no clear staff recruitment or selection procedures at all, nor any induction training for new staff.

All providers in Joyce's survey were asked if they had child protection policies in place in their services to deal both with the prevention of child abuse and any suspicion of child abuse that might arise. All responses to the question about prevention were negative, and nine out of the twelve had no policy with regard to dealing with suspicion. The remaining three responded that their policy was for staff to inform the manager, who would in turn inform the health board.

Joyce concluded that, given the centrality and importance of staff in the care 'package' offered to children and families, the clients of these pre-school settings were receiving an inadequate service with reduced opportunities for prevention and early intervention where children might be in need. She pointed out the difficulty for pre-school services inspectors in responding to situations where children's developmental needs were unmet and staff were insufficiently trained, in the context of inadequate legislative support. In her view, the Pre-School Regulations 1996 were not exacting enough to compel service providers to employ the sort of recruitment practices she felt were necessary to provide protective and developmentally appropriate care for children in pre-school settings. In addition to her recommendation for safe and consistently applied recruitment, selection and induction procedures, she strongly advocated review and clarification of the relevant section of the Child Care Act, 1991.

Child protection policies and procedures in services for adults and children with disabilities

As this section has already illustrated, organisations offering services aimed at promoting the welfare of children are now required to have child protection policies and procedures in place. The principal rationale for this is to enable staff to recognise signs of actual or potential child maltreatment and to understand the necessary steps to take in order to prevent its reoccurrence. Typically, these policies are aimed at protecting children from abuse by their families. However, two important areas to emerge from research and inquiry reports in recent years have been the potential for child abuse to occur within organisations where children are dependent on care from adults other than their parents for short or long periods of time (Finkelhor, 1988; Levy and Kahan, 1991; Department of Health, 1996a; Murphy, 1998, Waterhouse, 2000) and the vulnerability of persons with disabilities (Kennedy, 1992; Marchant and Page 1992; Westcott and Cross, 1996; Westcott and Jones, 1999; Marchant, 2000). The powerlessness of children in such settings has been highlighted, as well as the way that conflicting loyalties can act to promote denial and inertia by other members of staff who may suspect abuse.

Certain types of care situations have been recognised as particularly susceptible to what Wardhaugh and Wilding (1993, p.22) identify as 'corruption'. They claim that the type of inward-looking culture that can develop often fosters a rigid focus on 'control, order and the absence of trouble' and stifles any possibility of either challenging group norms or internal criticisms and complaints.

Services and organisations for persons with disabilities carry additional special features that can render them more open to targeting by potential abusers. Children and adults with physical and intellectual difficulties often lack the capacity to resist physical or sexual assault or communicate their reactions to it. They are made more vulnerable because of the number of people involved in delivering their care as well as their limited access to preventive programmes and to knowledge about child abuse and child protection. Feelings of disloyalty, or reluctance to jeopardise the availability of a scarce service, can impede their willingness to disclose or report abuse and they are less likely to make credible witnesses should a case be brought to court (Westcott and Cross, 1996).

Children First (Department of Health and Children, 1999) has now recognised the special requirements of organisations providing services for children, including children with disabilities, to produce child protection procedures that are consistent with the national guidelines, and to provide training for staff. These areas are the focus of the projects to be discussed in the remainder of this chapter. The first is a study carried out in 1999 by Liam Keogh, a social worker in St Michael's House, a voluntary organisation providing a range of community-based services for adults and children with learning disability.

At the time of Keogh's study, St Michael's House were in the process of establishing child protection procedures and setting up a specialist team to manage child abuse allegations that arose in relation to the users of its service. It was planned to appoint a designated person (the head social worker) to carry overall responsibility for this area of work, along with a multi-disciplinary team to assist in the implementation of the procedures. It was also envisaged that in the event of an allegation, the designated person would nominate a support person from the team to assist the local clinical team and ensure that procedures were followed. The aim of Keogh's research was to explore the type of knowledge and structures required by professionals to inform and support the implementation of the new system. He chose to include the experiences of agencies other than his own where child protection policies were already operational.

Keogh identified a sample of ten practitioners from three agencies, including his own, that provided services to people with learning disabilities. The group included two doctors, three psychologists, two social workers, one occupational therapist, a manager and a researcher/trainer. All had some level of knowledge and experience in responding to child abuse allegations and two of them were fulfilling the designated-person or support-person role in their own agencies. Keogh interviewed them, using a semi-structured format, and asked them about their current child protection policies and practices and their views on the knowledge, skills and resources required to enact their child protection roles.

The data indicated that the response to abuse allegations had become considerably more co-ordinated and focused since the appointment of 'support persons' in the agencies, one of the important effects being the availability of advice, knowledge and emotional support to staff. Roles differed from close involvement and facilitation of work to indirect consultation. It was seen to work best when support persons did not have to carry out child protection work in addition to their normal duties. Problems were identified with the role when it did not carry a mandate from senior management or when the demands became too onerous. It was also noted that the designated person was often at one remove from the event itself and that the potential therefore existed for distortion in reporting the details to the statutory authorities. The 'designated person' model operated in two agencies, with slightly different arrangements. In one, it was more administrative and concerned with staff training, and managing protocols for prevention, protection, reporting and treatment. The second model was similar but involved more direct work with persons involved in the allegation, ensuring that procedures were followed and offering support.

Whichever system operated, the common themes identified by Keogh were the need for support, good caseload management, good recording systems, clear procedures, a central person with responsibility for recording inform- ation, and the development of protective measures. Areas of knowledge considered important for a support/designated person included:

- child and adult development in order to recognise levels of functioning
- all aspects of interviewing and overcoming communication difficulties
- sexuality
- awareness of one's own attitudes in relation to sexuality
- thresholds for reporting, particularly in relation to neglect
- families' likely reactions to allegations.

Skills would be required in the following areas:

- communication
- administration and ability to record accurately
- ability to ask difficult questions, remain objective, appear confident and resist pressure
- diplomacy.

The need for a protocol on openness with families was identified, along with clarity about which agency or person should liaise with them. Suggestions for cultivating good relationships between voluntary agencies and health boards were offered by the interviewees, including the practices of getting to know workers and making informal inquiries, clarifying expectations and negotiating agreed goals, raising awareness about disability and expressing concerns in writing.

Issues in relation to allegations against staff were also raised, particularly the sensitivities involved, the requirement to manage information carefully and the need for the designated person to be conscious of the type of dynamics that can operate, e.g. power, denial, manipulation, bullying and creation of doubts.

It was acknowledged that the question of whether or not to report allegations of the abuse of adults is a complex one. However, it was generally agreed by staff that given the vulnerability of adults with learning disabilities, the practice of referring concerns about them to health boards should be continued.

Overall, Keogh concluded that the designation of a staff member to the co-ordinating role was necessary, despite the increasing streamlining of procedures within services. The potential for abuse to occur within organisations was cited by him as an important factor in the retention of a 'neutral' person as co-ordinator, though he agreed that the role needed to be reviewed with the aim of achieving a balance between its administrative and supportive aspects. He further recommended an increased focus on prevention and welfare including sex education programmes, treatment and openness with parents.

Child protection policies, procedures and practices in residential services for children
One of the points made by Keogh (1999) above was that the 'talk and chalk' stage of developing procedures was only part of the process of implementing child protection practices in an organisation. He argued that holistic and reflective understanding, along with sensitivity to the emotional process of dealing with child abuse, was also necessary. This theme was elaborated upon in three projects on the development and implementation of child protection policies in special residential services for children, one carried out in 1993, one in 1997 and one in 2000. The first of these was conducted by Gus Monaghan, a residential worker in a special child care centre in 1993. An incident in which one of the residents had sexually abused another had made staff in his residential unit acutely aware of their lack of experience and knowledge of the subject. It had also highlighted the need for a set of procedures to guide them and enable them to make an appropriate response in future. Monaghan was aware of the necessity to ensure that policies in his centre were democratically developed rather than imposed by management, and aimed to create a forum for discussion about the development of child protection guidelines that could be 'owned' by all the staff and residents.

An experienced group facilitator was engaged to chair a multi-disciplinary group, consisting of representatives of the care and teaching staff, the psychologist and a manager of the centre. The group met for six three-hour sessions over a six-week period. Its main objectives were to heighten awareness of child sexual abuse in the centre, develop a set of guidelines for dealing with child sexual abuse, review child protection policies in the unit, motivate staff to seek and participate in further training and raise staff morale.

Monaghan observed the process of the group and considered it to be cohesive and focused on the completion of the tasks it had set, while at the same time careful to retain clarity in relation to the issues involved. The principal themes for discussion were the extent and nature of child sexual abuse and its effects, the barriers to disclosure of child sexual abuse within the centre and procedures for handling disclosure. It was felt that the culture of the organisation acted to impede the potential for identification and disclosure. Cultural factors identified included the discomfort of the staff in discussing sexual matters as well as the perceived 'low' standards operating in relation to sexual matters, e.g. tolerance of sexist language and sexual talk and a resistance to communicating reports to management. The 'secure' identity of the centre which, according to the group, promoted a 'tough' image was also considered to act as an impediment against awareness and disclosure of sexual abuse.

The group determined a policy for dealing with child sexual abuse, including norms about confidentiality, reporting procedures, the provision of support for staff, and dissemination of knowledge about indicators. The role of other agencies was clarified, and the group discussed measures for dealing with allegations against staff members. They worked out a step-by-step approach to be taken when young people made disclosures, emphasising the need to assure, praise and encourage a young person to tell.

From his observation of the group in action, his discussion with the facilitator and his analysis of the evaluation sheets completed by participants, Monaghan considered the group process to have been generally successful. The aims of raising awareness and establishing a sound foundation from which to create a set of procedures had been met. He found the appointment of an external facilitator to be an important element in the success of the project in terms of enabling a more balanced discussion and enhancing the status and perceived importance of the group. At its conclusion, Monaghan observed an increase in the participants' confidence in discussing sexual matters and in their awareness of the potential for abuse to take place within the centre. The morale of the group members had, in his view, been enhanced by their sense of achievement. He emphasised, however, that the long-term positive outcome of the group process would depend on the willingness of management to finalise the suggested child protection guidelines and implement them as policy within the centre.

Another project on a similar theme was conducted in 1997 by Patricia

Flynn, the manager of a residential centre where children defined by the courts as 'young offenders' are placed under the 1908 Children Act which was in operation at the time. The aim of her study was to establish the level of staff's willingness to report incidents of suspected child abuse and see if their current child protection policies were adequate.

Flynn cited evidence of the high incidence of abuse in residential settings, focusing particularly on the Pindown experiment (Levy and Kahan, 1991), and the Madonna House inquiry (Department of Health, 1996a). She quoted inquiry reports and studies to show how abuse can vary from denial of basic rights, over harsh regimes, oppressive behaviour modification techniques and intimidation, to physical and sexual abuse (N.A.Y.P.I.C., 1989).

Flynn used previous research to show that inappropriate treatment by staff can often be treated as a personnel matter rather than a child protection matter and tends to be dealt with at an internal level by management (Singleton, 1983). She showed how reporting of their colleagues by staff members can be inhibited by absence of clarity about mistreatment, fear of retaliation, shame, counter transference or sympathy. She pointed out the conflicts of interest that can arise for investigators who are also managers, where fears of loss of credibility, loss of funding or bad publicity can combine to cover up incidents of child maltreatment (Nunno and Motz, 1988).

Modelling her research on a study previously carried out by Rindfleisch and Bean (1988) on the same topic, Flynn carried out her fieldwork in three separate centres, using a group administered questionnaire. She asked a total of sixty-six workers to consider two hypothetical scenarios and use rating scales to indicate their likely responses to the incidents therein. One scenario concerned a 13-year-old child's sexual relationship with her boyfriend and the second scenario gave an example of a staff member abusing his power over a child by making her participate in a sporting activity that she disliked. Staff were asked to indicate if they would do nothing, talk the incident over with the staff member involved, talk it over with his or her co-workers, tell an administrator, report to a statutory agency, and/or inform An Garda Síochána.

Like other researchers before her, Flynn found that incidents involving physical and sexual abuse were more likely to be reported than incidents of inappropriate behaviour by staff. In the first scenario, 96 per cent of staff indicated their willingess to report the incident immediately. She speculated that the incident described may not have evoked any feelings of supervisory responsibility from the workers, but was more likely to have been interpreted as the child's misbehaviour. Flynn wondered if this was the reason for the high rate of willingness to report. She noted that in relation to the second incident described, only 16 per cent of workers would challenge their colleague if they saw him or her acting inappropriately and attributed it to a lack of confidence. She observed a positive correlation between years of experience and certainty about responses that, in her view, had implications for training and supervision.

Taking the survey findings into consideration, Flynn later interviewed six residential managers to ascertain their willingness to report abuse to outside agencies and see if barriers to reporting influenced their behaviour. Contrary to some earlier research findings, Flynn found that managers were quite uninhibited about their responsibility to pass concerns about physical or sexual abuse to the health board and did not seem to be deterred by anxiety about retaliation or negative publicity. She noted, however, their acknowledged tendency to trust the accounts of adult witnesses over those given by children and their concern about the unpredictability of the health board's response to reports which gave them a sense of loss of control. In her review of their child protection procedures, Flynn noted the absence of any mention of 'independent' persons to act on behalf of child victims, or any advice on what to do if the alleged perpetrator was a manager.

While Flynn recognised the limitations of her study as far as the use of hypothetical situations was concerned, she concluded that more effort was required to ensure that child protection issues were incorporated into the general ethos of the units and integrated with a Charter of Rights. Such a charter, she suggested, should also outline the responsibilities of children to use the complaints system fairly. She pointed out that many issues that could currently be seen as complaints could be dealt with as part of the daily process of caring, providing staff with the opportunity to demonstrate their capacity to be fair and just and handle criticism openly. It would also, in her view, allow young people to develop the skills of being appropriately assertive and effective negotiators.

Flynn also advocated the appointment of an independent person and the provision of training to enable staff to discriminate between caring and potentially abusive behaviours such as over-familiar relationships or spending inordinate amounts of time with one child. She strongly recommended the use of weekly staff meetings as a means of generating discussions and raising consciousness of these issues. She emphasised the need for workers and managers to maintain an appropriate understanding of the potential for abuse within their organisations and never to assume that 'it couldn't happen here'.

That the existence of a child protection policy in a residential unit did not ensure its implementation was the subject of a project undertaken in 2000 by Michael Lynam, a residential worker in a unit similar to, though separate from, those studied in Flynn's research. While Flynn had confined her data collection to the perspectives of workers and managers, Lynam also sought the views of the children who were resident in his centre.

In the centre studied by Lynam, a 'Policies, Procedures and Protocols' document had been formally adopted in 1996 and included sections, amongst others, on rights of young people, child abuse definitions, bullying, and complaints procedures. The director had been designated as the child protection officer, the person with responsibility for responding to allegations of child abuse and reporting them to the statutory authorities. Lynam undertook a critical evaluation of the effectiveness of this document in 2000.

Lynam was aware from his experience and his study of the literature of the vulnerability and powerlessness of young people in care, particularly those in involuntary or court-ordered situations. He argued that children in such settings can lose their sense of safety and security, and would be unlikely to challenge the power of adults when they feel it is being exercised unfairly. The aim of his study was to see if the young people were aware of the policies in the unit, and would be prepared to use complaints procedures. He was also interested in ascertaining the views and perceptions of staff members.

Lynam interviewed eight of the young people who were resident at the unit, comprising four each from the senior and junior units. In addition, he interviewed four staff members and surveyed six other staff members by means of a questionnaire.

The interviews with the young people yielded disturbing data, revealing that they knew little of their rights and of what Lynam describes as 'a system that is supposedly in place for their protection'. Over half did not know the identity of the person designated to deal with child abuse allegations, or even what a child protection officer was. Over half did not know what emotional abuse was, and only one quarter understood the term 'physical abuse'. Seven of the young people had made complaints to the staff but three of them felt that it had not been a worthwhile exercise. None of their parents had been informed by the staff about the complaints. Most of the young people had not been given guidance about how to make a complaint, and half of them felt that it would be difficult. Though all said they would complain about staff, only half were prepared to complain about ill-treatment by their peers. While all the young people felt that staff were always prepared to listen to them, only half felt that they were understood.

Lynam also discovered that fewer than half of the young people had had contact with their social worker or probation officer in the previous month and only half of them had their social worker's phone number.

Understandably, Lynam considered his findings to be a cause for concern, pointing out that their lack of information, knowledge and confidence in the system greatly impeded their ability to make a complaint about abuse or any other difficulty. The fact that half of them did not feel able to report problems such as bullying by their peers illustrated their powerlessness, and the dearth of their contact from social workers and probation officers suggested isolation.

Data from staff interviews and questionnaires indicated that all staff did not actually have ready access to the Policies, Procedures and Protocols document, and were unsure about definitions of child abuse. The staff who were interviewed indicated that they felt insufficiently trained to deal with child protection issues and had some doubts about the availability of support for themselves should an allegation be made against them. As Lynam pointed out, the lack of support, training and information engenders unease, anxiety and ultimately defensive practice. His study revealed the need for an urgent review not only of existing policies and procedures, but of their implementation. He challenges the idea of a 'line management' approach to making complaints, raising the possibility that it can be used as a 'filtering tool' in the prioritising of complaints where self-interests can be protected.

Lynam specifically recommended training for the staff and young people, with the formulation of a clear step-by-step procedure for client complaints to be made available to the young people, staff groups, parents, social workers and probation officers. Lynam emphasised that child protection must become an integrated component of the care system and not a mere tool for responding to crises.

Child protection training in youth and community organisations

A consistent recommendation of all the projects carried out on the subject of identification of child abuse was the provision of staff training. As the Murphy report on child abuse in swimming (Murphy, 1998) illustrated, training in this area must not be confined to staff but extended to persons working with children in an unpaid or part time capacity, particularly within organisations who use large numbers of volunteers. Two projects were undertaken specifically to raise awareness and provide guidance on safe practices and child protection amongst volunteers and employees engaged in the youth sector. The first of these was conducted in Kerry in 1993, by Joe Coughlan, manager of the Kerry Diocesan Youth Service. His aims were to enable staff to define and recognise indicators of child abuse, and to understand the correct reporting procedure. His project consisted of identifying training needs and then conducting and evaluating a training event. He surveyed ten youth leaders in relation to their knowledge about child abuse, their understanding of issues like confidentiality and duty to report and their awareness of referral procedures. While he found that all of them perceived themselves to have an important role in promoting child welfare, the survey results illustrated gaps in their knowledge about duty to report and referral procedures as well as differing views about confidentiality. Coughlan prepared a training programme to address the identified needs.

Twelve youth leaders attended the half-day programme, which focused heavily on issues like understanding 'healthy' and 'unhealthy' sexual behaviour, indicators of abuse, cultural relativism and reporting responsibility.

He was particularly concerned to emphasise the impact of personal values on the process of forming a judgement. He evaluated the session by questionnaire. The findings of this exercise indicated that three quarters of the participants had found the day useful in terms of their ability to recognise children who might have been abused or were at risk of abuse. Most also indicated a good knowledge of reporting procedures. Interestingly, the questionnaire results demonstrated the number of personal dilemmas experienced by workers where there was a lack of clarity about concerns or suspicions. This indicated a raising of their awareness about the complexity of the subject and an increased likelihood that they would report suspicions in the future rather than waiting for confirmation or proof that their concerns were grounded. On the less positive side, the findings illustrated that most (87 per cent) participants were doubtful about the health board's capacity to make an effective response to reported child protection concerns.

On the basis of his findings, Coughlan planned to try to engage with health board personnel in his area in order to link his organisation with the wider child protection network. He planned to include health board staff in later training events so as to inform the youth leaders about health board child protection practices and build up a level of trust between the agencies. His recommendations included further training on the role of An Garda Síochána and inter-agency co-operation generally. He also planned to develop and implement a policy for the management of suspected abuse on the part of an employee or volunteers.

Another project on similar lines was conducted in 2000 by Bill Blake, director of training in the City of Dublin Youth Service, who undertook a pilot training programme for use in the youth sector. In designing his programme, Blake incorporated the key issues raised in child abuse inquiries, many of which were common to a range of organisations providing services to children. He highlighted the need for training in the following areas:

- awareness about the possibility of child abuse occurring and recognition of signs and symptoms
- the need for user-friendly complaints systems
- codes of behaviour between volunteers and young people
- development of a child protection policy
- clear procedures about the necessary steps to be taken if abuse is suspected
- providing and raising awareness about supports for volunteers
- the importance of involving parents in club activities
- responsibility to co-operate with a range of agencies and services.

Blake also consulted the literature about methods for training adults in sensitive areas like child protection. He noted the importance of ensuring that the content of a programme is relevant, that the mix of trainees is appropriate, that the context is considered, for example in relation to available time and resources, and that the trainer is appropriately qualified and experienced. In keeping with the principles of youth work practice which value learning through participation, Blake applied Kolb's (1988) learning model, which utilises the cyclical process of experience, reflection, conceptualisation and experimentation and builds in time for the participants to reflect on the material. A variety of training methods was used, including word-storming, role plays, group work, case studies and buzz groups. This was necessary to address the different learning capabilities in the group, and proved to be based on a correct assumption as it later transpired that two trainees had literacy problems. Blake was also aware of the possibility that some of the fourteen volunteers in his group may have been abused themselves and ensured that appropriate strategies and supports were in place for dealing with disclosure or addressing concerns.

The programme was limited by the commitment of the volunteers to two two-and-a-half hour sessions, the shortage of time inevitably restricting the content. Within these constraints, Blake was unable to cover all the areas that he considered necessary and confined the programme to strategies for identifying and responding to suspected child abuse and good practice issues in the context of youth work. He built in structures for formal and informal evaluation from the outset by designing questionnaires, including feedback sessions, and providing for communication of relevant issues to management of the different groups.

Among the process issues that arose was the need for the trainer to be flexible and sensitive to the mood of the group. For example, when they wanted to talk, this needed to be facilitated. Discussions that tended to be critical and negative about the child protection system had to be guided towards an understanding of other agencies' perspectives and constructive solutions. For example, through this type of 'neutral' discussion, the group became more aware that the ability of health boards to respond to concerns about child protection depends on the depth and quality of information referred to them. The group members showed particular interest in handling disclosures and ethical dilemmas about confidentiality and were provided with case studies as learning tools. While they discussed practice issues, they were constrained by time limits and unable to reach the areas of recruitment and selection.

The overall evaluation indicated that objectives had been reached, and that the group had gained considerable knowledge and improved their skills in the area of child protection, particularly in relation to handling disclosures, good practice and leadership in groups. As Blake had anticipated, two participants required further support in relation to personal issues, reinforcing, in his view, the need for trainers to be sensitive not only to the content of a programme, but to the manner in which it is delivered.

Not surprisingly, Blake recommended an extension to the programme to cover areas like policy, procedures, monitoring and review processes. However, he pointed out the difficulty common to volunteer groups of limited commitment to training, and suggested the introduction of incentives, such as making affiliation conditional on training or providing grants or certification for groups and individuals who have participated in training.

Conclusion

Taken together, the studies discussed in this section suggest that considerable progress has been made by professions and agencies to improve their potential for identifying and addressing children's protection and welfare needs. Though the individual projects have, in most cases, highlighted areas which require modification and further development, it must be acknowledged that collective professional attitudes about the unacceptability of child abuse and the responsibility to both prevent and address it are more closely aligned with officially recommended practices now than at any time in the past.

That being said, each of the studies raised issues of some significance. It was clear from the four studies conducted by public health nurses that their profession plays a vital and primary role in promoting child welfare and preventing a deterioration in the situation of vulnerable families. Each of the projects contributed to a further refinement of that function. However, it is also clear that the process of working with child abuse poses considerable challenges for public health nurses that must be addressed by the provision of a formal system of supervisory support. This is an issue that will be dealt with in later chapters, but the consistency with which it became apparent underlines its fundamental importance.

The studies that focused on early childhood and pre-school services raised some important points. The evaluation of IPPA policies highlighted the advantage of affiliation with a co-ordinating and development agency that can help to integrate services both within a community and in co-operation with statutory agencies, as well as the need for constant review of policies. The study on staff recruitment practices in private child care settings clearly illustrated the limited value of regulations if they fail to pay attention to the qualitative aspects of child care. It also showed, in an alarming fashion, the futility of official inspectorial functions if they cannot ensure a basic level of safety and protection for children.

The vulnerability and powerlessness of children who are dependent on others for their care, and the need for policies to ensure their protection and attention to their rights were made visible in the projects carried out in residential units. It is interesting that while two of the projects supported the appointment of a designated officer to deal with child protection issues, they advocated caution. They both illustrated in different ways the need for caution in relation to the extra obstacles to intervention that can be created in the process, particularly if that person has a management function. As they pointed out, administrative and therapeutic roles can become confused. Other projects highlighted the potential for conflicts of interest and the need for an alternative procedure if the alleged abuser is in a position of power within the organisation. The model of a 'neutral' or 'independent' person was posed and might seem to offer a useful alternative. The recent establishment in Ireland of the Social Services Inspectorate should serve to address some of these issues in the wider child care arena, but the fact that their remit is limited to health board funded children's homes means that all the organisations featured in the studies here would be outside their area of responsibility.

The thorny issue of inter-agency co-operation emerged with enduring consistency, specifically and repetitively in relation to the unpredictabilty and perceived narrowness of health board social workers' response to reports about child neglect, particularly those cases that fall into the 'grey' area between need, vulnerability and abuse. This is the subject of fuller analysis in Chapter Four, but the studies discussed here have highlighted the importance of maintaining links between voluntary and statutory agencies, to ensure that policies and reporting thresholds are agreed and consistently operated, to share concerns and provide mutual support. As Chapter Five will show, attention needs to be paid to the process of inter-agency working and any obstacles acknowledged. Importantly, as Stevenson (1999) argues, too much reliance must not be placed on informal consensus in inter-agency relationships, as goodwill may quickly evaporate in the event of a crisis – it is important to have formal strategies in place, mandated by senior management, upon which to base sound arrangements for collaboration and co-operation.

The need for training was consistently illustrated in the studies discussed here. The projects carried out within the youth sector provided particular insight into the most effective ways of imparting information, skills and knowledge to groups with varying education, experience and involvement in the child protection process. All cautioned against overloading training programmes of limited duration and usefully illustrated the importance of paying attention to the potential sensitivities of dealing with a subject as complex as child abuse. Training in child protection has, over the past five years, become almost an industry in Ireland, but like inter-agency co-operation, it must be complemented by policies and structures that continue to support staff, and by itself it should not be regarded as a solution to all the difficulties and complexities of child protection work.

As these studies have shown, the consciousness of professionals and agencies has been raised considerably in relation to the potential for children using their services to be abused by persons with responsibility for their care, whether they are parents, staff or volunteers. The existence of child protection policies and procedures, once they are disseminated and implemented, will enable practitioners to act on their concerns in an accountable, and hopefully, effective manner. Caution has been advised in relation to overemphasis on procedures at the cost of critical professional judgement (Buckley, 1996; Stevenson, 1999). However, what these studies have emphatically shown is that policies, procedures and protocols should never be regarded as a substitute for the consistent and conscious efforts of practitioners, whether they are professional staff or volunteers, to create anti-abusive environments that promote the welfare of children and respect their rights.

4

Responding to Concerns about Children's Safety and Welfare

Introduction

The obligation imposed on the health boards to promote the welfare of children who are not receiving adequate care and protection largely defines the philosophical thrust of the Child Care Act, 1991 as a broad-sweeping, pro-active instrument of law. Whilst the legislation contains mechanisms for operating sanctions against families who are seen to fail in their duty to their children, it is based primarily on the ideal enshrined in the UN Convention on the Rights of Children, ratified by Ireland in 1992, that children have a right to be brought up within their own families. The Child Care Act, 1991 clearly compels the health boards to facilitate this process where necessary.

Essentially, under the terms of the Act, health boards should operate services that are aimed to minimise potential harm to children and prevent them from being abused. This suggests that supports should be available to families before they reach crisis point. However, research carried out in the South Eastern Health Board during 1996 found that while social workers were quick to respond and offer services on a medium- to long-term basis when child abuse was identified, a number of families who were undergoing considerable hardship and had a myriad of difficulties including poverty, inadequate housing, children with behavioural problems and adults with mental health problems, were being filtered out of the system within a short period when signs of actual abuse were not identifiable (Buckley, Skehill and O'Sullivan, 1997). A similar trend was visible in a study carried out during 1997 in the Eastern Health Board, the largest health board in the country. There, the research found that health board social workers were operating almost exclusively as a child protection service. It was claimed that the bulk of resources available to the community care programme was being spent on safeguarding rather than promotional activities, and identified the need for a radical shift in direction (Eastern Health Board/ Impact, 1997).

This trend is by no means unique to Ireland. In Britain, a large programme of research carried out in the early 1990s has identified a similar trend (Farmer and Owen, 1995) and has also illustrated that, despite a high level of response to reports of child abuse, families in need receive very few services (Gibbons, Conroy and Bell, 1995). Thorpe (1994) found a similar trend in a comparative study carried out between Wales and Western Australia. He asserted that unless reported concerns about children conformed to a designated 'norm' of child abuse, they were likely to get a poor response from the services. Parton (1997) has argued that despite the aspiration of the Children Act [UK] 1989 towards partnership, participation, prevention, family support and a positive rethink on the purpose of care, child protection has continued to dominate the development of services in the UK. In a later paper, Parton (1998) analysed what he terms the new obsession with the elimination of risk and the desire for certainty, factors which have forced practitioners to adopt a focus that is investigatory and procedurally driven. He argued that the pre-occupation with risk has evolved from the numerous child abuse inquiries that were held in Britain during the 1970s and 1980s, in which blame was apportioned to professionals who were accused of failing to accurately assess the degree of risk involved in the individual cases. In Ireland too, we have had our share of child abuse inquiries and probably through lack of research on child protection policies and practices in our own country, have tended to follow British trends in service provision. It is possible to speculate that Parton's observations could accurately describe the way that child protection practice and policy has developed in Ireland over the past two decades, despite the cultural and administrative differences that exist between the two countries.

Following the recommendations of the Department of Health [UK] research programme, British policy in child protection has made efforts to 're-focus' services towards the identification of children in need and the integration of family support services with child protection (Department of Health [UK] 1995; 2000). In Ireland, *Children First* has attempted to prioritise child welfare by emphasising the necessity to consider optional ways of intervening early where children are at risk and emphasising the importance of providing family support. It remains to be seen, however, if this can be achieved and the proposed introduction of mandatory reporting may ensure that the balance remains tipped in the area of child protection.

However, though the domination of child protection over other aspects of child welfare has been criticised, it also has to be acknowledged that in Ireland, inadequacies in practice with child abuse have been justifiably highlighted in some specific instances. As the chapter on inter-agency co-operation will show, knowledge about child abuse procedures and recognition of individual roles and responsibilities by professionals involved fully or partially in child protection has needed to progress considerably in the past decade. Reporting practices have been poor and methods of assessment and longer term planning have been found wanting in several high-profile cases (Department of Health, 1993; Western Health Board, 1996; North Western Health Board, 1998). Whilst a lot of the problems were linked to structural inadequacies in the child protection and welfare system, it was also recognised that efforts were needed to raise awareness and improve practice skills. It was in this context that many of the projects to be discussed here were carried out. As the remainder of this section will show, a number of pertinent areas were addressed by either researching the need for a change in approach, or actually proposing and evaluating a procedure or programme of intervention. The projects to be discussed concern methods for reporting and communicating child protection concerns, assessment of children's needs and responding to child neglect and child protection interventions.

Reporting child protection concerns
Research in Ireland, the UK and Australia has shown a high rate of non-substantiated child abuse reports that has continued to rise in line with the increase in referrals (Department of Health, 1995a; Gibbons, Conroy and Bell, 1995; Thorpe, 1994, 1996). In order to find the most appropriate way of responding to this increase, Ann Logan, at the time a social work team leader in the South Eastern Health Board based in Wexford, undertook an action research project in 1997, with the intention of designing a workable protocol for the referral of child protection concerns. From the literature, Logan was aware that any measures taken to enforce the reporting of suspected child abuse, such as the introduction of strict guidelines or mandatory reporting, were likely to result in an overloading of the system. The aim of her project was to encourage *accurate* reporting by offering a guide to what she described as an 'assessment of concern'. In order to pilot her proposed protocol, she concentrated particularly on general practitioners and teachers. She selected general practitioners because she perceived them to be well placed to identify child abuse, particularly in a rural community where opportunities were available to get to know families over generations. Her choice of teachers reflected the commonly accepted view that teachers have unique opportunities to develop strong relationships with children and observe worrying behaviour or behavioural changes in a child (Gilligan, 2000a).

Logan designed an 'assessment of concern' form and presented it to a sample of five primary, secondary and vocational teachers, as well as four general practitioners. She conducted focus group with the teachers to ascertain their views on the form, and carried out individual interviews with the general practitioners who were not able to participate together in a group setting because of their limited availability.

The protocol consisted firstly of a guide to the process of completing the form, followed by a space for collecting details of the child's identity, age and family details. It then asked different sets of questions of the professionals regarding the nature and origin of their concerns, specifically:

- details of the manner in which the concerns were manifested
- the reason why the matter had now become a cause of concern
- the positive features of the child's behaviour
- the child's own views and the views of the parents in relation to the source of the concern
- any plan or action that the referrers could suggest or take in order to address the concern.

The response of the sample of general practitioners and teachers to the draft assessment form was generally positive, with the proviso that certain areas required modification. They were uneasy about the expectation that they could accurately assess behavioural problems, which they all felt was beyond their professional competence. Despite what is now known and accepted about the benefits of openness and honesty with parents and the rights of children to have their views heard, both the teachers and general practitioners expressed reservations at the requirement in the form to discuss their concerns with the parents and children. They considered such actions to be intrusive, awkward and impossible to imagine. This is an area that has since received attention in *Children First* (Department of Health and Children, 1999) and the Department of Education and Science child protection guidelines (Department of Education and Science, 2001) and it is interesting to observe how reluctant these professionals were, at that time, to respect what is now considered a right of families and children.

The general practitioners and teachers in Logan's study also expressed uncertainty about the requirement to draw up an action plan. As a result of this, Logan decided to consider 'reporting' and 'taking action' as two distinct phases, the latter being more dependent on further exploration of the issues. The participants also requested clearer indicators to guide them in making an assessment of problems in a child's environment, or the type of behaviour likely to arouse suspicion. Logan modified the form in line with the suggestions of the participants by offering more specific guidance on the identification of factors in a child's environment that may have affected their welfare, as well as ways of describing aspects of their behaviour. She outlined a plan to pilot and evaluate it with one professional group, probably teachers, for a given period. She also signalled her intention to discuss the implementation of the Assessment of Concern form with a multi-disciplinary group of health board staff, and to monitor the impact of new referral procedures on the substantiation rate of newly reported cases.

While official guidelines have now provided pro-forma reporting forms for professionals, it is undoubtedly the case that the implementation of assessment frameworks such as Logan's have provided professionals such as teachers and general practitioners with considerable assistance towards gathering their thoughts and focusing on the specific areas that cause them concern about children's safety and welfare.

Filtering out and fitting in

The tension identified in the introduction to this chapter, between child protection and family support, was the subject of a project carried out in 1998 by Sue Kane, at the time a child care worker employed by the Western Health Board. Kane set out to examine the role of the community care child care worker and took an unusual route by exploring the link between the timing and nature of referrals to the child care service and the type of assessment criteria operated by duty social workers. Essentially, she hypothesised that the reason why child care workers received referrals about cases at a fairly advanced stage, when a crisis had arisen, rather than sooner when the need for family support could have been identified, was because of the filtering criteria used by social workers. This, she believed, both stemmed from and fed into a lack of clear policy regarding the fit between social work and child care work in a community care setting. Kane had based her speculation on evidence in the literature (Buckley, Skehill and O'Sullivan, 1997; Parton, 1997) that social workers assessed the concerns reported to them in terms of the immediate risk that they appeared to pose for children, 'filtering out' rather than 'fitting in' alternative perspectives. She considered the extent to which the organisational culture of social work influenced the manner in which the role of the community child care worker was defined and determined. Kane also wondered if more active participation by child care workers in intake meetings might make a positive difference in terms of their ability to pick up referrals at a more appropriate point.

For her fieldwork, Kane studied the case records of a sample of twelve child protection and welfare cases that were referred to the duty system over a four-week period. She also conducted in-depth interviews with two community care child care workers, one social work team leader, one senior social worker and one child care manager. From her study of the records, which indicated that only five of the twelve referrals progressed into 'cases', she was able to ascertain that those involving fairly visible child protection concerns elicited an immediate response from the duty social worker. At the same time she found that those with no specific child protection concerns but with welfare needs were more likely to be directed out of the department to other services or else closed with no further action. None was referred to the child care worker despite the apparent need, in some of them, for family support. This represented an under-utilisation of a readily available resource.

From the data gathered by interview, Kane noted that no policy had been developed by management with regard to the use of the child care posts. She found that while her child care colleagues were clear about their role and function in providing family support, her social work colleagues and her managers had difficulty in specifying a particular role for the post. While the team meeting was the forum for determining the nature of intervention into families with child care or protection concerns, the decisions made there appeared to be framed almost entirely in line with social work priorities. These in turn were determined, according to Kane, by the level of risk currently being experienced by children. Risk, however, was defined in terms of harms that had happened or were likely to imminently happen to a child rather than a manifestation of a child's longer-term welfare needs. A social work manager interviewed for the study acknowledged that it was difficult, within the current context, to prioritise preventive work. Kane therefore found that not only was the role of the child care worker ill-defined but that an ambivalence existed regarding the value of preventive work.

While Kane was reluctant to make strong claims on the basis of her research, she raised several provocative questions regarding the manner in which the child care workers' access to clients was organisationally determined. She tentatively suggested that community care child care workers in her area were conforming to the cultural norms identified by Pithouse (1987) in relation to collegiality by never challenging or confronting their social work colleagues, and that social workers, acting within the same norms, were actively controlling the degree to which their 'territory' was visible and accessible to others. Kane also questions whether or not these practices reflect Hugman's (1991) theory about the higher status of 'problem solving and curing' social work over 'curing and tending' welfare or family support work. Kane's work raises another issue, later dealt with in detail by Skehill (1999) who argues that social workers, prior to the development of the child protection system, were still battling for space with the more 'legitimate' professions such as medicine and psychology and subsequently 'claimed' child protection as a way of validating their work and giving it status, to the extent that it began to dominate their professional practice from then on. These conclusions confirm the complex challenge that faces professions in adjusting to a change of focus.

Kane concluded that the potential role of the community care child care worker in providing early intervention would depend for its effectiveness on the establishment of clear policies and structures. She recommended :

- 'advertising' the child care worker service more widely
- defining a specific area of work for each child care worker to avoid the danger of being spread out too thinly
- restructuring the duty meeting to facilitate the process of early identification of children in need

- establishing a 'clinic' service for child care workers to meet clients and facilitate referral by duty workers.

Finally, she conceived of the way forward as focusing less on care workers' tasks and social workers' tasks and more on the task that they can share in providing a holistic child protection and welfare service.

Neglecting neglect?

Kane had suggested that the organisational culture of social work departments determined the somewhat narrow response that was made to child protection and welfare referrals. Following a similar line of enquiry, Brian Graham, at the time a social work team leader in the Eastern Health Board, undertook a study in 1998 to examine the way that community care social workers responded to referrals specifically concerning child neglect. This is an area that has received considerable attention in international research, many studies showing both the high proportion of neglect referrals made to child protection systems and the equally high rate at which these reports are eliminated from the system without the offer of services to the families involved (Dubowitz, 1994; Farmer and Owen, 1995; Gibbons, Conroy and Bell, 1995; Stevenson, 1998; Buckley, Skehill and O'Sullivan, 1997). It has also been suggested that the identification of child neglect is closely associated with dilemmas about 'cultural relativism' and the reluctance of workers to intervene in situations where the boundaries between inadequate care or welfare and other social problems such as poverty, disability, addiction, mental health and homelessness are blurred (Dingwall, Eekelaar and Murray, 1983; Stevenson, 1998; Buckley, 1999).

Graham speculated that the statutory obligations of health boards under the Child Care Act, 1991 to not only promote the welfare of children, but also take steps to identify such children, were a cause of considerable discomfort to health board practitioners. He also postulated that these statutory responsibilities were a source of conflict between the health board and other agencies. This was so, in his view, particularly in relation to neglect and emotional abuse. His project aimed to identify a group of cases referred to the health board social work department where concern had been expressed for a child's welfare, but where no specific allegation of physical or sexual abuse had been made, and to examine how this group of cases was processed.

Graham identified, from case records, eight 'neglect' referrals. His difficulty in actually isolating these cases from other referrals reflected, he believed, some of the dilemmas encountered by the social workers. For example, he found a lack of clarity in the referrals about categorisation and definition of the type of abuse alleged. He encountered very unspecific concerns and little documented linkage between factors such as homelessness and addiction with the welfare of the children concerned. These confusions were later mirrored in some of the assessment processes conducted by the workers.

In addition to his documentary analysis, Graham conducted in-depth interviews with the three social workers who had initially assessed the eight cases, as well as five of the professionals who had referred them. These included a head medical social worker, a Garda, a child psychiatrist and three public health nurses.

In his analysis of the 'neglect' files, Graham found five central themes:

- A considerable time delay between a referral of alleged neglect and its 'grounding' by a social worker. He found that once a decision had been made, even to send a letter, a feeling of containment appeared to set in and the matter lost its momentum until the next step materialised. This, he argues, illustrates the low priority assigned to neglect referrals
- Confusion and uncertainty about the referred information including doubts about its integrity and dissent about who should correct the confusion, ultimately resulting in a kind of stagnation
- A tendency for uncertainty about the referring information or any re-assurance about the family that emerged during the initial enquiry period to be used as a rationale for no further action
- No direct contact made between the health board social worker and the family in over half of his small sample (five out of eight)
- Decisions about a response made in terms of what, if any, immediate risk existed in relation to the child and the potential for changing unacceptable parental behaviour, but little consideration of the child's situation.

When he interviewed social workers about the neglect cases, Graham found them to be either 'overwhelmed' to the extent that they perceived their interventions to be of little use in the face of enormous and impervious problems, or 'underwhelmed' to the point where the workers tended to normalise the level of perceived neglect. The perceptions of the social workers suggested that they believed themselves to be working in a crisis-driven, overburdened system whose remit was tightly controlled and defined in terms of abuse in the very visible or active sense of injuries or assaults. They identified the fact that procedures and systems existed for the assessment and management of physical abuse and child sexual abuse but not particularly for concerns that were less clearly defined or identifiable. Graham argued that the underestimation of the significance of neglect by social workers was conditioned by the structures within which they were operating, which were inadequate to deal with the problems posed by neglect. He also, disturbingly, found, when he interviewed referrers, that they had little real expectation of a response from the social work department to their concerns about child neglect.

Graham understandably encountered inter-professional and inter-agency tensions around the making of neglect referrals, the health board social workers perceiving other agencies to be acting in an ill-considered and oppressive manner by 'dumping' cases on them when they had reached crisis point and the other professionals being highly critical of the social work response, seeing them as operating only a 'high-risk, high-return strategy where dramatic action might yield dramatic results'. Paradoxically, the more Graham recognised the lack of inter-agency work in this area, the more he identified the need for it if the cases were to receive an adequate response. He was forced to conclude that a mismatch had developed between community care social workers' operational strategies and priorities, their agencies' function and the sort of needs and concerns most frequently experienced by children and families. He made the following recommendations:

- a method of identifying child neglect to be adopted as part of the intake system
- 'masking' codes such as addiction and illness to be supplementary to and not instead of 'neglect' categories
- the development of universal, non-stigmatised, community-based support services
- efforts made to offer focused services to families where neglect is a concern in a supportive and facilitative rather than coercive manner that may be perceived as threatening
- a raising of awareness by social work team leaders and managers of the profile of neglect concerns in relation to local resource allocation and the development of locally-based services
- a broadening out of assessments to encompass, in a disciplined and analytical way, the needs of children in presenting situations
- the promotion of inter-agency work.

Finally, Graham argued for a restoration of the confidence of social workers to fulfil their responsibilities, so that, releasing themselves from the dilemmas of being over- and under-whelmed in the face of neglect, they can focus on what can, rather than what cannot, be achieved.

Assessment of children's needs

Graham's (1997) study illustrated the narrow approach being adopted by practitioners in response to concerns about children's safety and welfare. Two projects completed slightly later illustrate optional ways of assessing children's needs, taking approaches that go beyond immediate and visible signs of harm to considering other aspects of a child's family and community environment. The first study concerns the use of attachment theory as an assessment tool, and was conducted in 1999 by Liz Kennedy, a social worker in the South Eastern Health Board. Kennedy postulated that social workers were under-utilising a large body of available knowledge about the importance and quality of children's attachment to caregivers when making decisions about their current and future care. While she did not claim that attachment theory never featured in social work with children, she suggested that it was more likely to be 'stumbled upon' than it was to systematically underpin assessment, and that its use was largely implicit.

Kennedy's fieldwork for the study consisted of in-depth interviews with six social workers, four of whom were engaged in child protection work, one of whom specialised in fostering and one of whom was based in the maternity unit of a hospital. She then chose four of the cases currently open to some of the social workers and examined the degree to which attachment was a relevant issue in each one. Her objectives were:

- to examine the extent to which attachment theory was understood and utilised by social workers
- to demonstrate its applicability and its capacity to promote a more preventive approach to practice.

Drawing upon the works of Bowlby (1979, 1982), Ainsworth, (1991) Rutter (1981) and Fahlberg (1992), Kennedy argued that despite what she claimed was the changing orientation of child protection work and the pre-occupation with investigative procedures, attachment theory was as relevant as it ever had been. She claimed that Fahlberg's work in particular illustrates the way that attachment develops in an 'arousal-relaxation' cycle in a way that is accessible both to social workers and to those with whom they are working, particularly foster parents.

Having interviewed the social workers, Kennedy found that while they claimed to be familiar with the basic concepts of attachment theory, they did not tend to utilise it overtly in their practice, focusing instead on the presence or absence of risk in terms of children's safety from physical or sexual abuse. The exception to this was the worker in the maternity unit who would have worked from the outset with parents and infants and was very conscious of the need to observe their interactions.

When she examined the individual cases, Kennedy was able to identify significant attachment issues in each one. One of the cases involved a child who was reunited with his father following two years in foster care after his mother died. The worker had apparently paid considerable attention to the boy's relationships with his various caregivers and had made what seemed like correct decisions about his placement as a result. In the other three, however, two of which involved reunion, plans had been made, in Kennedy's view, without full consideration of the attachment issues involved. In one case, a three-year-old girl had been reunited with her mother after a prolonged separation for all of her first year. She had apparently never quite 'fitted in' and was later returned to the care of the health board following a non-accidental injury caused by her mother. Kennedy cautions against making a direct link between these two events and acknowledges that many other factors could have contributed to the outcome. However, she points out that the child's emotional safety did not appear to have been sufficiently considered when she was re-placed with her mother and that opportunities for preventive work may have been missed.

All the workers in Kennedy's study expressed enthusiasm for greater use of attachment theory in their work but argued that they were prevented from doing so by their heavy caseloads and lack of appropriate facilities for carrying out assessment. While Kennedy acknowledges that what she describes as the current 'defensive climate' does not facilitate the use of a broader approach to welfare work, she claims that considerations about attachment can be readily and usefully incorporated into child protection work. The result, she argues, would be the growth of more systematic and developmental approaches, the empowerment of caregivers who could gain insight into their parenting practices and better planning and decision making in relation to access and reunification for children separated from their families.

While Kennedy's focus was on the relationship between children and their caregivers, another study highlighted the importance of paying attention to the wider environment of families and children when assessing suspected child abuse, particularly neglect. Marguerite O'Neill, a senior clinical psychologist in the Mid-Western Health Board, conducted her project in 2000, and set out to explore four cases where child neglect was a concern. She looked at both the quality of caregivers' social networks and the emotional involvement of their children in the families. She was interested in finding out if any link existed between the two, with a view to making recommendations for practice.

O'Neill used two established research tools to carry out her study, the Social Network Map (Tracy and Whittaker, 1990) and the Family Relations Test (Bene and Anthony, 1985). She carried out structured interviews with four mothers and four of their children (two of whom were in care) who were known to a voluntary child care agency in her area. Neither the parents nor the children were previously known to her.

O'Neill presented her findings in relation to the mothers in terms of their social network 'maps'. She illustrated the amount and quality of support they received from their families, extended families, work or school, clubs or organisations, friends and neighbours. She found that in general, there was a paucity of support in the lives of the four women who had few friendships and no contact with their neighbourhoods. In two cases where the children were in care, the mothers did not include those children in their social networks. While O'Neill was cautious about inferring links too readily, she pointed out that lack of 'harmony and warmth' between parents and children is a feature of child neglect.

The children's emotional involvement with their families was examined by exploring a child's feelings towards various members of their families and their estimation of the level of reciprocity that existed. The findings, in O'Neill's view, were worrying as the use of the research tool indicated the presence in all the children of defence mechanisms such as denial and idealisation in relation to their families. In her view, this suggested that they were not as emotionally linked as they claimed, and seemed to have mixed feelings about their place in their mothers' affections. O'Neill found a clear dichotomy between the children who were in care and those living with their mothers, with a greater degree of apparent closeness between the children in care and their siblings than between themselves and their mothers. She concluded that for children who are part of families where neglect concerns exist, healthy psychological investment can be difficult. This, she suggested, can by compounded when their parents get little support from their social networks and lack internal as well as external resources.

On the basis of her findings, O'Neill recommended an emphasis on early intervention with a focus on attachment and emotional difficulties. She further recommended a broadening of the focus of statutory organisations with the goal of developing external or alternative supports for families in need. Finally, she endorsed the recurring recommendation for the ongoing provision of family support services.

Interventions

Graham (1998) and O'Neill (2000) have highlighted the necessity to take child neglect seriously and, together with Kennedy (1999), have focused on the specific factors in children's lives that must be considered when making an assessment of their situation. Two separate case studies presented as projects illustrate the types of intervention that work most successfully with cases of emotional abuse and neglect. The first was conducted in 1996 by Marie Faughey, then a public health nurse, who designed, carried out and evaluated a specific intervention. She focused on a case of non-organic failure to thrive (NOFTT) in 1996. NOFTT is, as it suggests, a condition where a young child's physical development is observably delayed with no obvious organic cause. It has been alternately defined as neglect (Department of Health [UK], 1991), emotional and psychological abuse (O'Hagan, 1993), psychological maltreatment (Wolfe and McGee, 1991) and emotional and physical neglect (Iwaniec, 1995). Acknowledging the lack of consistency in defining the cause and nature of the problem, Faughey adopted a definition drawn from the work of Gagan, Cupoli and Watkins (1984); Iwaniec, Herbert and McNeish (1985); and Weston and Colloton (1993), describing it as a condition in a young child where :

- weight is significantly below the expected standard (below the 3rd centile)
- there is objective evidence of weight loss or inadequate weight gain
- there is absence of a major organic condition that could directly affect the child's capacity to gain weight.

From the literature, Faughey was aware that, as well as little consensus on the definition and aetiology of NOFTT, neither was there much agreement on the treatment. There was evidence, however, that several multi-disciplinary approaches and methods may be required for effective intervention. She chose, for her fieldwork, to focus on a single case with which she was currently involved, where NOFTT had been identified. The case involved a child whom she called Joanne and who, at eleven months, was well below her expected rate of development. Joanne lived with her mother who had suffered from depression, had been a problem drug user, was taking care of five children with little support from her partner and was socially isolated from her family.

In order to inform her proposed intervention, Faughey interviewed a director of a voluntary drug agency, an academic with a special interest in addiction, a consultant paediatrician and a clinical psychologist. Using a framework developed by Iwaniec (1985), Faughey assessed Joanne's family composition, their financial position, their background, the health of Joanne's mother, the family's social support, the child's own history and development, her relationship with her mother and her feeding habits and patterns. On the basis of her assessment, Faughey designed a programme to be carried out over ten weeks, involving the family, herself and a community care child care worker. The intervention was aimed at:

- increasing Joanne's weight above the 3rd centile
- improving the parent/child interaction during feeding
- correcting the delay in Joanne's gross motor, fine motor and language development
- empowering the mother and raising her self-esteem.

Faughey outlined individual action plans designed to address target behaviours and problems and achieve desired results, identifying specific goals and proposed actions to be taken in relation to each of the difficulties identified. For example, she linked Joanne's lack of interest in food and poor appetite to a combination of factors, including her mother's depression and apathy, the fact that she wasn't sitting where she could see her mother and the way that she wasn't included in family mealtimes. Other areas targeted were the lack of routine and stimulation, Joanne's insecure attachment to her mother, the mother's sense of being overwhelmed by care-giving and the relationship problems between the mother and her (non-resident) partner. Many of the ameliorative strategies involved other personnel, including the community welfare officer, the community care child care worker, the general practitioner, the social worker, the addiction counsellor, staff in the day nursery and the paediatrician.

Faughey's own contribution to the multi-disciplinary plan of intervention was to visit weekly with the aims of tackling feeding in a constructive way, providing information, listening to the mother's concerns and positively reinforcing any changes that were observable. She also kept a diary in which she recorded events that affected the family, any changes, the content of each visit and observations of the mother/child interaction.

Although the mother and her partner were initially reluctant to participate, Faughey eventually managed to engage them and the programme worked according to plan. While she acknowledged that ten weeks is too short a period to achieve major change, the progress was very encouraging. Using a standardised measure, Faughey was able to demonstrate that the previously identified goals had been achieved in relation to Joanne's gross and fine motor development and the mother/child relationship. Joanne became far less insecure and her interaction with her mother became more positive and began to include smiles and laughter. Joanne displayed a new capacity to explore independently and seek comfort from her mother when she was upset, all illustrating a healthier attachment. Noticeable improvements were observable in relation to the mother's mental health and her interest in the programme. Goals in relation to Joanne's language, weight and feeding and the parents' relationship were partially reached, which is understandable within the time constraints. Joanne's developmental progress was confirmed by her paediatrician. Faughey emphasised that the progress was achieved not simply through her own interventions but in combination with the work conducted within the multi-disciplinary network.

Faughey concluded that the improvements achieved by Joanne and her family were significant and consistent with those identified in research, but cautioned that longer-term work was needed. She pointed out that despite the necessity, highlighted in the literature, for a multi-professional response to

NOFFT, she had encountered considerable difficulty in communicating with the other professionals involved in the case, either through their unavailability or apparent lack of interest. However, on the positive side, she suggested that similar interventions could provide exciting opportunities for public health nurses to engage in direct work with multi-problem families and avoid the proliferation of specialist referrals that often have a dis-empowering and marginalising effect on clients. Faughey makes the important point that even though special programmes are time consuming, her experience has been that the systematic management of work involved produces more positive outcomes.

The second project illustrating an intervention was conducted in 2000 by Fiona Ward, at the time a senior psychologist with the North Eastern Health Board. The subject of intervention was a twelve-year-old boy who had experienced serious adversity and was referred to the community care services with serious behavioural and attachment difficulties. In her study, Ward focused on the factors associated with positive change, and particularly emphasised resilience, turning points and relationships. She used a case study approach and obtained her data from a study of case records and semi-structured interviews with the child's mother, the family's social worker, the school principal and a class teacher, and a refuge worker who had known the family.

The child, who was known in the research as Michael, was the eldest of several siblings. Data from his case records showed that he had witnessed many incidents of domestic violence which understandably impacted on his mother's capacity to care for him and meet his developmental needs. Frequent moves and separations, including five periods in foster care, had contributed to an insecure attachment between Michael and his mother and had left the family isolated in the community. He suffered physical abuse from his mother's partners and manifested signs of emotional abuse and neglect. By the time he was ten years of age, he was displaying aggressive behaviour at school and, as Ward describes it, his early experience was characterised by 'insecurity, inconsistency, disruption and trauma'.

One of the challenges for the services was the negative relationship that existed between the family and professionals. However, during the period of intervention, the departure from the family of the mother's cohabitee represented a turning point as the mother now found herself in a position where she was able to recognise her need for help and avail of supports from the services. At the same time, the provision of a private counsellor for the mother (funded by the health board in order to provide the mother with a form of help that was acceptable to her) seemed to act as a bridge between the family and a range of other helping agents. The involvement of the same social worker over a long period was also a positive factor as she was able to engage the mother in a consistent, supportive relationship. Other intensive supports included a funded crèche placement for the youngest children and day fostering for the older two. The mother was offered therapeutic help by the psychology service. The multi-disciplinary health board group and the school made submissions to the Department of Education who provided an individual teacher to work with him, a factor which represented another important turning point. For the first time, Michael made positive relationships with school personnel and was able to take part in activities that fed into rather than diminished his self-esteem.

Ward identified all the foregoing factors as instrumental in initiating change for Michael and his family. However, the maintenance of change can be difficult to achieve and in Ward's view, several other important elements contributed to the continuance of progress. These included Michael's own resilience and positive qualities including his warmth, enthusiasm and sociability. Likewise, Ward identified the commitment of the workers and their overt values and beliefs, for example, the school principal's conviction that 'there's good in every child' once people are prepared to understand the meaning behind certain behaviours and feelings. All the professionals interviewed by Ward emphasised that future progress would only be sustained if the support offered at primary school was continued into secondary school.

Overall, Ward observed that four key themes emerged from her data that could be associated with the positive outcomes of intervention in this case. One was the importance of a secure base for a child, provided in this case by the school, which compensated for deficits in his primary relationships with caregivers. This illustrated the vital compensatory role played by social networks in situations where children and families have experienced adversity. The second was attention to a child's own resources and use of opportunities to build on existing resilience factors. In this case, the child's self-esteem was built up through facilitating him to partake in activities he enjoyed and excelled at. The third positive factor identified by Ward was the quality of relationships between families and professionals, a factor strongly associated with effective family support interventions (see Chapter Two) and also the long-term commitment of professionals to stay involved over the long haul. She cautioned that short-term focused interventions would not sustain change in cases where the impact of negative early experiences was profound. Finally, Ward emphasised the importance of core values such as empathy, inclusion and partnership between all actors in the network and taking a holistic view of a child and family.

In addition to highlighting the key elements of success in the case under study, Ward identified four important implications for practice arising from her research. Firstly, the building of trusting relationship between agencies, secondly, the recognition of the potential of school to promote positive change in vulnerable children, thirdly, the promotion of core values and finally, the maintenance of the belief that change is possible.

Evaluating child protection interventions and outcomes
The prospect of greater openness in the public service and the requirement to link inputs and outputs stipulated in the Government Health Strategy (Department of Health, 1994) led Gerry Lowry, at the time a senior social worker in the North Eastern Health Board, to consider how child protection practice could be effectively evaluated. In his project, conducted in 1995, he created a model for evaluation and used it to examine the objectives, services provided and outcomes for six child protection cases in his area that had been open for at least six months. Through semi-structured interviews, he ascertained the views of social workers responsible for managing the cases, together with those of parents in five out of the six sample cases.

Lowry pointed out that evaluation of child protection in Ireland has tended to consist of official investigations into cases that have had a high and negative public profile, such as the Kilkenny case. His study was an attempt to provide a way of analysing 'ordinary' cases in order to explore the processes involved and highlight, in a non-threatening manner, areas for improvement. He was aware of the difficulty of evaluating an area as complex and as dependent on social, cultural and organisational contexts as child protection and drew on existing models to illustrate the various elements and phases of a case career, i.e.

- referral
- investigation/assessment
- results of investigation/assessment
- decision to allocate services to some cases and not to others
- decision to close a case (Thorpe, 1994, pp 44-45).

Lowry pointed out that cases do not necessarily progress in a linear fashion, and highlighted the way they are also shaped by procedures and the outcome of negotiation around the creation of a casework relationship. He also emphasised that, even within this multi-dimensional framework, other factors could intervene to determine an outcome. Acknowledging the difficult nature of the task he had set himself and drawing on previously conducted evaluative studies (Corby, 1987; Thorpe, 1994) he designed an evaluation tool for use with interviewees. It consisted of three sections, looking at:

- the helping/ child protection process
- the service process

- outcome criteria – focusing on nine dimensions (after Parker, 1991) by which to assess the changes experienced by the child as a result of intervention.

While Lowry found that child protection appeared to be the first priority applied to cases, he also encountered a considerable degree of variation in the way that objectives were selected and understood by social workers and parents in the same cases. Some objectives appeared to be vague and long term while others were specific and short term. Even when the aim of intervention was described by social workers as therapeutic, parents appeared to perceive social work involvement as mainly protective. There also appeared to be a lack of harmony between social workers' perceptions of their own professional characteristics and the way that parents viewed them, with the parents being somewhat critical, though generally accepting of the social worker's approaches.

When inquiring about the provision of services, Lowry encountered differences between the responses of parents and social workers regarding the nature and usefulness of services, while both groups had difficulty linking services to outcomes. This, he concluded, probably stemmed from a lack of clear, agreed objectives and lack of built-in measures for judging the usefulness of services. Social workers' experiences of inter-agency co-operation and supervision were also mixed.

When perceptions of outcomes were examined, improvements in the individual children's situations were acknowledged by both parents and social workers, though Lowry found considerable variation in the extent, perceived source and understanding of the change. Social workers tended to focus on outcomes for the child, whereas parents gave considerable weight to the impact that intervention had on themselves as well. Satisfaction with outcomes depended on the way that families understood concepts such as 'emotional well-being' and their own wishes in relation to their children, for example where reunification was an issue. Social workers, it appeared, could appreciate when a positive outcome had been achieved, but were sometimes unclear as to how it had evolved. More complexity arose in 'neglect' cases than those concerned with physical abuse and sexual abuse, due, according to Lowry, to the uncertainty about definition and the difficulty in measuring progress where neglect was concerned.

While Lowry acknowledged that child protection is too complex and unstable an area for the application of one single model of evaluation, he concluded that the pursuit of key questions in relation to goals, methods for achieving goals and outcomes could result in more effective practice and better morale for workers and would have fewer resource implications. He strongly recommended the following measures to support the process:

- establishment of common definitions of abuse, risk and family support
- procedures and resources to support the system
- systematic questioning of intervention methods and processes
- the inclusion of consumer views in any evaluation
- the input of all members of the child protection network.

Research in the UK (Cleaver and Freeman, 1995) has indicated that outcomes in child protection work can be heavily dependent firstly, on the way that families experience the process of being investigated for suspected child abuse and secondly, on the nature of the relationship that exists between child protection workers, particularly social workers, and families. Cleaver and Freeman coined the term 'operational perspective' to describe the process employed by parents in order to make sense of and cope with an abuse accusation. Using a similar framework, Catherine Carty, at the time a child care worker in the Eastern Health Board, undertook a project in 1996 to explore what she termed the 'perception cycle' experienced by parents who came into contact with the social work department. Carty set out to conduct a retrospective study in which she interviewed a sample of clients who had been referred for the first time during a specific four-month period and whose files had since been closed. She chose her sample by applying these criteria to the ninety-nine referrals made in her area during the designated period and then randomly selecting and writing to ten of them. However, through this method she secured the agreement of only three clients for interview, so she asked her colleagues to put her in touch with others and by this means managed to interview two more. Ultimately, she interviewed three parents who were referred to the health board because there were concerns about alleged physical abuse and two where there were concerns about alleged sexual abuse.

Carty devised the term 'perception cycle' to illustrate the trajectory between pre-contact, contact and post-contact perceptions of clients. Her interviews with clients indicated a similar pattern whereby all of them experienced some kind of fear of either being judged unfit to care for their children, or having their children taken away. The fear had been present even when clients had self-referred to the health board and, as the interviews demonstrated, was associated with what Carty describes as their 'stereotypical' negative view of a social worker as someone who intervened punitively and removed children from their parents. When clients were asked how they found the actual interaction with the social worker, they described more fear, confusion about what was actually taking place or what might yet happen and reticence about asking for clarification. However, most of them ultimately considered the meeting to be useful, the most significant variable determining the change of attitude being the personality or personal qualities of the social worker. If she or he appeared caring, interested and non-judgmental the clients' fears generally subsided. In one contrasting case, the social worker was considered abrupt, not inclined to share information or to listen, and the client maintained her pre-contact negative view.

Carty found that four out of the five clients she interviewed had considerably changed their view of the social work service by the time the interaction with the social worker was over, particularly if they felt they had been 'listened to' and supported. In terms of the 'perception cycle' she considered that their attitudes could be constantly in flux depending on what was happening, but that a 'negative cycle' could be corrected by the substitution of a new worker or a more positive experience of the original worker. In analysing her findings, Carty made an association between the low participation rate of clients in her research and the negative pre-conceptions held of social workers by those that she did interview. She felt that both could be a result of certain factors such as negative views of the health board, suspicion that the health board was constantly 'checking up' on people, the threatening nature of child protection investigations, the family's standing in the community and the way that it would be affected if neighbours were aware of the health board's interest in them and the 'sacrosanct' nature of the Irish family. Data from the interviews confirmed that the negative image of child protection work had largely been created by the media.

Carty used the interviews to explore what areas, in the views of clients, could be improved in order to modify the negative attitude held about social workers in child protection. Suggestions included talks and presentations in schools and community groups about what social workers do and dissemination of information or booklets about clients' rights. Carty also felt that the issue of confidentiality needed to be explored by workers and explained more fully to clients in order to develop confidence in the child protection system.

Conclusion

The studies reported in this section highlight two important factors. One is the tendency, despite the statutory requirement of health boards to promote the welfare of children, for child protection services to assess concerns about children in a limited fashion. Several of the projects illustrated how responses of child protection workers focused on incidents rather than patterns of abuse and did so in an individualistic manner that took little cognisance of the child's ongoing developmental needs or the impact of external factors on the family system. Indeed, as Graham's study has shown, the object of assessment in cases of child neglect has tended to be parents, not the children, and the work that was done was determined by the structures and services that were available rather than the needs of the children. Essentially, as some projects illustrated, the 'child' in child protection is not always visible, a factor that has also been highlighted in child abuse inquiries and research (Western Health Board, 1996; Buckley, Skehill and O'Sullivan, 1997; The Bridge Consultancy, 1996).

The second factor is the effectiveness of focusing assessments on a range of factors in the child's context, as a number of the projects demonstrated. While some of the studies illustrated the failure of workers to respond to the less dramatic, more insidious problems and deprivations experienced by children, others have shown how the inclusion of easily accessible information regarding the child's physical and psychological development, and the family's social networks, can comprehensively inform an assessment and lead to appropriate and workable interventions.

In the United Kingdom, both Stevenson (1998) and Howe (1992) have protested that work with children and families, instead of adopting a framework based on professional skills, knowledge and values, has given itself up to a practice based on the technical rationality required by a heavily proceduralised system which stifles professional development. Gibbons, Conroy and Bell (1995), Farmer and Owen (1995), and others have shown through research that assessments carried out in a forensic manner can seem threatening to families and, in the long run, are not helpful to the majority who enter the child protection net.

The development of the child protection system in Ireland has been much slower than that in the UK, and has never been as bureaucratised. However, there is no doubt that a more defensive climate has developed in Ireland following the child abuse inquiries of the 1990s. A senior health board administrator (Doherty, 1996) has identified the 'moral panic' that has evolved in recent years which, he observes, is

> characterised by a desperate search for simple solutions based on unrealistic and often contradictory expectations, and a failure to grasp the realities of dealing with child protection situations (Doherty, 1996, p.103).

Most of the studies discussed in this section would in some respects reflect the sort of ethos that Doherty referred to, and would have justifiably criticised both the organisational culture and the structures that have influenced the narrowing focus of services. To reverse such developments in the current climate would be very challenging and require radical refocusing at a broad policy level, a point highlighted by Parton (1997) commenting on the UK situation. The development of support services and resources must support any broadening of assessment; otherwise it will be just a paper exercise.

On the positive side, the projects identified approaches that, even without a massive injection of resources, could provide a service that is far more child-centred and effective. As some of them illustrated, not all 'concerns' represent child abuse but still require attention at a multi-disciplinary level. Building on existing strengths is as important a part of intervention as the identification of difficulties. The recommendations made concerning the integration of the community care child care worker into child protection and welfare work at an earlier stage represent an efficient use of an already existing resource. The importance of raising the profile of child neglect has been emphasised, in terms of acknowledging the seriousness of its short- and long-term effects, so that it no longer gets sidelined in favour of the more visible categories of child maltreatment such as child sexual abuse and physical abuse.

This section has highlighted the importance of using a needs-based assessment, built on knowledge of child development, attachment theory and the effect of structural problems on families' ability to cope, in order to assess a child's needs, enable parents to understand the basis for existing concerns and, ultimately, connect them with external supports. Even though services may not be sufficiently developed at any given time to address the needs identified in the broader assessments suggested by these projects, the first step is clearly to highlight and document both the protective factors that need strengthening and the problems that need addressing. Providing evidence for both will, at the very least, outline a framework for the provision of new services. Finally, the two evaluations that focused on intervention illustrated the need for clarity in relation to objectives and strategies and the importance of linking them to a clear assessment of the presenting difficulties. Throughout, the emphases was on warmth, respect and honesty in the worker/client relationship.

The theme of inter-agency and inter-professional relationships permeated most of the projects discussed in this and earlier chapters. It will be dealt with in detail in Chapter Five.

5

Inter-Agency and Inter-Professional Relationships

Introduction

Inter-agency collaboration and co-operation have, for many years, been considered fundamental to effective practice, and have been enshrined in legislation and official guidance here in Ireland as elsewhere (Department of Health, 1987, 1995, 1999; DHSS [UK] 1991; DoH [UK], 1999). The 'ideal' child protection system presented as a multi-professional network, whose interlocking elements combine to produce a seamless, comprehensive and holistic response to the cases of child maltreatment that come to its attention. Since the development of the child protection system in Ireland, certain professionals have been regarded as central to the task of recognising and reporting concerns about children and working with children and families where risk has been identified. These typically include social workers in both statutory and voluntary organisations, public health nurses, general practitioners, teachers, child care workers, An Garda Síochána and hospital staff and, as this section will show, others whose significance and contribution is not always acknowledged.

Whilst there appears to be general agreement in the literature about the desirability of collaborative work, the complexities of trying to achieve it are well recognised. Irish child abuse inquiries go back as far as 1982 (Government Information Services, 1982). More recently, the Kilkenny incest investigation, and the Kelly Fitzgerald and McColgan cases have repeatedly highlighted instances where information was not shared and working relationships broke down (Department of Health, 1993; Western Health Board, 1996; North Western Health Board, 1998). It has been claimed that weaknesses in inter-agency work were fundamental to the inadequacies in practice identified in these high-profile cases. Not surprisingly, *Children First* has highlighted the importance of this area, outlining the personal and corporate responsibilities of professionals and organisations towards the protection of children.

However, professionals working in the front line of child protection will know that even mandating co-operation will not ensure that it happens and are aware of the dangers of over-simplifying its feasibility. Analyses offered in British, Australian and Irish literature would suggest that the problems can be structural in terms of inadequate resources, stringent gate-keeping, lack of inter-agency strategies, isolation of workers, non-synchronous work patterns, poor recording systems, high turnover of staff and unfilled vacancies. Some professional reasons for failure to work together have been identified as rivalries, differences in power and status, stereotyping, role confusion and disagreements about confidentiality and other ethical norms (Hallett and Stevenson, 1980; Reder, Duncan and Gray, 1993; Birchall and Hallett, 1995; Morrison, 1996; Butler, 1996; Scott, 1997; Buckley, 2000a). Many of these factors are almost imperceptibly built into professional and organisational culture and can be uncomfortable and in some cases, costly, to challenge. While research carried out in Britain has been useful, it is important to acknowledge the administrative differences between the British and Irish child protection systems. It is necessary, therefore, when making judgements about the feasibility of joint work between different agencies and professionals, to consider the context in which statutory and non-statutory staff delivering services to children operate.

It follows that, if inter-agency co-operation is to be realistically achieved, the essential elements that need to be developed in each situation must firstly be identified and, secondly, addressed in a realistic and achievable manner. This topic was the focus either directly or indirectly of a substantial number of projects produced by a range of professionals who found it to be of relevance to their own professional practice. Individual pieces of work were produced by members of An Garda Síochána, social workers, public health doctors, public health and community nurses, and a training and information officer. The necessity to address the working relationships between An Garda Síochána and the health boards received a considerable amount of attention, particularly as the requirement for joint notification and planning was introduced in 1995. Specific Gardaí/health board working relationships and strategies will be discussed in Chapter Six. The remainder of this chapter will discuss the projects that focused on inter-agency relationships at a wider level.

Inter-agency co-operation between members of the professional network
A number of projects examined co-operation and collaboration in the broad professional network. These studies included staff from different services within the health boards as well as teachers and general practitioners who have been identified in guidance and child abuse inquires as essential partners in child protection and welfare work. The projects varied from the exploration of attitudes and assessment of needs to the evaluation of specific programmes and events designed to promote inter-agency co-operation.

A project carried out in 1995 by Marie McNamara, then a public health nurse in the Mid-Western Health Board, explored the attitudes of a wide range of professionals in relation to child protection work. She interviewed nineteen members of the child protection network, including two Gardaí, two social workers, three public health nurses, two general practitioners, a home help organiser, a playgroup co-ordinator, three school principals, a foster parent, a youth leader, an area medical officer, a community welfare officer and a child psychologist. One of the most interesting findings was the degree to which professional perspectives on child protection differed by virtue of occupational orientation, and depended to a degree on local experiences, such as whether or not special training or policies had been recently implemented. McNamara found that individual professionals had extensive knowledge of their own child protection cases and their own aims and objectives, but lacked what she described as 'overall knowledge' about roles and the system in general. She also found that some professionals who regarded themselves as having a fairly significant contribution to make, such as home helps and community welfare officers, were disregarded by others as being peripheral to the work.

While McNamara found general practitioners to be alert to the physical signs of child abuse, she felt their perspective and their understanding of their own role in child protection was limited and the general practitioners she interviewed expressed reluctance to attend case conferences. In her view, the professions most likely to have a more holistic view of family situations, and therefore of the full context in which child abuse may be taking place, were public health nurses, teachers and community welfare officers. However, she observed that some of these professionals lacked guidance in how to recognise and assess risk.

Viewing her findings from a public health nursing perspective, McNamara acknowledged that the varied nature of the caseload of public health nurses might mitigate against their ability to devote enough time to child protection issues. However, she recognised the opportunities to be gained by their involvement in so many sectors and their ready access to families and recommended the development of the public health nurse role for those who have an interest in the area of child protection.

As well as role confusion, lack of feedback from social workers to other disciplines, particularly teachers, following referral to the child protection system was cited in many instances as a major impediment to inter-agency co-operation. This resulted, according to McNamara, in some professionals feeling isolated and ill-equipped to deal with the consequences of making a report and thus disinclined to refer again in the future. On the positive side, she found a lot of support for the concept of greater co-operation, particularly outside 'crisis' situations as well as a willingness on the part of most professionals to take part in any endeavours to develop it.

On the basis of her findings, McNamara recommended the implementation of strategies for inter-agency co-operation, but cautioned strongly against the elimination of debate and challenge – she reiterated the view of Blyth and Milner (1990) that working relationships that become too comfortable may generate a degree of unhealthy collusion. The methods recommended by her included training, particularly in relation to procedures and management of cases, to be delivered at a multi-disciplinary level as well as to specific groups such as playgroup leaders who may have little prior experience in child protection and welfare issues. She also recommended the streamlining of case conferences, with protocols and the development of a 'core' group of regular invitees. McNamara also recommended focused inter-agency meetings to discuss local social and health profiling, as well as local initiatives and the development of a format to improve communication and feedback. She suggested that these meetings would be attended by 'regular' child protection professionals with the rotational inclusion of other practitioners including foster parents. An important focus of inter-agency co-operation, in McNamara's view, was the development of a universal format for risk assessment, to be used by all professionals in the network.

Another exploration of inter-agency co-operation was undertaken in a slightly different, but very relevant, context in 1998 by Anne Pritchard, a community nurse based on a child guidance team delivering services in a rural area of the then Eastern Health Board. She set out to look at the working practices and working relationships between the child guidance team and the local community care team with a view to making recommendations for enhanced professional relationships. She carried out a total of ten interviews, four with the child guidance team, five with the community care team and one with a senior manager who had responsibility for both services. An important contextual factor was the recent amalgamation of the child guidance service with the Children and Families Programme of the Eastern Health Board. Pritchard acknowledges that the combination of a rural setting and the relative stability of staff in both services may have been contributory factors to what was a relatively harmonious relationship between the teams that may not necessarily be replicated in other areas.

Pritchard found that while some working practices differed, the factor that bound both services was their commitment to the promotion of child welfare and the provision of therapy to children in difficulties. She highlighted the necessity to develop good working relationships between the teams, following the assertion by Sanders, Jackson and Thomas (1996) that treatment services are an essential element of the child protection system.

Starting with the positive elements of the relationship between the child guidance and community care services, Pritchard noted the similarity of purpose shared between them, and the flexibility with which both agencies make and receive services from each other. However, she cautioned that not all child psychiatric services, including those within the same health board region, work under the same structures and that some insist on medical referrals before they will provide services. She also noted the high level of informal consultation between the services, though she once again pointed out that the unique context of a rural area and stable teams are significant factors. However, on the more problematic side, Pritchard highlighted the lack of formal structures for contact between the two agencies, apart from a 'case by case' approach which is more often than not crisis driven. She found that the presence of waiting lists in both services could be a source of tension between them. Recent and rapid administrative changes were also perceived to be a cause of strain, and while these may be once-off events, current trends would indicate that many services will be coping with differences in structure over the coming months and years. A factor that appeared to frustrate both services was the lack of 'mandate' held by professionals attending inter-agency meetings – for example, a representative from the child guidance team could not guarantee that a child would be accepted for treatment even if it was recommended. Similarly, community care personnel could not guarantee a service like family support or a residential place without further consultation. The degree to which child protection conference recommendations were binding or not was another source of tension, as was the view held by each team that professionals from the other specialties were not 'trained' to make decisions in their own field.

When Pritchard examined working relationships between the two agencies, she again found many positive factors, particularly associated with informal friendships between staff on the teams. However, she did pick up tensions around what is often perceived of as 'cherry picking' by the child psychiatric team, and a lack of agreement about whether treatment should take place before, after or during an investigation into alleged child abuse. An interesting insight from the interview data was the emerging view that each agency needed to pay attention to its own internal working relationships and structures.

Pritchard's findings led her to recommend bi-monthly meetings to discuss cases causing concern, which she believed would reduce anxiety, and demystify the reality of what each service had to offer. In common with other projects cited here, she recommended cross-agency training and more frequent contact on formal and informal bases. A significant, and very relevant recommendation is the development of a joint working initiative between child guidance, community care and possibly other agencies providing services in the area, to identify gaps and lobby for resources. Pritchard asserted that this would not only achieve a more comprehensive service to children and families at risk, but would alleviate the perception that services were holding back on necessary resources.

Inter-agency co-operation between teachers and health boards
John Kelly, at the time a social worker in the NWHB seconded to the Child

Abuse Prevention Programme, undertook a project in 1995 to explore the potential for schools to work together with community care services in a health promotion role. He randomly selected ten schools from the one hundred and eighty primary schools in Co. Donegal, and interviewed their principals. He was careful to focus his interviews on the potential for positive development rather than concentrating on the problems that existed between the health and education services. Kelly aimed firstly, to investigate schools' perceptions of their caring and health promotion roles with a view to suggesting a pilot project to progress any potential aspiration towards more integrated work. He found that teachers were very positive about the schools medical service as well as the public health nurse nursing service and the health education service offered by the health board. They were also happy with the child abuse prevention programme which, at the time, was delivered jointly by the education sector and the health board. Teachers were reasonably positive about contact with the social work service, though their experience was very limited. More reservations were expressed about the speech and language therapy service and the psychology service where inadequate resourcing and the need for more practical advice to teachers were identified. Where more general inter-agency difficulties were identified, they included the isolation of schools, the way that teachers are 'taken for granted' by other organisations and the apparent impossibility of 'off the record' conversations with social workers.

Kelly found that while teachers acknowledged their role as protectors of children and were keen to promote child welfare, their duty to report suspected child abuse caused them some discomfort. The guidelines in operation at the time (Department of Education, 1991) were not, it appeared, widely disseminated, nor were they considered useful.

The sort of pilot scheme proposed by Kelly on the basis of his findings from this project would consist of a body of teachers, with parent and pupil representatives, who would meet with health board personnel including speech therapist, psychologist, social worker and possibly the juvenile liaison officer from An Garda Síochána. The meetings would have the dual purposes of introducing personnel to each other, and focusing on specific, practical issues such as the delivery of services. School principals identified the benefits of such a project as facilitating communication, providing more mutual support, and enabling the early detection of abuse. While they saw the demands such a process would make upon school time as a potential difficulty, they were still in favour of such a venture. Kelly himself believed that a project such as this would eventually address some of the identified inter-agency difficulties and would lead to the development of a pro-active integrated service that would ultimately be of considerable benefit to children.

Carmel Keane, who was also, at the time, a social worker seconded to the

CAPP programme, based in the Mid-Western Health Board area, carried out a project in 1996 which also sought to explore the role of primary teachers in the early identification and referral of child abuse, and to identify the main issues that arose for them with regard to communication with health board professionals. She interviewed all the primary school principals (nine) in one health board sub-area, together with nine health board professionals – four social workers, four public health nurses and an area medical officer. Although it was not strictly speaking a case study, Keane loosely based her research on thirteen child protection cases that had 'shared' the involvement of health board and school staff the previous year. The majority of cases concerned child neglect, reflecting the local and national pattern in identified child abuse. However, Keane pointed out that this figure could have been artificially low as teachers may not necessarily recognise or define neglect as 'abuse'. She found that teachers were influenced in their referral practices by prior positive or negative experiences with the health board as well as their professional experience and local knowledge. Like Kelly (1995), she found that the Department of Education guidelines barely featured in schools' knowledge base on child protection.[5] She found little experience of teacher participation in case conferences and confusion regarding the type of information schools were required to pass on to the health board. Like McNamara (1995) Keane encountered dissatisfaction on the part of teachers regarding the lack of feedback from the health board following referral, or if they had a child in their school who was in care. This appeared to be an understandable source of great annoyance to them, given what they perceived as the demands for information made upon them by health board staff. Keane found, when she interviewed health board professionals, that they had quite a high level of understanding of the dilemmas experienced by teachers, particularly their fear of repercussions from parents and their feeling of being 'overwhelmed' when confronted with a case of suspected child abuse. Conflicting views and practices concerning the identification of teachers as reporters of child abuse were a cause of frustration to staff from both sectors. However, it appeared that when the rationale behind revealing a name was explained, teachers were prepared to accept it.

Keane found several discrepancies between the Department of Health child abuse guidelines and those operated by the Department of Education. Both have since been revised and are now more consistent with each other, but this project made the very important point that unless such guidance is agreed by

[5] The fact that the Department of Education guidelines have now been revised and will be disseminated possibly renders this finding out of date but underlines the need for wide and recurring distribution of such policies.

all parties likely to be involved in the work, confusion and resentment can ensue. In common with most inter-agency projects, Keane recommended regular inter-agency meetings and joint training. She also highlighted areas for attention in teacher training courses including the following:

- signs and symptoms of child abuse
- factors likely to lead to child abuse
- steps to be taken if abuse is suspected
- guidelines for referral
- guidelines on report writing
- the emotional impact of abuse on professionals
- overcoming barriers to co-operation.

Other recommendations included an emphasis on good practice in the health board with regard to providing feedback, and maximising the use of the school medical examinations to both facilitate the assessment of child neglect and emotional abuse and promote good inter-professional relationships.

Doctors and child protection

The involvement of doctors, particularly general practitioners, in child protection has been the focus of research studies and child abuse inquiries both in Ireland and the UK. It has been suggested that general practitioners fail to fulfil their reporting obligations and are poor at communicating child protection concerns or consulting with non-medical colleagues. It has also been suggested they assume a 'superordinate' role in child abuse cases, are poor attenders at case conferences, and show little commitment to child protection training (Dingwall, 1979; London Borough of Brent, 1985; Lea-Cox and Hall, 1991; Hallett and Birchall, 1992; Department of Health, 1993; North Western Health Board, 1998; Buckley, 1998; Polnay, 2000). Antoinette Rogers, at the time an acting Director of Community Care in the South Eastern Health Board, undertook a project in 1996 to explore the perspectives and practices of a randomly selected group of ten general practitioners in her area. As she pointed out, her research was based on the conjecture that doctors are not well integrated into the child protection system.

Rogers found that only half the general practitioners she interviewed were familiar with the 1987 child abuse guidelines which were operative at the time. Consistent with earlier research, Rogers found that general practitioners came into contact with very few cases of suspected child abuse. Despite this, however, she found that they had a clear perception of their roles and responsibilities in relation to reporting to the health board. Most of them had attended child protection conferences and were positive about their value, but would have had strong reservations about attendance if parents were to be present. Some of the general practitioners interviewed were critical of the management of case conferences and offered suggestions to improve efficiency and effectiveness. Anxiety was expressed by several of them in relation to the provision and circulation of written reports, as well as the extent to which they could reveal information about their patients. On the basis of her findings, Rogers highlighted the need to have some kind of liaison system between general practitioners and the health board in order to ensure a satisfactory flow of information, and suggested that the health board should take the lead in providing training. She added that doctors' suggestions regarding the management of child protection conferences should be taken seriously, with a view to increasing their participation overall. In general, she concluded that general practitioners were familiar with and interested in child protection to an extent far greater than she would have predicted, but acknowledged that her study was carried out relatively shortly after a high-profile child abuse inquiry in the area (Department of Health, 1993) in which the role of the general practitioner had been highlighted. She also conceded that the responses made to her questions might not necessarily be reflected in practice. Nonetheless, she claimed that significant progress appeared to have been made as far as the participation of general practitioners in the child protection system was concerned.

Taking cognisance of the broadening role of all medical doctors in child protection work, Mary Fitzgerald, an area medical officer in the Western Health Board, explored protocols for medical diagnosis and assessment of child abuse. Fitzgerald was aware from the literature of the necessity for doctors to develop methods for the accurate assessment of child sexual abuse in particular and for the utilisation of specialists in the conduct of physical examinations. She was also aware of the necessity for doctors to employ the type of 'jigsaw' approach recommended in the Cleveland report (Butler-Sloss, 1988) which would incorporate different levels of medical, social and psychological assessment to complete a picture of the child's condition. She sent questionnaires to all the Directors of Community Care (DCCs) in Ireland, medical doctors who were at the time responsible for the management of child abuse cases in their areas,[6] to collect data on prevalence and incidence, referral patterns and methods for assessing different types of child abuse. She also conducted an in-depth interview with a doctor from a

---

[6] Directors of Community Care, or their designates, are no longer responsible for the management of child abuse cases. This task has now been assumed by child care managers in each health board area.

child sexual abuse assessment unit. Less than half of the DCCs responded to the questionnaire and in Fitzgerald's view, this partly reflected the varying arrangements for the assessment of child sexual abuse in different health board regions as DCCs did not all consider themselves to be the most appropriate respondents to questions on this area. The findings revealed inadequate systems for recording referral rates, with a need for clearer definitions and guidelines for referral. Fitzgerald noted that reporting rates by doctors varied a lot, and speculated that the presence of paediatric and obstetric social workers on some teams may account for raised awareness of child protection concerns and therefore an increased likelihood of reporting in particular areas. She also noted a predominance of child sexual abuse referrals by doctors, as opposed to emotional abuse and neglect. She inferred from this that doctors were less inclined to look out for the latter forms of harm to children. Where evaluation of suspected child sexual abuse was concerned, Fitzgerald found that even though arrangements varied from area to area, there was an appreciation of the need for special expertise in physical examinations.

On the basis of her findings, Fitzgerald pointed out that the development of a central epidemiological data base on medical aspects of child abuse would enable diagnosis and thus facilitate treatment and prevention. She also recommended the clarification of potential therapeutic roles for referring physicians who, in her view, could help families to focus on positive outcomes.

As a second strand to her project, Fitzgerald established, on a trial basis, an inter-disciplinary forum to discuss and develop means of addressing child protection and welfare concerns in the region. On the basis of a preliminary meeting of the group, attended by medical and community care professionals and a member of An Garda Síochána, a proposal was made to form a smaller group to develop into an Area Child Protection and Welfare Policy Working Group. The first meeting raised a number of points to be addressed prior to developing policy, including: different professional perspectives, confidentiality issues, medical ethics, sharing of information, and the need to explore the dynamics and hidden anxieties underlying collaborative work. Fitzgerald recommended that the group then progress towards the development of guidelines on identifying and reporting child abuse along with protocols, the latter to include guidance on the management and feedback of information. She also recommended that the group develop a standard protocol for the medical evaluation of child abuse, based on her survey findings.

The use of inter-disciplinary meetings to progress fruitful working relationships was the subject of another project later carried out by a public health doctor. Mary Conway, an area medical officer in the South Eastern

Health Board, also proposed the development of local child protection network meetings and used this as the focus of her research in 1995. Mindful of the conclusions of the Kilkenny Report (Department of Health, 1993) regarding the lack of co-ordination and communication about professional activities, she had also become aware of the number of missed opportunities where concerns about individual cases was experienced by different professionals but not necessarily communicated to each other. This project proposed similar models to those suggested by McNamara (1995) and Kelly (1995) but differed from them insofar as the professional networks were in this instance intended to be health board staff only, and one of the functions would be the discussion of individual, known cases. Confidentiality was therefore a significant issue, but was addressed by the development of a set of norms to be agreed by participants and their managers. It was also necessary to confine the 'network' to a reasonably small area in order to ensure that participants were familiar with the cases and matters to be discussed.

Conway progressed her project further than the developmental stage by actually holding three network meetings on a trial basis and evaluating the outcomes. For the purposes of the initial meetings, she focused on a small geographical area, and included the local general practitioner, the public health nurse, the social worker, the community welfare officer and herself. The aim of the project was to establish a forum for discussion of issues arising in the local area and facilitate the development of good working relationships. It also had the practical objective of conforming with Section 3 (2) of the Child Care Act, 1991 to identify children in the area not receiving adequate care and protection. Conway initially selected the participants on the basis of the potential contribution of each one – for example, though she frequently shared premises with general practitioners providing a medical service, she had found it increasingly difficult to find the time to discuss cases with them. She was aware that the professional training of doctors encourages them to make decisions without consultation with others, and that the status of doctors makes it difficult for some of them to accept that a professional of a perceived lower status may have a greater understanding of a case. She therefore considered them to be essential participants in her project. While public health nurses and social workers were normally regarded as central to the child protection system, Conway was keen to involve community welfare officers, whom she regarded as well placed to detect families under stress and observe relationships between families and children. Like McNamara (1995), she identified the value of their involvement in child protection though it is not often recognised in official policy.

The three network meetings facilitated by Conway were specifically focused on different topics. The first one concentrated on building up an area profile. This meeting had the considerable benefit of highlighting not only information about the population, but also about the number of services, not known to every professional, which were being provided for families and children. The second meeting focused on risk assessment – a topic that had also been recommended for inclusion in McNamara's (1995) proposed network meetings – and provided an opportunity for discussion of cases which were of mutual concern. The third meeting focused on the exploration of professional roles in child protection. The third one, in Conway's view, was the most challenging as it obviously touched on an area that was not comfortable for an inter-professional group, that of assigning tasks to other professionals while still 'owning' cases.

Conway made a presentation of the network pilot project to colleagues in public health nursing as well as a group of area medical officers, a group of social workers and a multi-disciplinary community care group. All groups, as well as all the individuals who had participated, were positive about the benefits to be gained. Public health nurses were among the most enthusiastic, thus reflecting their sometimes isolated position. Area medical officers were also keen to develop the networks, though they expressed reservations about the demand on their time. Social workers were also interested, but expressed caution about the potential for an increased referral rate to them. The multi-disciplinary group recommended the inclusion of dentists and speech and language therapists. Conway herself concluded that child care workers, when they were appointed, would be a useful addition.

Conway felt that certain factors would be essential to the future success of network meetings in the area – the support of management, sharing responsibility for arranging and recording the meetings and the facility to discuss 'real' cases which meant keeping the networks local where possible. She recommended that bi-monthly meetings would suffice once the networks were established.

Multi-disciplinary training

A model for training in child protection at a multi-disciplinary level was designed and utilised by Patrick Gannon, at the time an information and training officer with the Western Health Board in Mayo, in 1994. Gannon traced the origins of multi-disciplinary community care work to the 'district care teams' devised by McKinsey (1970) when the health boards were first set up. He cited O'Mahony's (1985) evaluation of their poor development, which ground to a final halt in the mid-1980s, illustrating the complexity inherent in achieving collaboration even within a single agency. In his project, Gannon laid a lot of emphasis on management as a key issue in attaining teamwork, citing principles of mutual trust, mutual respect and the individual freedom necessary for exceptionally high employee performance.

Gannon's interdisciplinary workshop aimed to

- provide a clear outline of the legislative framework within which child protection work operates
- facilitate multi-disciplinary discussion on teamwork with emphasis on the obligation of the health boards to promote the welfare of children
- give information on and discuss current child protection development within the Western Health Board area
- identify the strengths and weaknesses of multi-disciplinary teamwork.

Following consultation with colleagues, Gannon confined participation in the first workshop to health board staff including administrative personnel as well as representation from the general and special hospitals programmes. It had been agreed that work needed to be completed at health board level prior to inclusion of representatives from other statutory and voluntary groups. Methods of evaluation were built in, comprising feedback sheets and a focused discussion.

As well as identifying barriers to collaboration – burnout, poor accommodation, isolation, competitiveness, defensiveness, lack of role clarity, poor feedback, lack of opportunity to meet, poor co-ordination and personality differences – the workshop participants identified and discussed ways of maximising the opportunities for team development. These included better planning and evaluation, better accountability, service development determined by 'quality' as opposed to 'quantity', innovative thinking, increased understanding and communication between disciplines, and the provision of better services to clients.

The feedback following the workshop was positive, not least because of the opportunity it gave staff to meet each other and spend time together. However, Gannon cautiously highlighted the important point that while issues had been brought out into the open, the mechanisms necessary to address them were not yet in place. He asserted that the training workshop should be seen as the beginning of a process, and not an end in itself. Its main achievement was to chart ways forward to the development of better child protection practice.

Conclusion

These studies have together provided a substantial body of knowledge on the issues involved in inter-agency co-operation and have gone further in many cases by suggesting and in some instances actually piloting some strategies to promote joint work. The studies that focused on intra-agency co-operation as well as inter-agency issues have highlighted different professional perspectives and perceptions about roles and responsibilities.

It is interesting to note the frequency with which inter-professional and inter-agency meetings are suggested as a solution to perceived inter-agency difficulties. These reflect both aspirations and experiences of professionals which have led them to believe that more frequent formal and informal contact will forge channels for communication. However, just as some of the taken-for-granted notions about Garda/health board relationships need to be challenged, the aspiration towards a permanent round of network meetings needs to be questioned as well. For staff working in increasingly pressurised organisations, the prospect of finding yet more time to participate in something they have heretofore regarded with ambivalence may prove off-putting. Several of the projects outlined in this chapter have shown that assigning a purpose to events and outlining a relevant agenda can ensure success in the short term at least. As Rose (2000, p.37) points out, effective collaborative work between professionals is built on purposive and planned activity, and clarity about tasks of leadership and co-ordination. In order to support and strengthen processes like this, strategies to improve inter-agency working arrangements must be put in place. They should address the issue of co-operation at several levels, often starting within the agencies themselves (Morrison, 1996). As some of the studies pointed out, workshops and training events are often only the beginning of a process, and team building within organisations is an important pre-requisite.

Another important point is the impact of rapid structural change on the willingness of staff to work with others, a factor previously identified in the literature by Hallett (1993). This is an increasingly pertinent factor for health board staff and will understandably have unsettling effects.

Child protection training on an inter-agency basis was recommended in many of the projects and is generally regarded as one of the most effective ways of bringing staff from different agencies together and challenging the boundaries that exist between them (Horwath and Morrison, 1999). As well as the delivery of information and the raising of awareness about child protection practices and policies, one of the perceived benefits of training is the opportunity it provides for staff to meet and 'put a face' on each other. However, it is important that inter-agency work goes beyond communication to real collaboration. Hallett and Birchall (1992) have emphasised the importance of informal relationships in promoting collaborative work, but caution against over-reliance on this factor, a point that is very relevant to Irish child protection work with the rapid turnover of health board staff. In the same vein, training in the absence of agreed strategies and commitment to the implementation of agreed plans provides only short-term solutions. It is important therefore for senior management in agencies to assume ownership of the responsibility to develop policies and arrangements.

One of the difficulties in implementing strategies, however, is the fact that in reality, no body or organisation actually exists that can adjudicate when one or other agency or profession refuses to co-operate. Even within a context of mandatory reporting of suspected child abuse, very few members of the child protection network, apart from those within individual management structures, would themselves be accountable to the other in relation to the quality or level of co-operation on an ongoing basis, and the overall 'umbrella' of the Child Care Act, 1991 appears to compel little liability from the non-statutory agencies. Whittington (1983), commenting on accountability within the welfare network, asserts that in the absence of joint rules, divisions of labour or an overall authority, agreement on courses of action have to be negotiated within the limits set by organisational factors and is worked out through the encapsulated view of the professional/occupational cultures of the respective workers concerned.

Some of the inter-agency models proposed by the studies discussed here could be seen as prototypes for the Area Child Protection Committees recommended in *Children First* (Department of Health and Children, 1999) and shortly to be initiated by the health boards. If successful, these committees could provide a framework from which inter-agency norms and practices would flow. As the representation on the committees is likely to be at a senior level, members would hold the sort of mandate needed to progress the development of policies and provide the necessary authority. However, as Sanders, Jackson and Thomas (1997) argue, caution is required to ensure equal representation and ownership of the committees at a multi-agency level in order to avoid further consolidating differences by allowing one or two organisations to dominate. Representative membership could be problematic for some sectors in Ireland, particularly education, as there is no regional body linking primary, secondary and vocational schools in a single area (Buckley, 2000b). Nevertheless, it is the most feasible model currently available and has the potential to make a considerable difference.

Ironically, though inter-agency co-operation is a much sought-after goal, it has to be pointed out that too much collaboration can be almost as dangerous as too little. As Crawford and Jones (1995) argue, conflict is not necessarily pathological, but if properly managed, can be socially constructive. Debate can not only open up awareness of competing perspectives, but can ensure that collusion, lack of accountability and informal decision making do not dominate decision making.

As Scott (1997) points out, in the field of child protection more is spoken about failure than success. She argues that learning should be gleaned from developments that are working well. She recommends the exploration of both developing and effective collaboration as well as elements of conflict that are within the capacity of agencies and workers to control. By this means, she points out, the conditions that need to be replicated will be made visible. In many respects, the studies discussed in this chapter have represented an example of this process in action, by highlighting small-scale projects in different health board areas all over the country and illustrating the elements that should be retained as well as those that require modification. Although the studies themselves are small, they have all been carried out within similar contexts, legislative and policy frameworks. To that extent, when taken together, they represent a significant body of work from which much may be learned.

6

Working Relationships between An Garda Síochána and the Health Boards

Introduction

Working relationships and arrangements between An Garda Síochána and the health boards were the focus of several pieces of work conducted between 1992 and 2000. Many of these projects reflected contemporaneous working practices that have changed considerably throughout the decade, yet have all highlighted factors that remain relevant to the present day. The Kilkenny report (Department of Health, 1993), identifying poor exchange of information and relationships between the South Eastern Health Board and An Garda Síochána, recommended the introduction of a protocol to promote better collaboration and suggested the appointment of liaison officers within An Garda Síochána to deal with child abuse cases. The introduction, two years later, of the national guidelines on co-operation between the Gardaí and the health boards (Department of Health, 1995) further progressed attempts to achieve co-ordination, but even earlier there had been awareness of the need to develop inter-agency strategies between the two organisations responsible for the investigation of alleged child abuse.

Collaborative work between police and social services in the UK has been developing since the mid-1980s and particularly since the publication of the Cleveland Report (Butler-Sloss, 1988) which identified serious difficulties between the two bodies. Research carried out in the early 1990s in Britain indicates that working relationships, though still problematic at times, have improved considerably (Hallett and Birchall, 1992) within a context where joint training, specialist teams and joint child protection units have been set up, and the requirement for co-operation has been enshrined in guidance (DHSS 1991, recently revised in 1999).

While the 1995 Garda/health board guidelines were welcomed by most professionals working in the area of child protection, they were introduced very quickly with no national plan for either training or specialist posts. Virtually no strategic arrangements were implemented on a national basis as a result. Research carried out in the SEHB shortly after their implementation revealed that, while the new protocol was considered useful, many of the formerly identified difficulties still existed (Buckley, Skehill and O'Sullivan, 1997). To address this area, *Children First* (Department of Health and Children, 1999) has outlined a framework for co-operation, emphasising the requirement to implement a liaison system as well as the necessity for multi-disciplinary and inter-agency training between An Garda Síochána and the health boards. However, as this chapter will demonstrate, such protocols can cause the required tasks to appear deceptively simple, obscuring many of the complexities that operate in the day-to-day reality of work.

The projects to be discussed were carried out by health board social workers and members of An Garda Síochána, the majority having been conducted by the latter. They were carried out both prior to and after the implementation of the 1995 guidelines. These studies have explored the topic in different parts of the country and offer insights into the process of inter-agency co-operation including factors that both facilitate and impede its development. Practice and training models have been suggested which, in some cases, have been operated on a trial basis and later refined.

Inter-agency co-operation between the health boards and An Garda Síochána
Bridín O'Rourke, at the time a Garda sergeant based in Templemore, carried out a project in 1992 on the promotion of inter-agency co-operation between An Garda Síochána and health boards. Her study reflected what she described as the traditional practice of An Garda Síochána to work as an individual organisation in the investigation of child sexual abuse, only contacting other agencies when court cases were finalised or when there was insufficient evidence to prosecute alleged offenders. O'Rourke pointed out that the Gardaí, at the time, had not sufficiently recognised that dealing with child abuse was fundamentally different from investigating other types of crime. She undertook to explore the potential for setting up specially trained mixed-gender teams of Gardaí to work with other professionals on cases of suspected child abuse. To achieve this, she carried out a survey amongst twenty Garda members who were based in rural areas and actively involved in child abuse cases, with the objective of identifying areas for attention. Some of the specific difficulties identified at the time were:

- an unsatisfactory level of co-operation between medical doctors and An Garda Síochána in the early stages of investigation
- lack of clarity in relation to the role of social workers
- frustration with the timing of referrals
- availability of health board professionals outside normal working hours
- disagreement regarding the timing of interviews with children and lack of training in this area.

On the positive side, O'Rourke found a high level of commitment and dedication amongst her colleagues in relation to the investigation of suspected child abuse, despite the absence at the time of specific training or support networks.

A similar project was undertaken in 1992, this time from a health board perspective, by Helen Buckley, then a social worker in the Eastern Health Board. Buckley interviewed nine members of An Garda Síochána and eight social workers. She found the same type of factors that were identified by O'Rourke, along with

- difficulty in accessing Garda records where the investigating Garda was not available
- some stereotyping and negative attitudes from both organisations
- conflict regarding the necessity to involve An Garda Síochána at the outset of investigations
- disagreements about confidentiality and the necessity to share certain types of information.

Buckley found a similarly high level of commitment and acknowledgement from both organisations of the value of working together. She also found that while social workers were not always comfortable with the Garda approach, they appreciated the authority lent to some of their investigations by a Garda presence.

Both of these projects highlighted what was, at the time, a significant gender issue whereby the majority of child sexual abuse investigations were carried out by female members of An Garda Síochána, and in-service training on rape and sexual assault was available only to female Gardaí. Training has developed considerably since that time, and modules on child protection are now delivered to all members. However, as later projects continued to illustrate, the burden of child sexual abuse investigations still falls to female Gardaí.

Both projects made similar recommendations, including the availability of training in child protection for all members of An Garda Síochána, particularly with regard to interviewing, the setting up of compatible arrangements for the storage of information, and the creation of specialist child protection units or teams both within An Garda Síochána and jointly between the two organisations.

Notification of suspected cases of child abuse between health boards and Gardaí

In 1995, procedures for the joint notification of suspected child abuse were published by the Departments of Health and Justice. For the first time, official guidance now existed which explicitly obliged health boards and An Garda

Síochána to notify each other of suspected child abuse cases that came to their attention. The guidelines outlined an administrative framework whereby a designated officer in the health board and the Garda superintendent in each area organisation would receive the notifications and assign staff to individual cases who would continue to liaise and exchange new and relevant information. The procedures also recommended that both organisations agree a strategy for proceeding with investigations and attempt as far as possible to prioritise the welfare of the children concerned. In contrast to the UK system, there was no recommendation for the permanent designation of police specialising in child protection, nor any suggestion regarding the use of joint investigative teams. While these guidelines have now been strengthened and elaborated in *Children First*, they provided the basis for joint work between health boards and An Garda Síochána, the most significant element of which was the requirement for the prompt exchange of information regarding reports of suspected child abuse.

Some of the projects completed following the implementation of the guidelines gave a sense of how the new arrangements were working, and highlighted some further areas for development. Ann Griffin, a Garda sergeant based in Galway, carried out a small-scale study in 1996 where she interviewed five social workers from the Western Health Board, five members of An Garda Síochána in Galway, and a middle manager in each organisation. Her project illustrates that some of the problems identified in the earlier studies still remained, despite the implementation of new guidance – non-synchronous working arrangements were proving problematic, there was no effective routinised exchange of information, and unless staff actually knew each other personally, there was potential for lack of trust between them. Drawing on British and Irish research (Waterhouse and Carnie, 1991; Burman and Lloyd, 1993; Metropolitan Police and the London Borough of Bexley, 1987; Horgan, 1996) to develop her own findings, Griffin suggested a number of practical measures and the use of specific criteria for the selection of Gardaí to investigate cases of child abuse. According to her recommendations, members of An Garda Síochána working in this area should:

- be confident in their respective disciplines and roles
- have sufficient professional confidence to adopt established techniques and practices and learn new ones
- be experienced in child abuse work and interested/sensitive to the needs of children
- be willing volunteers, given the nature of the work to be undertaken
- be selected from male and female members.

Griffin recommended the implementation of a strategy for exchange of information, including initiatives such as inter-disciplinary meetings. She was strongly of the view that single-agency and inter-agency training would enhance the quality of service provided at a number of levels. She also concluded that the establishment of specialist units would provide a strong focus for child protection and underline its value as well as improving communication and developing expertise. She noted, however, the view of Garda management that specialisation would be prohibitively expensive in terms of personnel. Griffin additionally highlighted the need to explore further the impact of gender and power in relation to inter-agency work between the organisations, particularly with regard to the establishment of specialist teams.

A later evaluation of the 1995 guidelines was carried out by Mary Delmar, a Garda sergeant in the Dublin-based Domestic Violence and Sexual Assault unit[7] in 1997. Delmar used a case study approach to examine, in depth, ten incidences of suspected child abuse that had been notified, five by An Garda Síochána to the health board and five by the health board to An Garda Síochána. She interviewed the investigating Garda and where possible, the social worker for each case (in two cases no social worker had been allocated) as well as a social work team leader and two 'nominated' Gardaí.

Delmar's findings were consistent with existing research carried out both in Ireland and Britain (Burman and Lloyd, 1993; Pence and Wilson, 1994; Horgan, 1996; Morrison, 1996; Buckley, 1997) which indicated certain barriers to joint working between police and social services. Additionally, she found local factors that added to the complexity, particularly in relation to the non-availability of social workers for allocation to cases, and the difficulties in tracking down individual workers from both organisations. The area selected by Delmar for her study was in the Eastern Health Board. It was well organised in respect of the procedures, to the extent that a system existed for referrals to be passed from the Superintendent to Gardaí who were assigned to work in the community (known as the 'Neighbourhood Unit'). They would in turn keep a record of the case before passing it on to the investigating Garda. Monthly meetings also took place between the social worker team leader and two of the Gardaí from the Neighbourhood Unit.

Despite these arrangements, Delmar encountered a low level of adherence to the 1995 guidelines. While Gardaí had managed, in general, to respond to notifications received by them, by meeting with a social work team leader, they found this to be an unsatisfactory substitute for speaking directly to the

[7] This unit was set up by An Garda Síochána following the publication of the Kilkenny Incest Inquiry. It was initially known as the Woman and Child Unit, and its name was subsequently changed to the Domestic Violence and Sexual Assault Unit.

social worker assigned to the case. In this small case study, Gardaí had only managed to achieve the desired level of contact in one out of five instances, having in each of two cases, made seven to ten unsuccessful attempts to contact the social worker. As a result they had, in more than one instance, called to the home of the alleged victim, with very little information. This was a problem also experienced by health board social workers who had difficulty contacting Gardaí when they were on the night shift. Altogether, though some form of contact had occurred in all ten cases, direct communication between the investigating Garda and the assigned social worker had only taken place in less than half. Staff interviewed from both organisations also commented that insufficient information was given on the notification forms, thus underlining the need for personal communication.

Delmar found that while there were no repeat medical examinations carried out on children in her study sample, two of the ten children were interviewed twice, once at the hospital-based assessment unit and once by the Gardaí. She noted that the requirement in the guidelines for both organisations to agree a joint strategy for investigation was adhered to only in a minority of cases and even then the contact was minimal. The 'ongoing liaison' stipulated in the guidelines had, in fact, taken place in only one out of the ten cases. However, despite the negative tone of her findings, Delmar found encouraging evidence that co-operation and co-ordination had improved in the area since the implementation of the guidelines, particularly the system of using Neighbourhood Gardaí as a liaison team, and the development of the monthly contact meetings. She noted a desire from both organisations to refine the system and create specialist teams, a theme which recurs in most of the projects on this subject. Delmar acknowledged that some differences still existed with regard to social workers' attitudes to having Gardaí involved in cases from the outset, but concluded that the main difficulties lay in lack of resources, with waiting lists for allocation of cases impeding co-operation on each side, and problems in communication. While she recognised that the question of resources needed to be addressed at a wider policy level, Delmar recommended the following:

- Where a social worker cannot be assigned to a case, An Garda Síochána should be given at least the name of a worker with whom they can share information. When a social worker is assigned, An Garda Síochána should be informed immediately
- The health board should inform An Garda Síochána urgently if the potential for forensic evidence exists
- A workable system of message taking and returning should exist in both organisations
- Notification forms should contain an adequate level of detail

- Both organisations should keep each other informed of the names and locations of social workers and investigating officers attached to each area. Lists should be kept up to date
- The monthly 'contact' meeting should be developed and used as a model for other areas.

The child protection practices of An Garda Síochána

In another piece of work undertaken in 1997, Karl Heller, at the time a Garda sergeant in Ballymun, explored the child protection practices of An Garda Síochána and the health board. He focused specifically on the attendance of Gardaí at case conferences and joint social worker/Garda interviewing of the alleged victims of child sexual abuse. Like Delmar, he chose a case study approach, focusing on the 52 cases of child sexual abuse that had been reported to the Gardaí in his district between 1 February and 31 December 1995.

Heller focused on child protection conferences on the basis that they represented an obvious vehicle for inter-agency co-operation and were a potential source of valuable information for An Garda Síochána. His interest in joint interviewing came from his concern that children could be subjected to repeat interviews which might be in conflict with their welfare. He also believed that the ongoing involvement of a social worker in any criminal investigation was essential to the future protection of the children involved. He had been influenced by the publication of the UK document, *Memorandum on Good Practice on Video Recorded Interviews with Child Witnesses in Criminal Proceedings* (Home Office [UK], 1992). Though this document concentrated primarily on electronically recorded interviews, Heller believed that it had much guidance to offer in relation to interviews conducted in other ways.

Heller used a questionnaire to survey the views of eight female and twelve male members of An Garda Síochána, a combination of uniformed Gardaí and detectives who had been involved in investigating the cases. He also carried out in-depth interviews with three uniformed Gardaí and one detective. He found that only just over one-third of the Gardaí involved in the sample cases had attended case conferences during the investigative stage. He also found that only just over half the cases had actually been allocated to social workers after notification had taken place and speculated that this may be linked with the lack of collaborative work. His findings on joint interviewing between Gardaí and social workers were rather more stark as he found that none at all had taken place.

Heller also encountered two other interesting findings that had not been the specific focus of his study. One was in relation to gender, a theme that has emerged in relation to most of the projects associated with An Garda Síochána. Heller found that even though female Gardaí represented only 11 per cent of the force in the district under study, they carried out 40 per cent of the work in cases of actual or suspected child abuse. He speculated that this was because women members were generally regarded as having better interviewing skills even in the absence of training, but recommended that the allocation of work be reviewed in the interests of fairness and non-discrimination. His other finding was in relation to the prosecution rate for sexual offences against children. In only 2 per cent (one case) of the sample had a prosecution commenced. Investigations were still ongoing in 67 per cent and the remaining 17 per cent had been closed. This led him to question why such investigations have to be so lengthy and to recommend that Gardaí receive guidance in relation to the preparation of files for the DPP. In common with the other studies reported here, recommendations from Heller referred to inter-agency training and the speedy allocation of cases. He also advocated that

- the Gardaí should recommend the holding of a case conference if appropriate and if the health board has not initiated one already
- the practice of having a social worker in attendance at Garda interviews should be encouraged as a first step towards the development of joint interviewing
- even when no social worker is allocated by the health board, the Garda investigation should commence immediately in order to avoid a prolonged process for the child.

Specific models for co-operation
A number of studies have proposed specific models or programmes to both develop and utilise the value of collaborative work. These include the participation of Gardaí in inter-agency training programmes, workshops and child sexual abuse assessment units as well as the use of liaison management teams. Deirdre Hughes, at the time a social work team leader in the Eastern Health Board, undertook a project in 1994 to identify the training needs of An Garda Síochána and social workers in relation to working together. This work was carried out prior to the implementation of the 1995 guidelines, but touched on factors that are still pertinent to both organisations. Hughes interviewed five members of An Garda Síochána, including a juvenile liaison officer as well as five social workers from the health board team in the same area. She aimed to explore the extent of their understanding of child abuse and current procedures, their understanding of each other's respective roles and their views on training. She also decided to explore their perceptions of the gender issues existing within and between the two organisations. Her intention was to make specific recommendations for a training module to be conducted on an inter-agency basis in each district of her community care area.

Hughes found that Gardaí and social workers had similar perceptions regarding child abuse though, unsurprisingly, the Gardaí tended to emphasise the criminal aspect. Her examination of their understanding of each other's roles revealed more differences between the professions, with the Garda emphasis on prosecution and the social work focus more on protection and welfare. When the issue of gender was explored, her findings were similar to Buckley's in 1992 and later, Heller's in 1997. Most staff felt that training and practice skills were more significant than gender itself, but the practice of allocating more child abuse cases to female Gardaí prevailed nonetheless.

Specifically focusing on training needs, Hughes found that staff in both organisations felt insufficiently trained in either working with child abuse or working with each other. Areas highlighted for particular attention were:

- understanding of each other's role and function
- the law in relation to child abuse
- theoretical knowledge of child abuse itself
- interviewing skills particularly with young children
- court room skills for social workers
- approaches to joint work
- secondment to each other's agencies
- child development and psychology for Gardaí
- personal issues arising out of the work
- communication strategies.

Hughes, recognising that training will only be effective if followed up by the implementation of strategies to support it, reported the views of interviewees that specialist units in An Garda Síochána as well as specialist workers on teams should be appointed. She also reflected the view that regular meetings, more inclusion of Gardaí at case conferences and the establishment of named link persons would greatly enhance co-operation. She made recommendations to this effect, and started the implementation of a training process in her own area in line with the outcomes of the project.

Another area of investigatory police work in child protection that requires the pooling of special skills is that of interviewing victims who have comprehension and communication difficulties. A project on this topic was carried out in 1999 by Donal Kiernan, a Garda sergeant. The research focused on the type of training required by Garda officers in order to enable them to carry out this type of work sensitively and effectively. Kiernan interviewed sixteen professionals working in the field of disability in order to explore their ideas on how a training programme for members of An Garda Síochána might be designed and conducted. The interviewees included fives social workers, two psychologists, two care staff and four administrators.

Data from the interviews highlighted the key areas to be covered in a training programme. These include the need for Gardaí to have a full understanding of the nature of individual disabilities and associated issues such as levels of comprehension and perception, effects of medication and the degree to which a victim's memory may be impaired by his or her disability. The optimal style of questioning was considered to be 'concrete' rather than open-ended and the use of other or additional means of communicating information such as drawing or role playing was advocated. The need for an interpreter and/or a supportive person to accompany the victim was emphasised, as was the requirement for the interviewer to have good communication skills. Interviewees commented on the importance of providing a full explanation at the outset of the interview, checking that the investigator's understanding of events was the same as the victim's, and providing regular breaks. The desired personal qualities in an interviewer were considered to be empathy, creativity, courtesy, knowledge of the issues, confidence and an interest 'in people as people'. While some respondents recommended the appointment of a designated and specially trained Garda to interview persons with disabilities, others cautioned against such an arrangement as this might mean that all related work was referred to one person, thus unfairly overloading him or her.

While many of the above attributes would be expected of professionals engaged in any type of investigative interviewing, Kiernan observed that respect for difference was a central requirement for interviewing any victim with comprehension or perception difficulties. This, he suggested, would flow from knowledge and information which would in turn challenge prejudices and myths about disability. He made the following recommendations:

- the implementation of a disability awareness programme in An Garda Síochána
- the employment of interpreters where any person with a disability is to be interviewed
- the employment in certain positions of persons with disabilities.

Finally, Kiernan recommended that further research be carried out on this subject among members of An Garda Síochána who have never been involved in interviewing persons with disabilities, and also among disabled persons, probation and welfare officers, solicitors and barristers.

Joint seminars
Most of the projects undertaken on the subject of inter-agency co-operation between An Garda Síochána and health boards advocated regular formal and

informal meetings, to be held locally. It was considered that these would provide opportunities for staff to meet each other and discuss pertinent issues. In 1998, Maire Lernihan, a Garda sergeant in Dun Laoghaire, undertook to organise and evaluate an inter-agency event with the aim of enhancing co-operation and collaboration between Gardaí and social workers in her own district.

Having reviewed the literature and familiarised herself with the most commonly identified impediments to collaborative work, Lernihan first met with the social work manager and the director of the hospital-based child sexual abuse assessment service for the area, both of whom were very supportive of her proposal and undertook to involve themselves in it. She then surveyed eight Gardaí and eight social workers to ascertain the degree of co-operation that currently existed in the area in order to prepare an agenda for the event. She found that very few of the social workers and Gardaí knew each other, possibly due to the high rate of staff turnover in the health board. She also encountered a reluctance on the part of social workers to make informal contact with the Gardaí, and subsequently linked these two findings. The questionnaires also revealed the difficulties encountered by staff from both organisations in maintaining contact once the initial notification was made. This was largely due to different shift arrangements and general difficulty in finding each other at their respective bases. In general, Lernihan's survey indicated a high level of willingness from both groups to work together and to support workshops, meetings and joint training.

The second phase of Lernihan's project, the inter-agency seminar, took place in the in-service training section of Shankill Garda Station in south county Dublin, and such was the level of interest that it was attended by more participants than those originally targeted. In all, twelve members of An Garda Síochána and fifteen social workers attended it. After short presentations by representatives from An Garda Síochána, the health board and the child sexual abuse assessment unit, participants were specifically asked to discuss the following topics:

- positive aspects of Gardaí/health board liaison
- issues that were causing difficulty
- suggestions for improvement in working practices.

Discussion at the seminar and feedback following it indicated that a lot of new understanding had developed about the professional perspectives of each group, with issues such as confidentiality and the implications of particular legal judgements being clarified in detail. Other issues discussed were the process of having children assessed for child sexual abuse, the attendance of parents at case conferences, ways of improving communication and feedback locally and the need for specialisation. It was decided to implement a system of face-to-face meetings immediately after notification, a proposal for tracking false allegations was outlined and agreement was reached on the designation of a liaison Garda to maintain contact between the two organisations. It was also proposed that a Garda attend the health board child abuse review meetings held fortnightly. Interestingly, the views on specialisation and the setting up of a specialist unit reiterated those expressed by Gardaí in Griffin's (1996) project carried out in the West of Ireland – that while it was an attractive idea, it was not certain that it would be an effective use of the valuable resources required, and did not seem viable for the present.

One of the important outcomes from the seminar was that personal relationships were formed, and in Lernihan's view this, in conjunction with the proposed strategies, would lead to a higher level of trust between the health board and An Garda Síochána locally. The recommendations stemming from this seminar reflected the outcomes of the discussion, and it appeared certain that more inter-agency events would take place in the area.

Special units

Nina Long, a Garda based in Limerick, explored the idea of a specialist unit in 1995 by examining Garda participation in the Mid-Western Health Board Child and Family Centre, where child sexual abuse assessments are carried out. She was particularly concerned about the repeated interviewing of children who had been sexually abused and was interested in exploring whether the establishment of a specialist unit might prevent this happening and promote inter-agency co-operation generally.

In order to explore the acceptability of her proposal, she interviewed professionals from the Child and Family Centre and six members of An Garda Síochána based in Limerick. In general, Gardaí interviewed by Long reported that they found the assessment unit to be a valuable resource and experienced good co-operation with the staff there, leading them to be positively disposed towards the notion of a specialist unit. Gardaí believed that in order for such a unit to work effectively, they would need specialist training on interview techniques, more insight into the roles of health board professionals working in this area and courses in personal development. The health board staff who were interviewed had also experienced positive working relationships with An Garda Síochána in the Limerick area. They identified the non-synchronous shifts worked by both organisations as an impediment to co-operation and, like the Gardaí, saw a need for training in several areas. The health board professionals were strongly of the view that specialist Gardaí needed to be designated to child sexual abuse cases. They expressed mixed views on the desirability of a specialist unit. Half of those interviewed believed it to be the best way forward but the other half expressed concern that families might find the presence of Gardaí at disclosure interviews to be off-putting, stating a preference for the partial involvement of a panel of specialist Gardaí. From her findings, Long concluded that the latter proposal might be both more acceptable and more practicable for both organisations, as long as the panel was comprised of trained personnel who were allocated to a specific area so that teams of investigators who knew each other could work together.

Long proposed a structure that conforms to the national guidelines, according to which allocated personnel from the health board and An Garda Síochána would co-ordinate the work from the time of referral to after a child protection conference, including, as well as the investigative interview, the following tasks:

- arrangements for the victim and others at risk
- action regarding the offender
- supervision of the family
- any further enquiries necessary
- recommendations to be made to a child protection conference.

Liaison management teams
Children First proposes the development of 'liaison management teams' comprised of social work team leaders and a district-based inspector or sergeant, whose functions would be to

- consider notifications
- assign personnel and supervise investigation
- review progress in a case.

Denise Walsh, a Garda based in Ballymun, carried out a project on the development of liaison management teams (LMTs) in 2000. *Children First* had not been implemented at the time, but she was aware of the existence within her district of similar models. Walsh was aware of the negative consequences of delays in pursuing prosecutions of alleged offenders and cited a recent court ruling where a judge had dismissed a case of alleged sexual abuse from her own area due to what he called 'unnecessary delays on the part of the prosecuting authorities (p.9)'.[8]

Walsh was aware, both from the literature and the outcomes from projects cited here, of the consistently expressed aspiration towards the development

---

[8] Geoghegan, Mr Justice (1999), *Judicial Review: Paul Phelan v. the DPP*. Law Society of Ireland

of specialist child protection units either within An Garda Síochána or jointly with the health boards. In her review of literature, she discussed the perceived benefits of such a system including better co-operation and the opportunity to build up experience and knowledge. She also highlighted the negative perceptions that had been identified in British research. These included the risk of burnout, the danger of police becoming 'de-skilled' in other areas of work and the potential for resentment from other members of the force of the 'elitist' image created by specialist units (Metropolitan Police and the London Borough of Bexley, 1987; Scottish Police College, 1991). Bearing in mind these factors, Walsh proposed that the development of LMTs would represent the first real effort to address cases in an orderly manner and may ultimately facilitate the development of effective child protection units in Ireland.

Walsh carried out in-depth interviews with two social work team leaders and two Garda managers. All of these staff had previous and current experience of working in teams that could be considered comparable to the model proposed in *Children First*. Walsh asked them to discuss their experiences of working within these models, and to discuss the benefits of LMTs and identify how they might overcome previously identified barriers to co-ordinated work. The interviewees identified the benefits as:

- better communication between professionals
- a more co-ordinated approach to cases
- better understanding of each other's roles
- better service to clients.

The liaison arrangements, according to interviewees, would overcome the problems caused by differing shift arrangements as well as conflict over the manner in which both organisations approached cases. More efficient case management was also identified, as was reduction of stress and trauma to victims by conducting a more co-ordinated and hence supportive approach. It was also felt that more prosecutions could be brought.

Walsh was careful to highlight the fact that barriers to collaboration could still exist, even within the recommended system. These can be caused by dependence on individual personalities, turnover in personnel and consequent changes in policy, the difficulty in keeping meetings going in a context of high pressure and a lack of consistency around the arrangements for meetings. Nonetheless, there was unanimous support from staff in both organisations for the formal development of LMTs. On the basis of her findings Walsh recommended that great care should be taken to ensure that LMTs are developed as 'meaningfully' as possible. This, in her view, would necessitate adequate resourcing and the selection and training of staff who have an interest in the area as well as the maintenance of quality standards.

Conclusion

Studies carried out in different parts of the country at different stages between 1992 and 2000 show an interesting level of consistency, and have highlighted both tensions and solutions that are not readily visible in official guidance, yet are fundamental to the understanding of inter-agency co-operation between An Garda Síochána and the health boards. On the positive side, they have illustrated the level of good will towards co-operation and commitment to making the process of a child abuse investigation more effective and less stressful for victims and their families. However, while personnel in both organisations clearly see a value in each other's involvement, the projects have consistently highlighted enduring difficulties as well as including serious structural differences – the fact that shifts are non-synchronous, the rapid turnover and difficulty in filling social work posts, and the mutual communication problems experienced by staff at the 'operational' end of the work. Some of the philosophical differences still remain and trust between the organisations continues to be fragile and difficult to maintain in any sustained manner. However, there has been an undeniable shift in attitude over the decade, with an increased acknowledgement of the value of joint work. Training and focused inter-agency meetings were found to be successful, with the caution that strategies and the implementation of practical suggestions emanating from these events would be the only means of ensuring their long-term effectiveness.

The combination of studies also challenges some taken-for-granted views. It is interesting to note that despite the frequently offered suggestion for specialist units or teams as a means of streamlining practice, a degree of ambivalence was expressed in relation to both the wisdom and long-term feasibility of such an arrangement in no less than four studies conducted in different areas when the implications were considered. The questionable cost-effectiveness, the danger of de-skilling and 'burning out' individuals and the risk of overwhelming clients were all cited as reasons for postponing the implementation of specialist teams for the present. While their existence in Britain has been credited with achieving much greater harmony between police and social services, Stevenson (1999) points to the risk that encapsulating child protection work within a small section of the force may result in 'ordinary' police being insufficiently aware of the links between crime and abuse, a matter of salience when juvenile offenders are from seriously neglectful homes.

The problem of the low rate of prosecutions was highlighted by some of the studies, and must raise questions about the best approach to take to ensure that children are not further victimised by a process that may ultimately fail to reach its target.

These findings underline the important point that what appear to be neat solutions are in fact very complex issues, and will not necessarily work in each situation. They illustrate clearly that collaboration between An Garda Síochána and the health boards must be addressed at several levels, from the strategy outlined in national guidelines to the sort of practical measures that have been suggested for each district and team. The findings may underline another important fact: that technical rationality will never replace sound professional judgement and that flexibility within a well articulated framework for practice is the key to effective child- and family-centred child protection work.

7

Violence and Sexual Assault against Women and Children

Introduction

This chapter will discuss a number of projects focusing on agency responses to the problems of domestic violence and child sexual abuse against women and children. The research to be reviewed concentrates primarily on services provided by social workers, family support workers and An Garda Síochána.

In common with many social problems, family violence has always existed, but has been historically and politically constructed in terms of the organisations and legal framework that have been created to address it. Acknowledgement of the unacceptability of physical and sexual violence against women and children has been associated with the rise of the feminist movement, which has not only drawn attention to its extent, but has raised public consciousness to the point where legislators and policy makers have been forced to take action (Gordon, 1989; Parton, 1990; Kelleher and Associates and O'Connor, 1995). The perceived slowness of the official response to the problem in Ireland has been linked with national denial and resistance to the notion of men's violence in the context of the family, a process that was not helped by the attitude of the clergy (O'Connor, 1996).

Domestic or intimate violence

In relation to what has become known as 'domestic' or 'intimate' violence, the Women's Aid movement which was established in Ireland during the mid-1970s, and the Rape Crisis Centre, have consistently lobbied for social and political change. These organisations have, over the years, challenged the theory that family violence is gender-neutral and that family preservation should take precedence over women and children's right to a life without abuse. A study commissioned by the Irish branch of Women's Aid in 1995, the first national survey of its kind in Europe, confirmed that 18 per cent of Irish women have been subjected to either mental cruelty, threats of physical violence, actual physical violence and sexual violence at the hands of their husbands/partners (Kelleher and Associates and O'Connor, 1995; O'Connor, 1996).

The Report of the Kilkenny Incest Inquiry (Department of Health, 1993) precipitated some major reforms in policy on domestic violence during the 1990s including the following:

- the establishment of the Domestic Violence and Sexual Assault Unit within An Garda Síochána in 1993. This unit initially served the Dublin Metropolitan Area but was extended in 1997 and given a countrywide brief
- the introduction in 1994 of the Garda Síochána Policy on Domestic Violence, a major recommendation of which was the duty of Gardaí to act as law enforcers rather than mediators in domestic violence disputes
- the implementation of the Domestic Violence Act, 1996 which allows persons whether married to each other or not, or health boards acting on behalf of individuals, to take civil action[9] to protect themselves and their children, and incorporates criminal aspects of domestic violence in relation to the power of An Garda Síochána to make arrests
- the appointment in 1997 by the Minister for Justice, Equality and Law Reform of the task force on violence against women which was intended to integrate the somewhat fragmented existing strategies and draw up proposals for the development of co-ordinated and coherent services for women who have experienced or been threatened with violence, including intervention programmes for perpetrators of violence and preventive strategies to address the root causes of the problem. The report of the task force made strong recommendations in relation to the provision of refuges, help-lines and other community supports, training for service providers, dissemination of information, increased provision of legal aid and intervention programmes for men.[10]

The emotionally destructive effects of domestic violence on children, as well as the links between domestic violence and child abuse, are well documented in international research (Dobash and Dobash, 1984; Stark and Flitcraft, 1996; Cleaver, Unell and Aldgate, 1999). However, research on practice has shown that this is an area that has received insufficient attention (Mullender, 1996, Hester, Pearson and Harwin, 2000). The Irish study commissioned by Women's Aid confirmed a trend already replicated many times in this volume, that the priorities operated by statutory social workers meant that unless children involved in domestic violence incidents were actually injured or considered to be at risk of harm, intervention was not normally offered and preventive work was non-existent in such cases (Kelleher and Associates and O'Connor, 1995). Likewise, research has shown

---

[9] Under the Domestic Violence Act, 1996 a District Court may grant a safety order, a barring order or a protection order depending upon the circumstances. Section 6 of the Act empowers health boards to apply for orders on behalf of a person who is deterred through fear or trauma from doing so him or herself.

[10] For a detailed account of Irish legal and policy developments in relation to domestic violence, see Holt (2000).

that women can be reluctant to seek help for their children from statutory agencies out of fear of a punitive response or the removal of their children to care (Kelly, 1996).

Critiques of agency responses to domestic violence are not confined to child protection and welfare organisations, but extend to the criminal justice system. British studies have documented the dismissive and derogatory way in which 'domestic disputes' are handled by police (Mullender, 1996; Hester, Pearson and Harwin, 2000) and research carried out in Ireland has illustrated inconsistent approaches on the part of An Garda Síochána together with differing interpretations of their powers of entry and arrest (Casey, 1987; Morgan and Fitzgerald, 1992; Kelleher and O'Connor, 1999). It is evident that informed and collaborative approaches to domestic violence need to be agreed between a number of relevant professionals. The projects to be discussed in this chapter will illustrate the nature of the endeavours already started. While it must be acknowledged that a number of the studies were carried out prior to some of the most significant recent developments, it is suggested that many of the issues raised still have currency in the present system.

The social work response to domestic violence

Mary Killion, at the time a social worker in the Cavan/Monaghan area of the North Eastern Health Board, undertook a study in 1992 with a group of women who had suffered domestic violence. The main focus of the research was on the women's experiences of the criminal justice system and the statutory social work service. Killion contacted her research participants through Women's Aid. In order to collect data, she conducted and analysed the content of six group sessions with an average attendance of five out of thirteen victims of domestic violence who were in contact with a refuge in the North East region. An average of three refuge staff members also attended the sessions and all were invited to comment on their perceptions of how the statutory services had responded to the women's abusive experiences.

The group discussions confirmed Killion's prior view that health board social workers were not perceived as particularly helpful by abused women or refuge staff. The women indicated a lack of awareness about the role of social workers, but also a sense that social workers were only interested in providing a service for children, particularly when children were being received into the care of the health board. The refuge staff participating in the study were also critical of social workers who, they pointed out, 'dumped' families in the refuge, failing to offer any follow-up service or assistance with pursuing legal matters or plans for their future accommodation. Refuge staff also offered the view that social workers seemed unsure of how to respond to abused women and appeared to have little understanding of the effects of domestic violence on children.

Similar views were expressed by the research participants in relation to the involvement of An Garda Síochána in domestic violence. While several of the women felt that the Gardaí were courteous and co-operative, most felt that they had little understanding of the problem and were reluctant to confront perpetrators or, indeed, to become involved at all. They gave examples of having to contact the Gardaí more than once in order to elicit a response and expressed dissatisfaction with the level of support offered to them, for example, in relation to transport to refuges after an assault. It was acknowledged by the women that frequent withdrawal of complaints by themselves against their assailants was a cause of frustration for the Gardaí, but still felt they might have received a more consistent and protective response.

Most of the women were positive about their experiences in relation to court and obtaining Barring Orders, though Killion considered this finding to be influenced by the fact that the judge who normally presided over the court in the area was particularly sympathetic to victims of domestic violence.

The research participants were also critical of the lack of treatment services available to themselves and their children, some of whom had experienced sexual abuse as well as the emotional impact of living in a violent environment.

On the basis of her findings, Killion identified the need for a more assertive and consistent response from An Garda Síochána particularly with regard to the arrest of perpetrators (this study was carried out before the 1994 policy on domestic violence was implemented by the Gardaí). She made the following recommendations:

- more education of child care professionals in relation to the dynamics associated with domestic violence and its effects on victims and their children
- the adoption of more creative interventions and programmes for working with victims and perpetrators of violence
- the adoption of consistent and co-ordinated inter-agency procedures for responding to domestic violence.

In relation to the provision of a more effective social work response, Killion reflected that her own research approach, of using discussion groups, had been empowering and positive for the women and suggested the adoption of this type of intervention.

The Garda approach to domestic violence
The focus of two projects conducted in the early 1990s was the Garda

response to domestic disputes involving violence to women and children. The first one, conducted in the Dublin area just as the Domestic Violence and Sexual Assault Unit was being developed, was carried out in 1993 by Lorraine Stack, a Garda sergeant newly appointed to the unit. Stack conducted a qualitative study of the experiences of eight female victims of violence inflicted by their husbands. Her principal aim was to evaluate the response of An Garda Síochána in each of the cases from the perspectives of the women involved. It must be pointed out that this study was completed prior to the introduction of the Garda protocol and the implementation of the Domestic Violence Act, 1996, but nonetheless raises pertinent issues that are still of relevance.

At the outset of her study, Stack drew attention to difficulties frequently experienced by An Garda Síochána when responding to domestic disputes, including their limited powers of arrest and their inability for insurance reasons to provide transport for victims. She acknowledged a point raised earlier in Killion's (1992) project, namely the tendency for victims to withdraw complaints and conceded that this influenced the attitude of investigating Gardaí. For her sample, Stack concentrated on reports received one year earlier, during the first week of May 1992, on the basis that the intervening period would have allowed the women to reflect on their experience sufficiently to be able to give an objective account of it. She chose eight cases at random, all consisting of married women who had been abused by their husbands, three of whom were still living in the family homes. Her choice of married women was designed to allow her to seek information in relation to Barring Orders and to try and explore the perceived effects of violence on the couple's children. All the women were interviewed by her in their own homes, some while their husbands were present in the next room. In Stack's view, all the women she interviewed were relieved to talk about their histories and spoke very freely.

The nature of the abuse suffered by the women was consistent – in seven out of the eight cases, emotional abuse had been a constant feature of their relationships with their husbands, later compounded by threats, actual physical abuse and damage to property. Most of the women reported that their children had been present during violent incidents and some of them had been threatened and assaulted. Negative effects manifested by the children included 'nervousness' and aggressive behaviour at home and at school. While these women were selected for the study on the basis of their contact with An Garda Síochána, most said that the majority of abusive incidents experienced by them had not been reported. At the time of the study, three women had Barring Orders in force, but five had no legal protection whatsoever and two of these said they were too frightened of giving evidence against their husbands to pursue any kind of order.

Five out of the eight of the women interviewed by Stack reported that the

Gardaí had responded speedily to their reports, a finding which contrasted with Killion's (1992) project where most participants had needed to make more than one call before Gardaí arrived. Like the participants in Killion's study, the women had mixed views about the attitude and level of understanding displayed by the investigating Gardaí, some finding them sympathetic and helpful, but about half finding them either indifferent or lacking in understanding. However, in general the interventions of the Gardaí were perceived by the women as having been 'useful' though it was generally felt that more arrests should have been made.[11] Most women expressed fear and lack of confidence in the court system, some saying that they would never have the courage to undergo a court appearance where they had to give evidence against their husbands.

Stack acknowledged that her position as a Garda sergeant may have influenced the generally positive view of Garda involvement expressed by her interviewees. Nonetheless her findings provide useful and practical insights into the ways of improving practice. It was clear from Stack's findings that a more consistent and informed approach on the part of An Garda Síochána was needed, for example increased understanding about the protracted nature of emotional and physical violence as well as more sensitivity to the women's fears, ambivalence and lack of confidence. Stack considered that while powers of arrest were not always available to the Gardaí, follow-up visits could have provided significant support for victims. Likewise, she suggested that referrals to and liaison with social work services could assist in co-ordinated and comprehensive intervention, particularly in relation to the children in the households. She recommended the provision of support to facilitate women in pursuing legal options open to them as well as provision of information and practical support in the form, for example, of transport to a refuge or accompaniment to court. Her most significant recommendations related to the necessity for An Garda Síochána to treat domestic violence seriously by responding to reports as they would to any criminal investigation. In order to facilitate this process, Stack recommended changes in the law, most of which were addressed later in the Domestic Violence Act, 1996.

Another project on Garda responses to domestic violence was carried out in 1994, this time in the South East of Ireland. Agnes Reddy, a sergeant based in Kilkenny, surveyed a random selection of forty-five Gardaí in the area about their perceived role in relation to domestic violence and child abuse as well as their professional experience of responding to reported incidents, including the outcome of each case. She received thirty-nine completed

[11] The 1996 Domestic Violence Act gave the Gardaí more extensive powers of arrest in cases of domestic violence. At the time this study was completed, their powers were limited to situations where victims had been actually hurt or an assault was witnessed.

questionnaires, giving a response rate of 86 per cent, representing 62 per cent of the total Garda force in her district. In addition, she contacted ten agencies likely to be involved with victims of domestic violence from Kilkenny and asked them to comment on the Garda response to crimes of this nature. She received four responses, from a voluntary social services agency, the adult psychiatric service for the area, a local women's study group and a women's refuge in the area.

Reddy found that two-thirds of the Gardaí she surveyed, including eight members in supervisory positions, had undertaken no training in the investigation of child abuse or domestic violence. The data also revealed that while the Gardaí participating in the survey had attended fifty-seven incidents of family violence, only five arrests had been made and files were completed in only four cases. Reddy noted that no action at all was taken in forty-seven of the incidents, acknowledging that this number was likely to be far short of the actual prevalence of domestic violence incidents in the area. She noted that only twenty-six of the fifty-seven incidents had been recorded in writing, indicating a poor level of record keeping that provided no information for other Gardaí coming on duty.

The idea of a specialist unit to deal with domestic violence and child protection was proposed by Reddy in her questionnaire and was considered to be a positive idea by two-thirds of the respondents, particularly the younger Gardaí. The negative views expressed coincided with those detailed in other projects discussed in this volume, mainly citing the limitations of isolating members in a single area of work.

Reddy noted a paradox in her findings, where almost all respondents declared their sense of responsibility towards victims of domestic violence and child abuse, yet acknowledged their lack of ability to do so in terms of training and information. She also noted the steady rise in reports of domestic disputes to An Garda Síochána over the most recent period. The issue of gender was also highlighted in much the same manner as it arose in projects completed by O'Rourke (1992), Buckley (1992) and Heller (1997), where the practice of female Gardaí carrying domestic violence and child protection cases conflicted with the views of respondents that it was an area of work that should be undertaken by members of both sexes.

The agencies that responded to Reddy's request for information highlighted concerns about some indifferent responses to cases of family violence from An Garda Síochána along with little assistance from them in terms of information or support. It was felt that greater co-ordination was needed between the Gardaí and other agencies in the community as well as better training, and more user-friendly services. The matter of gender was again raised, whereby respondents suggested that the delegation of domestic violence cases to female Gardaí could be interpreted as discriminatory and a signal that the Gardaí did not take them as seriously as other crimes.

Reddy was aware that the new Garda protocol was about to be implemented and considered that this may address some of the problems raised in her study. She made the following, additional, recommendations:

- inter- and single-agency training at all levels on domestic violence and child abuse to impart knowledge and understanding of the subject and attempt to ensure a co-ordinated and consistent response
- dissemination of information about services for victims of family violence
- development of a local protocol in conjunction with the South Eastern Health Board
- ongoing support by Gardaí to assist victims in pursuing services
- the establishment of a specialist unit in Kilkenny.

Overall, Reddy considered that her findings reflected not only inadequate practices on the part of An Garda Síochána in relation to domestic violence, but a sense of helplessness and frustration on the part of the Garda respondents. It should be acknowledged, however, that the many legislative, policy, training and operational developments which have taken place in relation to child abuse and domestic violence over the past decade have considerably influenced the Garda response and the operation of their duties in this area of work.

Interventions with domestic violence

The absence of a specific domestic violence policy initiative in community care social work prompted Stephanie Holt, at the time a social worker and co-ordinator of the family support service in an area of the Eastern Health Board, to undertake a project in 1999 focusing on the role played by family support workers in cases where domestic violence was a component. She sought to assess intervention from the perspective of service users and thereby identify factors in the family support service that facilitated and sustained change. Ultimately, she aimed to identify key factors for consideration in future development of the services.

Holt carried out in-depth interviews with six women who were victims of domestic violence and in receipt of a family support service from the health board. She also collected data by means of a self-completed questionnaire from the six family support workers and six other professionals involved in each of the cases. Information from case records was used to provide a profile of each case and indicated that the women suffered from a combination of social isolation, long-standing physical, social and emotional abuse, mental health problems and concerns about their children's psychological and emotional welfare. Half of them had a history of contact with the child protection services because of concerns about their children's safety and welfare. All the women had been initially referred to the family support service for reasons other than domestic violence and its prior existence as a problem was known to the referrer in only one case. These findings confirmed theories proposed in the literature, that victims of domestic violence can be so deeply affected and undermined by what is happening that they become immobilised and unable to contemplate either disclosing what is happening or attempting to leave the situation, leaving themselves to literally suffer in silence (Mullender, 1996; Kelly, 1996).

In all cases featuring in Holt's study, the women had first disclosed their experience of domestic violence to the family support worker. From that point, they appeared to be empowered to take some action. Holt sought to explore the factors that facilitated this sharing of information. It appears that the length of involvement of the family support service, varying from seven months to three years, was helpful in gaining the women's trust along with the pace of the work which was always matched to the women's ability to change and progress. The approach adopted by the family support workers, their focus on the women themselves, their support and encouragement and the way in which they gradually managed to raise the women's sense of self worth were all seen as positive factors in facilitating disclosure and positive action to protect themselves. The positive and non-threatening effect of the social support, concern and interest shown by the family support workers appeared to act in an encouraging and enlightening manner that enabled the women to identify alternative options for themselves and their children. In Holt's view, these findings highlighted the necessity for a service that provides long-term, intensive support to victims of domestic violence and recognised the problem as a process rather than a one-off event. The research data collected from other professionals involved in the cases indicated their positive attitude to the family support service, not only in terms of the beneficial outcomes for families, but because of the positive impact it had on their own ability to engage with the women in a real and meaningful way. In conclusion, Holt recommended the implementation of policies at local level to reflect an awareness of domestic violence and establish best practice guidelines for all personnel. In particular she advocated the provision of social support as a model of intervention for victims of domestic violence, with specialised and relevant training for family support workers.

Child sexual abuse

While the sexual assault of children by adults had been coming to the attention of statutory and voluntary child protection authorities for many years (Ferguson, 1993; Raftery and O'Sullivan, 1999) child sexual abuse as a specific concern was not really acknowledged in Ireland until the early 1980s, around the same time as it was gaining attention in the UK (Cooney and Torode, 1989; McKeown and Gilligan, 1991; McGrath, 1996). The inclusion of child sexual abuse as a separate category in the 1987 child abuse guidelines represented an official endorsement of growing concern around the increasing number of cases being referred to the health board and other agencies. The Department of Health responded by providing monies to the health boards for the establishment of child sexual abuse assessment units or teams. From 1991, the Stay Safe Programme, a culturally sensitive, developmentally staged child abuse prevention programme was gradually introduced into schools (McIntyre and Carr, 1999). During the 1990s, the Kilkenny Report (Department of Health, 1993), together with the West of Ireland Farmer Inquiry (North Western Health Board, 1998) and high-profile coverage of the 'X' case[12] as well as the Brendan Smyth affair ensured that child sexual abuse had a specific position on the social and political agenda and ensured that reports of child sexual abuse would be taken seriously.

Research on services dealing with child sexual abuse has highlighted a number of issues. In a study commissioned by the South Eastern Health Board and published in 1997, the assessment service offered to victims of child sexual abuse was considered to work well, but follow-up by either Gardaí or social workers was considered to be unsatisfactory. Families highlighted the lack of information given to them during the course of a prosecution as well as their disappointment at the low numbers of prosecutions obtainable. While the response of social workers to initial discoveries or disclosures of abuse was judged to be good, parents complained that once 'safety' issues were addressed, they were not given sufficient support to deal with the aftermath or the longer-term effects of sexual abuse on their children (Buckley, Skehill and O'Sullivan, 1997). Likewise, in a UK study carried out in the early 1990s, Sharland et al (1996) highlighted some shortcomings in the way that families of sexually abused children had been dealt with by the child protection services. The worth of medical examinations was challenged as it appeared that they rarely yielded important evidence and caused great distress; the lack of prosecutions was the source of great disappointment and frustration to families who had been led through a fairly detailed forensic style of investigation, and the degree to which professionals were able to appreciate

---

[12] The X case involved a fourteen-year-old rape victim who came to public attention when a court injunction by the Attorney General prevented her from travelling to England for an abortion. This ruling was later overturned by the Supreme Court, precipitated three national referenda on the subject of abortion and provoked major political controversy (McGrath, 1996).

the shock, trauma and sense of guilt experienced by families was considered questionable. In a study of mothers whose children were sexually abused, also carried out in the UK, Hooper (1992) found that child protection workers had unrealistic expectations of mothers' abilities to come to terms with their children's abuse, deal with the losses involved and cope with the aftermath for themselves and the children. The lack of treatment facilities for both victims and abusers was highlighted in all these studies.

Six projects completed between 1993 and 1999 directly addressed some of the issues raised in research, one addressing the needs of mothers of children who had been abused, another evaluating a group for male adolescent offenders, a third one on training professionals on how to prepare parents and children for child sexual abuse assessment, a fourth one on parental perspectives on the assessment service in a health board area, a fifth one examining Garda responses to sexual abuse and assault, and finally, a project that focused on ways of addressing the problem of child pornography on the internet.

Support for mothers of sexually abused children
In 1993, Anne Valentine, at the time a community care social worker in the Eastern Health Board, undertook a project which consisted of setting up, conducting and evaluating a self-help group for mothers of children who had been sexually abused by adults outside their families. Valentine was aware that assessment and treatment services were available for children who were the victims of child sexual abuse, as well as groups for adolescent offenders and their parents. However, she noted a dearth of services specifically for the parents, particularly where their children had been abused outside the family. This replicates findings in the Irish and UK studies already mentioned (Buckley, Skehill and O'Sullivan, 1997; Hooper, 1992; Sharland et al, 1996) where safety issues tend to dominate the initial intervention. This narrow focus meant that families who were deemed to be satisfactorily protecting their children from an 'outside' abuser were often left to cope with the aftermath without the assistance of the health board or other treatment agencies.

With the co-operation of her colleagues and the assistance of a student psychologist who acted as a co-facilitator, Valentine set up a support group for mothers whose children had been sexually abused. She justified her focus on mothers in terms of (a) their pivotal role in protecting the family and (b) the fact that they had been offered no therapy after their child's abuse. The aims of the group were to share their experiences, consider changes which may have occurred in their relationships with their children, share their feelings and attitudes towards the perpetrators, examine appropriate adult/child boundaries and discuss the area of sex education.

The group ran for six sessions, concentrating initially on building up trust and focusing on the aims that were initially agreed. It was attended by five women, each of whom were interviewed by Valentine prior to their inclusion in the group. Valentine noted the strong emotional responses expressed by the women in relation to their children's abuse. These included self-blame, guilt, anger, denial, powerlessness, sadness and a sense of loss, replicating the feelings noted in the British study conducted by Sharland et al (1996). All of the children had been assessed in the child sexual abuse assessment unit that served the area. While the mothers were satisfied with the assessment procedure, they expressed confusion about the fact that no treatment had been provided by the unit. They resented the fact that so many agencies had become involved in what seemed such a private matter to them and were critical of the insensitivity displayed by Gardaí who called to the house in uniform and in marked cars. The mothers expressed mixed feelings about the short-term nature of services offered to some of their children by child guidance clinics, most feeling that further help would be necessary at different times in the future. A range of behaviours had been displayed by their children following the abuse, including aggression, confusion, reluctance to discuss what happened, self-blame, school refusal, clinginess and loss of self-esteem. Fear was expressed by some mothers that their sons would repeat the abuse they had experienced.

The mothers availed of the opportunity provided by the group sessions to express their anger at the perpetrators of abuse and their disappointment at the leniency with which they had been treated by the law. Valentine noted the mothers' ability to understand their children's role as victims and their clear allocation of blame upon the perpetrators.

The later sessions concentrated on discussion around children's sexual development, values and behaviours including boundary setting at different developmental stages. The final session was dedicated to an evaluation of the group process. The mothers indicated how much they valued the support and learning they had gained through the group experience. Valentine acknowledged the need to be sensitive to the emotions experienced by mothers whose children are abused as well as the requirement to clarify information more than once to families who were traumatised by abuse. She recommended the co-ordination by the health board of the wide range of services needed for families of victims of child sexual abuse, including individual and group therapy for offenders, parents, children and non-abused siblings. She also recommended the delivery of preventive and educational programmes using a community-based approach for adults and children.

Training in the assessment and management of child sexual abuse cases
Since the late 1980s, all the health boards have developed systems for

specialist assessment of suspected child sexual abuse. Different arrangements exist both within and between the various boards, some assessment units being hospital-based and others situated in the community. In Limerick, as in other areas of the Mid-Western Health Board, child sexual abuse assessments are carried out in a unit known as the Child and Family Centre by a multi-disciplinary team of health board psychologists and social workers. Referrals to the assessment unit are normally made by professionals in the wider child protection network who may or may not be familiar with either the signs and effects of child sexual abuse or the operation of the unit itself. Understandably, the quality of preparation that families receive prior to their contact with the assessment unit can determine the way that children and families understand and experience the assessment process. This, in turn, will depend on the knowledge and experience of referring professionals.

Recent research studies have focused on best practice in interviewing children (Aldridge and Wood, 1998; Westcott and Davies, 1996) and it is now recognised as an area requiring sensitivity and care. In 1993, John O'Sullivan, at the time a social worker in the assessment unit, designed a training programme for community care personnel to enable them to adequately prepare children and families for the assessment process. From his experience, he was aware that the parents and children could present at the unit feeling confused and apprehensive. The time spent explaining the nature and purpose of assessment and helping families understand and become comfortable with the process added to the pressure on the service and in his view, contributed to delays in offering appointments to clients. He believed that if the preparatory work could be completed by referrers like social workers, public health nurses and area medical officers, the assessment process itself would not only be more acceptable but more effective for children and families. He proposed that a training programme would have the potential not only to enable professionals to prepare families for assessment but would also increase their knowledge base on child sexual abuse. It would, in his view, also have the function of encouraging them to reflect on their own practices, identify future training needs, and act as an initial step in both expanding the pool of expertise on child sexual abuse in the area and promoting inter-agency co-operation.

O'Sullivan designed a programme for a one-day training seminar. The aim was to give participants the opportunity to address their own professional and personal issues about child sexual abuse work. O'Sullivan chose a variety of training methods, using large and small group sessions and incorporating case examples. The material presented included information about child sexual abuse and the type of detail required by the team in order to proceed with an assessment. It also incorporated subjects like potential risks to children who have already been abused, the rationale for assessment, information on the assessment process as well as guidance on how to help parents to prepare children for assessment. Each session was followed by a period for discussion. The discussions following the presentations raised a number of points including:

- the Child Care Act, 1991 and its relevance to child sexual abuse
- the vulnerability of certain groups to child sexual abuse
- the wisdom or otherwise of a community care social worker interviewing a child
- the need to observe children's behaviour when suspicions have arisen
- the precise nature of information required in the referral
- social factors associated with risk of child sexual abuse
- the length and nature of the assessment process
- reasonable expectations to be held of parents
- the need for parental consent
- how interviewers explain their role to children
- prevention and treatment
- the emotional impact of assessment on children
- the type of advice to be given to parents.

O'Sullivan evaluated the training seminar through questionnaires and verbal feedback at the end of the day. Overall, the seminar was rated very positively by all groups, though the anonymity of the evaluation sheets meant that individual professional gains were not identified. Not surprisingly, the need for more time to be spent on each session was highlighted. One of the most valuable areas of learning appeared to be the nature and extent of information required by the assessment team from other personnel, particularly in relation to children's behaviour. O'Sullivan himself identified several other areas for future training including:

- partnership with non-abusing parents
- understanding of the effect of parents' own abuse on their ability to respond to their children
- professionals' expectations of parents
- child abuse procedures in relation to child sexual abuse
- individual professional roles in child protection.

In the meantime, he proposed making up information packs for circulation amongst health board staff. He recommended the establishment of inter-agency training and opportunities for inter-agency discussion in the region and suggested that preparation for assessment by social workers, public health nurses and area medical officers should be adopted as local child protection policy and reflected in local procedures and child protection manuals.

Parental perceptions of child sexual abuse assessment

In 1997, Samantha Ronan, a social worker who was then based at the Child and Family Centre in Limerick, undertook a project to examine the views of seven sets of parents whose children had undergone assessment at the unit. She explored factors influencing their perceptions of the service and the perceived impact of intervention on the entire family in each case. In addition, she sought suggestions for the future enhancement of the service.

Ronan used semi-structured interviews with parents, all of whom had contact with the service approximately eighteen months previously. She started by contacting the area social worker for each family in order to ensure that the timing of the interviews would not be either insensitive or inappropriate. Although only one of the seven was a one-parent family, Ronan was able to meet with both parents in only two of the remaining six and interviewed only the mother in those cases.

Data from the interviews indicated that, in general, none of the parents had been aware of the existence of the child sexual abuse assessment service at the time that concerns arose about the sexual abuse of their children. Most had been referred to it by other agencies. In five of the cases, the children had disclosed their allegations of abuse to their families prior to assessment and families then viewed the assessment process positively, as a confirmation of their children's statements. In two other cases where less evidence existed, the process was seen as more investigative.

While most parents found the somewhat dilapidated exterior of the centre to be unattractive and off-putting, they expressed positive views about the appearance of the unit once inside. They were equally positive about the professionalism shown to them by the staff at the unit. While the sample was small and the majority of views were favourable, the exceptions were accorded some significance by Ronan. These included instances where parents felt they had received no feedback following assessment, one where parents had felt that the questions were intrusive, and one where home visits by the staff were regarded as a very public breach of privacy. One parent was critical of the fact that the family had been interviewed by An Garda Síochána prior to involvement by the health board and found the process very dis-empowering.

Most parents interviewed by Ronan had found the assessment process to be of benefit to their children, the exceptions being where the disclosure had not been made beforehand. In both these cases, the parents had been somewhat reluctant to undergo the assessment and claimed that the children had found the process confusing and upsetting. One set of parents was critical of the lack of follow-up therapeutic work both for the child who had been assessed and the rest of the family who were still coping with the aftermath of the abuse. Some parents also expressed concern about the future healthy development of their children and queried the wisdom of so much concentration on 'good' and 'bad' touches.

In her analysis of the data, Ronan highlighted the importance of keeping agencies informed about the service offered by the Child and Family Centre, given the different pathways through which families are normally referred. She noted the importance of professional standards of behaviour including feedback and advice about treatment, as well as agreement between the health board and agencies such as An Garda Síochána about the best means of approaching families at the outset. She recommended that these issues be highlighted in supervision and training. In addition, she proposed that the health board should pay attention to the parents' negative impressions of the exterior of the Child and Family Centre and that the unit should consider a broader style of intervention to include whole families and maintain support over a longer period. She further recommended that the centre should widen its orientation, which was mainly towards small children, to include teenagers and to provide separate facilities for them.

Another study evaluating the impact of practices in the area of child abuse assessment was carried out in 2000 by Margaret Blake, a social worker in the Western Health Board, based in Galway. While Ronan's study concentrated on the perspectives of families, Blake focused her research on the perspectives of children. Her aims were to explore what the process of being interviewed was like for children, with the aim of promoting more effective and acceptable practices from their points of view.

Blake selected a number of cases involving children who were between twelve and sixteen years old and had undergone an investigative interview with the Western Health Board during the previous two years. She had hoped to interview the children involved. However, she only managed to recruit one child out of a possible twenty-eight and ultimately decided against carrying out the interview as doing so may have unwittingly identified the child.[13] Ultimately, Blake relied on the literature to provide her with evidence of children's views on the investigative interview process and surveyed a number of relevant studies to inform her research, principally Farmer and Owen (1995); Sharland et al (1996); Taylor, Roberts and Dempster (1993); Prior, Lynch and Glaser (1999) and Westcott and Davies (1996). In addition, she conducted semi-structured interviews with six professionals from her area who had been involved in interviews with children. These included two social workers, two psychologists and two members of An Garda Síochána.

The findings from Blake's interviews with professionals revealed that

---

[13] The reasons for failure to recruit were primarily refusal by the children concerned, the fact that some had moved and their whereabouts were unknown, the fact that appointments were failed, or that when they were contacted, it transpired that no investigative interviews had taken place.

children are not normally informed directly about interviews, nor are they asked to comment on the suitability of the interview arrangements. Most of the professionals interviewed acknowledged that the venues most commonly used were not child friendly, e.g. were without bathrooms or facilities for making tea, and often lacked toys or play materials. Both the waiting areas and interview room were considered to be too public. Practitioners reported that interruptions were common and the atmosphere generally lacked warmth. Lack of support for families during the assessment process was highlighted by the interviewees as a major deficit. The 'rush' of the administrative process of investigation was seen to contribute to a situation that centred more on the agency than on the child and family. The interviewees were particularly concerned about the inconsistent provision of therapy for children once the assessment process was concluded.

Blake noted that children were never asked for their view of the process, or invited to comment on what the experience of being interviewed had been like for them. In other words, no 'de-briefing' or evaluation was carried out. The provision of support and training for workers themselves was inconsistent. While most of the professionals interviewed found the work reasonably satisfying, it was generally agreed that regular support and training was necessary to obviate the potential effects of stress on the quality of work carried out.

Most of the findings emerging from Blake's interviews with professionals reflected the issues raised in British research that had been carried out specifically on children's perspectives. Informed by both these sources, she made the following recommendations to the Western Health Board:

- efforts made to directly facilitate children in relation to information, timing and location of interviews and the gender of interviewees
- improvement in interviewing facilities in terms of location, methods of ensuring privacy, provision of child-friendly materials like books, toys, and bathrooms
- the provision of support during and after the assessment process for children, their parents/carers and siblings, as well as therapy if appropriate
- the development of strategies for staff training.

Finally, Blake recommended that the service provision be evaluated on a continuous basis.

Treatment for adolescent abusers
In 1996, Raymond McEvoy, at the time a social worker in the North Eastern

Health Board, based in Co. Louth, undertook a study to explore the treatment needs of sexually abusive adolescents, as perceived by a number of professionals in the area. While differing definitions of abuse and the diverse pathways by which young abusers came to official attention made it difficult to determine the prevalence of the problem, it was known that a substantial number of serious sexual abuse offences had been committed by adolescents including some as young as twelve and thirteen. McEvoy was aware of an inter-agency treatment group operating in the Eastern Health Board area. However, he was conscious both of the lack of such a facility in his own area and the increasing pressure from An Garda Síochána and the education authorities for an urgent response to the problem.

From the literature, McEvoy was aware of the difficulty of making assumptions about the characteristics of young sex offenders or the origins of sexually abusive behaviour in childhood and adolescence. Likewise he was aware of the lack of agreement in research about the evaluation of treatment programmes. In order to ascertain which issues were most pertinent in relation to treatment of adolescent offenders, McEvoy carried out unstructured interviews with a number of professionals, including a senior probation officer, two health board social workers, a senior health board social worker, a senior social worker in the child and adolescent mental health service, the health board programme manager, a senior psychologist, a community worker, a garda superintendent and a head teacher.

The findings from the interviews illustrated the complexity of the problem. Most interviewees pointed out that adolescent offenders had a variety of needs. It was suggested that many had been abused themselves, some lacked sexual knowledge and others had little emotional support. The professionals generally acknowledged a lack of knowledge and information on adolescent abusers and emphasised the need to provide treatment as tertiary prevention to lessen the possibility of young people continuing to offend into adulthood. The programme manager in particular commented that evidence of the efficacy of treatment which might be provided by a treatment programme could serve to justify further investment of resources in this type of service. The Garda expressed a view that a treatment group could serve the purpose of helping young offenders to take responsibility for their behaviour. It was suggested by the head teacher that the establishment of a treatment group might prevent local people from taking the law into their own hands in response to incidents of sexual abuse. Social workers pointed out that a group would facilitate them to use the therapeutic skills that they already possessed.

McEvoy was able to conclude from his findings that a treatment programme was desirable and would receive the support of the child protection network in his area. He advocated the use of group-work, in order to enhance adolescents' social skills, self esteem and reality testing, as well as alleviate the sense of isolation often experienced by young sex offenders. He considered that a cognitive approach would be the most effective, and would work well in a structured group setting that would facilitate role playing, rehearsing and feedback. He recommended the use of systematic problem-solving strategies in order to determine the nature of problems, brain-storm plans, execute the plans and evaluate their effectiveness. The use of an assessment tool prior to the inclusion of individuals into the group would, in McEvoy's view, ascertain information such as the power differential between abuser and victim, type of sexual activity, extent of coercion, nature of fantasies involved and vulnerability of the victim. He was also aware of the sensitivity involved in dealing with an area of essentially criminal activity, and recommended that assessment be carried out after a court had established a finding of guilt. McEvoy proposed to initiate the group process based on his research findings. However, he cautioned that the identification of a long-term plan for a young person would require attention to his or her overall functioning, thus implying that a variety of interventions may be necessitated to meet his or her needs.

An Garda Síochána and child sexual abuse

The numbers of cases of sexual abuse being referred to An Garda Síochána for investigation rose considerably during the early 1990s, from 349 in 1990 to 850 in 1995. Bearing in mind the challenges now facing Gardaí in this line of work, Valerie Campion, a Garda sergeant based in Monaghan, carried out a project in 1999 to ascertain the extent of information about child sexual abuse held by investigating officers, their training needs in the area and their suggestions for the provision of a more effective investigatory process.

Campion carried out her research by means of structured questionnaires, distributed to fifty Gardaí operating in the Cavan/Monaghan area. She focused the questions on the length of experience and numbers of sexual crimes dealt with by each individual, the extent and perceived usefulness of their training in the area and their suggestions for a better service. She tested their knowledge of child sexual abuse, paedophilia in particular, by means of a quiz.

Campion received thirty-seven replies to the fifty questionnaires distributed. Not surprisingly, the findings revealed that those members who had the longest service had experienced the largest number of sexual abuse cases, though Campion noted that the number of cases held by younger members was proportionately higher. Likewise, the data indicated that younger Gardaí had undergone more training, having joined the force after the recommendations of the Walsh report[14] (1985) were implemented. Over half of the respondents indicated that they had undergone additional training in the form of seminars, including one that had been held in conjunction with the North Eastern Health Board. The limitations of short training and the need for additional input were acknowledged. Respondents highlighted a number of areas that they considered to be challenging, including interviewing child victims and trying to balance the child's welfare against the need for him or her to give evidence, dilemmas about breaking up families and the difficulty in getting suspects to account for their actions.

The responses to the questions posed about sex offenders indicated a high level of uncertainty and ambiguity where the members' knowledge base was concerned. For example, only just over half of the respondents were aware that paedophiles are not necessarily homosexual and only a small percentage were aware that non-fixated paedophiles would be willing to accept treatment. Campion concluded that most Gardaí worked on the basis of generalised 'practice wisdom' rather than reliable and evidence-based information. This, in her view, was unsatisfactory given the considerable body of knowledge that now exists in relation to sexual offences.

Respondents to the survey offered a number of suggestions to improve their skills in this area. Campion included these in her recommendations for regular and updated training in the skills and knowledge about sexual abuse and the provision of peer support as well as support from management in this special area of police work.

Child pornography on the internet
The advancement in technology and the wider availability of computer equipment has contributed to the problem of child pornography, a subject that poses considerable challenges to the police. This was the subject of a project undertaken in 2000 by Gerry Deegan, a Garda sergeant in the Domestic Violence and Sexual Assault Unit in Dublin. Deegan set out to critically examine the legislation available to the police in Ireland and compare it with that operating in some other European countries. He also aimed to highlight the problems and challenges posed by the availability of pornography and the need for collaboration between police forces and other stakeholders in order to address the issue effectively. Deegan explored existing policy measures set up to deal with the problem and carried out interviews with a group of fifteen trained Gardaí to establish their level of awareness in the area.

[14] The Walsh report recommended changes in the basic training offered to new recruits to An Garda Síochána. Training is now offered in five phases over three years, phases 1, 3 and 5 being conducted in the Garda College in Templemore, while phases 2 and 4 are carried out as fieldwork placements in Garda stations, under supervision. Basic training now covers social and legal aspects of child abuse.

Deegan identified a number of risks posed by the availability of child pornography on the internet. One was the actual abuse of children in the course of producing the material and another was the possibility that it may detrimentally influence children who viewed it. Deegan pointed out that the internet facilitates access to children by paedophiles who use it as a means of 'normalising' the notion of sex between children and adults and enables them to disguise their identities. The process of engagement taps into the vulnerabilities of some children by providing attention and a sense of belonging to a group. The Child Trafficking and Pornography Act, 1998 now provides for offences such as trafficking, publishing, printing, importing or selling child pornography and using children for the production of pornography. However, Deegan criticised its lack of specificity in terms of the grades of criminality to which it can be applied. He suggested that legislation in this area requires more consistency on an international level. For example, he argued that crimes should carry different levels of seriousness according to the ages of the children involved and the nature of any assault committed. Deegan pointed out that a higher level of uniformity with regard to punishable offences would not only enable juries to reach decisions more easily, but would eradicate conflicts and contradictions between different jurisdictions and ensure that such crimes were taken seriously on an international level.

Deegan used a questionnaire to explore the extent of knowledge about child pornography on the internet possessed by fifteen experienced Gardaí who were participating in a training course on the subject of child sexual abuse. He found that 60 per cent of the participants used the internet fairly regularly both at home and at work and just under half of these said they had encountered pornographic material. One of the questions concerned the legal meaning of the term 'pornography' and the wide range of responses indicated that the group in general were not aware of the wording contained in the legislation. However, from the answers given in relation to the nature of offences committed, Deegan concluded that the level of awareness about the problem was generally quite high. He noted the unanimous view of the respondents concerning the need for international co-operation whilst acknowledging the difficulties involved in policing it.

On the basis of his findings, Deegan recommended that the police response to the problem should be made at a global level, and that the co-operation of internet providers should be sought. He proposed further dissemination of education programmes concerning the dangers of paedophile activity on the internet and the development of a separate unit in each country staffed by personnel who are highly trained in computer technology. Finally, he suggested the creation of legal measures to compel service providers to report the presence of pornographic sites and to provide the police with any evidence that could be used in a criminal prosecution.

Conclusion

Though some of the studies reported here were carried out in different regions of Ireland at a time when services were developing rapidly, many of the issues raised transcend policy and legal modifications. Important practice issues have been highlighted, including the need for consistently sensitive, respectful and honest contact between service providers and the family who have been directly or indirectly affected by domestic violence or sexual abuse. The projects have also illustrated the value of ongoing specialist and in-depth work with different client groups in order to provide both practical support and therapeutic interventions. The empowering role that group-work and family support work can play with abused women was emphasised, the importance of the latter service being the enduring nature of the relationship formed between the workers and the victims of abuse which facilitated disclosure and change at an acceptable pace. Similarly, the necessity to provide support not just to child victims of abuse but also to those caring for them was illustrated. The concerns of a wide range of professionals in relation to adolescent offenders were highlighted and models for intervention were proposed. Importantly, the need for ongoing intervention after the initial crisis has passed was heavily emphasised.

In common with most of the other sections in this volume, the area of domestic violence and sexual abuse raises further gender issues, including the broad issue of abuse committed by men, the need for therapeutic services for male offenders, the focus on mothers as the protectors of their children, and once again, the question of whether the police dealing with family violence should be male or female.

The need for ongoing training and research in all areas of domestic violence and sexual assault was confirmed, in particular with regard to the dynamics and effects of both domestic violence and sexual abuse, as well as knowledge about sex offenders. The complexities involved in dealing with child pornography on the internet served as a reminder that despite the progress made, services will continue to be challenged. At the same time, it should be acknowledged that the many legislative, policy, training and operational developments which have taken place in relation to child abuse and domestic violence over the past decade have considerably influenced the Garda response and the operation of their duties in this area of work.

This section has reflected the voices not only of professionals but of service users and has elucidated the range of complex needs experienced by them at different stages in the process of protecting themselves and their children from violence of one kind or another. Probably the most important message to emerge from the studies is, not surprisingly, that a comprehensive approach to the problem of family violence requires effective partnership between professionals and agencies in order to assist parents and children to move forward.

8

Child Protection Conferences

Introduction

One of the central elements of the 'machinery' of child protection is the child protection conference, defined by *Children First* as 'an inter-agency and inter-professional meeting which is convened by the child care manager /designate, normally held when decisions of a serious nature are being considered that require the input of a number of professionals from different disciplines and agencies'. Its main functions, as stated in the guidance, are to facilitate the sharing and evaluation of information between professionals and carers, to outline the child protection plan and to identify tasks to be carried out by different professionals.

However, despite the pivotal position and perceived value of child protection conferences they are, by their very nature, prone to a range of factors that strongly impact on their effectiveness and have been the subject of numerous research studies. Current literature on child protection conferences tends to concentrate on three principal issues; one is the way in which information is processed and decisions made, another is the acting out of inter-agency and inter-professional rivalries and tensions, and the third is the matter of parental participation.

A study carried out in the UK by Farmer and Owen (1995) on the conduct of one hundred and twenty child protection conferences illustrated a number of weaknesses, including the unnatural degree of consensus and absence of debate at conferences, the unremitting focus on details surrounding single abusive incidents and the lack of attention paid by the conference to families' material circumstances. It was also critical of the lack of theoretical reasoning displayed about issues such as violence or family dynamics. The reluctance of social workers to 'own' their expertise by using theoretical linkages has also been highlighted by Stevenson (1995) and Bell (2000). In Ireland, a study published by the South Eastern Health Board in 1997 found that while case conferences were considered useful for the sharing of information, making joint working plans and allocating tasks, they were nonetheless subject to certain structural weaknesses and were dominated by reporting and discussion with little energy devoted to decision making or realistic planning. The data also indicated that most of the work was ultimately designated to social workers despite the multi-disciplinary make-up of the group (Buckley, Skehill and O'Sullivan, 1997).

144

While one of the essential functions of a child protection conference is the facility it offers for multi-disciplinary work, it also has the potential to both reflect and exacerbate existing inter-agency difficulties. As Reder, Duncan and Gray (1993) suggest, child protection conferences can be the objects of unrealistically high expectations, given the complicated nature of the processes involved. Several studies carried out in Ireland and the UK have criticised the low participation rate of general practitioners and teachers (Buckley, 1998a; Kelly, 1996; Hallett, 1995; Thoburn, Lewis and Shemmings, 1995), despite the central position ascribed to them in child protection guidelines. The absence of what are considered key professionals can have an inevitable and distorting effect on the nature of decisions made. Research has also illustrated how conferences can be used as platforms for the acting out of hidden agendas, professional rivalries and hostilities that have unwittingly dominated the discussion, relegating the needs of the children and families involved to a secondary position in the process (Hallett and Stevenson, 1980; Dale et al, 1986; Reder et al, 1993; Buckley, 2000a). Reder et al go so far as to recommend a clear acknowledgement of the naturally occurring dynamics at the outset of a conference in order to ensure a clear and unambiguous focus on the purpose of the meeting.

The issue of parental participation at child protection conferences has been explored in large-scale studies carried out mainly in the UK and a number of critical issues have been highlighted. Thoburn, Lewis and Shemmings (1995) found that the majority of practitioners and their managers were supportive of parents' participation, believing that the meetings were more effective and therapeutic and less liable to gossip and speculation when parents were present. However, when parents' own perspectives were sought and analysed, a substantial number complained that while they had been pleased to attend, the process and function of the conferences had not been adequately communicated to them in advance, and their views were not listened to or considered. In the Farmer and Owen (1995) study, the researchers were not impressed with the level of 'user involvement' that took place when parents and children attended, suggesting that an expectation existed that parents would not influence the conference judgment but would be influenced by it. Likewise, Cleaver and Freeman (1995) contrasted the positions of the two 'sides' at the outset of a meeting, with parents sensing that they are about to stand trial, while still experiencing the pain and distress of the accusation. On the professional side, Cleaver and Freeman observed that a professional consensus is frequently fashioned before the formal discussions begin. Similarly, Corby, Millar and Young (1996) sense a 'misplaced optimism' in the popular notion of parental involvement, suggesting that parental participation is more likely to be related to the 'compliance' rather than the 'openness' of parents. Their central argument is that the denial of the power differentials undermines the usefulness of involving parents at all. Bell (2000) also illustrates the limits to which parental participation at child protection conferences can be considered empowering. As she points out, when congruence is reached between parents' and professionals' perceptions of risk or abuse, parents can feel empowered to participate and be consulted, but when agreement is absent, their involvement is often limited to the exchange of information. She suggests that the term 'enabling' might be more appropriate than 'empowering' in restricted circumstances.

Whatever their weaknesses, child protection conferences will continue to play an essential role in the processing of suspected and actual child abuse and provide a unique forum for the exchange of inter-agency perspectives. The remainder of this section will discuss a number of projects carried out in different health board regions between 1992 and 1999, all of which deal with different aspects of the conference process. They concentrate principally on means of streamlining the process and ensuring more effective and focused decision making and highlight the important area of public health nurse participation.

Making child protection conferences more focused

An action research project carried out in 1992 by Una Ryan, at the time a social worker in the North Eastern Health Board based in Navan, Co. Meath, focused on the quality and value of the child protection conferences held in her area. Ryan was concerned that much of the value of the child protection conferences was lost through lack of focus and direction and her project aimed to provide a framework for understanding the essential nature of these meetings in the child welfare system. She set out to do this by exploring the nature of conferences as they were currently operating.

Ryan initially sought the views of colleagues who regularly attended conferences, by interviewing social workers, psychologists, area medical officers, public health nurses and community welfare officers. She asked them about the functioning of case conferences, their effectiveness, their purpose, the role of participants and the involvement of different professionals. In general, the respondents were positive about the opportunity for meeting with other professionals and sharing information but made a number of negative comments in relation to the process of the conferences.

Critiques in Ryan's study centred on a variety of factors. The absence of key personnel including general practitioners and teachers was identified by a number of respondents, who were also critical of the structure of conferences, the inadequacy of the normal venue used, the short notice usually given and the absence of written reports.

Several respondents expressed the view that case conferences were called solely as a matter of procedure and had an agency-centred rather than client-centred purpose. Lack of engagement by senior staff at the meetings with a corresponding lack of support offered to front-line workers was the subject of some comment. However, the principal criticism was made in relation to decision making. Decisions were perceived as vague, unrealistic, over-dependent on the capacity of one person to carry them out or not clearly allocated. This deficit was linked by some respondents to the lack of clarity about the purpose of the conference.

On the basis of these findings, Ryan designed and piloted a framework for the conduct of child protection conferences in her area. She incorporated the following elements:

- a standard agenda for each meeting
- a standard letter of invitation to be sent with the agenda, to contain a brief summary of the purpose and content of the conference and a list of participants
- a personalised letter to be sent to parents
- a pro forma case conference report sheet
- arrangements for taking minutes
- agreement on a review date
- a summary letter to be sent to parents following the conference
- a standard summary sheet to be sent to all participants following the conference.

Ryan had hoped to include the appointment of an independent chairperson and a change of venue but these tasks proved to be unachieveable at the time. However, the new framework was successfully applied to ten conferences over a two-month period. Ryan evaluated its effectiveness by surveying all participants using a post-conference questionnaire and analysing the case records. In general, the responses indicated an improvement in the conference process. Participation increased, a factor associated by Ryan with the explanatory nature of the invitation letter. Ryan pointed out that the preparation of the agenda gave a clearer focus to the meetings and the distribution of the summary gave the proceedings more positive meaning. In addition, she considered that those who had not been regular attenders were given more positive messages about their significance in the child welfare system. From the survey responses there appeared to be more understanding and agreement about the purpose of the meetings and the relevance of decisions. The fact that a review date was always set gave participants a sense of continued involvement with the cases. Parental participation appeared to work well and, according to the survey results, decreased the expression of hearsay and uninformed opinion.

Acknowledging the improvements, Ryan recommended that the health board should pay attention to the encouragement of fuller participation, and promote the more positive aspects of health board involvement in child welfare. This, she asserted, would alleviate misconceptions held by non-statutory professionals and indicate which professionals should be essential attenders. She pointed out that the area of parental participation required consideration and preparation in order to maximise the positive contribution that it can make. Finally, she recommended that an annual evaluation of the process and management of child protection conferences be undertaken by senior personnel in the health board.

A project similar to Ryan's was carried out in 1993 by Val O'Kelly, at the time a senior social worker in the North Western Health Board. Like Ryan, O'Kelly had been concerned at the lack of policy in relation to the conduct of child protection conferences specifically in relation to their purpose, organisation, inter-agency and inter-professional issues, parental participation and decision making. She employed what she described as 'an inter-disciplinary' dialogue in order to examine the current operation of conferences in her area, with particular reference to information gathering, decision making and parental participation. She focused on ten conferences, eight of which concerned allegations of sexual abuse and the other two being concerned with child neglect, and surveyed all the participants by means of a questionnaire. The principal participants at the conferences were social workers, Gardaí, a paediatrician and a psychologist. A general practitioner had been invited to one but was unable to attend. A total of twenty-four questionnaires was returned. In addition, O'Kelly carried out in-depth interviews with members of the 'core' group that attended all child protection conferences. This was comprised of the director of community care,[15] senior psychologist and senior public health nurse.[16]

Findings from the questionnaire survey revealed that participants had a clear knowledge of the purpose of the conference and were satisfied that information was satisfactorily shared. They also appeared to be satisfied that the concerns were clearly specified and that risks were assessed. However, in hindsight O'Kelly acknowledged a flaw in her methodology where she had basically asked yes/no questions in relation to these issues. Having received very monosyllabic answers, she later considered that she should have elicited specific detail on the perceived purpose and nature of the information and

---

[15] At the time this study was conducted, directors of community care were responsible for the management of child abuse in their areas and normally chaired case conferences.

[16] The core group would normally include the senior social worker. As O'Kelly held that role at the time she was excluded from the study.

concerns in each case, in order to ensure that they were, in fact, as clear as the participants claimed them to be. She noted a discrepancy in the responses to the question about the allocation of a key worker. The majority of participants had indicated that the social worker was allocated this role. This finding conflicted with O'Kelly's own observation of the meetings where, she claimed, the designation of the key worker had not been explicitly made. She concluded that the survey findings reflected more of the participants' *assumptions* about the conference process than the reality of what actually transpired in each case. This was illustrated by the majority response to the question about parental participation, where the consensus view was that parents should be invited to attend, but reservations were expressed in relation to each of the conference cases in the study.

O'Kelly's interviews with members of the core group yielded more detailed information. She focused specifically on how each of them perceived their own roles in relation to child protection conferences. The director of community care expressed some doubts about his own expertise and skill in relation to chairing meetings in such a specialised area and suggested that his responsibility might be more usefully discharged in an advisory capacity. While the senior public health nurse was satisfied with the role of her profession in relation to the conferences and to child protection work in general, the senior psychologist raised a number of questions and suggested that the role of the psychologist in child protection work needed to be clarified further.

While O'Kelly acknowledged that her methodological approach, particularly her use of the questionnaire, had not facilitated participants to consider their roles at the conferences in sufficient depth, she also concluded that many of them had never given serious consideration to the subject. Her project, she felt, could represent the beginning of a process whereby professional contributions and responsibilities would be reflected upon and re-framed where appropriate. She made recommendations for the more effective conduct of conferences which were similar to those advocated by Ryan (1992) including the appointment of a chairperson with special expertise, a clear statement of purpose for each meeting, the setting of clear agendas, the presentation of written reports, consideration given to parental involvement and efforts made to include general practitioners and other relevant personnel.

Parental participation at child protection conferences
The area of parental participation was given more detailed consideration in a project carried out in 1997 by Mary Coen, at the time a social worker in the North Western Health Board, based in Sligo. Coen was aware that while

some health boards had a definite policy of parental participation, the decision as to whether or not parents were invited to child protection conferences in her area was at that time to be taken on a case-by-case basis, by the senior social worker. She took the view, therefore, that the attitude of staff working with children and families would be influential in determining the level of involvement permitted to parents. The aim of her study was to examine the current practice in her area, with a particular focus on the views of health board personnel on the participation of parents in child protection conferences. She hoped, in carrying out her research, to provide a framework for understanding the complex issues involved and make recommendations to address them.

At the time this project was conducted, there was evidence in the literature of the intentions and aspirations of Irish health board staff to facilitate the fullest possible involvement of parents at child protection conferences (Buckley, Skehill and O'Sullivan, 1997; Gilligan and Chapman, 1997) but virtually no research had been carried out into the actual practice of parental participation. Studies in the UK, however, had elucidated the pros and cons of parental attendance and Coen reviewed the most recent literature and outlined the arguments on either side (Thoburn, Lewis and Shemmings, 1995; Farmer and Owen, 1995; Corby, Millar and Young, 1996). She quoted research suggesting that attendance at child protection conferences might be distressing and emotionally disturbing for parents who may become disruptive or upset. The literature reviewed by Coen highlighted the possibility that participants may be inhibited in making their contributions honestly if parents were present, may lack the necessary skills to deal with parents and may feel inhibited about expressing disagreement. The studies also illustrated how the aims and objectives of conferences could be diverted from the protection of children in order to prioritise parental rights and how confidentiality may be harder to maintain if parents are present. On the positive side, Coen quoted literature supporting the argument that parents have civil rights to receive information and to contribute to discussions about their children and that decisions should be made openly and in their presence. She made the important point that when parents are offered a realistic picture of professional concerns, they may be more committed to change.

For the purposes of her own project, Coen examined the records of twenty-two child protection conferences held in her area over a two-month period and found that parents had been invited to attend on only one occasion. The professionals who most commonly attended the meetings were social workers, public health nurses and psychologists. For this reason, she chose these professionals as her research subjects and adopted the methodological approach of holding focus group discussions with participants from each of the three professions. She conducted three groups with an average of five to seven participants in each one.

In each focus group, participants were asked to describe their roles in child protection. While social workers and psychologists saw themselves as having active involvement in assessment and intervention, public health nurses perceived themselves to be more involved in referring concerns and providing information. When asked to what extent they would share information with parents prior to child protection conferences, social workers and psychologists agreed that they would discuss the fact that a conference was taking place and explain what would happen in varying amounts of detail depending on each case. The public health nurses generally agreed that they would not discuss the conferences with parents, nor would they mention their own attendance. They expressed the view that such discussions were not their role and would be more appropriately carried out by social workers. The same norms appeared to apply following a case conference though there was some variation in the psychologists' role; if they were involved with the family for only a short period they felt that discussion might be more appropriately carried out by the social worker. Again, the public health nurses felt that it was not their role and that they did not have the skills to talk to families about the content of child protection conferences. Social workers pointed out that senior managers might take on the task of talking to families in certain circumstances where it was judged that more 'weight' was required.

While all the practitioners in the focus groups were familiar with the concept of parental participation at child protection conferences, only a small number had actually experienced it and, even then, parental attendance was only partial. The views they expressed conformed very much with those to be found in the literature. They pointed out that parents had rights, that hearing the concerns of professionals may be very effective in impressing upon them the seriousness of any risks being experienced by their children, that professionals may be more careful to present only informed opinion and that it would bring an air of realism to the conference proceedings when all participants were able to 'put a face' on the parents. On the negative side, concerns were expressed about the inhibiting effect that the presence of parents might have, particularly when sensitive information was known to some participants. The possibility of 'awkwardness' if parents admitted offences in the presence of An Garda Síochána was mentioned, and anxiety was expressed about the possibility of parents' misinterpreting the views or statements of professionals. The issue of inter-agency or inter-professional disagreements was considered to be potentially problematic and there was some concern expressed about the intimidating effect on parents of having to sit at a meeting where they would be considerably outnumbered by professionals.

When asked to consider what factors would facilitate parental attendance at child protection conferences, the focus group participants suggested that preparation would be important and should include a prior meeting with the chairperson. Practical suggestions included the provision of transport, childcare and an appropriate and accessible venue. Availability of clear information about the expected proceedings and a policy of introductions to all participants were emphasised. It was also suggested that parents should have a support person, either a professional or an advocate.

In contrast with findings from studies conducted in the UK which all recommend full parental attendance, most of the focus group participants in Coen's study appeared to favour a model whereby parents met the professionals at the outset, but attended only part of the meeting. Public health nurses in particular expressed the view that parents might feel more comfortable meeting with just one or two professionals after a conference. They expressed concern that their relationship with parents would be damaged if they were seen to be part of a child protection conference and suggested that as they were unskilled in dealing with parental aggression, they would require training if a policy of parental participation were to be implemented.

When Coen analysed her data, she drew attention to the variations in attitude and practice within and between the three professional groups. She noted that public health nurses appeared to feel unprepared for dealing with child protection issues and were reluctant to let parents know that they attended child protection conferences despite the fact that other professionals discussed the meetings with them. She attributed some of the differences to the lack of guidelines in the North Western Health Board, noting that none of the groups seemed to be conscious of the role of 'key' workers. Coen observed that while most of the professionals were familiar with and generally positive about the concept of parental attendance, their experience was low and suggested that, in the light of the data revealed in this study, it was timely for local practices to be reviewed. She suggested that the fact that most professionals favoured partial attendance could be a starting point, given the finding in British research that the more experience professionals have of parental involvement the more they are prepared to accommodate it to a point of full attendance.

Coen felt her project was useful in raising the consciousness of her colleagues in relation to parental attendance at child protection conferences, including their training needs. She felt that it had the further effect of generally raising practitioner awareness of the desirability of working with parents throughout all stages of a child protection case, not just the conference. She recommended that the health board prepare policy and procedures on the issue in consultation with practitioners and parents. She suggested that written information on procedures and child protection conferences should be made available to parents, and that the board should adopt a policy of inviting parents unless clear reasons exist for their exclusion. She proposed that parents be facilitated by the chair to contribute as much as possible and that procedures be implemented for informing parents who do not attend of the outcome. Finally, she recommended that child protection conferences be viewed, not in isolation, but as part of an ongoing process of parental involvement in child protection work.

The role and contribution of public health nurses at child protection conferences

Other projects discussed in this volume reflect the frustrations of public health nurses at the level of unsupported work they find themselves carrying in relation to cases where no other professional is involved. It would seem, therefore, that the child protection conference represents a venue where public health nurses are likely to find opportunities to draw attention to the nature of their work and receive tangible support in dealing with complex situations. However, research would suggest that public health nurses have found child protection conferences somewhat unsatisfactory in terms of providing either support or relief to them and in sharing responsibility for the management of cases (Butler, 1996). Three projects completed between 1995 and 1999 illustrated the difficulty sometimes experienced by public health nurses in communicating their concerns about children at conferences, and sought to find means of addressing this problem. A study conducted in 1995 by Agnes Durkin-Boyle, at the time a public health nurse in the North Western Health Board based in Donegal, set out to identify how public health nurses could be enabled to communicate their own detailed knowledge to their colleagues. Durkin-Boyle used a focus group to elicit the views of public health nurses and generate a discussion on the subject. Twelve public health nurses participated, all with three to five years experience and all of whom had attended child protection conferences.

Participants in the focus group were in agreement about the importance of their role in monitoring children's health and development and in the identification of risk. For this reason, they saw themselves as important members of the child protection conference. However, from the discussion it became apparent that public health nurses were frequently unhappy with both the process and outcomes of child protection conferences. While they believed that meetings like this were essential in order to facilitate the sharing of concerns in a multi-disciplinary setting, they were unsure as to how seriously their views were taken. They suggested that social workers were over-focused on evidence and reluctant to commit themselves to involvement in cases unless there were more explicit indications of abuse than the nurses were able to provide. The public health nurses in the focus group were resentful of the manner in which, at the end of a child protection conference, they were frequently left carrying the entire responsibility for a risky case with an expectation that they would visit daily and 'keep social workers informed'.

While the child abuse guidelines in operation at the time (Department of Health, 1987) allowed for the allocation of the role of key worker to public health nurses, most of the study participants felt that their caseloads were far too large and varied to permit them to take on such a time-consuming and responsible role. Yet, it appeared that they lacked the assertiveness to refuse this designation at child protection conferences and frequently ended up continuing 'surveillance' of families with little support. This, they felt, led to cases drifting until a crisis occurred, at which point a social worker would necessarily become involved. Resentment was expressed by the focus group participants about the way that social workers would then 'move in' on serious cases and rarely give credit to the work already done by public health nurses.

The focus group participants unanimously agreed that a good chairperson could make an enormous difference to their ability to contribute effectively to child protection conferences. They suggested that an independent chair would be free of associations with any particular profession, could keep the meeting focused and would prevent the discussion from straying or being 'hijacked'. The public health nurses agreed that they should prepare properly and bring reports written to a standard format. When the possibility of parental participation at conferences was discussed, most of the public health nurses expressed a positive view, but with reservations. Some said they would not feel free to express an opinion, given that families usually saw them as a help and not 'someone poking around the house looking for something to mark them down with'. In general, they expressed the view that separate time should be allocated for professionals to meet alone.

The public health nurses in the focus groups acknowledged that factors outside child protection conferences affected their ability to contribute. An important one was inter-agency and inter-professional relationships; most felt that if they availed of more opportunities to meet and get to know their colleagues, they would find it easier to debate and discuss issues with them at conferences. Another factor was supervision for public health nurses, a subject dealt with in Chapter Thirteen of this volume (Ryan, 1996; Fitzpatrick, 1997).

Durkin-Boyle's recommendations reflected the views of the focus group participants that the health board should adopt a protocol that outlines the role of the chairperson, the purpose of the conference and the procedures to be followed. She also recommended the streamlining of administrative services to offer both support and follow-up to the meetings and greater efforts at promoting inter-agency and inter-professional communications.

A study similar to Durkin-Boyle's was carried out four years later in 1999, in an area of the Eastern Health Board, by Bernadette Coggins, a senior public health nurse, who sought to explore public health nurses' current practices in relation to child protection conferences as well as their perceptions of their usefulness. She surveyed thirty-six public health nurses in her area, asking them for details of their experience to date, their views on the child protection conferences they had attended, and their opinions regarding parental attendance. She followed up her survey with a meeting attended by twenty-six public health nurses where she presented the survey data and facilitated an open discussion on their implications for future practice.

The results of the survey confirmed Coggins' earlier view that public health nurses generally found child protection conferences useful, leading to better work and more favourable outcomes for children and families. The most significant reasons offered for their worth included the opportunity for inter-professional discussion and improved teamwork. It was also felt that they enabled a degree of sharing of responsibility. The majority of respondents considered that their views were respected by other conference participants.

Although a total of seventeen child protection conferences had been attended by the nurses in her survey, Coggins noted that two hundred and thirty one of the families on their collective caseloads were on the 'vulnerable' register in the area. This was an indication, in her view, that public health nurses worked in isolation with a large number of families where risk was a factor but not considered serious enough for either allocation to a social worker or the holding of a child protection conference. The dissonance between inter-professional perceptions of risk between public health nurses and social workers is a point which has been made in several of the projects discussed in this publication (Leydon, 1992; Ryan, 1996; Fitzpatrick, 1997) as well as the literature (Taylor and James, 1987; Butler, 1996).

Another significant finding in Coggins' project was the low rate of report preparation and presentation by public health nurses attending child protection conferences. Two principal reasons were offered for this: firstly, that it was 'not the practice' and secondly, that reports were usually sent to the superintendent public health nurse prior to a child protection conference and not written specifically with the conference in mind.

Like Durkin-Boyle, Coggins invited the respondents in her study to comment on the usefulness of parental attendance. The response was similar, with the majority view in favour of partial attendance and the main argument offered for less than full attendance being the potential effect it might have on the parent/public health nurse relationship. The issues of inter-professional training and supervision also arose in the group discussion, replicating the findings of some other projects reported in this volume and carried out by public health nurses (Ryan, 1996; Fitzpatrick, 1997).

Overall, Coggins concluded that while public health nurses valued child protection conferences, they had little sense, at this stage in her area, of a clearly developed or defined role for themselves at the meetings. On the basis of her findings, she suggested that the 'marriage' of the two roles of child welfare and child protection was fraught with difficulty. While she considered the reasons offered for the low rate of report preparation and the nurses' ambivalence about full parental participation at child protection conferences, Coggins found them understandable, yet in conflict with developing norms. She suggested that the adoption of a protocol similar to that designed by Gilligan and Chapman (1997) which has since been adopted by *Children First*, would both prepare and enable them to challenge their traditional ways of working and develop a more open and positive approach to the child protection conference.

The public health nurses in Durkin-Boyle's study had raised the suggestion of a standard format for conveying their concerns to a child protection conference and this area was also an issue of concern for the nurses in Coggins' study. This was the subject of a project carried out in 1996 by Maria Ahern, at the time an acting superintendent public health nurse in the South Eastern Health Board. Ahern broadened her aims to include the development of a form of assessment that not only would enable a public health nurse to communicate child protection concerns, but would provide a framework for the identification of children and families in need of support and supervision. She designed a form that included a checklist of factors indicative of risk and a template for summarising concerns. She then invited seven of her colleagues to try it out and comment on its usefulness. Ahern subsequently interviewed each of the public health nurses individually to ascertain their views. The form was edited in line with their comments and piloted at a child protection conference after which it was evaluated by the multi-disciplinary group of participants.

The form consisted of four pages. The first page was designed to elicit family details including the names and relationships of all family members, the level of support available from the family and details about the accommodation. The second page covered maternal and child health, the child's developmental status, the quality of his or her attachment to his or her parents and parents' perceptions of the child's progress. It also included room for the public health nurse's observations. The third page focused on factors that may be causing stress to the family and on parent/child interactions including expectations, disciplinary techniques and the ability of parents to meet the child's needs. The fourth page elicited information on the family's social networks and supports and the family's interest in or use of existing family support services including the contributions of the public health nurses themselves. Most of the information was recorded by ticking one of a number of boxed options on the list.

The public health nurses who were asked to evaluate the form were invited to discuss its usefulness or otherwise at a meeting. While most had found the form useful and relevant, a few of them had found some of the questions to be detailed and repetitive, and they made suggestions for amendments. While they found it long, most acknowledged that a lot of questions could be answered fairly speedily. They agreed that the form enabled them to note significant issues that they may otherwise have overlooked, particularly in relation to maternal health, child development and the role of fathers. Some respondents raised questions about their ability to make judgements about attachment, suggesting that more training in this area would be useful. They also queried the value of quantitative information about stress factors, suggesting that families experience events differently depending on the level of support and the resources available to them. However, in general the public health nurses felt that the form challenged their current methods of assessing the quality of child care, broadened their focus on the family and triggered questions that they might not otherwise have considered.

The form was used by one public health nurse at a case conference following which Ahern moderated a group discussion on its utility with all the case conference participants. The public health nurse acknowledged that she had left some boxes on the form empty but would obtain the information at a later stage. However, she considered that the form had helped her to make a competent assessment and given her confidence to present her views quite clearly to the conference. The other conference participants generally agreed that the form comprehensively identified areas of potential risk as well as levels of formal and informal support available to the family. In particular, participants noted how the form illustrated the low level of contact achieved by public health nurses with fathers, highlighting this as an area for attention.

In her analysis of the data yielded by her study, Ahern acknowledged some of the shortcomings of using the form, e.g. its limited value as a means of appraisal. She emphasised that public health nurses carrying out assessments would need to be aware of their own standards, values and attitudes. She also suggested that nurses would need some form of induction or preparation in order to understand the rationale behind asking some of the questions. On the positive side, she considered that the use of the form provided a means of highlighting areas where the public health nurses most needed to expand their knowledge and skills, e.g. emotional abuse and its effects on children. She suggested that the form gave the nurses a channel through which they could articulate their concerns in relation to lack of resources and support services and draw the attention of management to these deficits. Ahern pointed out, on the basis of her findings, that the form could enable public health nurses to present informed and relevant information to child protection conferences in a confident manner. In order to further enhance the contribution of public health nurses in general, Ahern recommended that they receive ongoing training in identification and assessment of risk factors along with joint training with other disciplines to improve understanding and appreciation of each other's perspectives. Finally, she proposed the development of a multi-disciplinary system to review all cases causing concern to public health nurses.

Conclusion

The number of projects focusing on the conference process was quite small, but nonetheless yielded interesting information. The value of multi-disciplinary meetings was firmly endorsed by all the studies reported here. However, as several of the projects showed, unless the conferences are properly planned, well chaired and have an agreed and clear purpose and agenda, they can represent an inefficient use of time. The assumptions unwittingly made by participants about inter-professional responsibility and allocation of key tasks were illustrated in O'Kelly's study, where she was able to show the contrast between participants' impressions of the process and the reality of what actually transpired. Also on the theme of inter-agency work, the importance of identifying and facilitating the attendance of key professionals was emphasised.

The projects that focused on parental attendance at child protection conferences gave rise to what was at the time, in some areas, a new debate. They illustrated the gap that may still exist in relation to consumer participation, where, despite the current emphasis on facilitating parents and children to attend full meetings, the professional preference, particularly that of public health nurses, appeared to be for partial attendance only. The need for training and preparation was recognised, however, signalling the possibility of greater openness to full participation at a point where professional confidence would be strengthened.

The projects completed by public health nurses were of particular interest, highlighting the concerns of nurses about the most effective ways of communicating information. The research illustrated the frequent discomfort and frustration experienced by this professional group. In addition, the template suggested for compiling information provided a valuable framework for concisely communicating the type of information about children and families that is crucial to the design of effective child protection plans.

Since these projects were completed, considerable advances have been made in relation to the conduct of child protection conferences. *Children First* has adopted the protocol first implemented by the Southern Health Board (Gilligan and Chapman, 1997) which emphasises the importance of good chairing and the necessity to provide a sound infrastructure, as well as cautioning against over-use of conferences to compensate for inadequate supervision or poor inter-agency communication. The New Zealand family group conference model has been piloted in the Eastern Regional Health Authority and the first phase of its evaluation is optimistic about its effectiveness in particular circumstances (O'Brien, 2000). In the different health board regions where they were conducted, the projects discussed here have undoubtedly played an important part in laying the foundations for the development of this important element of child protection work.

9

Children in Out-of-Home Care

Introduction

Section 3 of the Child Care Act, 1991 articulates the principle that it is generally in the best interests of a child to be brought up in his or her own family, an aspiration that is affirmed in *Children First* (Department of Health and Children, 1999) which advises that separation of children from their families should occur only as a last resort. The rehabilitative ideal that currently dominates the child welfare discourse contrasts with the norm that prevailed in the early part of the twentieth century when, as Buckley, Skehill and O'Sullivan (1997) illustrate, the primary method of dealing with children in need was placement in residential care. An aim of the child protection and welfare system that has evolved over the intervening years has been to minimise the risks that might otherwise require children to be removed to the care of the state. Nonetheless, there are inevitably situations where a parent or parents cannot provide for their children's physical, psychological and emotional needs and the state has to take over responsibility in the long or short term. Children are admitted to care for a number of reasons and though the proportion of those who enter care under a legally binding arrangement has increased, the most recent statistics would still suggest that poverty, addiction, mental health difficulties, illness, stress and parental inability to cope are among the factors most strongly associated with separation, contrary to the popular belief that most children enter care as a result of child abuse (Department of Health and Children, 2001).

The numbers of children in the care of the Irish state has fluctuated from large numbers at the turn of the century, mainly in residential institutions of one type or another, to relatively low numbers during the 1950s and 1960s (Raftery and O'Sullivan, 1999; Gilligan, 1991). The numbers began to rise again during the 1970s, and with a trend towards the placement of children in foster care following the Report of the Task Force on Child Care Services (Department of Health, 1980), the balance has shifted to a position where most children in the care of health boards reside on a short- or long-term basis with foster families.

In both Ireland and the UK, the past three decades have seen growing concern about the welfare of children who are accommodated by the state. During the 1980s in the UK, research illustrated the worrying level of 'drift', lack of planning, failure to maintain links with families and poor outcomes for care-leavers in terms of educational levels, employability and homelessness (Rowe et al, 1984; Millham et al, 1986). In Ireland, recent revelations of abuse in the care system have dominated a range of similarly negative findings regarding the quality of care provided for children as well as eventual outcomes after leaving care (Department of Health, 1996b; Kelleher and Associates, 1998; Raftery and O'Sullivan, 1999). Despite increased resourcing of the care system, recent research continues to highlight deficits in an area that is becoming increasingly challenging as the full implications of the statutory obligations imposed by the Child Care Act, 1991 are becoming visible (Clarke, 1998). While legislation and policies governing the different types of state-regulated child care have existed in some form or other since 1862, the most significant developments in recent years have been the implementation of revised regulations for the placement of children in foster care (Department of Health, 1996b), and the establishment in 1999 of the Social Services Inspectorate under the Child Care Act, 1991. The Social Services Inspectorate published its first report in 2000, and it is generally anticipated that its influence will serve to ensure that standards and principles are imposed and maintained in residential care.

The projects described here represented initiatives undertaken in health boards and institutions in order to highlight areas where practices and services can be enhanced. This chapter discusses a number of projects carried out in different regions that covered specific areas central to good practice with children in out-of-home care including the process of emergency reception into care, children's own views on their experience in care, access arrangements, the review process, after care and direct work with children in care including the admission process, placement decisions, care plans, access, and career paths. The next two chapters deal with issues pertinent to residential care and foster care respectively, while the following chapter specifically discusses the degree to which parental involvement is encouraged and facilitated when children are in out-of-home care.

Emergency reception into care
While there is general agreement that careful planning and preparation should precede the placement of a child in a care situation (Triseliotis, 1993; Falhberg, 1992), the nature of child protection work is such that emergency placements are inevitable from time to time. The process of finding a placement and organising a move within a short period of time and often within an emotionally pressured context can mean that an individual child's needs and welfare are difficult to prioritise. This issue was the subject of a project undertaken in 1994 by Barbara Grossman, then a community care child care worker in the Eastern Health Board. Her professional experience had

illustrated how traumatic the admission process could be for children. She was also aware of how long it could take children to understand and make sense of what was happening to them during a move. She aimed, through her project, to explore the principal issues involved for children, foster parents and social workers. While she had originally intended to include residential workers and birth parents in her interview sample, circumstances and pressure of time prevented her from doing so and she acknowledged the limitations to her research caused by the omission of these key players. She ultimately conducted individual interviews with three children in out-of-home care, two girls aged ten and eleven and a boy of thirteen as well as with three female foster carers. In addition, she carried out a group interview with four social workers.

Grossman was aware from the literature on the subject that agreed norms existed in relation to good practice in the placement of children. She was also aware of the potential for feelings of grief, loss, anxiety, culpability and fear of the unknown to be experienced by children moving into placement, emotions that were likely to be exacerbated when moves were unplanned. Her findings from interviews with the children confirmed the frequency with which these feelings occur. Grossman analysed the data from the children's interviews in terms of negative and positive factors. On the negative side, the children described how they were left at times without clear knowledge of what was happening, where they were going or what had precipitated the move. Most notable was the tendency for children, particularly in the absence of information, to internalise responsibility or blame. The findings also highlighted the level of powerlessness, worry and anxiety experienced by children in relation to their new placement and the whereabouts of their families and personal belongings. Each of them in a different manner had expressed apprehension and a sense of lack of control in relation to their new circumstances, along with fear that their families would not know where to find them or that they would be left bereft of their toys or possessions when they moved. Two of them had witnessed social work staff on the telephone repeatedly trying to find accommodation for them, an experience that had increased their sense of helplessness and isolation.

However, Grossman's interview data illustrated some positive factors that had relieved some of the negativity surrounding the placement moves. The presence of a familiar social worker, efforts made to placate or amuse the children, the involvement, however slight, of their own parents or relatives, being placed in a familiar area and demonstrations of concern such as medical checks were all interpreted by the children as channels through which some comfort and sensitivity was delivered to them.

The foster parents who were interviewed by Grossman appeared to be generally tolerant of the difficulties caused by unplanned or emergency placements. They did, however, point out that some deficits like missing or incorrect information were virtually inexcusable and had impacted negatively on their ability to settle the children or ease the trauma they were experiencing. Replicating some of the points raised in the children's interviews, foster parents indicated that involvement or contact with the child's birth family and placement in a familiar area made the move somewhat easier. While the foster parents had been positive about the support received from their own social workers, they were less so in relation to the workers for the children whom they found less accessible and communicative.

The main issues raised by the social workers interviewed by Grossman concerned the conflicts involved in trying to access a placement while attending to a child's needs, the lack of resources and the difficulties in trying to ascertain what, if any, suitable placements were available. Social workers who were interviewed suggested that unrealistic expectations were often held of them by other disciplines and some non health board agencies. They also claimed that they had occasionally felt unsupported by their own agency when criticised, for example by the courts, because of the lack of facilities for children requiring placement. Overall, they expressed the view that responding to the crisis presented by the move tended to take precedence over attending to the child's needs.

On the basis of her findings, Grossman made recommendations for policy and practice in her agency. Notwithstanding the unpredictability of emergency placements and the attendant shortcomings, she suggested some strategies to reduce pressure on all concerned, decrease the level of trauma for children and facilitate more successful placements. These included:

- the provision of a computerised system in each board for the display of information about available placements
- the availability of information on foster families or residential units in a form that could be given to a child as part of preparation for placement
- the development of procedures for good practice in emergency placements including the availability of a second worker to support a key worker and ensure that the child or children's needs were addressed
- the provision of a child-centred environment where children can comfortably await placement
- adequate communication of information about the child to prospective carers.

Finally, Grossman advocated further and more detailed research into the process of emergency reception into care, including evaluation of practices.

Placement issues
A crucial determinant of the quality of a child's career in any care situation is

the decision-making process involved in the initial placement. Most health boards operate this process through the mechanism of a placement committee. However, the ability of the committee to make appropriate decisions depends on the means available to it and is thus only one element in the complex business of matching a child's needs to a family's resources. A project exploring the context of decision-making in relation to placements, with a particular focus on the workings of the committee, was carried out in 1992 by Róisín Maguire, at the time a social worker in the Western Health Board and based in Mayo. The specific objectives of her study were to examine existing decision-making processes, evaluate the appropriateness of current placement practice in her area and establish consistent procedures based on the views of professionals, caregivers and children.

Maguire carried out her study in two phases, the first one consisting of a prospective case study where she explored the process of matching children with foster carers in nine cases, and the second one examining three placements in hindsight. In order to gather data, she consulted written documentation submitted by the social workers seeking short- and long-term placements for individual children and administered questionnaires to the same social workers. In addition, she administered questionnaires to the members of the committee, known as the Fostering Case Committee, seeking information about the basis of the different matches made between children and families. Certain difficulties arose in relation to the data collection in the first phase, some of which had implications for her later recommendations. Firstly, it transpired that information was not always submitted in writing by social workers seeking placements, and secondly, they did not all return the questionnaires. While she was able to make general inferences from the available data on all nine cases, Maguire decided to carry out an additional piece of work by focusing specifically on the only case where complete information was available in order to elucidate a typical decision-making process. She interviewed a foster carer and the foster child in this case.

For the second phase, Maguire explored three cases where long-term placements had been made in order to ascertain, within obvious time constraints, whether the decisions made had been appropriate. She interviewed the three foster children concerned and two of the foster carers with whom the children had been matched.

When analysing the prospective part of her research involving nine cases and a total of fifteen children, Maguire noted that all requests for short-term or emergency care were met, though in two instances the preferred option of residential care was not available. While three of the cases involved sibling groups, it had not been possible to place the children together. In two cases, children were placed with relatives, a practice that was not particularly common at the time the research was undertaken. At the end of the fieldwork period, seven of the children still required long-term placements but none was currently available. Maguire noted that there was a high incidence of sexual abuse in these cases. In relation to the committee process, Maguire was critical of the lack of written information provided by workers which, she argued, inevitably impeded good decision making. She considered that this was unacceptable practice, even in the context of an emergency, and proposed the use of a fairly basic data sheet for workers to complete.

The single case on which data were available involved a teenage girl requiring first short- and later long-term placement. A primary concern was to provide a setting that would enable her to study for forthcoming examinations. Maguire evaluated the decision-making process in terms of how well it met the child's needs and the compatibility between the child and her ultimate foster carers. She found that, as she had predicted, the placement decision was determined more by the availability of a resource than the child's needs. It also transpired that the type of placement was not one originally envisaged by the foster carers who had originally opted to foster a younger child on a long-term basis. The principal requirement in relation to the placement, that it would facilitate the girl to study for impending examinations, was met. However, when Maguire examined the compatibility between the child and the foster carers, she found that, even though a certain amount of information had been available, it was insufficient and its inadequacy had hampered the committee in its deliberations. Ultimately, their decision appeared to have been based mainly on their knowledge of the foster carers. They considered that a match of a 'limited nature' had been made. Data from interviews with the foster mother, the child and the social worker, later confirmed that there were many irreconcilable differences between what the child wanted and needed and what the foster carers felt able to provide. This, in Maguire's view, illustrated the gap that can exist between the committee's view and that of the principal actors in the situation. While Maguire argued that this case example illustrated the need for a standard method of providing information to the Fostering Care Committee, she also acknowledged that the non-availability of suitable placements had an ongoing adverse effect on the decision-making process and ultimate placement.

Moving on to the retrospective consideration of placement decisions and outcomes, Maguire examined the three cases where long-term matches were made between families and children after a campaign seeking foster homes for a total of eight children. In each situation, she looked at the quality of information provided to the committee and the views of foster carers and children. She found the information supplied in each case to be comprehensive, though different formats were used for presenting it. The interviews with the children confirmed their wishes to have a 'normal' family experience, to remain with their foster carers on a permanent basis and have no threats to the security of their placements. The foster carers highlighted the importance of having an open relationship with their social workers and access to as much information about the children as possible.

The committee decisions had apparently been made on the basis of the families' wishes in relation to the type of child they were prepared to take, the age structure of the families, the children's needs in respect of access and education and how far the families' lifestyle suited the children. There were two particular criteria used in relation to specific children, one with a disability and one who had had previous negative experience with a father figure. In each case the committee was satisfied that the child's needs would be met by the selected families.

Having considered the findings from her study, Maguire concluded that even though uncertainty and unpredictability will always feature in fostering situations, certain basic elements will add to the potential success of a placement. These include considerations about permanence where appropriate. In order to avoid the tendency to base decisions on available resources, Maguire proposed that more options be made available by the provision of sufficient substitute care facilities including residential places and possibly professional fostering services. She suggested the reorganisation of existing residential services and the development of needs-related special residential and fostering schemes to address the needs of older and more difficult to place children such as teenagers, sibling groups and children who had been sexually abused. Having noted that decision making for long-term placements was more considered and carefully conducted, Maguire recommended the introduction of a standard protocol for short-term placements including a requirement for a minimum amount of written information on the child. Finally, she emphasised the need for an ongoing review of resource requirements.

The Carer's Project: specialist placements for adolescents
The contention that a child's past history of sexual abuse affects the nature of decision making in relation to his or her placement was also borne out in a project completed in 1991 by Anne Meehan, at the time a social worker in the Eastern Health Board. Meehan's study aimed to explore the factors that influenced decision making in relation to the 'Carer's Project', a specialist fostering project for the placement of adolescents. In addition, Meehan sought to establish the expectations of the key players in the Carer's Project at the outset and to identify the most effective means of preparing carers and young people for placement.

The Carer's Project was designed to place teenagers of between 14 and 16 years of age with carers in the community. Its core principles included the participation and willingness of the young person to take part in the project, the involvement of all persons of significance in the young person's life in the placement process and the ongoing availability of training to carers. Meehan noted that six of the twelve young people who were referred to the project had a history of experiencing or perpetrating sexual abuse, and she hypothesised that this issue alone would dominate the professional decision-making process. For the purposes of her study, Meehan focused on one case where a young person who had abused younger children was placed with a carer. She conducted an in-depth interview with the young person who was the subject of the case study, his key residential worker, his social worker and his carer. She also interviewed five other carers with a view to evaluating the impact of training on their willingness to consider caring for adolescents who had been the victims or perpetrators of sexual abuse.

Meehan used the case study and the associated interviews to try and get a sense of the perceptions and understandings held in relation to the project by the young person and his various workers and carer. Each of them, in different ways, described the placement as a new opportunity for him to spend some time in a family environment prior to adulthood and independence. Meehan noted that the placement committee had focused very specifically on an incident where the young person had sexually abused two younger children in a previous placement. For this reason they had made a decision to place him in a setting where there were no other young children, and they had requested additional information regarding his 'abusive' history. This had caused some unease to his social worker, who felt that too many people had been involved in discussing issues that were very sensitive and confidential.

The (female) carer with whom the young person was placed had initially thought that the sexual abuse was a highly relevant matter. However, as time went by it had apparently not affected their day-to-day lives together and gradually diminished in importance for her in relation to some of the other elements of the placement. The young person's former residential key worker considered the sexual abuse to be quite important in terms of the boy's potential to re-abuse and also his own development and sexual maturation. However, he was concerned lest it dominate the other professionals' perception of him. While the social worker also felt that the abuse was significant on several levels, she too was concerned that it might have affected the way that others perceived the young person to a greater degree than she considered relevant. She felt that it might have caused them to give less attention to other aspects of his social context. From the data obtained in the interviews, Meehan ascertained that the social worker and the key worker understood and explained the young person's abuse in terms of his early history and unmet needs in the context of his whole life history and experiences of rejection, lack of attachment and low self-esteem. The young person himself indicated in his interview that the incident where he sexually abused two younger children had a profound effect on the course of his life, causing two placement disruptions. He was also aware of the concern that it caused all the professionals involved with him. He said that he dearly wished to let it go and put the experience to the back of his mind and he did not consider it relevant to his day-to-day life with his new carer.

When Meehan interviewed the larger group of carers in order to judge the impact of training on their attitudes to caring for adolescents with a history of abuse or abusing, she found that covering this topic had not greatly altered their original decisions or views. They claimed to have learned a lot from the sessions on sexual abuse, finding them informative in terms of its prevalence and the impact that it had on young people's lives and behaviour. This confirmed Meehan's view that training should involve a discussion to check carers' myths and assumptions about sexual abuse and present clear and accurate information. While she considered it important that carers are made aware of the signs and consequences of sexual abuse, she felt it would be unhelpful if they were encouraged to link it to all the difficulties experienced by young people.

In her analysis of the findings, Meehan noted that all the young people involved in the project had been referred to it for reasons other than their involvement with sexual abuse. Yet, this area had received more attention and response from the placement committee than any of the young persons' other needs. As this was likely to be an ongoing issue for the project workers, she made the following recommendations in relation to the placement of adolescents:

- that all persons involved in a placement have clear information about sexual abuse, including any risks associated with a potential placement
- that the conflict between meeting a young person's need for placement and the responsibility to protect families with children from the risk of abuse be acknowledged and addressed
- acknowledgement that the experience of sexual abuse is possibly only one of a number of significant events in a young person's life in care.

Finally, Meehan urged the employment of caution in relation to the handling of private and sensitive information, bearing in mind the manner in which it may be interpreted.

Life in care from the perspectives of children
By the 1990s, a certain amount of Irish evaluative research had been carried

out into different aspects of the care system (The Kennedy Report, 1970[17]; Department of Health, 1980; Richardson, 1985; O'Higgins and Boyle, 1988; Streetwise National Coalition 1991), but up to that point, the voices of children accommodated by the state in various settings had really not been heard. In light of this deficit, a project carried out in 1993 by Anne Tighe, a social worker in the Western Health Board, sought to examine the quality of life experienced by children in care, from the perspectives of the children themselves. She was particularly interested in comparing foster and residential care and in researching the extent of children's participation in decision making about their lives. She also sought to examine their understanding of the roles of social worker and key worker, the degree of information that children possessed about their families, the level of contact with their families, their willingness to talk about being in care, their school experiences, their preparation for leaving care[18] and their health needs.

Tighe interviewed ten young people over the age of twelve who had been in care for an average of two to five years. Five children were in foster care and five in residential care. Half of the children had experienced more than one placement. All the children were given free choices regarding their participation in the study, and the necessary consents were obtained in each case.

Findings from the interviews indicated that, in terms of the areas under examination, the quality of life for children did not differ greatly according to whether they were in residential or foster care and all the children interviewed indicated that they were happy in their current placements. Certain differences emerged, however, particularly in relation to health board reviews of their placements. Although reviews of children in residential care were conducted regularly at the time, reviews of children in foster care were not statutorily required. However, in practice most foster placements were reviewed regularly but normally without the children present, while it was relatively normal practice for children in residential care to be invited to attend the meetings. Interview data revealed that attendance at reviews by no means guaranteed real participation, with most of the young people indicating that they did not look upon the meetings as a means of making their opinions and wishes known. In general, it appeared that children in both types of care understood their social workers' roles and were satisfied with the service they received, though the data indicated that children in residential care were seen more frequently by social workers than those in foster placements. The children in residential care all had key workers and were generally satisfied with them.

---

[17] Reformatory and Industrial Schools Systems Reports (The Kennedy Report) 1970.
[18] The subjects of access and preparation for leaving care are also dealt with in detail in later sections of this chapter.

While all the children had some degree of knowledge about their families, only one had a life storybook and none of the others had any kind of written information about themselves or their families. Tighe particularly noted the lack of information possessed by the children regarding their fathers, notwithstanding the fact that most parents were either unmarried or separated. Where contact with families was concerned, three out of the five children in residential care had regular contact with their families, as did four out of the five in foster care. However, 'family' tended to mean mother and siblings. Only one child had contact with his father, and eight out of the ten had no contact with grandparents, aunts or uncles. Tighe found that distance from home was related to frequency of family contact for children in residential care, but not in foster care. However, the sample was too small to make any meaningful inferences from this finding.

Tighe's interview data indicated that the young people in care had difficulty talking about their birth families and their placements to friends and acquaintances. They all attended school regularly and appeared to like it and feel supported in their education. There was, however, evidence that a significant number of the children were educationally delayed, indicating that special help should be available. While the general health of the children was good, Tighe noted that those in foster care had less regular medical checks than those in residential care. She also found that the degree to which the children were being taught domestic skills and prepared for independence probably did not differ greatly from children living with their families, but pointed out that the likelihood of children leaving care and ultimately living on their own was greater, thereby highlighting the importance of adequate preparation. On the positive side, Tighe found that all the children were encouraged to have hobbies and participate in community activities, thus building up their social networks and availing of opportunities to build up their self-esteem.

Tighe presented her findings to residential care staff and social workers who agreed that children needed to be prepared and enabled to both participate in reviews and talk about their care situation with their peers. They acknowledged that information exchange needed to be improved and that more attention should be paid to making regular medical and dental appointments as well as providing educational help. Agreement was also made in relation to improved contact between children and their fathers and grandparents.

Career paths of children in care

It is becoming increasingly recognised that children who have grown up in the care of the state tend to be disproportionately represented in the ranks of the homeless and other disadvantaged groups (Kelleher and Associates, 1998). A project was undertaken in 1998 by Renee English, then a social worker based in the Eastern Health Board, who undertook to explore the career paths of children received into the care of the state. She subsequently produced an interesting overview of a cohort of children who were accommodated by the health board during a specific period. English focused particularly on the circumstances which led to the separation of children from their parents, the degree to which plans were outlined and operated and reviews were carried out and the career of the placement over a period. Aware of concerns about 'drift' of children in care (Millham et al, 1986; Gilligan, 1996) and poor outcomes after leaving care (Kelleher and Associates, 1998), English's aim was to highlight pertinent issues and make policy recommendations.

English focused her project on the total number children who were received into care in one community care area between 1 July and 31 December 1996, consisting of eighteen children from twelve families. She studied the files of the children involved and carried out in-depth interviews with nine social workers and one child care worker involved in the cases, including five staff members who had changed employment in the meantime. The care arrangements consisted of three placements with the Carer's Project,[19] seven placements in supported lodgings, one in day care, one in relative foster care and the remaining six in 'standard' foster care. None of the children in the study was currently in residential care, reflecting the national trend towards the use of foster placements.

When she examined the environmental profiles of children admitted to care, English found that the typical picture was one of a deprived, lone parent family. Only two of the families in the sample consisted of parents who were married to each other and six of the families were headed by a single parent. Two of the largest families were members of the Travelling community. Only one family lived in owner-occupied accommodation, with the remainder in dwellings rented either privately or from the council. In just over half of the families, neither parent was working. Legal measures had been used to separate the children from their parent/s in only two of the families and the most frequently cited reason for reception into care was stress or illness on the part of the mother, frequently described as 'inability to cope'.

There was evidence to show that planning meetings had been held by health board staff in some cases, principally those where legal proceedings were pending or where risk to the children had been identified by more than

---

[19] The carers project was set up by the Eastern Health Board in 1988 to cater for adolescents who had spent time in residential care.

one source. However, English found no formal care plans in the case files and evidence that reviews had taken place existed in only three cases. These lapses were in contravention of Department of Health regulations (Department of Health, 1995b).

The findings from the records and interviews indicated that contact had been maintained between children and their families in all but the very short placements. Access had been arranged informally between parents and foster families in three-quarters of the cases studied. By the end of the period under study, ten of the eighteen children were no longer in the care of the health board, those remaining representing the group that had been in care for the full six months.

Through the semi-structured interviews, English examined the context in which work with the children and families involved in the study had taken place. She sought to highlight any issues that may have had relevance either for the original reception into care or the nature of interventions carried out in the meantime. She found that all the social workers were carrying high caseloads and that it had not always been possible to allocate newly referred child protection concerns. As a consequence, cases that were not in 'crisis' tended to be left on a waiting list for a considerable length of time, which obviously impacted on the level of preventive work taking place. It was considered that in at least one of the cases where children were later received into care, early intervention may have pre-empted the ultimate outcome. The case where day fostering had been provided was cited by a social worker as an example of early intervention that possibly averted a full-time placement. While English noted the implementation two years earlier of a standardised recording system, she found that there was considerable variation in the quality of record keeping, reflecting the competing demands on social workers' time and also making it difficult to ascertain the nature and process of decision making.

The sort of community services that may support families under stress and prevent reception into care also seemed to have been in short supply. English found, for example, that child and adolescent psychological and psychiatric services in the area operated within quite rigid constraints with the result that services for young people with behavioural and emotional problems were difficult to access. A scarcity of addiction services catering for teenagers was also noted, this deficit being particularly pertinent as problem alcohol and drug use frequently featured in the caseloads of workers. Social workers who were interviewed acknowledged that their involvement with Traveller families tended to operate on an 'all or nothing' basis with either scant involvement or reception into care, affirming the point that more attention was needed in relation to this group.

While the fact that foster placements were available for all the children received into care was positive, English noted that some placements had been delayed because of the difficulties involved in trying to place large numbers of siblings together. She also observed that children were at times being placed inappropriately. For example, the families who provided supported lodgings had not been trained or assessed for the care of younger children, yet were being asked to foster them when other placements were not available.

On the basis of her findings English concluded that preventive services and early intervention with community-based services may have precluded the admission to care of at least some of the children in the cohort under study, particularly in those cases where the families were already known to the health board. She noted that some family support initiatives were underway in the area and recommended their further development. She suggested that record keeping, together with care, planning and regular review of children in care should receive priority in the area. In response to the shortage of psychological and psychiatric services for young people, she recommended the development of a consultancy service to advise and assist social workers in meeting the needs of families where children were experiencing behavioural and emotional difficulties. Likewise, she proposed that social workers should make links with Traveller organisations in order to receive training and plan joint work and thus provide a more effective and culturally appropriate service.

Finally, English acknowledged that even with the development of family support and preventive services, there would always be a need for admission to care for some children on a short- or long-term basis. She recommended a strengthening of the number of available placements with an increase in the range of options available to meet ever-changing needs.

Supported lodgings for young people out of home
There is a particular group of children for whom health boards have responsibility, but whose needs are defined in a less clear manner than children who are the subject of child protection proceedings. These are juveniles who present to the services as homeless. This category of vulnerable children has increased over recent years and has been the focus of a number of policy initiatives (Forum on Homelessness, 2000). Section 5 of the Child Care Act, 1991 obliges the health boards to enquire into the circumstances of a child who appears homeless, and if he or she is not received into the care of the board, must make available suitable accommodation for him or her. One of the services that developed during the 1990s to meet this need has been 'supported lodgings'. Different models of supported lodgings have been developed by the various health boards. While it is seen to be a reasonably appropriate way of addressing the problem of teenage homelessness, there

have been many concerns about the safety and welfare of children cared for in what is seen to be a less regulated and more informal manner.

A project carried out in 1998 by Breege Mangan, then a social worker in the North Eastern Health Board, aimed to develop a satisfactory supported lodgings scheme in Co. Louth. Mangan surveyed the available information on the way that type of care was provided in all the country's health boards, and attempted to identify the essential elements of a safe and effective service. First, she endeavoured to seek a reasonably universal meaning for the term 'supported lodgings'. According to the norms operating in different regions, it appeared to Mangan that the minimum accommodation to be provided was bed and board. The environment was expected to be 'hospitable'; service providers were expected to work with the health board and agree to certain standards and the health boards paid the service providers a fee for their work.

Mangan carried out in-depth interviews with social workers in her area to see how and to what extent they were currently meeting the requirements of Section 5 of the Child Care Act, 1991. She also interviewed three adolescents, two of whom were in supported lodgings at the time and one of whom was in residential care, in order to elicit their views of the quality of the service being offered to them. To gain some insight into what was being offered in other regions, she interviewed two social workers from two other health boards, and finally, she interviewed a service provider in another health board area.

The child protection social workers in Mangan's own area confirmed that the number of referrals concerning juvenile homelessness had increased since the implementation of Section 5 of the Child Care Act, 1991. All of the social workers agreed that lack of suitable accommodation caused them the greatest difficulty. They felt that this had the unintended consequence of diverting their energy into seeking accommodation when they could have otherwise spent time with the young person and their family trying to work towards returning the young person home. They suggested the development of a specialist service with purpose-built accommodation, linked with community and voluntary groups. All felt very uneasy about placing young people in bed-and-breakfast accommodation without parental consent or the protection of the young person being officially 'in care'.

One of the three adolescents interviewed by Mangan had been in bed-and-breakfast accommodation for seven months. Another had been in similar accommodation for three months. The third young person interviewed had been in residential care for seven months. Two had left home because of 'problems' and the third had become homeless because her foster placement broke down. The two who were living in bed-and-breakfast accommodation said that they missed a 'family atmosphere' and were lonely. They found it hard to finance their daily living costs like lunch, toiletries and laundry. The young person in residential care expressed unhappiness at his sense of 'not fitting in' and being placed with children who had 'much bigger problems'. While all three had positive comments to make about their landladies and the residential staff, they were generally dissatisfied with their living arrangements.

The interviews with the two social workers from other health board areas who were involved with supported lodgings schemes confirmed that the problem of juvenile homelessness is generally on the increase and putting an intolerable strain on existing services. One of the boards had a policy of eight-session assessments prior to the approval of service providers for the supported lodgings scheme, similar to those carried out with foster parents. The other board carried out a shorter, three-session assessment. Both boards put a lot of emphasis on carers' experience and expectations. Likewise, both were careful to ensure that Garda and medical checks were completed and referees interviewed. In each region, the service was co-ordinated by one social worker who was responsible for supporting the service providers, a factor that was considered to be vital. Payments varied slightly between the two boards. Difficulties that had been experienced to date included problems in moving young people on, allegations of abuse made against service providers, over-burdening of service providers and lack of out-of-hours social work support. On the positive side, supported lodgings was viewed by the social workers interviewed as a useful resource for respite from other forms of care.

Mangan interviewed a service provider from a health board region adjacent to her own. The service provider had become involved in the scheme through her experience of providing bed-and-breakfast accommodation to young people referred through the health board. While she generally found the work satisfying, she confirmed that support from the project workers was essential to help her cope with day-to-day problems.

Mangan concluded that the health boards were generally not satisfactorily fulfilling their obligations under Section 5 of the Child Care Act, 1991, mainly because the necessary structures had not been put in place. She also felt that the practice of placing young people in bed-and-breakfast accommodation without parental consent was legally unsafe. On the basis of her findings, she suggested that a properly resourced and serviced supported lodgings scheme could enable young people in their transition from residential care to independence, allowing them to take greater responsibility for their lives while still having someone to turn to for support. She pointed out that an appropriately resourced supported lodgings scheme would, in fact, be more cost-effective than the provision of bed-and-breakfast accommod-ation over the longer term. She argued that an important element of the assessment of potential service providers should be their own understanding of the needs of adolescents and clarity about their expectations. Importantly,

Mangan felt that there should be a co-ordinated range of options available for young people. She made the following recommendations to her health board:

- the provision of appropriate accommodation for young people under Section 5 of the Child Care Act, 1991
- the development of an appropriately funded supported lodgings scheme
- the development of Leaving Care schemes as an integral part of the child care system
- the conversion, in appropriate cases, of foster placements to supported lodgings placements in keeping with the current needs of the young people placed there
- the development of transitional housing as a bridge to greater independence for children leaving care.

Mangan's proposals were approved by the child care manager in her area and piloted following the completion of her study.

Leaving care

Section 45 of the Child Care Act, 1991 provides for the health boards to assist children leaving care up to the age of 21, or thereafter if they are still engaged in full-time education. While the legislation is enabling rather than obligatory and the assessment of whether or not a child is in need of assistance lies with the health board, the provision of aftercare has now been recognised as part of the responsibility of residential institutions and is enshrined in the *Guide to Good Practice in Children's Residential Centres* (Department of Health, 1997a). The importance of a successful transition from care is vividly illustrated in a study undertaken in Ireland. Kelleher and Associates (1998) illustrate the disadvantaged status of young people leaving care, with a low level of educational qualifications and consequently lowered prospects for training and employment, vulnerability to problem drug and alcohol use and ultimately, homelessness. Conversely, the same study showed that children who have had a planned and supported exit from care are less likely to experience these adversities.

Four projects completed between 1995 and 1999 focused on the preparation of young people for independent adulthood after leaving care. They were carried out in the North East, the Mid West, and the Eastern Regional Health Authority areas and reflect the needs and experiences of young people in both residential and foster care.

In 1995, Valerie Minogue, at the time a child care worker in a residential centre in Limerick, undertook a study to explore the attitudes of care workers, social workers and young people on the area of leaving care. She was aware from her experience and research on the subject that not only had contact between families and children in residential care been insufficiently fostered in the past, but unrealistic expectations existed about the capacity of young care leavers to live independently. The decline in the involvement of religious orders in the provision of care was, in Minogue's view, an important factor in relation to planning for after care as many orders would have traditionally offered support on a long-term basis. Changes in the nature of care from long- to short- and medium-term stays were also, in her view, significant influences on the ability of residential units to offer longer-term involvement and increased the risk of care leavers becoming homeless. Her aim in undertaking the research was to seek professional perspectives on the type of service to be offered, elicit young people's views on the nature of preparation needed and outline a policy for adoption by her own agency.

In order to conduct her fieldwork, Minogue firstly convened a meeting of child care workers in her agency to elicit their views on the key issues involved in after care and to identify potential obstacles to its provision. She then carried out interviews with five health board workers who were in contact with her organisation and five child care workers from separate units within the service. She also interviewed four young people, three of whom still lived in the centre and one of whom had left within the previous three years. The interviews with social workers and child care workers contained open-ended questions to facilitate free responses, while the interviews with the young people contained more closed questions.

The group discussion involving the child care workers yielded some important data. It was generally agreed that young people leaving care are immature and vulnerable to isolation and loneliness. Most of the workers expressed a view that lack of resources and the necessity to prioritise the needs of current residents were the main blocks to providing a service to them.

The interviews with social workers and child care workers explored their perceptions of the needs of care leavers and the essential elements of an after-care service. They also asked the question of how and by whom the service should be delivered and focused on the adequacy or otherwise of the provisions of the Child Care Act, 1991 in relation to after-care. In general, the responses from social workers indicated that a service should meet the young person's needs for life skills, formal support systems, information about services, education about drugs and alcohol and counselling in relation to relationships and personal development. Preparation for leaving care should, in their view, be an integral part of the care plan for each child, with links set up between child care workers and social workers. Co-ordination of networks and information services was emphasised strongly and the establishment of an adequately staffed, separate after-care unit was recommended, where plans could be reviewed. There was strong support from the social workers for the idea of a multi-disciplinary after-care team, made up of various professionals involved in the children's lives.

Interviews with the child care workers illustrated the need for support, guidance and practical advice for care leavers. They recommended a preparation period of at least one year prior to leaving with a continuing service including the establishment of a semi-independent transitional unit. The need for inter-agency co-operation was also stressed.

Minogue invited the young people whom she interviewed to complete questionnaires indicating their perceptions of the level of useful life skills they possessed. They were also asked to give information about their plans, their knowledge about accommodation and budgeting, their contacts with family and friends, their own personal strengths and resources and their hopes and worries for the future. The young people were between fourteen and twenty years old. Minogue was concerned that less than half of them seemed adequately prepared for independent living, all expressing a lot of apprehension about leaving care. While they rated their personal skills and resources fairly highly, their knowledge about finance, accommodation and useful life skills was low.

Minogue concluded that there was no real evidence that any kind of after-care service was currently being offered to care leavers. She recommended urgent attention to this area, starting with a meeting between the residential manager and social work management in the area, to be followed by a submission to the health board outlining the necessary resources. She proposed that this exercise be followed by the establishment of a working party to decide upon a course of action and develop an after-care programme.

A project similar in many respects to Minogue's was carried out in 1999 by Seamus Hally, a senior child care worker in a residential centre for adolescent girls who were admitted to care via the juvenile justice system. While it provided care on a medium- to long-term basis, the length of stay was determined by the courts and was, on average, eighteen months. One of the distinct elements of the care provided was its 'secure' nature whereby the girls were not normally allowed to leave the unit. The average age of the girls was fourteen years.

Hally's study explored the perceptions of ten young women who had left his centre within the previous eight years about their experiences of leaving care. He also sought the views of staff at the centre about the type of service they offered to the young people on their departure. He then combined two sets of data to identify key elements of a quality after-care service.

Hally conducted in-depth interviews with his respondents, covering subjects with the ex-service users such as their feelings when leaving care, their contact with staff afterwards and their views on what type of help would have been most appropriate at the time. While, in general, the young women had been glad to regain their 'freedom', most of them recalled feelings of apprehension, sadness and loneliness. Some had been worried about re-offending; others had been nervous about re-joining their families and generally 'fitting in'. Hally noted that seven out of the ten ex-service users had been living on the streets prior to being remanded to the centre, but that most of them had had contact with their families while in care. However, the level of support they received from their families diminished when they left and became low in the majority of cases.

Over half of the ex-service users who were interviewed remembered receiving help from staff when they were preparing to leave, in the form of advice, assistance in getting jobs and accommodation. A smaller number said they had been offered ongoing counselling and support. A minority of ex-service users expressed the view that the help was insufficient and did not prepare them for the reality of leaving such a sheltered environment. When asked to identify the types of help that would have been most effective, six out of the ten identified general support as being the most important. Others suggested different areas where some assistance would have enabled them to adjust better, including help with finance, adjusting at home, finding accommodation and with their efforts not to re-offend.

Staff members in the centre were asked by Hally to give their views on the type of preparation given to young people leaving care. He also asked them to identify the sort of difficulties the young people were likely to encounter when they left. Most of them commented on the level of dependency created by the 'confined' nature of the centre and the restriction on the young people's freedom. This, the staff suggested, was at the root of some of the difficulties in adjustment experienced by the young people after they left. They suggested that more links between the centre and the community might lessen the 'gap' between them, for example a drop-in centre, an extension of the practice of peer support, or an outreach service staffed by personnel from the centre. It was suggested that greater efforts to work with families while the young people were still in care should be made by the centre.

Hally concluded that the care environment provided by the centre appeared to offer safety and respite to the residents but at the cost of creating and maintaining dependency which ultimately undermined their ability to make a satisfactory adjustment to living in the community. He supported the view that a 'step-down' facility should be developed to enable an easier transition, and emphasised the need to maintain links between the young people and their families. In order to lessen the possibility of young people moving frequently and ultimately becoming vulnerable to homelessness, he proposed the provision of more support during and after the transition period. Echoing the change in terminology proposed by Maluccio, Kreiger and Pine

(1990) Hally suggested that the term 'interdependence' rather than 'dependence' would challenge unrealistic expectations that young people leaving care can automatically adjust, and would signal the shared responsibility of professionals and families to offer help and support on an ongoing basis.

In relation to his own centre, Hally recommended that a greater effort be made to prepare young people for leaving care. To facilitate this, he proposed the development of an ethos of working in partnership with parents, the allocation of a specific number of hours per week to the provision of support to residents after they left, and the submission of a proposal to the Department of Education outlining the need for after-care. Finally, Hally recommended that his centre campaign for a change in legislation to enforce the provision of after-care as a statutory right of children leaving the care of the state.

While the projects completed by Minogue and Hally concerned children in residential care, two projects carried out in 1999 concentrated mainly on care leavers who had been in foster care or supported lodgings for their last placement. They were conducted by Heather Ritchie, a social worker in the North Eastern Health Board, based in the Cavan/Monaghan area and Laura Nee, a child care worker with the Mid-Western Health Board, based in Clare. Ritchie interviewed five young people including three who had left the care of the North Eastern Health Board in 1998 and two who were still officially 'in care' with foster families. In addition, she administered questionnaires to twelve professionals including social workers, child care workers, family support workers and managers. Nee interviewed thirteen young people who had left the care of the Mid-Western Health Board between 1995 and 1998, eleven of whom had been in foster care, one in relative care and one in residential care. Both studies sought to identify current policy, and the perceptions of young people regarding their needs when leaving care, and make recommendations accordingly.

Of the three care leavers interviewed by Ritchie, one was still living with her foster family though not officially 'in care' any longer and two were living independently. All of the respondents were involved in education or training. The young people were positive about certain aspects of moving on and rated independence very highly. They were not entirely free of anxiety about the future, however, and all expressed apprehension about possible financial or accommodation problems and potential loneliness.

Of the thirteen young people interviewed by Nee in the Mid-West area, seven were still living with their foster families and two more visited their former foster families every weekend. Eleven of them were in school, training or employment. Of the remaining two, one was in part-time employment and the other was caring for a dependent relative. However, Nee noted that four out of the thirteen did not hold any educational qualifications, a factor that may later impede their employment opportunities. Interviewees in both studies indicated that their main sources of social support and contact were their birth or foster families. In both studies, social work support had diminished since the respondents left care. This had been anticipated and both sets of respondents reported that their social workers had made it clear they were available for further support, with the onus being on the young person to initiate any contact.

While most of the young people interviewed were leading what they described as happy lives and coping with either the actuality or the prospect of leaving care, over a third of those interviewed by Nee had recently been ill and half of them had either lost or gained significant amounts of weight since leaving care. In addition, nearly half of them had reported feeling 'down' since they left care. Like the young people in Ritchie's study, some of them worried about loneliness and experienced a lack of certainty about the future.

While the young people in both studies felt they had been given a reasonable level of preparation for independent living, including practical skills, they considered the cost of accommodation to be a major factor in their ability to live independently in the future. The young people interviewed in Ritchie's study identified a need for an information booklet to provide detail on financial, medical, counselling, and education and training services. They also expressed interest in knowing about employment, law and information centres, health board contacts, complaints procedures and how to get access to their files. The young people in Nee's research had similar suggestions, and also identified the desirability of a help line and/or advice service, help with making friends and coping with bullying, services for people with learning difficulties and services for care leavers who become parents.

The professionals who were interviewed by Ritchie were unanimously of the view that the issue of after-care had not been adequately addressed by the health board. They suggested that an after-care policy should deal with finance, accommodation, education, training, health and all forms of social and familial support. They also considered that standards and methods of evaluating practice should be an integral part of any policy. While they generally supported the idea of an information booklet for care leavers, concern was expressed about the need to ensure that the resources were available first.

A number of fairly significant points emerged from both these projects. One was the important part played by foster families, many of whom were still providing support and practical care for the young people in addition to, in some cases, full-time accommodation. Both studies recommended that the health board continue to encourage and provide financially for ongoing post-placement support of foster parents who play such an important and often unacknowledged role in after-care. Secondly, the importance of designating a specific post in health boards to the provision of after-care was illustrated. The studies both demonstrated the reluctance of young people to return to their former social workers. Yet, the need for a skilled professional to give practical advice and emotional support was clearly highlighted. Finally, the studies illustrated a factor which needs little elaboration, the need for not just an after-care service, but a quality experience for children right through the care process, with particular emphasis on stability of placements and contact with birth families. Both projects showed the difference that these aspects of life in care could make to a young person's readiness to move on.

All the studies on this area recommended that the Child Care Act, 1991 be amended to make the provision for after-care compulsory. They also recommended that each health board develop a written policy to help young people through the entire process of the transition from care, the appointment of an advocate or key support person, and the provision of information booklets. Nee and Ritchie both pointed out that a young person's ability to progress without difficulty from a care situation will depend not only on the existence of an after-care policy, but on the quality of the placement in the first place. Both their studies recommended that after-care should be seen as one of the last steps in a long preparatory process.

Conclusion

This chapter has focused on various aspects of a child's path through the care system. It has illustrated how good practice and decision making can be impeded both by the urgency with which placements are needed and the availability of the right type of placement. It became clear that in a number of instances, albeit small, the nature of placements was determined by availability rather than the identified needs of the children concerned. Notwithstanding the unpredictability of the work and the need for more placement provision, the projects underlined the importance of having protocols in place to ensure that minimum standards were met in relation to, for instance, the provision of written information and the minimisation of trauma for the children involved. Likewise the need for standardised methods of recording information and case plans was highlighted. Whilst acknowledging that children will inevitably continue to enter the state care system, the data reported in this chapter again demonstrated examples of where early intervention may have prevented more traumatic and undesirable outcomes.

The need for health boards to formalise the supported lodging schemes which had emerged in response to the problem of juvenile homelessness was clarified, with emphasis on the safety issues involved in placing children without parental permission. The notion of 'interdependence' to describe the period of transition between full-time care and living away from foster families or residential units was aptly used to describe the needs of young people who are progressing out of the care system. The inadequacy of the Child Care Act, 1991 in terms of the obligation placed on health boards to provide after-care was highlighted in all of the research, and specific frameworks for the provision of a service were outlined.

The next chapter focuses specifically on foster care, and highlights a number of key factors in the provision of a consistent, safe and nurturing environment for children who have been separated from their families.

=10=

Issues in Foster Care

Foster care in Ireland has grown at an enormous rate since the early 1970s to a point where in 1998, 88 per cent of children looked after by the state lived with foster carers (Gilligan, 1999a). The nature of foster care has also changed with a movement towards relative foster care; in 1998 almost half of the children in foster care in the Eastern Health Board region were placed with relatives, compared with a tiny percentage (37 out of 542) in 1993 (Eastern Health Board, 1998). In addition, as this chapter will show, special projects whereby emergency and long-term carers are recruited for children aged 12+ have been started in some regions. Irish and international research shows that while foster care can be a rewarding experience for children and families, the issues associated with recruiting and retaining foster carers and supporting placements are universally complex. Health boards recruiting foster carers have always relied on the availability of a pool of mainly female parents who do not work outside the home, a factor which is changing rapidly as the numbers of women returning to the workforce has increased. Concerns about the possibility of allegations by children against foster carers and an increased sense that children coming into care are showing an increased rate of emotional and behavioural problems also appear to have contributed to a decline in the number of prospective carers coming forward (English, 2000; Berridge, 1996; Triseliotis, Borland and Hill, 2000).

Two significant changes have occurred in relation to foster care over the past number of years. The first one is that it is now a much more regulated process; since the implementation of the 1996 regulations, regular reviews are now a statutory requirement, and the involvement of the children in their own reviews is a right rather than a concession. The second change is more subtle but no less important and reflects new insights into the needs of children who are separated from their families. Professionals have become more aware of children's differing requirements and now acknowledge that placements must be more tailored to suit individual situations and cultures. It has also been acknowledged that some placements may fail, despite the best intentions of all concerned. As a result of this knowledge and experience, a range of new challenges now present themselves for practitioners and policy makers. The projects discussed in this chapter give examples of how some health boards have attempted to meet these tasks. The topics covered include the involvement of adolescents in placement reviews, the provision of culturally appropriate foster care for Traveller children, emergency placements, placement breakdown and the sensitive issue of allegations made against foster carers by children. The discussion will start, however, with a more traditional subject, the training and support of foster carers.

Training and support of foster carers

Many of the projects discussed in this section highlight the need for training of foster parents, particularly in relation to the maintenance of links between children and their birth parents. Addressing this issue as well as the more general training needs and experiences of foster carers, Kevin Montgomery carried out a project in 1994. As a social worker specialising in fostering in the North Western Health Board, Montgomery was aware of the developing expectations of foster carers as the problems experienced by children entering the care system are better understood. He was aware that training was a key issue, and sought to try and probe the attitude and feelings of foster carers towards training, seek the views of social workers in relation to issues raised by foster carers, and make recommendations for future training and support.

Montgomery carried out in-depth interviews with ten sets of foster carers from different parts of Donegal. He later addressed a meeting of five social workers and discussed the findings from the interviews with them to ascertain their responses. Subsequent to this, the findings were discussed at a training day for foster parents.

Both parents were interviewed by Montgomery in eight of the ten families with one parent interviewed in the remaining two. Most families conformed to the 'conventional' model suggested by Bebbington and Miles (1990) of two parents with two to three children and one member working full time. A majority of the families had had foster children placed with them on a long-term basis for more than five years with regular contact between the children and their birth families. Eight out of the ten families had undergone some form of training, but only four had been trained as part of the assessment process. The training experience had been generally valued in terms of its educative and social value while the process of sharing experiences with each other was considered to be a central element. The carers expressed a preference for small and informal groups with multi-professional input. They emphasised the value of involving carers in developing the training programme. The issue of sexual abuse was considered to be important; foster carers suggested that training could help them cope with the effects of abuse and assist them to understand the therapeutic and legal framework. It was also felt that training could help them to avoid stress and deal with challenging behaviour without taking it 'personally'. Interestingly, the foster carers argued that their own commitment to the children and the personal investment involved were the most important factors in fostering, and that while training was considered helpful, it was not a priority.

In the discussion with social workers, a number of complex issues emerged. Workers expressed some confusion about the status of foster carers as colleagues, clients or partners and appeared unsure as to how they should be regarded. There was also a view that consensus between foster carers and social workers was lacking in relation to goals and expectations of the service and it was felt that training should specifically address this area.

The third phase of the project, the foster parents' training day, was attended by thirty foster carers including five of the couples who had been interviewed. The agenda for a the day was based on some of the issues highlighted in the interview data. At the end of the day, participants were asked to identify additional training needs. They recommended that training should incorporate areas such as talking to children, answering 'hard' questions, the lack of privacy and isolation experienced by foster carers and the impact of fostering on a family. However, the principal emphasis was on the need to develop good working relationships between social workers and foster carers, including mutual agreement on the foster care task.

Montgomery concluded that the commitment offered by foster carers must be affirmed by acknowledging their 'wisdom' and utilising it by giving them a primary role in training new and aspiring foster carers. He suggested that consensus on good foster care practice may be reached through training programmes delivered jointly by foster carers and social workers, focusing on specific areas like behaviour management. He therefore proposed the following:

- development of ongoing training programmes to be delivered jointly by social workers and foster carers
- mandatory training for new foster parents
- a review of the social work service to foster families and children focusing on service goals, expectations of foster carers and the working relationships of all parties involved.

However, Montgomery emphasised that while training was a key element in preparation and support for fostering, informal groups and meetings were equally essential and could combat the isolation experienced by some carers.

The involvement of young people in foster care reviews
Under the Foster Care Regulations (Department of Health, 1996), the health boards have adopted the practice of facilitating children to participate in review meetings. In 1999, Josephine Murphy, a social worker in the Western

Health Board based in Mayo, undertook a project that was designed to reflect the voices of adolescents who had taken part in foster care reviews. Murphy was aware from the literature that young people frequently feel unprepared for reviews and despite their inclusion, often feel they have no role in decision making (Horgan, 1996) and used her study to explore the views of a sample of young people in relation to their own reviews.

Murphy carried out in-depth interviews with six young people between thirteen and eighteen years of age who had been in foster care for at least a year and had attended at least two reviews each. She first secured their agreement along with the permission of their birth parents and foster carers. The choice of venue for the interviews was decided by the interviewees, most of whom opted for a location away from the foster home. Having considered the application of the Brief Solution Focused Model (BSFM)[20] to the review process, Murphy also adopted it as part of her overall research approach.

Five out of the six young people were positive about being in care, their feelings ranging from 'OK', 'settled' and 'happy', with one person expressing unhappiness. All had a level of preparation from their social worker before each review but generally considered it inadequate. All interviewees reported feelings of powerlessness and anxiety, and five out of the six said they felt nervous and embarrassed at the meeting. When asked if they felt that their views were listened to, only one responded with 'sometimes' but the other five gave a definite 'no' in response to the question. Murphy suggested that there was a general belief amongst the young people that the views of foster carers and social workers were given more consideration than those of anyone else. Most of the interviewees commented that unanticipated issues were raised at the reviews, including negative and embarrassing factors like poor reports about school or work experience. Half of them pointed out that they became confused at the meetings and did not always understand the decisions that were made. Most did not consider the review forms to be particularly relevant or useful and felt that the venues should be less formal than they tended to be.

When the young people were asked to think in terms of solutions, they unanimously expressed a wish for social workers and foster carers to listen to them more and make clear decisions. They expressed a preference to be consulted about the most suitable time and venue, to be told beforehand about everything to be discussed, for the reviews to be smaller, shorter and to start on time, and to be assured that their views would be taken seriously.

---

[20] The Brief Solution Focused Model (BFSM) is based on core principles of (a) empowerment of clients to enable them and find their own solutions, (b) focus on clear, specific, attainable goals, (c) building on clients' strengths and (d) the facilitation of growth by the therapist (Walsh, 1997).

On the basis of her findings, Murphy, who at the time had particular responsibility for chairing reviews in her own area, suggested that short- medium- and long-term changes should be made to the process. In the short term, she proposed that more consideration be given to practical matters such as the attendance, venue and timing of reviews. For the medium term she proposed that a working party, to include an adolescent representative, be set up to draft and implement new, relevant and user-friendly review forms. In addition, she suggested that workers should be trained in how to involve teenagers in review meetings. Murphy's recommendations for the longer term included the implementation of a 'Review Process Model' and the adoption of the principles of the BFSM. The adoption of these recommendations would, she pointed out, increase the young people's ownership of the meetings and make the process more focused and meaningful.

Providing culturally appropriate care for Traveller children

Research in Ireland confirms that Traveller children are particularly vulnerable to placement in substitute care. O'Higgins (1993) who was commissioned to carry out research in the Mid-Western Health Board region, attributes this fact to the displacement of Travellers in Irish society which involved the loss of their economic independence. She argues that in the latter part of the twentieth century, Travellers became a 'small, uniquely disadvantaged, minority subgroup, living on the periphery of Irish society' (p.147). O'Higgins' research also indicates that Travellers have more health problems, lower education and employment levels than the parents of other children in care, that parents had less contact with their children in care and that they had less support from kin or neighbour. It also appears that they receive a differentiated service from public bodies, even those charged with promoting the welfare of children. Buckley's (1999) research showed that social workers employed by health boards made little attempt to grapple with the dilemmas presented by cultural or social differences or try to educate themselves in relation to the implications of diverse patterns of child rearing by Traveller parents. The challenge therefore is to overcome cultural indifference when dealing with child protection and welfare issues in relation to this and other ethnic minority groups. This section deals with the issue of providing culturally appropriate substitute care and discusses two projects completed in 1993 and 2000 respectively.

Special residential units for Traveller children had been in existence in the Eastern Health Board area since 1975. At the same time, large numbers of Traveller children had been and continue to be placed in 'settled' foster care in the different health boards. As society became more aware and respectful of the cultural identity of ethnic minority groups, the importance of promoting and maintaining the children's sense of self while they were resident in substitute care was being increasingly recognised. Research had also shown that more promising outcomes could be predicted for children who were placed in the appropriate cultural environment (Keats, 1997; Shine, 1998). In 1991 a 'Shared Rearing' Project was initiated in the Eastern Health Board area by an agency called 'Traveller Families Care' in partnership with the Eastern Health Board, with the objective of providing foster placements for Traveller children within their own communities. The benefits of this type of placement are obvious; the child would not be separated from his or her community, he or she would have the benefit of a positive family experience and it would not be difficult to maintain contact with the birth family. Travellers were consulted before the project became operative and expressed interest and enthusiasm for it. However, in order to function effectively, the project required a considerable amount of information about the extent and nature of placements likely to be required. Data concerning Travellers have tended to be fragmented, with the collection of census information complicated by the nature of the population itself, where literacy could not be assumed, and mistrust of official organisations mitigated against the collection of statistics by standard means. However, even where information was relatively easy to access, there appeared to be little commitment to collecting it. For example, health boards kept no statistics detailing the numbers of Traveller children in care, thus making it very difficult to plan specific services to meet their needs.

In an effort to assist the development of the Shared Rearing project, Regina Comerford, at the time a child care worker in a residential service for Traveller children, undertook a project in 1993. Her specific objective was to survey Traveller children in care in the thirty-two community care areas. She sent a questionnaire to each area which sought to ascertain how many Traveller children were currently in substitute care, which areas had the highest numbers, where they were placed, what age they were at placement and what happened to them on leaving care. She looked for detail regarding their ages, gender, number of siblings, length of current placement and any difficulties with finding a placement. She also sought to find out if the option of the Shared Rearing Project would have been acceptable to social workers had it been available when the children were being placed.

The survey results indicated that there were 183 Traveller[21] children in health board care, of whom 60 per cent were in long-term foster care, 5 per cent were in short-term foster care and 4 per cent were living with their

---

[21] Comerford acknowledged that confusion can sometimes exist about a child's identity as a Traveller, and that the true number was likely to have been higher than 183.

extended family. The remainder, with the exception of six children about whom there was no information, were in residential care and almost half of those (13 per cent) were in special units for Traveller children. There were slightly more male than female children in care and over a third of the children had been in care for between five and ten years. Two-thirds of them had moved placement at least once, and under half were placed with siblings. One-fifth of the children had been considered difficult to place. The majority of the fourteen Traveller children who left care in 1992 (88 per cent) were re-united with their families, with 6 per cent going to B & B accommodation. Out of those returning to their family, six out of the fourteen went to live with extended family, raising the question of why placement with the extended family had not previously been considered.

Over half of the social workers surveyed said they would have opted for the Shared Rearing Project had it been in operation when they were seeking placements. Their comments indicated that the likelihood of Traveller children losing contact with their culture was higher than for settled children because of the mobility of their families, and concerns were also expressed about the limits to which settled families understood the Traveller culture.

Based on available information about the numbers of Travellers in the general population, Comerford estimated that the children of Travellers were six times more likely to enter care than children of settled parents. Nearly two-thirds of Traveller children in care were placed in long-term situations before they were four years old, and the majority tend to stay in care for a long time. Comerford considered that the long-term placements were similar to adoptive placements, as the children seemed to be more or less permanently separated from their families. The inference drawn from this by Comerford was that little effort is made to reunite Traveller children with their families. She also found it of concern that just over half of them were not placed with siblings, resulting in total isolation from their culture and family. While Comerford did not have information on the level of contact between parents and Traveller children in care, she speculated that access might not be sufficiently facilitated. She also suggested that the involvement of Traveller parents might not be encouraged in relation to decision-making, child protection conferences or case reviews. These issues should, in her view, be explored in further research.

Overall, Comerford considered that the information she had gathered gave considerable credence to the concept of Shared Rearing. She acknowledged a number of dilemmas in relation to this form of care, including placement in what might be considered sub-standard accommodation and the norm in the Travelling community of early school leaving. Notwithstanding these problems, she advocated the expansion of the project and made a number of recommendations to support it, including

- the increased employment of Travellers by health boards in order to enhance work with Traveller families and educate other staff in relation to cultural issues
- a commitment to place Traveller children within extended families, placing them with Traveller foster families under the project only if the first option is not possible
- increased community-based services and support for Traveller parents of young children by outreach workers
- equality of opportunity, including the availability of day care for Travellers
- inclusive practice with parents when Traveller children are taken into care
- research into access patterns, outcomes for Traveller children leaving care, the medical implications of inter-marriage.

Finally, Comerford reiterated the need for systems to collect statistical information on Travellers.

While the Shared Rearing Project is obviously a desirable form of substitute care for Traveller children, it has not been available on a broad enough scale to meet the demand, and a high percentage of Traveller children still spend long periods in foster care with settled families. In 2000, Tara Kelly, then a child care worker with the Eastern Health Board, undertook a project to explore the level of importance afforded to the issue of cultural identity by the key care givers of Traveller children placed in settled family care. Kelly encountered the same difficulty met by Comerford seven years earlier, that is, the absence of statistics identifying the status of Traveller children in care. From local information, she estimated that 23 children out of the 138 children in care in her community care area in 1999 were Travellers. She selected four foster families for interview who, between them, were currently fostering seven Traveller children and had had five others in their care in the past.

Kelly found that the foster families she interviewed were unanimously of the view that the children in their care should be made aware of and given information on their cultural backgrounds. Opinion on how this should come about varied between families and the level of knowledge about Travellers possessed by the families themselves depended on how far they had sought it as well as the type of contact they had had with Travellers in the past. Health board social workers had responded to requests for information but had not initiated it, and the contact between the children and their social workers was variable. Kelly was concerned that the experiences of Traveller children in settled foster care are so dependent on the different attitudes, expectations and beliefs of the foster carers. Yet these areas did not appear to have been specifically addressed in their training. She felt that even where foster families were interested and committed to providing the children with information, they would need assistance with imparting it in a positive way in order to encourage a sense of pride and positive self-identity.

In order to fulfil this aim, Kelly recommended the use of advisory panels to provide a forum for consultation on cultural issues where Traveller children were placed with settled families. She further suggested that specific training should be provided to foster parents to enable them to understand and value the Traveller culture in a positive way. Finally, she suggested that social workers continue to prioritise the assessment of personal values and attitudes of prospective foster parents so that children are matched appropriately in placement. She cautioned that failing to name cultural identity as a specific consideration could undermine the experiences of Traveller children in settled family care.

Emergency placement service for teenagers

One of the most vulnerable groups of children out of home are 13-18 year olds who, unless they receive an immediate and appropriate service when their living situation breaks down, can be vulnerable to crime, substance abuse and other 'street' hazards. In order to provide a response to young people in crisis, the Eastern Health Board initiated an 'Emergency Carers' project in 1992. The service was designed to provide a safe environment for young people while their circumstances were being assessed and the various options open to them were explored. The project was attached to the juvenile homeless section of the community care social work service and provided family placements for a period of time up to a maximum of eight weeks. Young people were referred by health board social workers for a variety of reasons, including disclosures of abuse, incidents where parent-teenage relationships had deteriorated to a critical degree or where respite was requested by foster carers. In some instances, young people had abruptly left residential care. The criteria generally applied for placement included the level of need, the likelihood of a young person being able to settle with a family, whether or not the young person was linked in with a daytime activity, and the geographical location of the available placement in relation to that activity. Young people who were currently abusing drugs, were suicidal or had a history of serious violence were not considered for placement (for a fuller discussion of this project, see Connolly, 1997).

By early 1995, thirty-nine placements had been made with six emergency carers under the scheme and a review of its effectiveness in meeting the needs of young people was carried out by Siobhán Connolly, at the time the only full-time social worker with the project. She was aware from the available research of the high rate of placement breakdown when children were in their teens (Rowe et al, 1984; O'Hara and Dewar, 1988) and was interested in exploring the underlying reasons. Her aims in this study were to build up a profile of the young people placed, measure the outcome of the placement in terms of success or failure, and identify factors associated with either of these outcomes.

Connolly collected data on each of the thirty-nine placements from agency records and enquiries from area social workers involved in the different cases. A successful placement was regarded as one where the young person stayed for the agreed period and then transferred into a positive situation. An unsuccessful one was defined as one where the young person left, either by choice or request, prior to the agreed date of departure. She acknowledged the complexity of measuring 'success' using crude measures that did not take account of the quality of placement, the types of benefits experienced by the young person or the longer-term outcome. However, she considered the measures that she applied to be meaningful when the stated aims of the project were considered. To provide contextual data, Connolly also interviewed three of the six carers involved in the scheme.

Data from the case records indicated that the largest single group (59 per cent) represented in the number of young people placed through the project were 14-15 year olds. Over half of the total group had been in a placement within the previous two years. A third had been physically abused and just over a third had been sexually abused at some point in the past. In addition, 41 per cent of them had engaged in what Connolly categorised as 'streetwise' behaviour, defined by her as involvement on more than one occasion in shoplifting, substance abuse or staying out most of the night. Two-thirds of the total group were involved in a daytime activity during the placement.

According to the case records, some behaviour problems were also exhibited by the young people during placement with the project, the most common being refusal to accept limits, staying out all night and lying. Overall, according to the measures used by Connolly, 49 per cent of placements had a positive outcome. When she explored the factors associated with negative and positive outcomes, Connolly found that young people who had engaged in streetwise behaviour prior to placement were less likely to experience a successful outcome to their placement. Those who had been in 'less stable' situations, for example staying with friends or relatives, or in a B & B, or sleeping rough, were also less likely to have a positive outcome. In contrast, those who had come from home, from residential care, or whose carers requested respite were likely to have a more successful outcome.

Interviews with the carers highlighted factors that supported or created difficulties for them during the placements. Most found it difficult to cope with young people who had difficulty accepting limits, though they found it helpful if the area social worker supported them in challenging the young person's behaviour. If they had not been given sufficient information about the young person, or if they felt the social worker did not know the young person, the placement was often difficult to sustain. Most carers, however, were prepared to be very flexible about the criteria used to select young people for placement and were open to giving the young people an opportunity.

When Connolly analysed her findings, she acknowledged that the factors associated with placement success and breakdown, i.e. stability in previous placement and previous engagement in streetwise behaviour, were predictable. However, she noted that the majority of breakdowns were associated with the young people themselves opting to leave. This, she suggested, could infer a mismatch between the placement and the needs of the young people concerned. Another important factor, in her view, was the fact that lack of information at the time of placement could undermine the confidence of the carers. As she pointed out, the challenge was to gain a balance between the ability to make an emergency response and ensuring that a minimum level of information was obtained. She recommended the development of a more efficient system, including guidelines, with regard to the passing of good quality information on the young persons placed to the carers. She also suggested that more emphasis should be placed within the project's own training programme on how to present and negotiate house rules with young people. At a broader level, she recommended the development of community-based resources in order to divert young people from becoming engaged in the street scene, a factor that was shown in this study to militate against successful placement. Finally, Connolly recommended the ongoing monitoring and evaluation of the emergency placement service.[22]

Allegations of abuse against foster parents

Children First, in classifying children most at risk of abuse, identifies children who are being cared for outside their families as a vulnerable category. Paradoxically, there is evidence that children separated from their families because of maltreatment have, on occasions, been subject to harm in situations that were intended to protect them and keep them safe. The late 1990s saw many revelations of abuse perpetrated against children in the care

---

[22] This service ceased to operate centrally after 1996, at which point all the social work teams in the health board area had been resourced to provide their own service. Some modifications were made, including a widening of the age range, and more flexibility about the length of placement.

of the state (Department of Health, 1996a; Raftery and O'Sullivan, 1999). However, the incidence of abuse in foster care has received little attention in Ireland, despite having been the subject of some high-profile cases elsewhere (Nixon, 2000).

A project completed in 2000 examined the issue of abuse allegations in foster care. It was carried out by Karen Buckley, a social work team leader in the Mid-Western Health Board. Her intention was to establish, with a small sample of foster carers, the sort of situations in which allegations of abuse occur. She aimed to find out the level of support offered to families in those circumstances. She also sought to examine the extent to which foster carers were aware of health board policy in relation to allegations.

As Buckley argued, the likelihood of foster parents being accused of abuse of children in their care has increased, for several reasons. These include the perceived increase in the severity of foster children's problems and the possibility that children who have been abused have a higher propensity to elicit an abusive response from others (Mid-Western Health Board, 1997). She was also aware of the potential for children in foster care to make allegations because of confusion or a desire to disrupt the placement. While Buckley asserted that the investigation of complaints about the safety and welfare of children in care should be taken as seriously and conducted as thoroughly as allegations made about children in any family setting, she highlighted the particular difficulty in providing support to foster families in such circumstances. As she pointed out, the status of the relationship between carers and the health board changes from that of colleagues to that of clients in the course of an investigation and inevitable tensions occur.

Buckley carried out interviews with eight randomly selected sets of experienced foster carers and four randomly selected social workers. She found that four out of the eight foster carers had undergone the experience of having a foster child make an allegation of abuse against them. Two of the allegations concerned physical abuse and the other two concerned neglect. While the health board had carried out an investigation in response to each allegation, none of the children had been removed from his or her placement as a consequence. Three allegations were considered unfounded and one was confirmed.

When asked about the experience, some of the foster carers raised the issue of delay between the complaint and the investigation. One carer had found it hard to believe that the health board had taken seriously a complaint that the family had considered spurious. All had been informed of the outcome of investigation; one of the four considered that they had been offered good support, one described the level of support given as average and two felt the support was not good. Two out of the four felt that their children as well as the parents had been supported.

Buckley found that five out of the eight families were aware of the health board's guidance on safe care, and those who were unaware of it included three of the families against whom allegations had been made. Four of the families suggested that the health board should provide extra training and guidance on this area as well as ensuring that the fullest possible information was given about the children when they were being placed. The foster carers suggested that investigation of complaints should be carried out within a time limit and that a worker should be allocated in order to keep them updated and provide them with support. They also felt that specially trained workers should carry out the investigation, and that counselling should be made available.

Three of the social workers who were interviewed were, by coincidence, those who had dealt with three of the families against whom allegations had been made. Their responses regarding the level of support offered and the manner in which information was shared roughly matched those already given by the foster carers, though their view of the quality of support offered was marginally more favourable. Recommendations from the social workers included an increase in available staff, more post-approval training and the availability of support groups.

Though her sample was small, Buckley argued that it illustrated the increased rate at which allegations were being made against foster parents by children in their care. Commenting on the practice in each situation, she considered that the concerns had been satisfactorily pursued and that information regarding the process and outcome of investigation had been communicated adequately. However, she noted that a certain amount of discretion appeared to operate in relation to whether An Garda Síochána were involved. She also suggested that the lack of satisfaction with the levels of support offered reflected role confusion on the part of social workers assigned to work with foster carers. Overall, she concluded that foster carers and professionals needed to be more prepared for the possibility of allegations being made against them, and that training and guidance should be strengthened to ensure that such eventualities were properly addressed and resolved. She specifically recommended the following:

- that safe care be considered an essential component of training for foster carers
- that child protection guidelines should contain specific sections on investigation of alleged abuse in foster care
- that investigations be time limited and prompt
- that the outcome of investigations should be conveyed to families
- that training in this area should be provided on an ongoing basis to staff
- that the fullest possible exchange of information and provision of advice be carried out with foster carers.

Finally, Buckley recommended that foster carers should be advised and encouraged to develop safe care practices within their homes.

Placement breakdown

Research in Britain has identified predictive factors associated with the breakdown of foster placements and has highlighted themes common to the actual process of breakdown and removal of children (Fitzgerald, 1983; Triseliotis, Borland and Hill, 2000). The fact that no Irish research had been conducted in this area prompted Vera Lally, at the time a social worker in the Western Health Board, based in Galway, to undertake a project in 1991 exploring a number of cases where breakdowns had occurred. She sought to identify salient factors, examine practice in relation to the cases and develop a procedures manual to guide staff in the handling of future breakdowns. During the previous five years, twenty-two children in her area had been placed in long-term foster care and six placements involving eight children had subsequently broken down. While the term 'disruption' is sometimes used in the literature Lally chose instead to use the term 'breakdown' to signify the reality and the high level of emotion associated with the termination of a fostering arrangement.

Lally undertook her research in five phases. First, she established the exact numbers of breakdowns during the previous five years. She then examined all the social work files on the relevant cases. Following this, she interviewed the social work manager, the four social workers involved in the cases and a residential manager who had a close involvement with one of them. She subsequently contacted the six families where the fostering breakdowns had occurred and secured agreement to interview four of them. In spite of the difficult and painful experiences they had undergone, the foster parents expressed agreement to be interviewed in order to assist other families who may be facing the same difficulties. Finally, Lally designed a procedures manual for use when breakdowns occur.

On the basis of her interviews and examination of the case records, Lally found that many of the predictive factors identified in the literature were present in the totality of cases in the sample, as well as a number of common themes. These included the children's early experiences, their attachments, their behaviours and the ages of the other children in the family. The lack of foster parents' experience also appeared to be a significant factor. In some cases, unpredictable events occurred, such as marital difficulties or discovery of previously unknown information. Lally also found instances where the foster families were left with a persistent sense of deep loss and grief, in some cases feeling resentful that early warning signs had been ignored, angry at the way the child's move was handled, a belief that they were 'rejected' as unfit foster parents and a sense that they had no part in the final negotiation of events. The interview with the residential manager illustrated how residential workers can feel excluded and judged as a 'last resort' when in fact they could have a useful part to play in supporting placements and addressing crises.

From her analysis of the data, Lally concluded that requests for help such as respite care must be taken seriously by social workers and not interpreted as rejection of the children. She also suggested that if foster parents were allowed to feel part of the decision making process, they would be better able to cope with the pain of separation. Their need to express anger, she believed, could be more satisfactorily met if they were allocated a 'neutral' social worker. Lally suggested that families had different ideas of how the child's move should be handled and that each option deserved consideration. Finally, she highlighted the way that families can feel they have failed and recommended sensitivity to their sense of rejection and consideration of their ability to foster in different circumstances.

For the second phase of her project, Lally developed a procedures manual drawing on the work of Fitzgerald (1983). She divided it into three sections. The first section dealt with the process to be followed during placement when difficulties begin to manifest themselves. It focused on developing a team relationship, hearing what each party has to say, listening carefully to the child and foster family, assessing the situation from a broad perspective, acknowledging difficulties and responding quickly to any concerns expressed without either minimising, apportioning blame or providing premature reassurance. It recommended allocating separate social workers for child and family, meeting with social work managers and fostering panels, informing the birth parents and meeting with the child and foster family to work out a time table. It emphasised the need to assure foster parents that the child would have benefited from their love and care.

The second section of the manual addressed the period of the breakdown. It highlighted the need to ensure that the child and family have someone to talk to, and to encourage the family to join with the social worker in explaining the reason for the move to the child and acknowledge the pain and grief involved for all concerned. It included advice on helping the child to move and on ensuring that the social worker has support for him or herself. The third section dealt with the period after the breakdown has occurred when the child has moved. It pointed to the need to help all parties concerned to resolve their feelings, and encourage links between the foster family and the child. It emphasised the need for follow-up contact with the foster family to help them work through the pain of separation and consider what kind of contact they would like to maintain with the child, to give them information about the child and to discuss their attitude to fostering another child.

Lally found that her study was of enormous benefit to her team, particularly in relation to ensuring that all parties involved in fostering breakdown were able to participate in decision making and were facilitated to maintain links. She also found that highlighting the common factors associated with breakdown assisted the process of matching children with potential long-term families.

Conclusion

The projects discussed here have highlighted some aspects of foster care that may be very pertinent for parents and children but might not have heretofore had a particularly high profile in the provision of a foster care service. While the research raised genuine concerns about the difficulty of supporting placements, it also showed that certain factors are relatively simple to address, e.g. commitment to the early exchange of accurate information between workers, children and foster carers. It has also addressed the challenge of preparing foster carers for the task ahead, supporting them and acknowledging that despite the best efforts of all involved, the placement may not always endure. It has illustrated the importance of sensitivity, understanding and learning when a placement terminates prematurely.

While there is an increasing movement towards the active participation of children in planning and reviewing their own placements, this chapter has shown that participation that is meaningful will need to go beyond the obvious and ensure that children are treated sensitively, fairly and with respect when attending formal reviews. Links between the maintenance of cultural identity and the child's ability to maintain links and strong relationships with their families were demonstrated as well as the importance of not unwittingly excluding parents from ethnic minority groups from actively participating in decision making about their children.

What this chapter has emphasised above all is the familiar tenet that good professional practice is the main ingredient required to support placements. It has shown that information must be exchanged fully and honestly. It has also demonstrated that if complaints and allegations are responded to rapidly and if the potential for breakdown is accepted and addressed before a full-blown crisis has developed, the outcomes can be contained and can sometimes be viewed positively by foster parents and children alike. Not surprisingly, this chapter has highlighted that the personal commitment of foster carers is one of the most significant factors of successful placement. Likewise, it has shown that children's sense that they are being respected and heard will enable them to capitalise on the benefits of living with foster carers. Good practice will nurture and build on these elements and enhance the possibility of successful outcomes for all concerned.

=====11=====

Issues in Residential Care

Introduction
As Chapter Ten has pointed out, the nature of out-of-home care has changed in the past thirty years to a point where now the majority of children who are accommodated by the state are placed in foster care. However, residential care is still seen as the preferred option for a small number of children with particular needs. The past decade has seen considerable changes in the legislative and policy framework underpinning the provision of residential care in Ireland. As in other areas of child protection and welfare, reported abuses in major institutions have raised public and professional awareness of the additional risks faced by children who are looked after in this way. Disturbing accounts of punitive and abusive regimes that operated up to the 1950s and 1960s in orphanages and industrial schools were publicised in television documentaries and books (Raftery and O'Sullivan, 1999), precipitating an apology from the Taoiseach and the development of the Commission to Inquire into Child Abuse. More recent malpractices in residential care were highlighted in the Report on the Inquiry into the Operation of Madonna House (Department of Health, 1996a). The Madonna House report also pinpointed practices which, while not abusive, could be seen as depriving children of their rights and failing to provide the most appropriate setting for their psychological and emotional development. Research in other countries had simultaneously highlighted weaknesses in the residential care system (Levy and Kahan, 1991; Westcott and Clement 1992; Stein, 1993).

As the Madonna House report acknowledged, the most effective method of reducing the risk of institutional abuse is the development of residential care as a quality service, guaranteeing children a higher standard of care than they would have received in the community. A study commissioned by the Mercy congregation in 1997 reviewed the operation of a number of centres and made significant recommendations in relation to care practices that had relevance for the provision of residential care on a national basis (Clarke, 1998). The establishment in 1999 of the Social Services Inspectorate, which is expected to be placed on a statutory footing by 2002, has meant that all residential centres under the control of health boards are subject to regular inspection. Residential centres are now expected to conform to the standards derived from government policy and legislation, including the child care regulations.

These measures have combined to strengthen the existing policy framework of best practice principles.

The projects to be discussed in this chapter outline the steps taken by different residential centres and health boards to improve practices in line with new policy and legislation. They cover areas that, if properly addressed, can act to minimise risk within residential care and enhance the quality of life for children. These include care plans, direct work with children, safe care and behaviour management and the provision of special residential care for children with intellectual disability. They also tackle less visible and more complex issues such as gender in residential work and inter-agency relationships and links between residential care and the community.

Care plans for children in residential care

Under the 1996 Regulations (Department of Health 1997b), health boards and residential centres are obliged to prepare plans for the children in their care that specify the aims and objectives of placements, the support to be provided to children, access arrangements and arrangements for reviews. A project carried out a year before the regulations were introduced outlines the key areas that residential staff should cover when formulating plans. The study was carried out by Martina Grant-Murphy, at the time a senior house-parent in a residential centre catering for eight adolescent boys. Grant-Murphy was aware that although the operation of the centre was based upon its mission to promote the development of the boys' physical, emotional, intellectual, social and spiritual needs, it lacked a systematic format for recording and reviewing the career and progress of each resident. She was aware, from her own practice as well as from literature on adolescents in care, of the special needs likely to be experienced by the boys. She was also conscious of the undesirable outcomes for children in care where planning was absent, and of the harm experienced by omission as well as commission (Kahan, 1979).

Grant-Murphy's study focused on the development of a process for designing and implementing care plans as a standard procedure. She devised a framework for assessing the needs of the boys in her centre with a view to constructing a plan to address areas of concern. She used Parker's well-established theoretical model as a basis for observing the spectrum of development along which children progress. The dimensions are broken down as follows: health, education, identity, family and social relationships, social presentation, emotional and behavioural development and self-care skills (Parker, 1991). For the purposes of her research, Grant-Murphy asked two key workers on the staff of the unit to use the model of assessment on two teenage boys aged fourteen and fifteen with a view to developing the basis for a care plan. She and the key workers met each of the boys separately prior to the project in order to outline its purpose and ask for their co-operation. Following the meeting, the key workers met with the boys individually over a number of weeks in order to elicit information about their development. Grant-Murphy then met each worker over four separate sessions to supervise and support them in the work. At each session, tasks concerning the assessment were agreed and reviewed at the following session.

The assessments revealed that medical knowledge was scant in relation to the two boys and highlighted the fact that they both required dental check-ups and in one case, an ophthalmic examination. Focusing on their educational progress illustrated the difficulties that were being experienced by both and highlighted the importance of liaison between the centre and the schools involved. Problems between the boys and different members of their birth families emerged during the assessment of their identities and family and social relationships, and areas where behavioural difficulties were inhibiting their emotional and psychological development were targeted for change.

Addressing the issues that arose during the assessment, the key workers carried out various tasks, including making medical and dental appointments, updating health information, meeting teachers and developing study programmes, setting up meetings with family members and social workers, working towards raising the boys' self-esteem, enabling them to express their feelings and working on practical skills like cooking and budgeting. As both boys exhibited challenging behaviour in certain circumstances, methods were devised for establishing clear limits, enabling the boys to take appropriate levels of responsibility and form healthy attitudes.

The key workers, with Grant-Murphy, presented the outcomes of their assessment at a staff meeting. In general, they had found the experience time-consuming but worthwhile. Additionally they considered that the exercise had helped them to become more focused in their work and gain insight into the overall needs of the two boys. Areas that were particularly highlighted included the need for a standard method of recording information and the frequent lack of information about a young person's state of health. The workers also drew attention to the requirement for time and space to work with the residents, the need to focus on identity building, family contact and the significance of behaviour on a young person's development. The need for training and supervision in working with difficult teenagers was emphasised.

On the basis of the project's success in providing a basis for planning, it was decided to adopt the framework for all residents coming to live in the centre with the long-term aim of involving the young persons' social workers in formulating care plans. Grant-Murphy made a number of recommendations, including the provision of time and space for the assessment and longer-term work, ongoing and regular review of care plans at weekly staff meetings, opportunities for staff to train and develop skills for working with young people with complex needs and regular supervision and support from management.

Direct work with children in residential care

Direct and individual work with children provides a means of enabling them to express their feelings, learn abut themselves, look at their personal, family and cultural histories and resolve some difficulties that may have impeded their normal developmental progress. It can take many forms and may be defined differently according to the context in which it is carried out. This section looks specifically at the process of direct work with children in residential and foster care, analysing its individual elements and highlighting some of the issues involved for workers. Three projects were completed on this area, each focusing on unique factors involved in working with children, but between them illustrating a number of issues that are common to this type of activity. The first two to be discussed concentrate on the concept of the 'special' or 'quiet' room within a residential setting.

In the early 1990s, a room known as the 'special' room was set up as a residential unit for Traveller children, most of whom were girls. A project to review its use was carried out in 1991 by Anne O'Neill who, at the time, was manager of the unit. After a period of training with a play therapist who emphasised the need for individual work with children, O'Neill and her staff had set aside a location in a quiet part of the house. They furnished it in soft, warm colours and fabrics and equipped it with art and play materials. The aim was to create a safe and secure environment where children could explore feelings and where sensory stimulation and nurturing experiences would be provided in an atmosphere without interruption. In the room, the children could do artwork, listen to music, role-play, experiment with the sensory materials, bathe, use self-care materials like creams and make-up in front of a mirror and play musical instruments. These activities were geared at improving the children's self-confidence and concentration, develop their senses, allow them to work through feelings, increase their self-awareness and enhance the image they held of their own bodies.

The aim of O'Neill's project was to see how the children made use of the room, and to explore how the staff felt about its effectiveness in achieving its objectives. She asked key workers to complete questionnaires on behalf of twelve children. In addition, the five key workers were asked to complete questionnaires on their own perceptions of the special room.

The questionnaires on the use of the room showed that the children highly valued the privacy and confidentiality afforded to them. Most of them enjoyed the sensory materials and particularly liked the objects that were pleasant to touch. When asked to describe what they thought about when in the room, many of them mentioned their families in either a positive or a negative way, indicating that they used it to resolve aspects of their relationships. In some instances, the children had role-played interactions between themselves and their parents.

The key workers valued the opportunity to spend individual time with children and while some found it difficult to decide between a directive or non-directive approach at the outset, they became more comfortable over time with allowing the children to take the lead. Importantly, they found that the time spent with the children gave them a very good sense of the quality of the children's attachments and provided them with an opportunity to resolve and work on them from a secure base.

The key workers' responses highlighted some interesting issues. An important area was the sharing of information disclosed to them by children in the quiet room. While confidentiality was considered significant by the children, the workers were aware that they needed to share important information with the rest of the team, particularly if disclosures of abuse were made. O'Neill concluded that while the therapeutic function of the room might be limited by the inability of staff to offer confidentiality, it could represent a beginning process for children and prepare them for therapy in another setting. The fact that the children had shown an inclination to talk about their families in the special room prompted the key workers to think about trying to work more closely with parents. They felt this might help the children to feel more accepted and trusting. The necessity for team-work was also highlighted and it was acknowledged that the special room could only work if everyone was committed to facilitating its use.

The issue of Traveller culture was raised, with some staff suggesting that the play materials should be more reflective of the Travellers' way of life. Other workers suggested that the raising of the children's self-image was an important element in helping them accept their Traveller identity.

O'Neill concluded that the special room made a significant contribution to the positive experience of the children in the unit. She acknowledged that it was a constantly evolving concept that would need to adapt to the changing needs of the children in the unit. She made the following recommendations:

- policy on confidentiality should be clarified
- team work in relation to the special room should be promoted
- options for children over twelve should be explored
- the use of time should be 'led' by the children as opposed to being used by staff to deal with behaviour and individual incidents
- key workers should be empowered to engage more closely with the families of the children.

Finally, O'Neill recommended that the special room be used for the promotion of healthy relationship building, using non-directive and child-directed approaches.

In 1992, Paddy Ormond, at the time the manager of a small residential unit for pre-teenage boys in the inner city, carried out a project on the development of a unique method for working individually with children, using a particular setting. The research consisted of a period spend organising a location for the work, followed by a review of its use. The review was carried out by means of questionnaires which were completed by key workers in respect of each of twenty-five sessions held in the room, and discussions with each of the key workers on their own perceptions of its use.

Several months before he began his project, a room had been set aside in the centre for the purpose of providing separate space for individual work with the children resident in the unit. However, in Ormond's view, the room had not been systematically utilised and the potential for its effectiveness had not been reached. He had identified as a major difficulty the lack of time available to staff to spend with individual children in the room. As a consequence it had been used in a 'chaotic' unplanned way and had been of little extra benefit.

Ormond directed his project at establishing a more systematic approach to use of the room in a way that would reflect the child-centred philosophy of the unit. He consulted with staff and together, informed by recent 'In touch with children' training as well as literature on play (Oaklander, 1978; Axiline, 1969; Winnicot, 1984), they agreed on an overall therapeutic approach. The main purpose in having what he described as a 'quiet' room was to cultivate an atmosphere of safety and security that would encourage the children to play in an exploratory fashion within a non-threatening environment. The chosen activities were play therapy and sensory stimulation, the selection having been informed by what was known from the literature about the beneficial effects of working through the different mediums available. Ormond considered it important to offer a wide variety of techniques to allow for children to respond differently to the experience of using the room. He acquired figures for fantasy and role play; musical instruments, objects with strong smells and a kaleidoscope to assist sensory development; taped stories, modelling clay and a sand box.

One of the most important elements of the new framework for use of the quiet room was the establishment of ground rules. It was decided that children would only use the room in the company of their key-worker. It was also agreed that nobody outside would be allowed to disturb them, that individuals had to respect each other and the equipment while using the room and that equipment and material would never be removed from the room.

In his review of the room's use and impact, Ormond noted that the primary difficulty continued to be the lack of staff time available to spend with children in the room. Many of the children in the house had grown up in chronically disorganised environments, a factor that was often reflected in turbulent behaviour in the residential unit. As a result, the management of the unit absorbed a large proportion of staff time and reduced the possibilities of doing what Ormond had hoped would be 'planned and positive interaction' through individual work. Nonetheless, all the children spent an average of one period a week in the quiet room.

The review of the sessions in the room indicated that sensory exploration was popular and evoked an enthusiastic response from the children. Other areas of play appeared to give children opportunities to act out and deal with some of their fears and anxieties. Ormond noted how some children whose concentration was known to be poor were able to engross themselves in activities and that the sense of privacy and individual attention available to them seemed to be beneficial. Discussions with the key workers indicated unanimous support for the use of the room as a method of therapy and direct work with the children. They also indicated an interest in acquiring more skills.

While the brevity of the time-scale involved meant that his evaluative review was of limited value, Ormonde was confident that the more systematic approach being employed was working well. Overall, he considered that the project had resulted in significant gains for the children. He acknowledged that he had been over-ambitious in anticipating that staff would be able to spend two sessions with each child every week. Ultimately he hoped that effective use of the quiet room would diminish the possibilities of intense acting out around the house through providing opportunities for a more constructive resolution of dilemmas. In the meantime, he concluded that the available time was worthwhile and would progress the work of compensating children for deficits and providing opportunities for further growth and development.

Safe care and behaviour management in residential centres

The issue of discipline and control in relation to the behaviour of children in residential care, particularly those who are considered difficult to control, is one which has received much current attention in the media, largely as a result of the report issued by the Irish Social Services Inspectorate in relation to Newtown House (ISSI, 2001b). The problem of managing challenging behaviour has been a pre-occupation of practitioners and policy makers for several years and was the subject of a study undertaken in 1995 by Andrew Fagan. At the time, Fagan was manager of a unit that had been set up to specifically cater for young people whose needs were not being met by existing services. The residents, as Fagan pointed out, were perceived as amongst the most difficult to care for. The unit operated an 'open' policy and did not use either medication or locked rooms to control the young people's behaviour. However, the rate of violent assaults committed by the residents against each other and against staff members was a serious cause of concern. Fagan's project aimed to explore this problem in order to find out the nature of those situations that could be considered 'unsafe', i.e. vulnerable to violence. Additionally, he sought some means to reduce the potential for violence in each situation. He ultimately hoped to use the findings from his study to influence policy makers in relation to the manner in which staff were recruited and employed.

Fagan drew on the notion of attachment to provide a theoretical framework for his research, particularly the concept of a secure emotional base as a foundation for the containment and modification of behaviour and the reduction of violence by young people. He was aware from existing research that young people in residential care often experience feelings of powerlessness and dependency that give rise to aggression (Holmes, 1993). According to the literature, this tendency can be exacerbated when a residential unit fails to provide a secure base for the young people who must live there. Fagan therefore speculated that factors such as staff turnover made the maintenance of stability more problematic and consequently the containment of violence increasingly difficult.

Fagan conducted a documentary examination of records for the year 1994 to ascertain the number of violent assaults and noted that ninety-nine separate assaults occurred, fifty-four of which were officially notified to management in the health board. He found a correlation between the number of assaults committed by a young person and the shortness of their time in the unit; the longer that young people were resident, the less assaults they were likely to commit. This, argued Fagan, could be construed in terms of the length of time available to them to make attachments to staff members. He found that the majority of assaults occurred when there were one or more temporary staff members on duty, with multiple assaults occurring three times more frequently when there were two temporary staff members on duty compared to when the shifts were completely covered by permanent staff. Because a number of permanent staff had left, and there was a high rate of sick leave during the study year, there was a significant reliance on temporary staff. There was also a correlation between a high rate of assault and the absence of the unit manager for a continuous period of six weeks. On the positive side, an association was found between less frequent violent assaults and occasions when the staff on duty were members of the same, small team.

Fagan was aware of limitations in his research, and acknowledged that the factors precipitating violent assaults by young people are complex, including their sense of powerlessness and dependency in care and the fact that many of them had been the victims of violence prior to their admission to care. He argued, however, that attending to the need for a secure base for young people as well as the provision of a secure base from which staff can work should help to reduce the number of assaults. He advocated a commitment to mutual respect between all persons involved in the unit, regardless of status, with all agreements negotiated between staff and young people. He suggested that structuring the staff in small teams with team leaders would create a core of senior staff and lessen dependency on the manager. Within this structure, Fagan advocated minimal change or shift-swopping in order to provide stability. He suggested ongoing training for staff to improve and maintain their understanding of the causes of violent behaviour and most effective ways of managing it.

Fagan suggested a protocol for dealing with violent assaults, including involvement of An Garda Síochána, case review and a measured and non-judgemental approach to the incident. Importantly, he suggested monitoring and review of the rate of violent incidents with appropriate response from health board management.

Special residential educational provision for children
Up to the 1970s and 1980s it was necessary for many children with special learning needs to avail of residentially based education. This was largely due to the scarcity of appropriate community based special schools, particularly in rural areas. By 1990, however, special education had been developed to the extent that children no longer needed to depend on residential services and could normally attend school in their own localities whilst living at home (Report of the Review Group on Mental Handicap Services, 1990). However, circumstances still exist where residential provision is the more appropriate option, for example where the child's educational difficulty is negatively affected by conditions in his or her home situation or where his or her needs are very complex. A number of services in Ireland continue to offer five-day residential care for this reason. However, little research exists in relation to the populations of children for whom this facility is being provided. As a result, policies that operate within the services may not be sufficiently focused to meet the needs of residents in the most appropriate or effective manner.

A project conducted in 1992 by Emer Gallagher, at the time a senior social worker in a service for children with general learning difficulties, aimed to fill this gap by creating a profile of the thirty-eight children who 'boarded' for five days a week in the school where she was based. She was concerned that, while criteria for enrolment in the school existed, there were no actual criteria for residential admission. This, she claimed, reflected the lack of information about the residential population and implied that no particular measures were being taken to ensure that the purpose of admission to residential care was either clear or achievable. The objectives of her research were to analyse the available information on the students and their families, identify the reasons for their residential placement, examine the review system in operation and explore the level of contact between the children, their families and the staff.

Gallagher conducted her research by surveying the records of twenty-five students in five-day residential care in her service. In addition, a number of consultation meetings took place with the child care staff and members of the social work and psychology departments which provided additional data on the young persons. As residential provision in the service was single-sex, the research subjects were all male. They were aged between nine and eighteen and the largest single group, comprising one-third of the students, were fourteen years of age at the time of the study. Gallagher found that just over a third of the students were from the local area, while all but one lived within the health board region. While almost half of the students had been assessed as functioning at the level of a general learning difficulty, 48 per cent had been assessed as functioning above this level.

When Gallagher examined the family circumstances of the students, she found that just over two-thirds were from two-parent families. The majoirty were from lower socio-economic groups and 92 per cent of the families were described in the case files as experiencing 'significant problems' including drug and alcohol abuse, marital disharmony, financial difficulties and violence. The most frequently recorded difficulty, occurring in two-thirds of families, was limited parenting skills. The most common apparent factor for admission to residential care was recorded as 'adverse family circumstances'. Gallagher observed these to be a combination of problems, most of which were associated with children's behavioural difficulties and poor parental management. As far as Gallagher could ascertain, the most frequently cited aim of placement was the provision of a structured and consistent environment for the students.

It appeared that different types of 'reviews' were held on most of the students during each year, but the majority of these involved only care staff and excluded parents. There was little apparent contact between care staff and families, though key-workers, comprising social workers or psychologists, frequently met with families either through home visit, meeting, phone or letter. The majority of students had little contact with their families during their weekly placements, but did return home at weekends.

Gallagher noted that many of the students who were functioning at levels above general learning difficulty could have been placed in mainstream education but because of behavioural difficulties, required residential placement and were thus placed in special schooling. She considered this finding to reflect a general failure of mainstream education to meet the needs of certain students and a subsequent mis-placement in special schooling. She also observed that the files contained no evidence of the intended length of placement, which, along with the variable review system, could potentially cause students to drift and remain in residence for longer than necessary or beneficial.

As many of the children actually came from the local area, and from families described as having significant problems, particularly with regard to parenting, Gallagher concluded that home circumstances rather than factors associated with education were the primary reason for their admission to residence. She therefore identified work with families to assist them in coping with their difficulties to be an important goal for the service, while at the same time she noted that there was a lack of clarity in the records about the aims of the placement.

Gallagher concluded that residential special education services should be included in the spectrum of services available for children and families who are in difficulty. On the basis of her data, she argued that while provision of a structured and consistent environment would benefit students who needed it, it was equally important for the service to try to achieve improvement in the children's family situations to facilitate their return. For this reason, she felt that it was vital for placement objectives, including expected duration of placement, to be clarified. She recommended the implementation of a consistent and inclusive review system, involving all personnel working with the child as well as the parents and students themselves. She suggested that mid-week contact between students and their families, including phone calls, should be encouraged. Given that deficient parenting skills were so commonly identified as the principal reason for the children's admission to residence, Gallagher proposed that the care staff should attempt direct parent training and increase their contact with the children's families. She emphasised the need for staff training to support this activity. Gallagher hoped that, by adopting her recommendations, the service could ultimately achieve an ideal of shared care between staff, families and students in a manner that recognised the importance of each individual in the process.

Decision making about the placement of children in high support units
While the young people residing in the setting discussed by Fagan (above) were termed as the most 'difficult' in the child care system, the centre was run, as he described it, on 'open' lines. From the mid-1990s, however, a number of high court rulings determined that health boards had to make accommodation of a secure nature available for certain children whose behavioural problems meant that they could not be safely cared for in other

children's residential centres. Several of the country's health boards were, therefore, obliged to establish what became known as high support units to cater for the needs of these young people. The features common to these centres include the necessity for young people to be kept under detention orders with a high staff/child ratio and security based normally, though not always, on a locked door policy.

Critiques of high support units include the suggestion that resources that might otherwise be invested in family support are now being diverted to expensive services. It is also suggested that the health boards' decisions to operate high support units are driven more by pressure from the judiciary than an informed analysis of the best kind of integrated service to provide for troubled children (Kenny, 2000). It has also been argued that high support units emerged largely as a consequence of the repeated failure of the state to provide adequate accommodation for homeless children and that the mere availability of secure accommodation means that it is considered a viable alternative when practitioners feel under pressure to find a placement for a child (Children's Legal Centre, 1997; O'Sullivan, 2000).

A high support unit was set up to accommodate up to three children in the Midland Health Board area in 1998 following a judicial review of a child in care and a ministerial directive. A project carried out in 1999 by Annette Maguire, a social work team leader in the region, set out to explore the sort of factors that influenced the decisions to place children in the unit. It also asked the question whether, had resources been available in the 'open' system, alternatives could have been satisfactorily offered. Maguire was aware from the literature that absconding, offending and violence were the three main factors associated with the placement of children in secure accommodation (Harris and Timms, 1993). Research had also indicated that the decision to place a young person in a special unit was a consequence of failure by the 'open' sector to meet their needs (Cawson and Martell, 1979).

Maguire carried out a documentary analysis of case records of two adolescents already in the unit and one seeking admission, in order to obtain a clear picture of the young persons' case histories and their individual profiles. Her primary source of data came from semi-structured interviews carried out with eleven professionals, four of whom were in management roles and had direct responsibility for decision making about the development of the unit and about which children were deemed suitable or not for admission. She was thus able to compare the responses of managers with those of practitioners.

The two young people placed in the unit had a history of placement breakdown, and had experienced some form of child abuse as well as rejection by family or other carers. One of them had been placed in a special school prior to admission to the unit. But this had been deemed unsuitable for him because of his young age and vulnerability. The other young person had been 'specialled' in a bed and breakfast establishment as no placement had been available. The child awaiting admission was residing at the time in a special school where he was considered to be unsuitably placed. One of the questions raised by Maguire concerned whether or not the needs of these two young people might be met in a properly resourced open unit.

The managers were asked about their previous knowledge of high support units, the rationale behind the establishment of the unit, the health board policy concerning the unit, the most suitable type of young person for the unit, the objectives of the unit and the back-up resources available. None of the respondents was familiar with existing research in the area. Two had prior knowledge of the operation of secure units in countries outside Ireland but none was specifically aware of the criteria that determined the MHB unit's status as 'high support'. They were not uniformly aware of the rationale for setting up the unit, and none of them was aware of any written health board policy in relation to it. They all saw its secure status as short term and as a step to a more open type of service, representing a phase of 'intensive assessment and treatment'. Their views of the type of child most appropriate for the unit were consistent with the literature, identifying children who had tendencies to abscond or whose behaviour was dangerous or violent. However, one respondent in this group expressed reservations about the secure nature of the unit, suggesting that young people exhibiting this type of behaviour did not necessarily require to be locked up and that more resources should be invested in open units. There was a concern that the current shortage of residential places may inevitably result in young people being placed in high support units because no suitable alternative existed.

The practitioners who were interviewed consisted of a senior social worker, two team leaders and four social workers who had been working with the children placed in the unit as well as the young person awaiting admission. None of them had any previous experience of high support units, and like the managers, could see no obvious difference between high support and secure units.[23] They all concurred that the reason the young people had been admitted to the high support unit was because no other options were available. None was sure of the length of stay intended but all perceived the admissions to be short term.

[23] There is in fact, no legally defined difference between high support units and secure units, though there is a tendency for health boards to describe the units which they have established recently as high support units, and a general belief that the level of security, i.e. locking up, is less in a secure unit. Under the Children Act, 2001, provision is made for what are termed Special Care Units, where non-offending children can be kept in secure accommodation under a court order called a special care order.

Six of the seven practitioners interviewed expressed the view that, had another appropriate open service been available, they would have chosen it for the young people concerned. While the young people already resident in the high support unit were considered to have made progress, this was attributed not to the secure nature of the centre but to the stability they experienced. This meant that the young people had not been threatened with expulsion and had received positive reinforcement from the care workers. The practitioners considered that the decision to admit the children had been made by management in response to legal and media pressure. The degree to which practitioners were involved in decision making appeared to be limited, with only two stating that they had an equal input to it.

The findings confirmed Maguire's sense that all the professionals involved in the unit had only limited knowledge of what constituted 'high support'. This, she pointed out, was not helped by the absence of written policies and procedures, a factor that was not conducive to the safe care of the young people involved. The absence of legislation specific to the area meant that there was no provision for reviews, independent representation for children or consistency about the manner in which detention orders were being made. She argued that the potential for appropriate placement was severely curtailed by the confusion and lack of clarity experienced by the professionals involved. She suggested that the lack of clear definition about high support tended to deflect professionals from the issue of detention and its implications. She argued that the manner in which high support units have been developed in response to litigation means that the nature of services is now being dictated by the courts, with the consequence that provision is piecemeal and on a case-by-case basis. This, she believed, was confirmed by the lack of availability of supplementary residential placements.

Maguire concluded that the most important challenge to be faced when dealing with troubled young people was the development by open services of methods of intervention and the provision of a safe and homely environment. She made the following specific recommendations:

- the development of legislation in respect of detention of young people
- the development of clear and comprehensive policies in respect of high support units
- adequate resourcing of residential centres to meet the complex needs of the older, more troubled, child
- horizontal planing of services to ensure continuity of care.

Finally, Maguire recommended the development of services in response to need rather than demand.

Links between residential care and community based organisations
Chapter Five has dealt in detail with inter-agency and inter-professional co-operation between agencies and professionals providing services for children, particularly in relation to the management of child protection and welfare cases. However, the issue of co-ordination has relevance for all elements of child care work and is particularly crucial in order to enhance the quality of life experienced by children in residential care. Residential units need to have useful contact and co-operation with other community based organisations in order to maximise the amount of support available to the children and enhance their social networks.

The important role of education in the development of a child's positive self-image and self-esteem has been well established (Gilligan, 1999b; Daniel, Wassell and Gilligan, 2000). It has also been argued that school can act as a powerful protective factor and a safe haven for a child whose domestic environment is unstable (Rutter, 1985). At the same time, it is acknowledged that children in care tend to have lower levels of educational achievement than their peers in the general population, thus lessening their chances of employment and rewarding experiences in later life (Jackson, 1988). It follows that the attitude of care staff to education, along with the relationship between a school and a residential centre, can be a crucial influence on how far a child in care can maximise his or her educational attainments and ultimately, life chances. A project carried out in 1993 by Phil Canny, at the time a child care worker in Mount St Vincent's residential centre in Limerick, sought to explore the relationship between the centre and some local schools in the community. The study aimed to improve channels of liaison and support between the unit staff and teachers.

Canny was aware that some of the children from the residential centre found it difficult to settle in school and presented challenges to the staff there because of their sometimes disturbed behaviour. She was aware of the necessity for constant communication between the school and the unit staff and the potentially positive outcomes for the children when contact was maintained in a constructive manner.

Canny conducted her study by means of discussion groups involving care staff from Mount St Vincent and teachers from four local schools. She specifically sought to explore current attitudes and practices of teachers and child care workers in relation to education, with a view to establishing a mutually agreed structure and policy with regard to school placements. Her initial intention was to include three post-primary schools, three primary schools and a special school for children with mild learning disabilities. However, the first two approaches she made to post-primary schools met with negativity and disinterest respectively on the parts of the principals, so she ultimately decided to include only the three primary schools and the special school. She facilitated three discussion groups, the first one with residential child care staff including senior management, the second one with the same residential staff and eight teachers including two school principals and the third one with the residential staff.

The first discussion group focused on four different areas: the importance of education for children in care, areas of special concern, the value of including teachers in planning for the children and issues about the sharing of personal information about the children. There was consensus about the importance of education, particularly as an aid to the personal development of the children and an enabling factor in the formation of interpersonal relationships. The consistency and stability that education provided for children was recognised as well as the importance of encouragement and commitment on the part of residential care staff. Concern was expressed regarding the low level of educational functioning of some children who had experienced trauma and disruption as well as the behavioural difficulties exhibited by some of them. It was suggested that care staff sometimes minimised the difficulties likely to occur when referring a child to school in an effort to ensure that he or she was accepted.

While it was felt that it would be unrealistic to expect teachers to attend planning meetings in respect of the children, the importance of giving feedback on care plans to schools was acknowledged.

The group discussion involving the teachers highlighted the lack of clarity with which schools regarded the residential unit. The teachers stated that they had made implicit assumptions that the children in care in Mount St Vincent were from 'problem' backgrounds. However, the role and function of the centre in the community had never really been considered by them. The child care workers used the discussion to inform the teachers about the unit and its policies, particularly the importance of care plans and case reviews. While the teachers were familiar with the term 'review' they had not hitherto been sure what it meant, so this input proved very useful for them. When their perceptions of child care workers were discussed, the teachers were generally positive about their contact with them. However, they acknowledged that they had sometimes found the workers to be 'guarded' and protective of information, sometimes raising the teachers' suspicions that there was something to hide about a particular child. They also pointed out the frustration of dealing with several different workers about the one child and suggested that the care workers sometimes appeared to hold unwarrantedly high expectations of the teachers' capacity to give a lot of attention to a child's individual needs. They were not necessarily familiar with the terminology used within the unit and this impeded their ability to understand and respond to children's chat and questions. In general, the teachers felt it would be helpful to have some general background information to enhance their understanding of the different events in the children's lives. It was ultimately agreed that information exchange should be confined to a 'need to know' basis but that it would be helpful for schools to have a basic idea of the child's care plan.

The teachers pointed out that some of the children from the unit seemed to have serious behavioural and emotional difficulties and that their achievements were often at a lower level. On the positive side, they revealed that the children in their schools from Mount St Vincent were generally quite open about where they were living and spoke freely about the centre.

The advisability and utility of having an information pack for schools about the centre was agreed and the value of face-to-face contact between key workers and teachers was affirmed. While they found the fact that the children often had to start school in the middle of a school year somewhat disruptive, the teachers expressed willingness to support the children through the experience.

The third discussion group drew together the findings and recommendations of the previous two and provided a template for the development of a policy document for Mount St Vincent on education, to be ultimately agreed by all parties who had been involved in the project. It was agreed that the document would contain information on the unit and its operation, a statement of intent to support the children in schools, and procedures for referral of children and liaison between schools and the child care unit. Canny argued that the commitment underlying its implementation would raise the awareness of teachers in relation to the difficulties encountered by children from residential centres when they start a new school, and form a basis for future working relationships.

Another project was conducted in 2000 on a similar theme, this time on the working relationship between health board social workers and residential child care workers. The research was carried out by Colette McLoughlin, a social work team leader in the South Western Area Board of the Eastern Regional Health Authority. McLoughlin was aware from previous research carried out in Ireland of certain tensions between social workers and residential care centres. These mainly concerned factors such as admission policies and the belief that centres were more disposed towards holding on to children who were less troubled and letting go those who were more challenging. Research had also highlighted a lack of clarity around complaints procedures and the sudden discharge of children for whom there was no other placement (Clarke, 1998). McLoughlin aimed to add to existing knowledge on this subject by exploring the relationships between social workers on her own team and staff in two of the residential centres within the same community care area. She also sought to identify their understandings of each other's roles, identify factors that both supported and impeded good working relationships and make recommendations for improvement.

McLoughlin gathered her data by conducting three focus groups, one comprising social workers from the area and two others each comprising residential staff from two different centres. One of the centres offered short- to medium-term care and the other offered medium- to long-term care. In addition, McLoughlin interviewed a newly appointed residential manager of one of the centres.

Findings from the focus group discussions revealed issues similar to those noted in previous research on inter-agency co-operation and partnership in child protection and welfare work (Hallett and Birchall, 1992; Reder, Duncan and Gray, 1993; Buckley, 2000). The professional factors included misconceptions about the extent and limits of each other's roles and responsibilities in relation to, for example, who should liaise with parents, who was most appropriate to do direct work with children and who should be available to a child in crisis. Differing attitudes in relation to disciplinary regimes in the residential centres and norms about involving parents were also identified as potential sources of conflict. The groups highlighted structural issues such as failure to communicate basic information, the amount of support offered by management and pressures of work that sometimes resulted in children having no allocated social workers. Interpersonal issues such as a tendency to criticise, stereotype and hold unrealistic expectations of each other as well as the importance of positive personal relationships between individuals from both professional groups were also raised for discussion. The need for each group to support the other in difficult work was emphasised and both sets of professionals affirmed the importance of complementary practice in relation to ensuring that a child's needs were being met.

Factors contributing to the strain on working relationships that were specific to work with children in residential care were identified. These included admission policies that were considered too narrow and the social workers' sense that they were being unnecessarily used as intermediaries between the residential centres and the parents of the children. Other factors were lack of dialogue about medical treatment for the children and sudden discharge of children without consultation or agreement. Communication difficulties included failure of social workers to return calls made by residential staff as well as failure to inform the centres about staff changes. Tensions appeared to be exacerbated when social workers prioritised other work ahead of contact with children in the units; instances were cited where residential workers had sensed that their contributions to care plans were ignored or undervalued.

Reviews of children in care present obvious opportunities for the sharing of information and ideas. However, McLoughlin encountered a great deal of confusion about the review process. Neither professional group seemed sure about whose responsibility it was to call or chair the meetings, where they should be held, or who should attend them.

The groups identified a number of elements that facilitated healthy working relationships between them. These included good management, low staff turnover, agreement from the beginning of a placement about clear, realistic and mutual expectations of each professional's role and responsibility. Other important factors were communication between key people and a reasonable fit between what was considered best for the child and the capacity of the centre to provide it. Appreciation of each other's work, mutual respect, pooling of suggestions and positive feedback between the two professional groups was accorded a lot of importance.

Both groups offered recommendations for enhancement of working relationships and the sharing of skills and knowledge. These included joint pre- and post-qualification training, joint professional conferences, commitment to joint work with families, joint preparation of reports and co-working with children in care. Clear channels of communication were suggested together with the development at management level of agreed standards and strategies to promote joint work. Importantly, the two groups emphasised the need for a forum whereby difference of opinion and grievances could be resolved.

Findings from McLoughlin's study also confirmed that whatever protocols and local arrangements were agreed, working relationships would continue to be strained as long as structural factors such as staff shortages and lack of placement options continued to prevail. She concluded that these pressures not only caused inter-agency and inter-professional tensions but negatively affected the potential for placements to meet the needs of children in care.

The role played by men in residential child care

While there is a large literature on gender in child protection and welfare work (Ferguson and Sinnott, 1995; Kelly, 1996; Milner, 1996; Buckley 1998b), men as foster carers (Gilligan, 2000b) and men in social work (Christie, 2001; Pringle, 2001) there is less about the issue of male staff in residential child care. This was the subject of a project undertaken in 2000 by Mary Kennedy, a residential manager in a centre catering exclusively for young males between twelve and eighteen years of age. She was concerned about the lack of gender balance in residential child care despite the popular belief that young people in care need to experience positive role modelling from male and female carers. Her research aimed to establish the gender balance in a sample of residential centres and find out if and why the proportion of men training for and entering child care work had declined over the past ten years. Her primary aim, however, was to examine the views of service users and child care workers on the role of male staff working in residential centres.

Kennedy gathered her quantitative data by means of a survey of twenty-five residential centres and all the colleges in Ireland operating child care courses. She made contact with the Department of Health and Children to establish the numbers of male and female children in care in Ireland and carried out an internet search for statistical information on children in care in England and Scotland. The qualitative data were gathered by means of twenty in-depth interviews with five male residential care staff, five female residential care staff and ten young men, one of whom was living in the unit she was managing, and nine who had recently left residential care.

The survey data showed that there had been a decrease in the number of male staff working in residential units over the preceding ten years, with female staff now outnumbering them by two to one. The data on children in care in 2000 indicated that males outnumbered females by 1 per cent in Ireland, with a slightly higher percentages of boys in care in Scotland and England. There was a low response to questionnaires sent to colleges conducting child care courses, with only three replies. However, the data indicated a sharp decline over the preceding ten years in the proportion of males undertaking child care training.

The interviews with service users indicated that most of them had experienced a good overall relationship with the staff. Interestingly, a majority of them did not perceive that the male and female staff did the 'same job', some specifying that the female staff were more open and more inclined to help and spent more time listening to their problems. Responses suggested that the female staff did more basic household chores while the male staff 'just watched' and that the male staff tended to behave in a more 'authoritarian' manner. However, most of the service users expressed a preference for going to the male workers to discuss 'male' issues and were positive about the presence of male staff, some suggesting that it had changed the negative perceptions of men that they had formed prior to entering care. Some respondents commented that the male staff seemed to understand their experiences of adolescence and they found this reassuring.

When female staff members were interviewed about their perceptions of the male child care staff, they unanimously agreed on the importance of having male staff to act as positive role models for the residents. They also felt that it was good to show the young people an example of males and females working on equal terms. However, a majority suggested that male staff can be undermining of their female colleagues, and that male staff found it difficult to ask for support when under pressure.

The male staff who were interviewed were also positive about their capacity to role model and their ability to empathise with male service users. They acknowledged that the 'macho' ethos that operates amongst male staff can militate against good child care and that they can be too easily seen as authority figures, which they found uncomfortable. When asked for their view on the declining numbers of men in child care work, only a minority mentioned the fear of abuse allegations, but some acknowledged that amongst their peers, child care was often seen as 'women's work' and considered an inferior career option.

Both male and female staff commented that the positive role modelling of male staff had the potential to prevent or challenge the development of sexist/racist and homophobic attitudes in the young people. In her analysis of the data, Kennedy expressed concern about the extent to which males were considered authoritarian, 'macho' and reluctant to acknowledge their vulnerabilities. She suggested that these factors were, in accordance with the literature, reflective of the sort of socialisation processes to which the workers had been subjected (Ferguson, 1998) and considered that the function of the research in raising general awareness of this amongst the staff may lead ultimately to change. She recommended that these issues be given priority in the training and supervision of staff, and suggested the development of group work with young people by male staff to focus specifically on the area of masculinity. Given the importance placed on the presence of male staff in residential care, Kennedy advocated more active promotion of child care as a viable career option for male students.

Conclusion

The projects discussed in this chapter have highlighted the way in which certain weaknesses in the residential care system can be tackled. While some of the projects were completed before the implementation of the child care regulations or the establishment of the ISSI, the issues raised in them are still pertinent. The legal requirement to formulate and review care plans was emphasised with some of the projects, illustrating how lack of formal care planning can lead to the postponement or neglect of basic tasks like regular dental and medical checks. Importantly, these studies also showed how lack of clarity about aims can be reinforced by the absence of a care plan and can ultimately lead to 'drift' in placement. The importance, not only of involving key agencies such as schools in the design and review of care plans, but also the need for effective liaison between residential units and other child care organisations was emphasised in a number of the studies discussed here.

Interesting and effective ways of working with children in care to restore their capacity for forming healthy attachments were illustrated in two projects. They also gave the strong message that opportunities for direct work rarely occur naturally in busy settings but must be included as part of a structured plan that allows sufficient time for staff to engage with children on their own. The issue of staff support and team stability was again reiterated in relation to safe management of behaviour and prevention of violent incidents, a factor that has been a cause of increasing concern in residential care work. The controversial subject of high support and secure units was discussed in a project which illustrated the complexity of placing children with challenging behaviour in a context where decisions are increasingly being determined by case law.

The inappropriateness of providing a time-limited residential service for children from troubled backgrounds without also providing a family support and intervention service was demonstrated, particularly as it is clear that placement in residential special education is often linked with stressors in the family home. The question of gender and residential care was discussed in a highly original project that examined the role of male staff in residential settings and highlighted dynamics that require to be challenged through training.

Chapter Twelve will return to the issue of residential child care and will develop a theme that has already been raised, that is the importance of maintaining contact between children and their homes, by involving their families in the day-to-day activities of residential units.

12

Parental Involvement with Children in Out-of-Home Care

Introduction

The importance of parental participation in child protection and welfare work is becoming increasingly recognised and has been enshrined in *Children First* (Department of Health and Children, 1999). The Task Force Report (Department of Health, 1980) was one of the first Irish policy documents to advocate the involvement of parents in the assessment of their children's needs. In the meantime, research carried out in Ireland and the UK has demonstrated the degree to which the failure to keep parents informed of and involved with the work of child welfare professionals has not only represented a lost opportunity, but has impacted on the effectiveness and outcomes of the tasks involved (Millham et al, 1986; Buckley, Skehill and O'Sullivan, 1997; Cleaver and Freeman, 1995). Thoburn, Lewis and Shemmings (1995) offer three reasons why involvement in the child protection process is important to families and professionals:

- it leads to better safeguarding of the child's welfare
- it recognises that family members possess unique knowledge about their own and each other's strengths and weaknesses
- it acknowledges explicitly the rights of family members which in turn helps to develop trust.

The norms and ideals described above in relation to parental involvement in the child protection process apply with equal weight to situations where children are either temporarily or permanently in out-of-home care. Research findings indicate that, up to the 1970s, Irish children who were separated from their parents through legal or voluntary means were frequently cut off from their families in what was assumed to be their best interests (Raftery and O'Sullivan, 1999). Studies carried out mainly in the UK during the 1980s highlighted the desirability of parental access both to maximise the possibility of rehabilitation and to enhance children's emotional stability while they were being cared for out of home (Millham et al, 1986). Practices in Ireland changed considerably following the child care reforms of the 1980s. Research conducted in a large organisation offering residential care during the mid to late 1990s reported that 76 per cent of children had contact with their families at least monthly, with the encouragement of care staff and management (Clarke, 1998). However, despite stipulations in the 1996 Department of Health Child Care Regulations, the same research found that few efforts were being made by residential centres to communicate basic information about their operation to parents, a most basic step in encouraging their participation and involvement.

Parental involvement with residential child care centres is the subject of most of the projects discussed in this chapter, the care situations ranging from a residential assessment centre to short- and long-term placement facilities and a unit for deaf children. The facilitation of access between parents and their children in both residential and foster care is a core element of this process and is extensively addressed.

Parental involvement in residential assessment

The aspiration to modify the focus of residential assessment from the 'problem child' to one that recognised the 'myriad effects of a web of relationships' underpinned the project undertaken in 1996 by Danny Lynch, assistant manager of Finglas Children's Centre, a facility to which juvenile (male) offenders are remanded by the courts for assessment. It had been the practice in this unit to confine parental involvement in the assessment to one interview, with a psychiatrist. Concerned about the narrowness of this approach and its inherent limitations, Lynch decided to carry out action research to pilot a new model of assessment that incorporated an additional number of interviews, to be conducted between the child's key worker and his parent or parents. He speculated that this change in practice would create viable ways for families to have an input into the process and that, as a result, the outcome would be more acceptable to all parties and ultimately more successful. One of the primary aims of the parental interviews was to elicit information on the family from the family themselves, rather than from the perspectives of other agencies as had formerly been the practice.

Lynch regarded his action research as part of a process that would generate further, informed debate. It was acknowledged that the staff at the children's centre had to operate within the constraints of a court system, inasmuch as their assessment was based on the principle that the child's welfare was paramount, but it was the judge who ultimately decided on the disposal of the case. Lynch postulated that an assessment that reflects the perspective of families would assist the judge to make a more informed decision.

For the pilot project, Lynch selected six assessments, held over a two-month period and conducted by five workers. In consultation with the workers, a strategy for including parents was negotiated which involved outlining key areas to be covered in the interviews, arranging meetings with the parents and facilitating their attendance by providing them with travel passes and meals on arrival. The number and times of subsequent meetings were determined by the parents and workers in each case. The workers documented the outcome of their meetings and used them to inform their assessment reports. Lynch then discussed the progress of each case with the workers concerned, thus accessing material for the project and at the same time sustaining the motivation of the staff member.

In each assessment, it was possible to identify a number of key areas where the impact of parental input was obvious, particularly with regard to the way that family dynamics now became visible and parental interest, motivation and concern became apparent. It became possible to clarify conflicting 'histories' from different agencies and understand the background to particular incidents or behaviours. It also created what Lynch described as dialogue through which negotiation with parents became possible.

Following the pilot period, it was agreed that flexibility would be needed in the future to take account of the way that the different circumstances of each family impacted on their take up of the invitation to participate. Lynch noted that, as in many action research projects, the research itself brought about change. Parents who had participated in the study continued to have active involvement with the staff as well as with their child in the unit, and appeared to be less constrained than non-participating parents in their communication with the staff. He also noted the increased satisfaction of the staff with their assessments.

Lynch was satisfied that his project had 'tested positively' the ability of the staff to change their practices and thus broaden the focus of the assessments which he felt were now conducted 'with' rather than 'to' families. He also claimed that the new, purposive approach assisted in diminishing the dis-empowerment previously experienced by parents by acknowledging their strengths and abilities. He planned to further extend the practice of parental participation by making contact with parents following the first court appearance of a child, sending them a booklet about the unit, with a contact name and initiating personal contact between key workers and parents at the earliest possible opportunity prior to the child's admission.

Parental involvement with their children in residential care
Another project on facilitating the development of positive attitudes towards the involvement of parents in children's units was carried out in 1992 by Lorna Wogan, then a senior houseparent in Mount St Vincent, a centre offering short-term care to children. While Wogan acknowledged that her unit reflected the policy of the Mid-Western Health Board to promote partnership in practice, she saw a need to progress existing links with parents

towards a policy of 'inclusion' within her own organisation. Her study sought to clarify the views of residential care workers with regard to parental links and to explore how the process of including families in their work would operate. She also elicited the views of professionals outside her organisation and the perspectives of the parents of some children in her unit with regard to the service that was being provided. Her ultimate goal was to facilitate the development of skilled and appropriate family work by staff in her unit.

In order to start the process of change within her organisation, Wogan decided to involve staff from each of the residential units in her study. She ran four workshops, the first two with residential child care staff whom she described as the 'core study group', and the last two involving, respectively, community care social workers and parents. Each of these events involved a focused discussion on the potential benefits of links between children and their families, the process of including families and the issues that it raised for all concerned.

The core study group acknowledged that greater parental contact would reassure children and lessen their anxiety about their parents. Additionally, they pointed out that parents, having been given a greater sense of control and inclusiveness, would be in a position to give their children positive messages about the unit, allowing them what Wogan described as the 'necessary permission' to grow, develop and thrive while in care. The core study group appraised and challenged their own assumptions and practices about parental involvement, concluding that there was much room for development. Interestingly, the residential workers expressed a concern that they may be encroaching on social workers' territory by seeking to involve parents. This was later discounted by the social workers participating in one of the workshops but it was an interesting example of a misperception that could have acted to undermine staff's motivation to change their practices.

Specific opportunities for parental involvement were identified by the core study group such as participating in everyday activities like bathing and reading stories, or taking their child for a routine medical examination. The workshop involving social workers highlighted the more frequent level of contact between child care staff and parents and the positive move towards partnership in planning, involving parents, health board staff and child care workers. These trends were perceived to both reflect and reinforce greater parental participation, and lessen the potential for collusion of two parties against the third, for example a parent requesting a child care worker to conceal information from the social worker for fear of the consequences.

Staff in the workshops were encouraged to visualise the parents' perspectives and understand the embarrassment, upset and awkwardness that may be experienced by them when visiting the unit. The learning from this was greatly reinforced by the sessions in which three parents participated, where they were able to convey their perceptions very vividly and made what Wogan described as a powerful impact on the group. Parents described their initial fears, their visions of the unit being like a prison or an old-style orphanage and their feelings of hurt, rejection and guilt about not parenting their own children. While they acknowledged that they experienced a reasonable level of involvement already and noted several positive factors about the unit, including its homely atmosphere, some spoke very movingly about their sense of separateness. They described a feelings of disappointment that the staff had not always enough time to talk to them, a sense of not hearing enough information about their children's progress, their lack of control over simple matters like their children's haircuts and their apprehension and confusion around review meetings. They expressed a strong desire for greater involvement and displayed considerable motivation to play their part.

Wogan's evaluation of the workshops was positive – she had observed a significant shift in attitude on the part of staff, increased motivation to include parents as much as possible, and a dispelling of the fears or myths around 'family' work. She was pleased to note the ownership adopted by the group of the responsibility to operationalise their ideas, and acknowledged that they would need the involvement and support of senior staff. On the basis of her findings, Wogan designed a set of guidelines for practice to cover the span of a child's residence in the unit: the period during which the child is in care, and the periods immediately preceding and following discharge from care. She also outlined several areas where policy might be modified, for presentation to senior management.

Preparation for return home

The preparation of families for the return of their children from residential care was one of the core objectives of a project carried out in 1993 by P.J. Fegan, manager of a residential centre for boys, the majority of whom were detained by court orders. A small study carried out within the unit in 1990 had clearly indicated the need for what was described as a 'Through-care/Aftercare Support Service'. The service had subsequently been established in Dublin, as most of the residents in the centre came from that area, and most ultimately returned to their families of origin there. Fegan's project arose from an additional need identified in the earlier study, the benefits of encouraging family participation in their children's placements with a view to enabling them to cope with their children's ultimate return to them. The project consisted of seven pre-planned and focused group meetings with six sets of parents. Most took place in the Dublin centre and the final two were conducted with the same groups in a respite centre owned by the organisation and based in Waterford.

Fegan addressed a number of issues in preparation for the group meetings, namely, whether parents were interested, what form the group should take, the level of resources required, which parents to invite, how to negotiate the finances necessary to run the meetings. He decided to start with a group of parents whose sons would be due to leave within the following year or two years and he visited them to ascertain their interest. Having been assured that they would attend the meetings, Fegan estimated the projected cost and negotiated the funding for the project from the management of his organisation.

The meetings were structured in advance and families were sent a copy of the proposed dates and agendas. It was planned to include probation and welfare officers and staff from the residential centre at different meetings to make presentations but there was also a heavy emphasis on interaction and discussion within the groups. The first one was introductory and touched on the area of family dynamics and coping with behaviour, a theme that was continued in the second meeting. Parents were given handouts to keep and to use as aids to discussion. The third meeting was attended by senior house parents who gave an account of the operation of the unit and discussed ways of managing behaviour, then facilitated a discussion about how parents could have a more meaningful role in communicating and receiving information. The fourth meeting concentrated on the parents themselves, their problems and the supports available to them. The fifth meeting was attended by a teacher from the unit and most of the discussion centred around school-related matters and educational difficulties and attainments.

The two final meetings took place on two consecutive days in the organisation's respite centre in Waterford, the parents having been transported there by the minibus belonging to the centre. The aim of moving the meeting out of Dublin was to give parents a break and create a relaxed atmosphere. The first meeting in Waterford was chaired by a probation and welfare officer who was the founder of a group called the Munster Parents Network, and consisted of a talk and discussion about the impact that the parents' own difficulties may have been having on family relationships. The final meeting was attended by all the staff who had previously participated. The main purpose of the session was evaluation and feedback and the making of future plans.

Attendance at the group meetings was supported by the provision of transport or bus fares and had been good, with two-thirds of the invited parents attending on average although fathers or mothers' partners attended less frequently than mothers. The principal issues that had arisen in discussion concerned communication between the centre and families, the support available to parents from the unit and from each other, and parents' own concerns about the future management of their sons' behaviour. Recommendations emerging from the project included:

- the formalising of information exchange
- more meaningful involvement of parents at case conferences
- the development of a social support network to enable the young people to have outside interests while in care
- the provision of ongoing support to parents on a countrywide basis by a team from the centre
- the development of a parents' network for mutual support.

Fegan considered the project to have achieved its aim of preparing parents for the return of their children. Additionally, he felt that it gave parents a more positive view of the care process as well as a degree of support and a sense of participation in their children's lives.

Links between parents and special residential schools
The development of stronger links between parents and the residential settings in which their deaf children live was the subject of a project undertaken in 1998 by Eileen Johnson, a house parent in a unit for deaf boys. Johnson was conscious that deaf children can have limited ability to develop social and problem-solving skills. She was also aware that because the nature of services provided for deaf children in Ireland often led to their placement in residential schools at a considerable distance from their homes, parents had only limited involvement in their children's care. The resulting separation and isolation, in her view, exacerbated the already existing communication problems caused by many families' inability to use sign language and the children's limited social networks.

The combination of these factors, as well as the available research about child abuse and disability, led Johnson to hypothesise that the deaf children in her care were vulnerable not only to abuse but also to deficits in their general welfare and emotional development. She therefore aimed, through her project, to encourage greater involvement of parents with the residential unit, with the ultimate objective of enhancing their children's well-being and safety. She was also particularly concerned to promote partnership between the residential staff and parents so that concerns about the protection and welfare of individual children could be shared and addressed in a united way. In order to start the process, she decided to target her project at parents whose children were entering a residential setting for the first time.

Johnson designed her fieldwork by first consulting with three social workers who had experience of working with deaf children. All three confirmed her view that the skills and knowledge required to work with a combination of child protection and disability were rarely found in one single profession or service. The social workers agreed that there was a need to develop suitable education and prevention programmes in addition to providing support and information to deaf children and their families so that a collaborative effort could be made to enhance the protection of this very vulnerable group.

Johnson then designed a questionnaire and circulated it to the parents of the thirteen children in her own unit, to elicit their views on the type of involvement they would favour and the nature of any information that would be of value to them. She received six replies, which yielded useful data, indicating that all parents wanted, on a regular basis, both information and reassurance that their sons were safe in the residence. They also expressed an interest in more meetings with staff and the promotion of greater links with home by letter and also through other appropriate channels like fax and email. Parents replied positively to questions about information on child protection, and agreed that they would like a forum for discussing complaints or behaviour problems.

On the basis of this small survey, Johnson set up a meeting that was attended by herself, staff from the unit and seven parents, some of whom had to travel long distances. Several significant issues were raised including parents' difficulties in communicating with their deaf children, their sadness at their child's isolation and lack of friends in a hearing community, their hurt at the sense of stigma their children sometimes experienced, their problems around discipline and behaviour and, in some cases, their over-protectiveness. One of the significant difficulties identified by parents was their perceived inability to discuss sexual matters with their sons because of a combination of unease, anxiety and the difficulty in knowing the correct sign language and communicating in an understandable way. At the same time they recognised their children's vulnerability and expressed anxiety about their protection. They also greatly feared that their children would be bullied by hearing children. These concerns confirmed Johnson's sense that the already existing problems of isolation that had been experienced by the children in their own communities could be compounded by their separation from their parents and that their resources for protecting themselves were likely to be very low.

As a result of the meeting, staff and parents agreed to have further regular meetings and exchanges of information, particularly in relation to dealing with adolescent and sexual behaviour in both a supportive and protective manner. In order to provide a tangible source of information, Johnson designed a booklet for parents that described the way the unit operated, the type of work carried out with the children, and policies on child protection and related matters. She also designed and implemented a phased pre-placement programme to enable the children to settle in more easily.

Johnson made further recommendations for adoption by the residential unit, including the following:

- attention to promoting of communication between children, care staff and their families through letters, 'home' books, telephone, minicom, faxes, email and newsletters
- the promotion of a friendly and welcoming atmosphere, including the offer of free accommodation to visiting parents
- the involvement of parents in social and fund-raising functions
- the representation of parents on committees and governing bodies.

Overall, Johnson believed that her project had achieved its aims and while the questions of service provision and society's attitude to deaf children were beyond her remit, she considered that greater parental interest and involvement in their children's care would make a useful difference.

Access between parents and children in the care of the state
A large body of research underlines the current view that children in short- and long-term care benefit considerably from regular and good quality contact with their families of origin (Millham et al, 1986; Berridge and Cleaver, 1987; Quinton and Rutter, 1998). To complement these findings and contextualise them in an Irish situation, a number of projects were carried out with the aims of exploring the nature of access, mainly to children in foster care, and making recommendations about good practice in this area. Through these studies, the views of birth parents, foster parents, social workers and children are expressed and analysed and essential issues that reinforce or undermine the potential for effective contact between parents and children are illustrated.

In 1991, Colm O'Doherty, at the time a senior social worker in the Southern Health Board, carried out an action research project which initially studied four cases in some depth to examine the frequency, nature, purpose and quality of access between the parents and children concerned. In each case the children had been in care for longer than six months. O'Doherty then made interventions on the basis of his findings with a view to enhancing the contacts and raise awareness of the practice issues involved. Using a model proposed in Millham et al's (1986) study, O'Doherty looked at barriers to access in terms of specific and non-specific restrictions and determined how to overcome them.

In two of the cases, access was quite frequent, less so in the other two. A striking trend was that in three cases, it seemed to be parental, mainly maternal, motivation that determined the frequency rather than any agreed arrangement between all the stakeholders. In two cases, fathers had availed of access when the children first entered care but by the time the study was conducted, had ceased contact altogether and in a third, there had never been contact between the children and their father. In one case where a hostile relationship existed between the family and the health board, access had been infrequent. In another case the visits took place in the birth parents' home, but the presence of the foster parent was resented by the birth mother. While others took place in the health centre or social work department, O'Doherty noted how the cramped and unsuitable facilities available for access negatively affected the communication between parents and children. He also observed how practical difficulties for the parents included the distance between their homes and their children's placements as well as the fact that some had other children that needed minding.

During the action phase of his study, O'Doherty made interventions in each of the cases with the intention of removing barriers to effective contact. He found that in one case, the mother's demands were very reasonable but had not really been heard by the social workers involved. In two of the cases, O'Doherty found that the foster parents were contributing significantly to the obstacles to access by failing to acknowledge its value and by prioritising their own relationship with the foster children. He mediated in each of the above cases to try and effect better communication and ensure that the value of access was understood by all the parties involved. In the case where contact had ceased, he managed to reinstate regular visits by approaching the parents as a 'neutral negotiator' with a positive suggestion about access and ensuring that the setting for the visits was practicable and child-centred and would be enjoyable for the children. Where parental motivation was low or ambivalent, or where for example, a co-habitee was less enthusiastic about access, O'Doherty spent time with a parent to discuss her children's need for contact, her rights to see her children and the potential for their return home. In the fourth case, he addressed the birth parents' need for re-housing, which had been perceived as a significant obstacle to reunion.

On the basis of his study of the cases and his action research, which showed largely positive outcomes in terms of increasing the frequency and improving the quality of access, O'Doherty raised a number of issues. He advocated more in-depth training, assessment and support services for foster parents to clarify the requirement for their co-operation in access and facilitate them in participating. He proposed the provision of an adequate, family-centred location for visits, and for some consideration to be given to the practical difficulties that travelling to see their children posed for birth parents. He emphasised the necessity for access arrangements to be based on 'all party agreement' including residential staff where relevant.

Whilst acknowledging the agency and resource implications in making a stronger commitment to enhancing the frequency and quality of access, O'Doherty felt that one of his most significant findings concerned the value attributed to contact by social workers. He pointed out that while the motivation to support and encourage access may have been somewhat undermined by case overload and ambivalence about its worth at times, neglect of this area could be detrimental to children's overall development and progress whether they remain in care or return home. On the basis of his study, he suggested that agencies adopt, on principle, a commitment to the enhancement of access that would, in his view, be greatly facilitated by partnership between all key actors.

The implementation of Section 37 of the Child Care Act, 1991 carries with it certain implications for all parties involved in the placement of a child in health board care. For the first time, facilitation of access between children and parents or any other person who has a *bona fide* interest in the children is specified as a responsibility of the health board. In the event of a dispute, the court may now 'make such an order as it thinks proper'. The implications of the legislation were examined in 1994 by Nuala O'Regan, at the time a social worker in the South Eastern Health Board, based in Carlow. The relevant section of the legislation had not yet been implemented, so the study focused on the likely impact of the changes it was expected to bring about. O'Regan interviewed three social workers, three birth parents, three children and three foster parents in order to elicit their views on current access arrangements between parents and children in foster care and their reactions to the new legislation.

While the social workers broadly welcomed the changes in the new legislation, they expressed some concern about the discretion available to judges who, it was felt, may not always understand the different needs and complexities associated with each case. It was also feared that the demands that access arrangements would make on social work time may not be appreciated. The workers identified a need for a specific code of practice in relation to access, as well as information leaflets on each aspect of the process and official forms to be used in relation to agreement on access arrangements.

The interviews with birth parents, children and foster parents illustrated the different factors unique to each child's care situation. The children had different expectations and desires in relation to visits with their parents. In general they enjoyed and wanted the contact, but specified different likes and dislikes in relation to which parent, how often and in what context they wanted the visits to take place. One child asserted her wish to see her siblings and cousins more often. Two of the three children firmly stated that they did not wish to see their fathers.

The birth mothers' wishes for involvement varied according to their personal situations; one mother had a mental health problem and found the access visits fairly challenging. Another spoke movingly and at length about her sadness at not being able to parent the children, her frustration at the scarcity of time she was permitted to spend with them and her sense of powerlessness about changing the arrangements. The third mother also described her dissatisfaction about her current access arrangements and her concern that protesting might work against her and ultimately deprive her of contact.

The five foster carers who were interviewed, which included two couples and a foster mother, very clearly demonstrated their commitment to facilitating access and their view that it was beneficial for children. They were frank about the difficulties involved including the effect on the children's behaviour prior to and after the visits, but generally seemed willing to deal with each issue as it arose. They expressed strong views on the location and arrangements for the visits, and the two foster fathers expressed some caution about the possibility of the courts becoming more involved in decisions on the frequency of visits.

O'Regan acknowledged the need to review some of the arrangements in response to the different issues raised particularly in relation to introducing a level of flexibility about the nature and location of access visits. She recognised the heavy demands on social work time made by access, but recommended that priority be given to working with birth parents both before and following contacts with their children, and suggested that self-help groups for parents with children in care could provide additional support.

Noting the lack of involvement of birth fathers even in this small sample, O'Regan recommended that stronger efforts should be made to engage them. Finally, she concluded that there was not sufficient awareness on the part of any of the participants in her research of the longer-term implications of the provisions in the Child Care Act, 1991 regarding access. She recommended both the dissemination of information and training for foster families and practitioners. Finally, O'Regan concluded that while overall standards and principles must apply, it was not possible to 'standardise' access arrangements, given the range of factors that impacted on each situation, but that each case must be considered in relation to its own unique set of circumstances.

Two factors are notable from O'Regan's project, one being the infrequency of access in the small sample, from six weekly to thrice yearly. The other is the absence of fathers in the lives of their children.

A project carried out in 1997 by Eileen O'Neill, at the time a social work team leader in the Midland Health Board, provided some useful contextual information in relation to the family type and age of admission of children in care in her area as well as the nature and frequency of their contacts with their parents and siblings. She carried out a survey of forty-eight children in care, based on structured interviews with thirteen social workers and reference to agency records. On the basis of her findings, she was able to make links between certain factors and, accordingly, to propose recommendations for policy and practice.

O'Neill approached her study on the basis of evidence from the literature that contact between children in care and their families is essential to their well-being. She was also aware from research that for a number of reasons, the frequency and quality of access can be overlooked and receive a low priority in relation to other aspects of their lives in care.

O'Neill's research produced a substantial quantity of useful information, based as it was on the total number of children in care in the Laois/Offaly region during a specific period. She found that the largest number of children in care came from (mainly female) lone parent families where the parents had either never been married or were now separated. The principal reason for entry into care was neglect, with 'mother unable to cope' coming second. O'Neill noted the gendered manner employed for framing the reason for entry into care which replicated the trend noted in research that responsibility for coping with children appeared to reside with mothers (Farmer and Owen, 1995; Buckley, 1998). Interestingly, the rate of access was higher for parents who lived alone than for those in couples whether married or not.

O'Neill explored 'contact' in terms of letters and telephone calls as well as access visits. She found that only one-seventh of the children had letter contact with parents, with only one-third having telephone contact. The data indicated that 54 per cent of mothers visited their children regularly, with frequency of visits declining as children got older, replicating a trend found in Irish and British studies (O'Higgins, 1996; Millham et al, 1986); only 27 per cent of fathers ever visited. Of that number, only fathers who had at one point resided with the children visited and their visits were less frequent than mothers'. While O'Neill found no link between the children's length of stay in care and the status of care (that is, whether it was voluntary or a result of a court order), she found that access was most frequent between mothers and children in voluntary care. Fathers' average rate of visiting differed only slightly in relation to the status of care, with less visiting when care was the result of a court order.

When she explored the rate of sibling access, O'Neill found that while two-thirds of the children who had siblings in care were placed with at least one of them, nearly three-fifths of the total number of children in care had a sibling in a separate placement instead or as well. She found that three-quarters of children who had siblings in another placement had at least monthly and often more frequent contact. However, she found a direct correlation between distance between placements and frequency of visiting, with the same trend apparent in relation to maternal access.

The most significant findings in O'Neill's study were the number of children of unmarried and separated parents in care, and the paucity of contact between children and their fathers. These factors highlighted, in her view, the need to provide early interventions to lone parent families so as to prevent entry into care, and the necessity to both research further and encourage paternal involvement with children in care. O'Neill further suggested that the trend towards decreasing frequency of contact as children got older underscored the need to develop a policy of planning for children in care with active facilitation of access and the identification of goals shared by birth parents, children and foster carers. This, she asserted, is particularly important given the link identified in the literature between frequency of access and potential for children to re-join their birth families (Millham et al, 1986; Berridge and Cleaver, 1987; Triseliotis, Sellick and Short, 1995). The link between geographical proximity of sibling placements and frequency of contact between siblings was also highlighted by O'Neill as an important pointer for planning.

O'Neill made recommendations in relation to the provision of resources, including social work time to plan and review contacts, recruit, train and support foster parents, provide transport for access visits if necessary, and provide comfortable and child-centred locations. She proposed practice improvements for social workers in particular, in relation to care plans, with explicit and agreed goals. O'Neill also recommended that foster carers be provided with and avail of training. In her view, their commitment to and assistance with visiting is a key determinant of success and effectiveness. Finally, O'Neill reiterated the importance of including birth parents and children in the formulation of visiting plans. She concluded that quality access must be

- reflected in the child care principles adopted by the agency
- resourced by the agency
- given meaning through policy and practice.

In a project carried out in 1998, Margy Dyas, at the time a social worker in the North Eastern Health Board, based in Dundalk, undertook to explore the perspectives of six children between ten and twelve years old in relation to the access visits they had with their families of origin. Dyas was conscious of the dearth of research, particularly in Ireland, reflecting children's views of foster care and contact with their families of origin and the importance of including their perspectives when making any judgements or planning policies. The children were selected through their social workers and Dyas used methods that were as child-friendly as possible, interviewing the children but allowing them to use whatever medium they found comfortable to make their replies. For example, as well as talking, they drew or chose cartoons to represent their feelings, or wrote what they thought.

Dyas used the interviews to explore the children's senses of identity, their feelings about being in foster care, their knowledge about their families of origin, the frequency of their contacts with their birth families, what they thought about the venues in which the visits took place and their views about the meetings along with any suggestions about how to make them different or better. She also asked them to draw or write one wish about their birth or foster families.

In general, the children had what might be described as a strong sense of identity in relation to their families; they knew what their mothers and extended family were called, where they lived and what they did. However, a notable finding was the absence of contact with fathers for four out of the six children. While they had a good knowledge in general about their families of origin, only two children in the sample knew where their fathers lived. All of the children had contact with their siblings and expressed positive views about its value. Five out of the six had frequent contact and expressed a wish for eventual unification; the sixth child had only three-monthly contact with his mother and while he did not appear to aspire to return home, he said he would like his sister to join him in his foster family.

The children's views on the location of their visits illustrated that a range of options should be available. For some, the health centre or their foster home was the preferred venue, but others expressed a desire to have more variety in the environment and liked shops and other distractions. Some liked playing, some liked 'making things' and others liked 'just talking'. Dyas considered these findings to signify the importance of paying attention to the choices that children themselves made in order to make the visits more purposeful. She pointed out that children's views might vary as they pass through various developmental stages and that their needs and wishes may differ according to which member of the family they are meeting. All the children in the sample claimed to enjoy the visits although two of them found the travelling time very tedious. The importance of contact did not appear to diminish even when the children had been in care for several years.

In addition to interviewing children, Dyas interviewed seven social workers in relation to the organisation of access. Most saw it as an important and worthwhile function, albeit time-consuming and sometimes difficult. Some expressed regret that the business of making practical arrangements had to take priority over considerations about the process and quality of the contacts and interactions. Most commented that training and a code of practice or policy on access would be of great benefit to them.

Dyas acknowledged the limitations of her study on a number of counts. Firstly, the sample was small and secondly, the children who were selected tended to see their families frequently which may not be the norm for many children in care. However, the exploratory nature of the research highlighted a broad range of views held by the children and, to that extent, she felt that it was a valuable piece of work.

On the basis of her findings, Dyas strongly recommended that workers specifically elicit the views of children with regard to the way that visits with their families are arranged and managed. She also proposed that training should deal with the subject of access, and that local policy should be developed in order to provide guidance on best practice.

Conclusion

The projects discussed here have illustrated a range of potential strategies for greater parental participation in the child protection and welfare system. They have also shown, through the successful trial and implementation of proposed models, that while parents may still experience many of the difficulties that led them into contact with the child protection system and feel a range of emotions specifically related to their children's involvement with the service, they continue to wish for meaningful inclusion in their children's lives. The different studies highlighted the prerequisites for effective involvement and participation – respect for the views of parents, appreciation of their knowledge and opinions, acknowledgement of their importance to their children, understanding of their problems and sensitivity towards their feelings. While most of the projects concentrated on situations where children were being looked after outside their families, the same principles can be applied to parents in any situation where their children are the focus of concern.

The projects illustrated how small gestures like the offer of transport or busfares can encourage and enable parents to attend meetings and access visits, and how acknowledgement of their own problems and difficulties can engender a sense of trust. The anxiety experienced by parents about managing their children's behaviour together with the grief and guilt associated with having children cared for out of home was movingly portrayed. It was also interesting to note the enthusiasm with which staff in all the services under study responded to the ideal of involving parents and shared the tasks involved in setting up the project.

It is sobering to observe that even with the notable improvement in care facilities themselves and the positive attitude of staff, it cannot be taken for granted that parental involvement is high on the agenda of any service. As Clarke (1998) in her review of the services provided by the Sisters of Mercy argues, many of the parents of children in care come form the poorest sectors of society and may have direct experience of being in care themselves. They may lack the confidence to deal with those whom they perceive to be in authority, and are likely to be reluctant to initiate contact themselves. Clarke points out that it is not enough for residential centres to deal only with 'co-operative' families, but that they must at the very least give written information to parents, invite them to reviews while providing preparation and support and, ideally, invite them to undertake some parenting tasks like helping with homework. As Clarke points out, greater involvement with families not only demands change in thinking and attitude, but requires more, not less, staff activity in support and supervision, points that were clearly illustrated in the projects discussed here.

While the demanding nature of access work and the frequent difficulties encountered were not minimised, the projects on this subject indicated that the mindset of practitioners and carers together with their commitment to promoting good-quality access was as essential as the availability of resources to carry out the work. It was notable that despite a common perception that contact consisted of access visits with parents, many children availed of telephone communication and letter writing and valued contact with siblings whether they were at home or in alternative placements. Several of the studies emphasised the need to include the views of birth parents and children regarding the nature and quality of contact to take place. Once again, the issue of involving fathers received a high profile as several different projects showed that contact between children and their fathers, whatever the circumstances, was very much less frequent than that with their mothers.

It is understandable that professionals, burdened with the pressures of child protection work or the responsibility of trying to run a service with the increasing problem of retaining staff, may have reverted to traditional ways of dealing with parents. However, these projects have illustrated the necessity, which has now become established in policy and practice, to acknowledge the needs and rights of children and parents to remain involved with each other's lives, whatever circumstances led to their involvement with the child protection system.

=====13=====

Supervision, Case Management and Support in Child Protection Work

Introduction

The issue of supervision and staff care has been a recurring one in child abuse inquiries both in Ireland and the UK (Department of Health, 1993; Western Health Board, 1996; London Borough of Greenwich, 1987; Butler-Sloss, 1988). In focusing on perceived errors of judgement and omission along with poor case management, communication and recording practices, these reports have recommended improvements in professional support systems for all disciplines working in the field of child protection. Ironically, the inquiry reports themselves have engendered a further challenge for practitioners. Doherty (1996), commenting on the aftermath of child abuse scandals, acknowledges that staff are increasingly operating in the knowledge that every action and decision they take may, at some point in the future, be scrutinised and judged from the perspective of hindsight. However, notwithstanding the powerful and anxiety-provoking effects of public scrutiny and high expectations, there is a strong desire amongst professionals to maintain good standards of practice and uphold professional principles in order to provide the best possible service to children and families. In order to do this, they require a structure that can enhance professional development in a supportive environment.

The stress inherent in child protection work has been noted in child abuse inquiries, but in day-to-day practice its acknowledgement is not always regarded as compatible with individual professionalism. Morrison (1997, p.204) illustrates how staff who feel helpless in relation to their work experience a sense of shame and receive the message from their agencies that those in the helping professions are paid to be 'copers' and not expected to be in need of support. Yet, child abuse work can evoke very strong emotions not only of stress and anxiety but of personal pain, often mirroring the experience of the client. As Murphy (1997, p.250) points out, it is commonly assumed that service deliverers leave their individual selves at home and become truly selfless parts of the child protection machine.

Child protection work takes place in a complex environment, influenced at the same time by prevailing political dogmas, gender and social class issues, conflicting ideologies and priorities, and sometimes clashes between personal value systems and agency norms. By its nature, the work involves balancing scarce resources, not least of which is time itself. In addition, workers are increasingly dealing with organisational change. Within such a turbulent milieu, it is not surprising that a powerful effect of the work on staff can be the potential for distortion of reality and a loss of direction.

There is ample evidence in the literature to illustrate the dangerous professional behaviour that can potentially occur if staff are left unsupported (Dale et al, 1986; Reder, Duncan and Gray, 1993). In a study carried out in the 1960s that has relevance for all child protection staff today, Menzies (1961) observed the behaviour of nurses in busy hospital settings. She suggested that, in order to combat the unresolved feelings that could be triggered off by stressful events, staff tend to adopt strategies that she called 'socially structured defence mechanisms' which eventually take on an external reality. Some of these include depersonalisation, denial of the significance of the individual and the attempt to eliminate decisions by ritual task performance. Responsibility could also be disclaimed and consequently reduced, by the act of forcing tasks 'upwards in the hierarchy'. As Menzies pointed out, the negative effects of such defensive practices are considerable, inhibiting full development of the individual's understanding, knowledge and skills, and ways of dealing effectively with anxiety. Ultimately, she argued, the inhibition of self-knowledge prevents individuals from realistically assessing their performances, and creates a vicious circle, by impeding them from realising their potential or strengthening their self-esteem and confidence.

British research on cases where children were fatally abused also illustrates the distorted interactions that can occur between abusing families and child protection workers, often going undetected. Reder, Duncan and Gray (1993) identified 'disguised compliance' operated by families, where workers were unwittingly persuaded that risks to children had abated because the parents operated a sort of superficial co-operation, particularly if they acted in a friendly, unthreatening manner. Because of a natural tendency to respond positively to compliant behaviour and avoid conflict, workers were lulled into a false sense of security, not noticing fundamentally important issues like the absence of a child during a visit, or the lack of opportunity to observe a child's physical state or emotional well-being.

Morrison (1997), adapting Summit's (1983) theory of the 'child sexual abuse accommodation syndrome' offers an example of the way that staff stress can be 'accommodated' by workers in child protection. He shows how workers can go through the same stages of secrecy, helplessness, entrapment (where they see their self-doubts and anxiety as unprofessional), disclosure and retraction (where they feel abandoned and fear that they will be written off as incompetent). This pattern of behaviour leaves them stuck, unable to acknowledge their difficulties and ask for help, and thereby unable to act as effective change agents themselves.

Much of the available literature on this area concentrates on the pressure that child protection work brings to social work staff, but as Murphy (1997) points out, the tasks are not the sole domain of field social workers, and their primary responsibility in this area does not diminish the role of other professions and agencies. As he points out, the personal costs of the work, in terms of anxiety and emotional distress, are felt by all staff participating in the network, and there is need for a flexible multi-disciplinary staff support system to be included as part of each child protection system.

This section will discuss a number of studies carried out in the area of staff support, case management and supervision in child protection work. The projects were conducted by a variety of professionals in different disciplines, illustrating the relevance of these elements to child protection work carried out in multi-disciplinary settings.

Stress in child protection work

Two non-social work professions in which stress has been associated with child protection work are An Garda Síochána and public health nursing. Two similar projects were carried out on the requirement for and use of support in work with sexual assault cases in 1996 and 1998 respectively by Gillian Ryan, then a member of the Domestic Violence and Sexual Assault Unit based in Dublin, and Mary Doherty, a uniformed Garda sergeant based in South Dublin. Ryan's study was carried out in a North Dublin District by means of qualitative interviews with an (unspecified) equal number of male and female members. Doherty's was conducted in a South Dublin District and used a survey method on thirty-six Gardaí representing six stations, from which she received twenty-two replies. An interesting gender issue arose in relation to the responses. Doherty's questionnaires were distributed to more female than male members, but as it turned out, more male Gardaí responded. As the sergeant in each area was responsible for distributing questionnaires, Doherty had no idea of the identity of the respondents. While Ryan interviewed equal numbers of male and female members, she found that she had to structure her topic guide differently for male Gardaí as they were far less talkative and needed to be drawn out more on topics. It could be inferred from this that male Gardaí are just as subject to stress as their female colleagues, but less willing to discuss their experiences when their identity is known to the researcher, particularly when they are speaking face to face with him or her.

Both pieces of research aimed at establishing the level and nature of stress experienced by Gardaí in the course of investigating sexual abuse crimes, and Doherty's project also sought to establish whether members were aware of and willing to utilise existing support networks within the force. Three types of employee assistance services existed at the time in An Garda Síochána. There was firstly, a welfare service, consisting at the time of four trained welfare officers (including three Gardaí), for the entire force. There was also a 'peer support' service, consisting at the time of a Garda in each division who had been on a ten-day training course and whose role was to respond on behalf of local management whenever a member was the victim of a traumatic incident, or was experiencing the effects of post-traumatic stress disorder. While this service was available to all members, Ryan considered that it was primarily aimed at Gardaí who had been called to armed robberies or fatal traffic accidents. The third type of support service was the 'contact persons' system which was set up to address complaints of sexual harassment. This system was operated by a number of designated female Gardaí throughout the country.

Both Ryan and Doherty established through their findings that female Gardaí were carrying a higher proportion of sexual abuse cases than their male colleagues. As Doherty's study highlighted, the majority of respondents felt this division of work to be understandable but in practice unnecessary and inappropriate. This finding had also been encountered by Heller (1997) in his project carried out in a different Garda District. A cause of frustration identified in both studies was the expectation that the women members had to carry these cases in addition to all the other work they shared with male colleagues. Participants in Ryan's study expressed frustration that if the cases suddenly became what they described as 'high profile' and due for hearing in a higher court such as the Central Criminal Court it was likely that they would then be managed by a sergeant or the District Detective Unit, leaving them with a lesser role to play.

Both studies indicated that stress about various aspects of their work is commonly experienced by Gardaí and is particularly associated with the investigation of sexual assault and rape. Likewise, both studies reflected a lack of support from senior officers to Gardaí working on sexual assault cases. This replicates a research finding in the UK by Gallagher et al (1996) who attributed it to the lack of experience or training in child protection on the part of senior officers. Respondents in Doherty's survey considered the following elements of their work to be most stress-inducing:

- listening to details of sexual abuse or rape
- dealing with the families of victims
- working in isolation on sexual assault cases
- a general feeling of lack of control over the response of the health board, the Director of Public Prosecutions, or the predicted outcome of a court case
- taking statements from alleged abusers.

While the respondents in Ryan's study believed that there was satisfaction to be gained when a perpetrator was convicted, they experienced immense frustration at the low numbers of prosecutions generally and were often ambivalent about the value of their work. This was exacerbated in cases where the investigatory process was obviously distressing for the victim. In some cases, according to the Gardaí in Ryan's study, the process of making a formal statement could be a healing one for the victim but the investigating Gardaí could find it an anxious, embarrassing and unpleasant experience despite the professionalism they displayed during the process. They were often appalled at the level of abuse and its effects on victims. Most Gardaí in Ryan's study felt they could not do that type of work on a full-time basis and believed it would cause them mental health problems and difficulties in their personal relationships.

When Doherty explored the level of Garda awareness about existing support systems and their willingness to utilise them, she found that only half of them knew of the Welfare Officers, one-third were aware of peer supporters and only one out of twenty-two respondents knew about the contact persons system. When asked what mechanisms they would use to deal with stress, the respondents said their normal methods of coping would consist of talking to family and friends, participating in sport and going for a drink. Nobody at all reported using the Garda support systems. When this was explored, it appeared that confidentiality was a major issue, together with a suspicion that admitting to stress might harm individual career prospects. There was no evidence whatsoever that existing welfare and support services breached confidentiality, but the perception of respondents still indicated a lack of trust.

Both studies made recommendations for training. Ryan suggested that officers in supervisory roles should be trained to communicate more supportively with their subordinates. She believed that this would be a cost-effective strategy, ultimately reducing stress and stress-related absence from work. Doherty recommended dissemination of leaflets giving contact details about confidential services within the force, as well as courses updating members on existing support systems. She recommended that the courses would also cover the symptoms and effects of stress and trauma as well as self-awareness and coping techniques. Doherty felt that support services should recognise that staff members may have themselves been the victims of sexual abuse or have difficulty with the subject of sex, sexuality or sexual abuse. She also recommended the appointment of a psychologist in the force to monitor vulnerable members and examine the area of stress and its implications both for sufferers and the performance of the force.

The fact that the two studies on the impact of sexual abuse work on members of An Garda Síochána studies were carried out in separate areas using different methods adds considerable weight to the value of the findings.

In each of these projects, participants pointed out that the question of their emotional and psychological reactions to child sexual abuse investigations was an issue that had never been considered either by themselves or anyone else, testifying to the commonly held notion that police officers are always able to cope emotionally with the nature of the crimes they encounter.

Another area where the acknowledgement of work-associated anxiety has tended to be low is public health nursing. A project carried out in 1992 by Triona Leydon, at the time a public health nurse in the North Western Health Board, claimed that while research into stress in nursing has concentrated on technical and 'high visibility' areas such as intensive care and neo-natal care, very little investigation has been carried out into what she describes as the 'less glamorous' and less financially supported community nursing services. She interviewed ten public health nurses to explore their perceptions of their professional roles, and devise strategies for supporting them and preventing burnout. Most of the nurses were covering large patches in remote rural areas, so that issues like isolation and difficulties in accessing management support were particularly relevant.

Leydon's project illustrates the varied role of the public health nurse and puts into context the number of other responsibilities carried by them in addition to their child protection roles. In 1992, when this study was conducted, very little of the Child Care Act, 1991 had been implemented and there had been virtually no training about its implications for public health nurses. It did not therefore feature very markedly in their perceptions about their professional roles. However, they had a strong commitment to preventive work with vulnerable families, an area that they felt was moving quickly out of their grasp due to increasing demands on their time.

The amount of record keeping, much of which was regarded by the nurses as unproductive and unreflective of their input into families, caused them immense frustration. This was compounded by the absence of secretarial back-up and access to computers.

What was perceived as the existence of a 'major divide' between public health nurses and senior health board management was believed to have a number of implications. It was felt that work was imposed on them without prior consultation and that there was no opportunity for them to have an input into planning services that were relevant to their practice, such as immunisation schemes or patient care plans. Lack of access to senior or superintendent public health nurses was a problem for them because of the geographical distances involved. The lack of supervision was cited as a missed opportunity for dealing with professional issues and allaying anxiety.

The need for further training in medical areas such as midwifery, public health and child care was also identified by the nurses participating in the project. Though Leydon acknowledged the limitations of her study size, she noted that a high proportion of nurses participating in it suffered a lot from headache, backache, skin problems and gastro-intestinal problems. She speculated that these were job-related, due to relentless pressure and rushing around, having to lift heavy patients without assistance, and constant contact with heavy duty cleaning materials.

Leydon made a number of recommendations which she presented to health board management in her area. These included:

- reduction in administrative work by provision of secretarial help and computers
- participation of public health nurses at a decision-making level in the health board
- availability of a senior or superintendent public health nurse for consultation
- attention to health and safety matters, for example, training on the prevention of back injury and provision of protective gloves and garments
- training on nursing and child protection issues
- resources to carry out preventive work, such as mother and toddler groups
- a system of peer supervision, to deal with professional issues.

Leydon presented her findings to management in the North Western Health Board with the expectations that a review of the public health nursing service would follow.

Supervision and training of public health nurses

Supervision of staff is regarded as a crucial element in the process of imparting knowledge, understanding and skill to front-line workers. It achieves the function of management, support and education, and importantly, provides a mechanism to enable staff to cope with the anxiety that naturally occurs in such an uncertain area of work. The need for supervision of public health nurses' practice has been consistently identified in studies carried out in different health boards. It has also been highlighted in child abuse inquiry reports. In the UK, the Carlile (London Borough of Greenwich, 1987) and Aston (Lewisham Social Services Department, 1989) inquiries specifically mentioned the need for professional supervision of health visitors, and in Ireland the Report of the Kilkenny Incest Investigation (Department of Health, 1993) emphasised the need for all child protection staff to have regular supervision. A number of projects considered in this publication indicated its absence in day-to-day practice (Devlin, 1993; Meehan, 1994; Madden, 1997; Leydon, 1992). Taking this idea further, two action research projects were conducted in which models of supervision were piloted. One was carried out in 1996 by Breda Ryan, then a senior public health nurse in the Mid-Western Health Board, and one in 1997 by Margaret Fitzpatrick, then a senior public health nurse in the Eastern Health Board. Both studies identified not only the absence of a supervision structure within public health nursing, but what might be considered as traditional obstacles to its implementation. Quoting Cloke and Naish (1992) Ryan points out that community nursing is normally associated with professional autonomy, a notion not consistent with surveillance by management. In a similar vein and referring to Byrne (1994) Fitzpatrick asserts that clinical supervision has often been linked by nurses to inspection, criticism and discipline. Both of these perspectives may have operated to slow down or even impede the implementation of a supervision structure for public health nurses.

While they raised many similar issues, the two action research projects differed in some fundamental respects. Ryan's study was aimed at highlighting key issues relevant to public health nurses in child protection and welfare work *through* a supervisory process, whereas Fitzpatrick's focused more on the *nature* of the supervisory process. Both authors carried out focus group discussions with nurses over whom they had direct line management and were aware of the limitations that this may impose. However, in each case every possible effort was made to establish internal validity in the research process and avoid bias. Ryan carried out four group sessions with an average attendance of between seven and eleven public health nurses and Fitzpatrick conducted two focus groups and five pilot supervisory sessions with six public health nurses.

Some of the highlighted concerns were common to the two projects, and had also been raised by the participants in Leydon's (1992) project. Public health nurses in both areas acknowledged their increased duties under the Child Care Act, 1991, including more frequent attendance at case conferences and monitoring of vulnerable families, often without the input of any other discipline. Anxiety was expressed in relation to the likely impact of their new responsibilities on their relationship with the families, about their duty to refer suspicions of child maltreatment to the child protection notification system and the requirement for them to inform families of their actions. The need to acquire knowledge and skills through ongoing training was recognised in both groups, particularly in relation to record keeping, assessment of vulnerability and articulation of 'gut' feelings as well as policies and procedures and provision of evidence in court cases. Inter-agency and inter-professional tensions and the perennial problem of not receiving feedback from social workers following referral were also raised for discussion. In both studies, dissatisfaction with the level of support from management was expressed, particularly when compared with that offered to hospital nurses. Public health nurses in the two areas highlighted the need for access to support services, and in Fitzpatrick's study, it was decided that they should pursue the matter with evidence-based proposals for service provision. Both Ryan and Fitzpatrick acknowledged that supervision could only go so far in resolving these issues, but argued that it provided a useful channel through which their concerns could be made collectively visible and communicated to management.

Both of the supervision models proposed in the studies included sessions where actual cases could be discussed by the nurses in a group setting. These were considered beneficial in terms of the support they offered individual practitioners in difficult situations as well as the opportunities presented for sharing experience, knowledge and skills. Ryan in particular found the sessions valuable as venues for deciding on standardised nursing practices like record keeping, identification of vulnerability, report writing and criteria for visiting. In Fitzpatrick's project, in addition to the case discussion, there was a formal presentation in each session on what she described as an educational issue, like report writing, and these were considered valuable by the participants. Her group also agreed to develop standard definitions and referral practices.

Similar dynamics appeared to operate within the groups involved in both projects. Ryan found that the mood in her groups vacillated between great enthusiasm and anger at the outset. When participants were given an opportunity to vent their feelings on particular grievances, she found that constructive discussions developed and a lot of learning appeared to take place. Fitzpatrick found that, in keeping with the literature, the public health nurses in her project were initially very suspicious and uneasy about the concept of supervision, seeing it in critical and negative terms. However, they became quite comfortable with it as the research progressed.

Both projects recommended continuation and development of the supervision model that had been proposed. While these two pieces of action research highlighted the need for and value of supervision, the number of issues raised within the sessions underlined the need for a strategy whereby the concerns of public health nurses can be communicated, illustrating a deficit in their organisational structure that had not previously been as obvious. Fitzpatrick noted the need to provide for consultation between individual nurses and management, particularly in crisis situations, and Ryan pointed to the need for case review at a multi-disciplinary level in addition to supervision groups.

The projects enabled both Ryan and Fitzpatrick to identify other areas requiring attention, including guidelines clarifying the role of public health nurses in child protection, the need for public health nurses to have access to family support services, the requirement for certain types of uni- and multi-disciplinary training, the development of strategies for inter-agency co-operation and systems for case review.

The issue of training for public health nurses in child protection and welfare is clearly an important one, and was the subject of a project undertaken in 2000 by Mary Kingston, at the time a public health nurse in the East Coast Area Board of the Eastern Regional Health Authority. Kingston's study aimed to identify the specific training needs of public health nurses operating under the Child Care Act, 1991. She decided to focus specifically on the area of report writing and giving evidence in legal proceedings as this was an area where public health nurses were becoming increasingly involved.

Kingston used qualitative and quantitative research strategies. She conducted a focus group with nine public health nurse colleagues, but prior to doing so, had administered questionnaires to the same participants and, in addition, a group of non-nursing professionals including social workers, child care workers, psychologists and pre-school services officers. The questionnaire survey aimed to establish the level of legal training that had been undertaken by each professional group. The results showed that while social workers had received specific legal training at undergraduate and post-qualifying levels, they still found the experience of report writing and giving evidence to be very daunting and challenging. The child care workers reported that they had received no training and considered themselves to be too incompetent to appear in court. The two psychologists who were surveyed had both had pre- and post-qualifying legal training but had found it unhelpful when it had been delivered by trainers with no experience of child welfare issues. While one of the pre-school services officers had received legal training, this had been in a separate context where she had been involved in delivering a multi-disciplinary child protection training programme herself. It was notable that the public health nurses in the survey had received no training at all.

Other projects reported here have indicated the importance placed by public health nurses on 'gut feeling' in relation to assessments. The nurses in this study were no different and the focus group discussion identified the difficulty of framing intuitive responses to vulnerable situations in a manner sufficiently compelling for court proceedings. They expressed concern at the prospect of being named as key workers in supervision orders, particularly in cases where the public health nurse was the sole professional involved with a family where children were considered to be at risk. All the focus group participants identified their lack of confidence in report writing, identifying the need for clarity regarding both the purpose and the required content of court reports.

Four of the nine public health nurses participating in the focus group had appeared in court on behalf of the health board over the previous five years.

All claimed to have felt ill-prepared and unsupported, and had found the pre-court assurances offered by the solicitors to be of little use. They felt resentful that the expectations held of them by the health board were not matched with guidance and direction about how to handle the process. They were frustrated and annoyed, in all four cases, that they had not been automatically informed of the outcome of the court proceedings and had to make, in some cases, repeat phone calls to find information. In one case, they had only learned of the outcome from the family whose child was the subject of the court case.

Kingston noted that the provision of training for child protection court work was inconsistently offered to different groups of professionals with divergent practices operated by different boards. She recommended the provision of co-ordinated training to be delivered at a multi-disciplinary level, incorporating report writing and specific preparation for court appearances. However, she acknowledged that training alone will not improve the child protection practices of public health nurses in the absence of role clarification, controlled case loads, regular supervision, professionalism, co-operation between disciplines, support from management and a satisfactory administrative structure.

Supervision of social work practice in child protection
While supervision has been more traditionally associated with social work, child abuse inquiries in Ireland have shown that it is not always carried out on a consistent basis (Department of Health, 1993). It is also necessary to ensure that the quality of supervision is appropriate to the area of work being undertaken (Gadsby-Waters, 1991; Hughes and Pengelly, 1996). A project on supervision practices in child protection social work teams on a national level, culminating in the development of a supervision model, was carried out in 1991 by Pat Kenny, at the time an acting senior social worker in the North Western Health Board. This work was carried out prior to the publication of the Report of the Kilkenny Incest Investigation, the Kelly Fitzgerald report and the West of Ireland Farmer report. However, Kenny had identified the recurring themes in British child abuse inquiries, notably those examining the Beckford, Carlile and Cleveland cases. He found some of the conclusions from these inquiries to be over-simplistic, failing to acknowledge the complexity of the social work task by assuming that adherence to legal requirements was a primary consideration. However, he noted the frequently highlighted lack of policies and frameworks for the conduct of child protection work and speculated that the same situation may apply in Ireland. Another of his concerns was the lack of explicitness around the theoretical perspectives and models for decision making and intervention that tended to

exist in relation to child protection work generally. In his view, a more visible policy framework together with greater clarity of purpose and understanding of the process would empower social workers and reduce their sense of being overwhelmed and directionless.

Kenny carried out his project in two stages. He surveyed all senior social workers, consisting of thirty-two, in the eight health boards that existed at the time. With the exception of five head social workers in the Eastern Health Board area, these social work managers were responsible for the supervision of social work staff. He sent the same questionnaire to the thirty-two directors of community care. The purpose of the survey was to ascertain the perceived level of support available to social work staff to deal with stress, the existence or otherwise of standards for social work practice and the nature of supervision practices. Kenny planned to evaluate the process of supervision of two social workers his own area. His aims in regard to the latter were only partially fulfilled as the task proved more complex than anticipated, but yielded some interesting data.

Questionnaires were returned by twenty-two senior social workers, and nine directors of community care. According to the findings, managers believed that high levels of stress and burnout were being experienced by social workers in over two-thirds of the areas involved in the study. These were manifested by frequent periods of sick leave, apathy, tendency to blame management for their problems, pessimism and negative attitudes to clients. The supports offered to the workers to manage their stress consisted of participation in team meetings, informal groups and case conferences, supervision and training. Kenny was critical of the reliance placed on case conferences to provide support for key workers, and cited literature to illustrate how these meetings can often intensify rather than correct dysfunctional processes (Hallett and Stevenson, 1980; Dale et al, 1986).

As Kenny had predicted, the majority of respondents to his survey indicated that no policies or procedures for child protection work or standards for social work practice existed in their areas. In his view, this deficit had implications not only for social work practice, but for the multi-disciplinary assumption of responsibility in child protection cases.

When supervision practices were examined, Kenny was surprised at the high priority ascribed to this area by managers, given the anecdotal evidence from informal discussions with social workers that seemed to indicate it featured low on managers' agendas. Overall, however, practices varied widely in relation to frequency and length of each session, the average being one and a half hours once a month. This, in Kenny's view was insufficient to deal with any more than the administrative dimension of supervision, and left little time for reflection or expansion of the workers' knowledge or skill base. He also questioned the value of supervision that took place in a context virtually devoid of policies and procedures. On the basis of his findings Kenny considered that social workers were receiving inadequate support and inferred a link between this and the high level of perceived stress.

For the second phase of the project, Kenny contracted to provide supervision for two social workers in his area to be conducted in individual and joint sessions over four separate days. They planned to address four areas:

- the social work task
- the clinical context
- administrative issues
- methods for evaluating progress.

However, establishing agreement between Kenny and the social workers in relation to the first two tasks proved so time-consuming that the latter two were not completed as part of the project. At the same time, Kenny believed that they raised interesting issues. Identifying the social work task provoked discussions about the conflict between the policing and therapeutic aspects of the work and illustrated the ambivalence of the workers. Ultimately, they agreed upon a definition according to which the social workers described themselves as 'being involved in empowering individuals or groups of individuals to negotiate various social systems'.

Undertaking the second task, both social workers had difficulty in identifying a particular theory or model of work that they consistently applied. Kenny used an example to show that one of them was using a systems approach. However, in failing to acknowledge this fully by consciously exploring all the dimensions of the theory, the worker had jettisoned it prematurely in response to a challenge and became unsure of how to proceed. Kenny concluded that practice was not being informed by theory, but was shaped in response to current circumstances.

While it was not possible to cover the areas of administration or agree on methods for evaluating the exercise, he was optimistic about the usefulness of his supervision model. The social workers involved had shown enthusiasm for continuing the process, and it was planned to develop it further.

Kenny acknowledged the limitations imposed by the short time scale of this study and recommended that further research be carried out on this subject. He suggested that the impact of caseload sizes, difficult cases and the links between sick leave and stress should to be explored further, along with methods for maintaining and improving inter-agency co-operation. He warned against the assumption that implicit policies and procedures existed and strongly recommended the formalising of such protocols on at least a regional basis. These should include, in his view, an explicit statement about professional tasks and objectives with children at risk. Finally, he recommended the provision of supervision that identifies, in a reflective sense, professional tasks and objectives with children at risk. This, he believed, would help social workers gain a more positive perspective of the intrinsic value of their practice.

The implementation of regional and national child protection guidelines has become widespread since 1991, when Kenny's study was undertaken. These have provided at least an administrative and practice base for supervision. However, his findings in relation to the need for a structure to focus on practitioner's theoretical reflectiveness and self-awareness in relation to the ambiguities and dilemmas inherent in child protection work are both enduring and useful.

Support from colleagues was identified by the participants in Kenny's project as a means of reducing stress. This is a factor highlighted by a British academic, Andrew Pithouse (1987), who conducted ethnographic research on social work norms and practices. The 'collegium' is the term Pithouse used for the collective entity from which social workers drew support and validated their professional identities. In a project on the provision of supplementary supervision for social workers carried out in 1994, Breda Dunne, at the time a social worker in the North Eastern Health Board area, sought to formalise the informal consultation and collegial support offered by practitioners to each other. She was responding to a perceived gap in the availability of supervision from the senior social worker and the needs of team members in the absence of a team leader post in the area. She designed a project whereby supervision was provided by an experienced social worker (herself in this instance) to less experienced and more recently qualified staff. The process was not intended to replace supervision by the senior social worker, but to offer additional support and guidance in a more accessible fashion. While the need for a practice like this has largely been obviated by the appointment of team leaders in all community care areas over the past five years, it raises interesting issues for supervisors. The model may also be of interest to practitioners in other disciplines, or non-health board agencies.

Dunne planned her project in stages, the first being the administration of a questionnaire to her five colleagues in order to assess their supervisory needs. She then planned and conducted four individual sessions each with five workers and two group sessions with all of them. She underwent two supervision sessions with her senior social worker and administered an evaluative questionnaire at the end of the project.

In order to clarify the boundary between her own function as a supplementary supervisor and the line management role of the senior social worker, Dunne agreed a contract with the social workers, to the effect that communication between them and the senior social worker would remain unchanged and that he remained responsible for the management of all cases where children were at risk and where legal proceedings were under consideration. It was also agreed that a list of cases discussed at each session would be made available to the senior social worker, and that management issues would be reported directly to him.

In response to the initial questionnaire, workers confirmed that they considered supervision to be encouraging, supportive and to have positive effects on the quality of their work. Most of them felt that they were not receiving adequate individual supervision, a particular frustration being the amount of interruptions that occurred during it. Its relative scarcity in relation to their needs was viewed to be a cause of anxiety, forcing them to inappropriately use team meetings to release frustration and stress. The social workers expressed a need for more formal, structured supervision that would be focused and offer feedback, support and recognition and sharing of responsibility.

During the individual sessions with the participants, Dunne addressed the areas of case management, case closure, engaging with clients, working with involuntary or resistant clients, planning for children's long-term care, assessment of child neglect and issues arising from working with child sexual abuse. She felt confident after the sessions that she had been able to facilitate the workers in appraising their interventions and planning their work and had been able to positively reinforce their achievements.

The group supervision consisted of case presentations and discussions. Norms about confidentiality needed to be established, and once it was acknowledged that each case discussion would be limited to a certain period of time, the outcomes appeared to be useful in terms of the feedback and advice given to each worker. Dunne found that the most important elements of her own role were time-keeping, ensuring equal participation and pulling together the various themes discussed.

During her own supervision session with the senior social worker, Dunne was able to deal with her anxieties about 'switching perspectives' between the clients being discussed and the social work supervisees. She found that the process helped her to identify the dynamics that were operating between the workers and their clients, and gave her confidence.

The final evaluation, which was conducted by questionnaire with the participating social workers, indicated that they had gained affirmation for their work, and felt they had been able to share responsibility and ideas. In addition to support, they claimed to have gained information and practice knowledge, and that relationships between team members had become stronger. There was a consensual view in favour of continuing supplementary supervision with the suggestion of fortnightly individual sessions and monthly group sessions.

Though Dunne had been apprehensive about taking on a supervisory role with her colleagues, she encountered no difficulties in that area. The key elements that contributed to the success of the project were identified by her as a clear understanding of the boundary between her role and that of the senior social worker, the preparation carried out before each session, the clear focus of each session and the fact that the sessions were held away from base and therefore not interrupted. Essentially Dunne defined the function of supplementary supervisors as preventing the individual resources of the workers from becoming over-stretched and envisaged the primary task as the provision of certain support and guidance functions as delegated by the senior social worker. She recommended that the role could be filled by a team leader when posts became available. In the meantime, she suggested that the provision of supervision become a specialist responsibility allocated to an experienced team member with a pro rata reduction in caseload, or a rotating responsibility to be carried on a yearly basis by an experienced worker, with a similar pro rata reduction in case load.

Caseload weighting and review systems

One of the weaknesses of a supervisory system in child protection work is the amount of unobserved activity that takes place between workers and clients. This means that essentially, what workers bring to supervision sessions are their own 'versions' of the work. Pithouse (1987) highlighted the sensitivity of the process, where it is possible for practitioners to believe that, because their work is not visible to the supervisor, the focus of evaluation is therefore upon themselves and their methods of coping with the work. This can mean that their work with clients is portrayed in a way that conforms to the supervisor's expectations. Supervisors in turn know that they need to rely on the practitioner's account, and are aware that, if this is going to be forthcoming, the workers need to be able to anticipate a helpful response. Thus, both sides contribute to what Pithouse has described as the 'supervisory dance' which, if unchecked, can pre-empt any exposure or challenge of inappropriate practice.

One way of avoiding this type of unhealthy collusion around supervision is to have tools through which changes in cases can be made visible. Three projects focused on this area, two carried out in 1991 and one in 1993. The first one reported here is on the development of a caseload weighting system, the second concerns the implementation of a case review system and the third focuses on record keeping.

Manus McDaid, then a senior social worker in the Western Health Board in Co. Mayo, devised an instrument in 1991 for the weighting of child protection cases on two dimensions, the substantive content of the case, and the context in which the social worker was operating. He was aware that the number of cases carried by a single worker gave only a crude estimate of the demands on that worker's time. He also felt that issues of accountability could be addressed through systematic organisation of work, while assisting the worker to identify progress or otherwise, including any impediments to intervention.

McDaid began by reviewing cases that had been referred to his department over the preceding nine months. His aim was to highlight elements of significant and frequent social work activity and create an instrument for weighting them. In what he called Part A, he identified the following six aspects which featured quite significantly in day-to-day *practice* with individual cases:

- urgency of the work
- clarity of focus of the work
- clarity about objectives
- frequency and intensity of the work
- co-operation of the client
- statutory profile of the case
- frequency of contact with other agencies.

He weighted the cases by assigning a points scale to reflect the intensity of each aspect. For example, he gave a higher weighting when work was urgent enough to require an immediate response, and a lower one if it needed follow up within two days, or longer. The frequency and intensity of work was measured by noting whether there were more than two substantial contacts per week. Other factors were weighted similarly, with higher points being given for the most urgent, most intense and so on. By this means, he created a template to enable workers to identify the cases that demanded urgent and extended interventions. However, as he recognised, the substantive content of a case presents only one dimension of the demands it places on a worker, the remainder being determined by the availability, knowledge, skill and experience of the individual workers and the degree to which their environment is supportive. Therefore, in order to enable a practitioner to establish his or her work *context*, he created Part B, consisting of four categories as follows:

- existing caseload based on weighting
- workers' experience and knowledge of the relevant professional area
- availability and use of colleagues for professional support
- support of line management.

These were weighted in a similar fashion. For example, a high caseload would be regarded as twenty four or over. Experience and knowledge could be low, medium or good depending on whether they were newly qualified, had between one and three years post-qualifying or relevant experience, or had over three years experience.

For the purposes of the research this model was then adopted for use by social workers on his team for a ten-week period. They concentrated on new referrals, and those that had been made during the three weeks prior to the commencement of the project. The process followed four stages, firstly, the allocation stage where the worker and client met, secondly, when information had been collected and the worker and client agreed a contract of work, thirdly during the intervention stage and fourthly at the evaluation and review stage. Ten social workers used the tool on nineteen cases. The model was then evaluated, using a questionnaire.

Eight out of the ten staff reported that they found the Part A instrument useful, with two reporting mixed feelings. Nobody had found it too demanding of time, most had found it helped them locate difficulties in working with clients, and most found it an aid to planning their work. The two areas that evoked reservations were 'clarity of focus' and 'co-operation of client'. The former raised questions about the judgements involved in making the focus clear, and the latter because the clients could be a parent and a child in, for example, a child sexual abuse case, where levels of co-operation might differ. McDaid had originally put a higher premium on short-term work, and a lower one on long-term work. Responses to his evaluation suggested that this should be reconsidered. With regard to Part B, all the staff found it useful, though they expressed reservations about encouraging peer support as they felt it could be overused.

The social workers had found the tool useful in facilitating the decision to close a case, and had helped them to keep track of their work in the ones that remained open.

On the basis of the responses, McDaid decided to refine Part A in order to address the concerns about judgements and different levels of co-operation along with the premiums put on short-and long-term work.

In McDaid's view, two important issues were highlighted through the study, firstly, the link between a worker's practice and his or her training and experience, and secondly, the importance of staff support in relation to the quality of work undertaken. While he acknowledged that his study was limited by its brevity and scale, he felt it had illustrated the potential for use of case-weighting in social work.

Terry McAuley, at the time a social worker in the South Eastern Health Board, carried out a study in 1991 on the use of a case review worksheet. The worksheet was intended to assist social workers in establishing goals and reviewing their cases, facilitate planning, assist supervision and allow workers to evaluate their own practice and identify progress. It was planned that the worksheet would indicate the level of risk for clients and social workers in order to avoid overloading individual workers with stress-related cases. McAuley also intended the worksheets to help social workers distinguish between short- and long-term cases, and provide evidence for management in order to highlight training and resource needs.

The worksheets were piloted by four members of the social work team for three months, and were used with a mixture of five newly referred child abuse cases and five other cases where family support needs were evident but the case had not been categorised as child abuse. The sheet was designed to fit folded onto the inside cover of a case file, and contained boxed spaces for factual information, causes for concern, family and child factors, a risk category and an action plan. It also included explanatory notes to help ensure a consistent approach. It was anticipated that the sheet would help the worker clarify the reasons for referral, goals for intervention, resources needed and possible obstacles to the achievement of goals. The cases were to be reviewed at one month and three months from the date of referral. If the case still required involvement at three months, it would then be considered long-term, with appropriate reviewing plans. At the conclusion of the project, McAuley interviewed the four workers who had used the sheet and administered an evaluative questionnaire.

Feedback from the workers indicated that some changes needed to be made to the review sheets. Two workers found the sheet cumbersome, and felt it needed to be reduced in size without losing the categories; another suggested that there should be longer gaps between review periods to allow for progress to be made. Three out of the four found that the worksheet helped them to structure their intervention; they had a clearer sense of direction and a stronger commitment to action as a result of recording their goals. Various workers commented that the process had highlighted the importance of recording and reviewing cases, and all felt that they would consider using it on an ongoing basis, provided it was used in conjunction with regular supervision. It was suggested that the explanatory notes needed to be revised and clarified.

Reviewing the cases upon which the research was based, McAuley found some interesting trends. She noted that in all five of the cases that were eventually closed, there was evidence of lack of parental co-operation, even though there was some element of successful intervention in each. This led her to suggest that assessment and goal setting processes might be usefully reviewed with a view to more client participation which might ultimately engender greater co-operation. She also noted how the reviews highlighted the lack of community based family support services. One of the most important outcomes, in McAuley's view, was the way in which the review system not only facilitated social work intervention, but allowed workers to acknowledge and celebrate their successes.

The issue of parental involvement in child protection work raised by McAuley was also a core element of the project undertaken by Mairéad Holten, a social worker in the North Eastern Health Board, in 1993. Holten set out to devise a recording system that respects and promotes the rights of services' users while simultaneously meeting professional and agency requirements. Record-keeping is an essential tool for supervision and, as Holten's project shows, it performs not only the administrative task of accounting for practice, but can be used creatively as a means of elucidating trends in casework and highlighting areas for intervention. Though Holten's project was carried out prior to the implementation of the Freedom of Information Act of 1997, its aims were entirely consistent with the principles of the Act insofar as it sought to achieve openness and transparency as well as a sense of shared participation with clients.

Holten referred to critiques of social work recording practices, one of which was described by Kinnibrugh (1984) as 'verbosity', whereby social workers recorded their practices in detail in what was described as an unwieldy, expensive and often unethical fashion, the latter connotation being applied to those records that ignore citizens' rights to personal privacy. Critiques offered by the British Association of Social Workers suggested that records were often used as vehicles for self justification and the writing of unsaid feelings about clients. The case for user access of records had been proposed by Kinnibrugh, and Holten argued that his reasons for doing so were relevant to the Irish context. These were as follows:

- The ethical consideration implies that the information belongs to the client who originally supplied it and the client therefore has the right to control how it is used
- Access would reduce the power balance between worker and clients in which the former has an unfair advantage in any dispute through his sole access to the file
- Access would help to ensure the accuracy and completeness of information on which decisions are based and make workers more careful and objective in what they write
- The client's suspicions and discomfort over being written about would be reduced
- Sharing the record and recording might even have a therapeutic value.

Holten was also aware that pressure of work often relegates recording to a low position on the social workers' agendas, as evidenced in the Report of the Kilkenny Incest Investigation (Department of Health, 1993), and acknowledged that recording in an area that involved such a human content and amount of subjective judgement, while paying due regard to norms of confidentiality, is a very challenging task. She decided to adopt a model of recording that had previously been in operation in a N.I. Social Services Board, and implement it by means of a training day, facilitated by her senior social worker who had experience of using the system. This was to be followed by the piloting of the model by her social work colleagues and finally, it was to be evaluated.

The training day was attended by the senior social worker, five community care (child protection) social workers, and partially attended by two social workers from other health board services. It focused on:

- a review of the theoretical framework for open access and shared records
- an outline of the principles to guide implementation of the system
- description of the purpose and use of standard forms
- discussion of the issues raised.

Discussion at the training day focused on confidentiality, for example, where records would be stored, by whom and which persons would have access to them. It also raised issues about the nature of restricted information. Overall, Holten felt that the day had served to foster individual and team commitment, raising questions that could only be resolved by practical application of the system.

Following two team meetings, it was decided that each social worker would try out the system on two cases, employing a commitment to apply it as far as possible and generally be more open with service users about the recording process. Case files were restructured into six sections, each to contain the following:

- fronting sheet (to be signed by the service user as well as the social worker)
- contact sheets
- assessment data
- reports and correspondence
- restricted information.

Interviews with the social workers following the trial period highlighted some pertinent issues. For example, the need for written consent from service users for the release of information in certain circumstances was identified. While it was decided that approval would not be explicitly sought from other agencies to share third party information, it was proposed that letterheads should carry statements of the health board's intention to allow clients access to their files. It was decided that restricted information would apply in situations where it was advisable to keep the identity of complainants confidential, a practice that is consistent with the since implemented Freedom of Information Act.

The social workers who tried out the system agreed that the policy of openness helped them to focus their recording on facts and informed opinion, and to check the purpose of each entry. Modifications to all the individual forms were suggested, but it was agreed that the format should be retained.

Sharing of information with service users was not an entirely new experience for the workers, as it had been their practice to share reports prior to case conferences. However, they had not been accustomed to this level of openness. The trial period gave them the opportunity to voice some reservations. One was in relation to timing. It was felt that sensitivity would be required to judge the right moment to share case files, particularly if clients had been through a particularly traumatic or highly emotional experience. The fact that clients sometimes gave false information, or objected to their situations being recorded at all, was noted. The reluctance of anonymous referrers, or couples who are in conflict, to sign fronting sheets was also noted. The possibility of impaired mental or intellectual capacity of the service user, and the potential for threats of violence to workers, were also raised as challenging issues, and the rights of the child versus the rights of the parent in terms of access to information was also highlighted.

Holten pointed out that the workers' difficulties in sharing records was possibly associated with the absence at the time of a legal mandate (now imposed by the F.O.I), resistance to change, the threatening nature of the proposed practice, and dilemmas and ambiguities associated with the role of social work in statutory settings where it is sometimes perceived that aspirations to 'partnership' are unrealistic and dishonest. She was confident that the commitment made by the social workers would override their reservations in time.

Support in working with children in care
As this volume has shown, professionals engaged in child protection and welfare frequently express unease with the way that work tends to revolve around crises, leaving little time or opportunity to carry out direct work with the children who are the subject of concern. Chapter Eleven has detailed some methods of direct work employed in residential units and has illustrated their value. However, practitioners in the community can find this area of work difficult and challenging, and may not always make it a priority. A support group for professionals undertaking direct work with children was set up and evaluated in 1992 by Helen Culhane, at the time a social worker in the Mid-Western Health Board. The Mid-Western Health Board had conducted a series of training courses on working with children, with staff from different

disciplines, yet it appeared to Culhane that very few professionals had actually put their training into practice. Her aim in setting up the support group was primarily to encourage practitioners to undertake direct work with children, and her specific objectives were to improve and share professional knowledge of child development and growth and to give workers the opportunity to express their own feelings in this very demanding area of practice.

Culhane facilitated the support group, which consisted of a residential worker and two health board social workers. They met for six two-hour sessions and rotated the locations for meetings between their four workplaces. The group quickly discovered the importance of putting by specific and uninterrupted time periods for the sessions which were tape recorded in order to alleviate the necessity to take written notes. Each of them selected one child from their caseload and used the sessions to discuss their individual work with the children and share skills and advice. The principal areas of discussion included the usefulness of flow charts to plot significant moves and separations in a child's life, the impact of early deprivation on children's sensory development, ways of communicating the importance of direct work to foster carers, techniques for engaging children, the necessity for linkage between social workers and residential staff and the need to use simple and everyday objects in work with children. Importantly, the sessions enabled the participants to acknowledge the personal feelings of loss and pain that this type of work can evoke for practitioners as well as children.

At the final session, the participants expressed very positive views on how the groups had educated and supported them. They confirmed that the process had taught them to organise and plan clear goals, and had enabled them to cope with the intensity of feelings that arose during the sessions. They also felt that the sharing of experiences gave them confidence and a feeling of competence. Importantly, the group process had encouraged them to prioritise this type of work and persist even when it appeared, on the surface, to be progressing very slowly. The perceived success of the group confirmed Culhane's view that professionals undertaking direct work with children need to be supported in dealing with the many and complex issues that arise. Her principal recommendation was that learning from training courses should be nurtured and developed through the establishment of ongoing support groups in each area.

Staff care

Two areas of child protection work that require attention are the retention of personnel, and support for staff who have encountered violence from clients. These are areas outside, though not unconnected with, the remit of case management and supervision. They each require a concerted response at organisational level, and are fundamentally important to the overall health of an organisation and, by inference, the quality of service provided.

There has been, for several years now, a concern about the numbers of staff leaving child protection work, some of which has been attributed to the negative public perceptions emerging from child abuse scandals, where media attention focused primarily and narrowly on what had gone wrong. One of the consequences of a rapid turnover in staff is shrinkage in the proportion of experienced personnel, with the result that front line staff, forced to adopt premature responsibility, are often young and inexperienced (Doherty, 1996). Statistics published by the Mid-Western Health Board and the Eastern Health Board in 1998 indicate that the ability of health boards to retain social work staff in particular, is being seriously challenged.

As a manager leader in a densely populated area, Enda Fulham, then a social work team leader in the Eastern Health Board, carried out a study in 1997 on the retention of social work staff. In her own sector, one third of the staff had resigned during the previous year and this trend was replicated in the other sectors of her community care area. Her objective was to seek causative factors and recommend solutions to the problem.

Fulham points out that, at the outset of her study, she had been operating on the belief that employing organisations in the health and social service area had given little consideration to the issue of staff retention due to their traditional concentration on staff recruitment. This emerged from her own experience as a team leader where she had frequently been asked how many staff she managed or how many posts she had in her area, but had never been asked how many of her team had resigned. She was surprised therefore when she consulted policy documents produced in the past two decades, to find evidence that staff retention had been a matter of concern for at least the previous seventeen years, starting with the INBUCON management consultants report in 1982, reiterated in the Committee on Social Work Report (Department of Health, 1985) and appearing again in the 1995 Eastern Health Board report on the adequacy of child care and family support services (Eastern Health Board, 1996). All of these policy documents had made recommendations in relation to planning, training, career structures and review groups with a view to stemming the tide of social work resignations, but as Fulham observed, they had to date been largely ignored.

In order to explore the issue further, Fulham administered a postal questionnaire to ten social workers who had resigned from two different community care areas in the Eastern Health Board during the previous year. She sought their views in relation to three principal factors: their early experiences in the job, their reasons for leaving, and the conditions under which they would consider returning to the health board.

Two-thirds of the social workers in Fulham's survey had no previous experience of working in community care child protection work prior to starting their employment, and one-third received some form of induction training. Over two-thirds received a case load on their first day, with the remainder being given a full case load within one week. She noted that a high proportion of them, over two-thirds, had been recruited by the head social worker in the area rather than the personnel department, and that 90 per cent of them started work on a temporary basis. Not surprisingly, the social workers had experienced a range of emotions and impressions, including confusion, powerlessness, and a sense of chaos. Some complained of a lack of information about services or agencies in the area. Although the majority of social workers were professionally qualified, they felt that their training was too general and had ill-prepared them for the type of work they were expected to undertake. As Fulham pointed out, happy memories of the first twelve weeks of their employment with the health board were scarce, with the strongest perceptions being of stress, unmanageable case loads, lack of resources and feelings of worthlessness. However, on the positive side, most respondents commented on the high level of support offered to them by team colleagues, a point previously highlighted in this chapter by Dunne's (1994) project and replicating trends in the wider literature (Pithouse, 1987). The negative experiences just outlined were the factors identified by respondents as reasons for their ultimate resignation, in half the cases, within a year, and in most of the others, within two years.

When asked to suggest the sort of conditions that would entice them back to community care child protection work, the most often cited were reduction in court work, provision of resources, better management support, controlled case load and better structures. Factors like promotion prospects, better pay and a lower staff/team leader ratio were mentioned, but were given a far lower priority than the formerly mentioned factors. When asked to identify the elements that made their current jobs more attractive, the respondents named the lower stress levels, more access to resources, job satisfaction and a sense that they were 'not being treated with contempt and negative suspicion'. Eighty per cent of respondents commented that they would not return to community care child protection work under any circumstances.

In Fulham's view many of the negative factors highlighted in the study could be reasonably addressed at an organisational level. For example, induction training and a reasonable 'settling-in' period would help new staff to adjust. Fear and apprehension about giving evidence in court could be alleviated by the provision of legal training. She also recommended the implementation of the following elements:

- in-service training to cover management and professional development issues

- a clear statement of objectives, policies and procedures in child protection work
- strategies to move from child protection work to pro-active prevention work.

As Fulham argues, the attainment of these objectives would be expensive in economic terms, but could be justified in terms of the long-term costs of ongoing poor quality service to children and families in the context of rapid turnover and low morale in staff.

Violence to child protection staff and its aftermath

Child abuse inquiries in Ireland have demonstrated the level of violent and aggressive behaviour that can be directed at child protection staff. For example, the public health nurse visiting the house of the family concerned in the Kilkenny case was intimidated by the father, and the social worker visiting the family in the West of Ireland Farmer case was threatened with dogs, again by the father. A study commissioned by the South Eastern Health Board showed that nearly 90 per cent of the sample of professionals interviewed had experienced threats to their personal safety throughout the course of their work (Buckley, Skehill and O'Sullivan, 1997). Thankfully, incidents where injuries are actually inflicted to workers are few, but nonetheless, there is a need for workers and management alike to practise protective strategies when encountering potentially dangerous situations.

The effect of violence or threats of violence on child protection practice was the subject of the project undertaken by Pauline Underwood, a social work team leader in the Mid-Western Health Board, in 1999. Underwood was aware of the considerable body of literature about violence against child protection staff (Hester, 1994; Biddy, 1994), but had found a dearth of information on the impact of violence on professional practice following an actual or threatened incident. She was aware on an anecdotal basis that services could be withdrawn from a family following an incident, and was concerned whether, in such circumstances, the health board was fulfilling its obligations to the children in the families concerned under the Child Care Act, 1991.

Underwood interviewed seven staff members of the Mid-Western Health Board who had experienced violent incidents. These included five social workers, a child care worker and a public health nurse. She was aware of the sensitivity of her topic and its potential for upsetting her interviewees, and therefore took appropriate measures to reduce the negative effects. She chose interviewees who had experienced the event more than six months previously, and secured the agreement of the health board regarding the provision of support for them should it prove necessary. The identity of the interviewees was not revealed to management, and Underwood did not interview anyone for whom she herself had line management responsibility.

Underwood sought to identify the work context in which the violent incidents occurred, the agency's response in the aftermath of the incident, the extent to which the health board fulfilled its child protection functions following the incident and the strategies employed for so doing. Finally, she sought to make recommendations regarding child protection practice where there is a risk of violence to staff.

Underwood's findings replicated those of Fulham's (1997) project in the Eastern Health Board area, which showed that most workers operate in an environment characterised by high case loads and inconsistent supervision arrangements. In common with the South Eastern Health Board study (Buckley, Skehill and O'Sullivan, 1997), Underwood found that several health centres were overcrowded and insecure with no means of preventing clients from having direct access to offices.

The violent events that had been experienced by the interviewees consisted, in five incidents, of hitting and punching, sexual assault in one case, and threatened stabbing in another case. Four were perpetrated by three women (the same woman had assaulted two different workers) and three by men. Most of the respondents interviewed by Underwood had not anticipated the incident and in some cases workers were visiting for what they described as quite unthreatening reasons, such as making access arrangements or collecting a child's clothes. However, Underwood found that social workers may have taken risks even when violence had been a feature in the case, if the pressure of work dictated it. For example, they would sometimes call to houses alone, or out of hours. Though a specific section of the Mid-Western Health Board child protection guidelines was devoted to staff safety, six of the workers interviewed by Underwood were not aware of them. However, as she pointed out, a number of the incidents took place prior to the publication of the guidelines and also in the context of a less well-developed and resourced system of management, particularly in the social work department.

The project showed how the responses offered by managers in the Mid-Western Health Board to the incidents varied considerably. In the majority of cases, respondents had received a supportive and sympathetic response, but there were exceptions. In one case, a worker received no follow-up from management, and in another, the worker had to go unaccompanied to An Garda Síochána to make her statement. In two cases, the health board had not offered to pay medical expenses. Underwood pointed out that a minority of respondents still felt aggrieved at the lack of support for them at the time of the incident. Supports such as time off, counselling or the opportunity to transfer the case were offered in most situations. However, while these offers were made in good faith, they were not always effective in practice. Some respondents were critical of the expectation that they would avail of counselling from health board colleagues and one commented that the offer of time off was of limited value as no arrangements were made to cover her work in her absence. Likewise, in one case no alternative worker was designated, so the worker who had been assaulted had to resume contact with the client who had attacked her. Underwood focused on two areas where child protection practice was affected by the incident. One was the response of the health board to the families in question and the other was the overall impact on the workers themselves. In relation to the former, the violent incident resulted in withdrawal of services either temporarily or permanently in four cases, and three other cases were brought to court for various purposes, though this process often took several months. As Underwood points out, the child protection concerns had in most cases been quite serious, the incident itself had provoked no fresh comprehensive risk assessment and in some instances, it was several weeks before families and children were visited again.

The impact on individual professionals' practices was quite marked. All respondents acknowledged that the incident had affected their work. Positive changes were associated with high levels of managerial support at the time of the incident and resulted in workers being more security conscious and careful about how they handled potentially threatening situations, taking care to do so with another colleague and during working hours. A number of workers described adverse effects on their practice, citing how they had begun to prioritise their own safety over their child protection roles. High levels of fear were reported, along with tearfulness and a sense of wanting to get out of the job.

On the basis of her findings, Underwood concluded that the stressful environment in which child protection workers were operating affected their ability to both anticipate risky situations and recover from the aftermath of an abusive incident. She argues that the absence of firm policies for responding to workers who have experienced violence reflects a lack of serious consideration on the part of the agency. Given the correlation that she found between support and recovery, Underwood emphasised the importance of addressing this.

Underwood pointed out that the withdrawal of services or cessation of home visits to families following a violent incident decreases the health board's ability to fulfil its child protection responsibilities. As she argues, there is ample evidence from child abuse inquiries that closure of contact between statutory services and families can precipitate serious incidents of child abuse (Reder, Duncan and Gray, 1993), and the health board's expectation that families will instead visit the office or health centre is both inadequate and unwarrantedly optimistic. She pointed out that while Mid-Western Health

Board procedures suggest an 'alternative strategy', it offers no specific guidance on the nature of such strategies. Underwood highlighted a number of vital issues that need to be addressed:

- strategies to ensure that child protection concerns continue to be addressed in situations where workers are assaulted, including the use of supervision orders, automatic re-assessment of children's needs and child protection conferences
- dissemination of existing guidelines on personal safety of practitioners
- training and awareness raising regarding the dynamics of violence and methods for self-protection
- a protocol, to be consistently observed, to respond to workers who have experienced violent incidents, to include the provision of support to workers taking legal action against perpetrators
- appointment of a staff counsellor / health and safety co-ordinator by the Mid-Western Health Board.

Finally, Underwood advocated the provision of supervision to practitioners in order to help them identify the impact of violence on their child protection practice and devise strategies to minimise any negative effects.

Conclusion

The importance of good management in child protection work is the strongest message emanating from the works discussed in this section. It has clearly shown that the emotional competence of professionals to undertake their tasks in a stressful area of work cannot be assumed and it has also clearly illustrated the association between this factor and the quality of child protection work undertaken.

Interesting issues have been raised in relation to different areas of work. For example, the tension between acknowledging stress and conforming to professional expectations was highlighted in relation to An Garda Síochána, particularly in relation to male officers. The high level of physical strain experienced by public health nurses, together with the contrast between their working environment and that of hospital nurses was illustrated. Neither of these areas has received much attention in the literature, yet they are clearly prevalent, and require to be addressed.

One of the important questions raised here concerns the nature of staff supervision, a practice traditionally associated with social work. It has been shown that all professions in the child welfare area require the supports provided by supervision and the studies discussed here have highlighted its different and necessary dimensions. The need to conduct supervision in a purposive and structured fashion has been emphasised, ensuring that practice is reflective and informed and that issues of agency responsibility and accountability are addressed. The projects also demonstrate that paying attention to the emotional demands imposed by the work is a challenging role for management. It has been shown that fulfilling one of these functions without the others is simply not enough to either ensure a quality service or prevent staff from becoming overwhelmed. Useful models of supervision for different staff have been presented in this section. To support these, the tools of case-weighting, case review and recording practices have been demonstrated as useful methods of rendering work more visible and accountable to management and as a means of facilitating practitioners to carry out self-evaluation and clarify the focus of assessment and intervention. Importantly, they allow for affirmation of successful outcomes in different dimensions of the work.

As the projects have shown, the issue of staff retention continues to be a pertinent one for health boards. It must be acknowledged that, as well as the stresses inherent in the work, a significant underlying factor in the high level of staff turnover is the availability of a range of new positions following unprecedented developments in the child protection field. However, in another sense these developments have polarised some of the 'nastier' elements of the work from what are sometimes regarded as safer and more comfortable options. As a consequence, workers in the frontline can often regard themselves as simply serving their time before moving on. This unfortunately means that a crucially important area of work is often relegated to inexperienced and, it would appear, not particularly well-supported staff. This can only perpetuate what is clearly an undesirable and potentially dangerous state of affairs.

The need to create and maintain good standards of practice in line with new learning and development has been highlighted in the studies, along with the provision of infra-structural supports such as administrative assistance and computers to achieve greater efficiency. The requirement for refresher training courses for different disciplines, not just in child protection, but in other related areas, including public health and management, has been emphasised. However, probably the most significant factor made visible by the projects discussed in this section has been the interplay between the nature of child protection work, its impact on practitioners and ultimately the degree to which these affect the quality of work carried out. This is not a issue to be taken lightly in a context where the safety and welfare of children and families is the focus of intervention. Child protection and welfare organisations therefore have a responsibility to promote what Morrison (1997, p.206) terms 'emotional competence'. Strategies suggested by Morrison include the promotion of openness, facilitating the expression of 'healthy uncertainty and difference' and acknowledgement of the unresolvable nature of some problems. With good quality management, he suggests, an organisation can own anxiety but also know how to deal with it and equip its staff accordingly. Continuing attention to role clarity is an essential part of the model, as is the provision of an immediate response to an expression of distress or an unwelcome event such as a violent assault. Morrison emphasises that 'restoration' to positive functioning is important, even if this includes making clear the need for the practitioner to change his or her behaviour, or a review of the size and appropriateness of their workload.

The studies here are supported by a broad range of literature in the child protection area. They demonstrate that the costs of ignoring management and staff support factors will be difficult to retrieve. The ultimate goal is to create a healthy and energetic working environment, and enable staff to maximise the strengths and the potential of the children and families they work with rather than mirror their helplessness and distress.

=====14=====

The Child Care Act, 1991

Introduction

One of the most fundamental changes in the child protection and welfare system over the past ten years has been the implementation of the Child Care Act, 1991. The new legislation, which was to replace the Children Act, 1908, began its life as the Child Care Bill, 1988. It was duly amended and signed into law by President Robinson in 1991 to be ultimately implemented in full in December 1996. The Child Care Act, 1991 is the first piece of modern legislation in Ireland to deal with children in a comprehensive manner and, for the first time, as Ferguson (1995, p.21) points out, transcends the 'negativity' of the Children Act, 1908 which concentrated very much on crimes committed by and against children. Importantly, the Child Care Act, 1991 also clarifies the role, duties and powers of the health board.

Specifically, the Child Care Act, 1991 for the first time extends the legal definition of a child to eighteen years. In philosophical terms, its central, pro-active tenet is reflected in Part II, which, having regard to the principle that it is generally in the best interests of a child to be brought up in his or her own family, gives the health boards responsibility to actively promote the welfare of children who are not receiving adequate care and protection. It also enables them to offer voluntary care where appropriate, provide family support services and enable voluntary bodies to do so, address the needs of homeless children, provide an adoption service, and importantly, account for the adequacy of child care and family support services. In order to streamline the previous powers of the health boards, the legislation provides a range of new court orders, introduces the use of care orders and the possibility of obtaining assessments on children. Supervision and assessment orders increase the powers of the Gardaí in relation to children at risk. The rights of children are underlined in terms of the Act's obligation to regard their welfare as paramount in any disputes, their right to be independently represented in Court, and in modifications in Court procedure which are aimed at rendering the process more 'child-friendly'. The rights of parents, already enshrined in the Constitution, are strengthened in terms of the health boards' requirement to facilitate their access to children in care, and provide after-care support for children who have been in state care. For the first time, pre-school services come under the ambit of legislation, and the health boards are compelled to account for the adequacy of their services through regular reviews.

The Child Care Act, 1991 began its slow establishment in 1991. The first two sections, comprising Part I of the Act, empowering the Minister to bring the provisions of the Act into effect, and defining a 'child' as a person up to eighteen years old, were implemented in 1991. In late 1992, Part II was implemented. However, in keeping with the 'genteel pace of reform' (Gilligan, 1991, p.366) the full implementation of the new legislation was phased over several years. The sections dealing with protection of children in emergencies, the taking of care proceedings and regulations around the placement of children in care were not implemented for another three years. The procrastination which resulted in so many years of the Act remaining 'in the pipeline' rather than becoming operational appeared to have its roots in political inertia (O'Sullivan, 1993). The main impetus for its implementation eventually emanated from a child abuse inquiry described by Ferguson (1994) as a 'powerful symbolic event' which focused public and political interest on the subject of child abuse in a way that would ensure that it was unlikely to disappear for some time.

While most of the chapters in this volume have illustrated the operation of the Act in relation to different aspects of child protection and welfare work, this section discusses research projects undertaken in relation to specific sections of the legislation that introduce new mechanisms for use by practitioners. It concentrates particularly on the remit of the legislation to promote the welfare of children not receiving adequate care and attention and focuses on studies carried out in relation to supervision orders, assessment orders and the provision to appoint a *guardian ad litem*.

Promoting the welfare of children

One of the recurring themes in this volume has been the perception that despite the underlying orientation of the Child Care Act, 1991 towards promoting the welfare of children, the focus of practitioners and agencies providing services has been on the protective aspects of the work. Yet, as the literature increasingly shows, the latter can only be adequately provided if the former is fully considered. A central tenet of the promotion of welfare is the requirement to provide a full assessment of children and families' needs. This is an area that is currently receiving the attention of policy makers and researchers in the UK (Department of Health [UK], 2000; Horwath, 2000) where practitioners are now encouraged to explore the way in which children's physical, emotional and psychological development is facilitated or hindered by other factors in their environment. One of the core elements of a comprehensive assessment is multi-disciplinary involvement. This was the focus of a study completed in 1998 by Monique Liberman, a psychologist in the South Eastern Health Board. In the course of her research, Liberman demonstrated the important role played by the psychology service in her area in working alongside other child protection and welfare practitioners. The project sought to explore how much consideration in assessment was given to four areas of a child's life, namely

- the family's general welfare
- the attitude of the child's parents
- the child's broader environment and social network
- protective factors in a child's life.

As a basis for her research, Liberman drew on the assessment framework presented by Reder and Lucy (1995) which lays emphasis on the way in which stressors in parents' life impact on their maturity and psychological availability to children and the way in which children experience and can be protected from adverse factors. Her study was further informed by theories on attachment (Bowlby, 1982; Rutter, 1981) and she sought to explore the degree to which all these areas were considered by frontline workers in their investigation and assessment of child care concerns. Her primary objective was to see how far services were meeting the requirement of the Child Care Act, 1991 to promote the welfare of children.

Liberman used a case study approach to examine seven cases of children who had been ultimately referred to the psychology department because they were deemed to be experiencing behavioural and emotional difficulties. She interviewed the referring professionals in each of the cases, comprising two social workers, one school principal, two public health nurses and two general practitioners.

Analysis of the findings indicated that in relation to the first factor, the family's general welfare, respondents were more concerned with parent's socio-economic circumstances, their health and to a limited degree, their relationships than they were about factors in the child's early life, for example, stress during pregnancy and the neo-natal period. Liberman also found that respondents were less concerned about issues such as the stress caused to families by a child's anti-social behaviour. Interestingly, she found that there was a correlation between concerns about family privacy and lack of probing for detail about marital relationships and family background. When she examined the data in relation to parenting, including psychological availability of parents, Liberman found that the degree to which a child's physical needs were met took priority over attention to their psychological and emotional welfare. She noted that in two of the seven cases, the children themselves had not been seen, so that their relationship with their parents was not observable, and nor was the child's own perspective considered.

When Liberman analysed the interview data in relation to the child's environment and social network, she found that while the teacher and social workers had a good knowledge of the significant aspects of a child's social life and social network, the general practitioners and public health nurses took a narrower perspective, concentrating on health and education. In relation to the fourth area, the protective factors in a child's life, Liberman found from her responses that two important factors were largely ignored, these being the child's early attachment experiences and the part played by and the attitude of the child's father.

On the basis of her findings, Liberman recommended a course of in-service training directed at improving the quality and depth of comprehensive assessment. She suggested a strong focus on the following:

- factors of parental vulnerabilty
- evaluation of emotional factors in parents' ability to care for their children
- impact of parenting on all areas of the child's development and functioning including his or her ability to make friends and maintain a satisfactory social network
- evaluation of the protective factors in a child's life including early attachment, father's/partner's equal ability to care for a child and parental motivation to do whatever is necessary in order to meet their child's needs.

Importantly, from the perspective of the psychology department, Liberman emphasised the need for a joint and consistent approach from all professionals involved in child protection and welfare which would consider not only the physical/socio-economic aspects of a child's life, but their emotional and psychological welfare.

Supervision orders
The Child Care Act, 1991 reflects the constitutional right of children to be brought up in their own families. To promote and support this right, section 19 of the Act makes provision for a supervision order to be made where a child's safety and welfare is considered to be at risk, but where the risk is not considered serious enough to warrant separation from his or her parents. A supervision order permits a child to remain at home under the supervision of the health board, and stipulates the conditions under which a child will be visited. Anyone who breaches a supervision order is liable on conviction to a fine not exceeding £500 (€635) or imprisonment for a term not greater than six months, or both.

While the Child Care Act, 1991 was a long time in gestation, child protection professionals and policy makers had been, up to its implementation, generally positive about the potential of the proposed supervision orders. The three child abuse inquiries that focused on intra-familial abuse (Department of Health, 1993; Western Health Board, 1996; North Western Health Board, 1998) all implied that the absence of a legal provision for supervision by health boards added to the potential for abuse to continue. Each of the inquiry reports emphasised the very limited power that was available to practitioners to insist on either seeing the children or subsequently making interventions to protect them. There was an implicit suggestion that had such powers been available, more effective intervention would have taken place. It was also believed that the supervision order would provide more options for child protection workers and in some instances obviate the necessity to apply for care orders. Research had illustrated the high number of poor outcomes for children in care (Millham et al, 1986). Although the Child Care Act, 1991 was drawn up prior to the revelations of institutional abuse that have been a feature of the recent past (Department of Health, 1996a; Raftery and O'Sullivan, 1999) it reflected the ideal that children should only be separated from parents as a last resort.

It may be assumed, therefore, that consciousness about the potential of supervision orders was prevalent in health boards prior to the implementation of section 19 in October 1995. In preparation for its implementation, a study was carried out in 1994 by Máire Churchill, a social worker in the Mid-Western Health Board. Her objective was to explore the perceptions of field social workers employed in child protection work in relation to the future use of this legal measure.

Churchill interviewed twelve workers, including two community care child care workers. She asked them to identify cases where they felt that a supervision order would be appropriate, to identify the grounds for an application, and to discuss the reasons why they would go for that particular option.

The interview data reflected a degree of uncertainty on the part of workers as to the threshold for defining 'reasonable grounds' to justify an application for a supervision order. This was understandable given the fact that the provision had not yet been implemented. What was more certain, however, was the extent to which workers considered that the extension of legal powers provided would be useful. It was suggested that the orders would provide workers with the necessary authority to intervene effectively where children were at risk. Examples were given of situations where children were being neglected over the long term rather than experiencing acute physical risk, of where children had frequent and unexplained admissions to hospital or of where a history of violence existed in a family situation. It was considered by research respondents that resistant families, and those who had the capacity to adequately parent their children but had not taken full responsibility for carrying out this duty would be suitable candidates for supervision orders.

A factor that was considered crucial to the effectiveness of a supervision order was identified as parental capacity to change. Reservations were expressed in relation to the potential for inappropriate use of social workers' power and the undermining effect that extra vigilance might have in cases where parenting skills and self-esteem were limited. The limited usefulness of supervision orders was acknowledged in cases where, for example, children lacked the courage or trust to disclose abuse, where children were out of their parents' control or where parents were co-operative but possessed only limited capacity or motivation to meet their children's needs. A fear was expressed that supervision orders would be handed down as a 'lesser tariff' in cases where grounds for an application for a care order were not obviously and immediately life threatening, and that such orders could not provide round-the-clock protection. Likewise, it was feared that they would 'mushroom' and stretch an already over-pressurised service. Concern was also expressed at the unintended consequences for children if their parents were unable to pay the fine incurred through failure to comply with the supervision order.

However, in general, the workers were positive about the potential opportunity to observe children more closely at home, and to offer support to enhance their situation. The granting of statutory authority was perceived as a form of empowerment for health boards and for the role of social workers and child care staff generally. The need to consider the perspectives of children was considered as well as the need for the establishment of 'common ground' between workers and parents to ensure shared understanding of the terms of any order. It was emphasised that an effectively discharged order would need to improve the quality of a child's life or meet his or her needs in a very concrete way.

On the basis of her findings, Churchill recommended the development of clear guidelines for workers in relation to the type of thresholds to be reached before applying for an order. She strongly advocated training and the sharing of perspectives between workers operating the orders and the judiciary that granted them. She emphasised the importance of supervision for workers as well as an acceptance by all concerned parties of the limits to which a supervision order can achieve protection and promote the welfare of children.

Another study concerning the use of supervision orders was conducted in 1999, four years after the implementation of Section 19, and it usefully complemented Churchill's earlier work. It was carried out by Anne McCormack, a social worker in the Western Health Board, based in Galway. McCormack focused on five case studies involving sixteen children who had been the subject of supervision orders for at least six months. She sought to establish (a) the context in which supervision orders were sought and (b) the views of social workers involved regarding the effectiveness of the orders. She also sought to identify the main features of the cases and the process of professional intervention prior to and following the granting of supervision orders. McCormack elicited her data by studying the records and interviewing the social workers involved in each case, as well as interviewing the senior social worker for the area and the health board solicitor.

McCormack found that alcohol abuse and single parenthood featured in four out of the five cases, sexual abuse was a concern in one and domestic violence in another. Overall, the main concern in relation to the children was neglect of their basic needs. In each case the supervision order had been sought on the recommendation of the social worker. The reason for the application for supervision orders was, in all cases, non-compliance with the services, though it was clear from the data that the decisions to take this course were also determined by the unavailability of foster placements and a resistance on the part of professionals to the separation of children from their parents.

McCormack's findings highlighted some key issues. One is that the level of compliance with services did not particularly improve overall after the granting of a supervision order. While it was agreed that the children's protection and welfare were enhanced in three out of the five families, this was directly attributed to the increased assistance of extended family members in two of the cases. Yet, it was noted that the involvement of extended family had not been specified as a source of support in any of the supervision orders even though their existence may have precipitated its initiation. Overall, the social workers found the supervision orders useful in terms of the increased access it gave them to the children which, it was argued, would enable them to make a more convincing case in court should they wish to pursue a care order. The senior social worker and solicitor, together with most of the social workers, agreed that the involvement of the judicial system helped to convey the seriousness of the situation to parents. Another important observation made by McCormack was the lack of preventive and family support services available to the families prior to the granting of the supervision order. This led her to make the following recommendations:

- the provision of family support prior to the application of a supervision order
- attempts made to engage members of the extended family at an early stage
- training and supervision of individual workers to increase their awareness of the dangers and implications of disguised compliance, closure and withdrawal by parents.

Importantly, McCormack stressed that supervision orders should not be used to compensate for inadequate provision of resources by the health board, and that their limits should be acknowledged.

Section 20 reports

Section 20 of the Child Care Act, 1991 links with other legal proceedings, specifically those of the Guardianship of Infants Act, 1964, the Family Law Act, 1995 and the Family Law (Divorce) Act, 1993, in cases where the court has concerns over the welfare of children, or the 'delivery or return' of a child. Basically, this means that when a court has a concern over whether or not a care or supervision order should be taken out on a child in any custody proceedings under the above acts, it can adjourn the case and direct the health board to make an assessment of the child's circumstances. In making its report, the health board should indicate why, if it decides against recommending a care or supervision order, it has done so, along with its recommendations for any other service or action that needs to be taken in relation to the child.

John Edwards, a lawyer in the Mid-Western Health Board area, who had frequently represented the health board in child care cases, undertook a study on the use of section 20 reports in 1997. His motivation for undertaking the research stemmed from his perception that this frequently invoked judicial measure was being used inappropriately and ineffectively. He sought to find out, in his own words, if section 20 was a 'useful tool' or 'useless toil' in relation to the many hours of preparation that it entailed.

Edwards based his study on nine cases where judges had directed the health board to produce assessment reports on children under section 20. He had initially intended to undertake a study of the relevant health board records, but ethical reasons prevented him from accessing the files, so instead he confined his fieldwork to in-depth interviews with the five social workers and the four judges involved in the cases.

The data highlighted several important issues, firstly in relation to the manner in which the direction to carry out an assessment is communicated to the relevant health board. As section 20 directives apply to cases where the health board is not already involved, it is necessary for the court decision to be passed to the board in order for the work to be allocated and completed. Obviously this task needed to be completed expeditiously. Edwards found that while the social workers (who usually carried out the assessment and wrote the report) were normally informed of their duty by the health board solicitor, the manner in which the health board solicitor was informed varied from quite formal communication to serendipitous situations whereby he or she just happened to be in court when the direction was made. This was despite the existence of a specific communication protocol set out in the District

Court Rules, known as a 'Form 32'. Ultimately, these forms had been received by social workers in under half of the nine cases, and one social worker claimed that it was not uncommon for a month to pass before she was notified that a section 20 directive had been made on one of her cases. The interviews with social workers also indicated that in most cases, inadequate information was passed to them by the courts and they had to make extensive inquiries in order to inform themselves of the concern that precipitated the direction. Likewise, they were not supplied with terms of reference and normally had to guess what the judge specifically wanted to know. In general, it was assumed that the court was concerned that the child at the centre of the investigation was being abused by one of the parties contesting custody. The judges interviewed by Edwards agreed that clearer terms of reference should be given, and that District Court rules regarding the communication of information should be adhered to.

With regard to the requirement for the health board to comment on the desirability or otherwise of pursuing an order under the Child Care Act, 1991, eight out of the nine social workers interviewed felt that this issue was irrelevant and claimed that the judiciary had not been seriously contemplating making care or supervision orders in the cases involved, but were simply using the section 20 procedure as a means of getting a social enquiry report.[24] Two of the four judges who were interviewed by Edwards concurred with the social workers' perception, acknowledging that section 20 reports were effectively replacing social enquiry reports that had formerly been supplied by the Probation and Welfare Service.

Edwards found that there was considerable variation in the length and style of reports compiled by social workers. While the basic tasks of finding out information, interviewing protagonists, checking professional networks and sometimes interviewing children and relatives were similar, the depth of investigation and probing differed. Some reports were five to six pages, others as long as seventy pages, reflecting the worker's difficulty in working without a protocol. All of the judges indicated a preference for short and succinct reports of under six pages. Likewise, the time taken to produce the report varied, not unconnected with the variation in communicating the information that a direction had been made in the first place. While the judges indicated their willingness to be flexible in relation to the timing of reports, they suggested that four to six weeks should be the maximum time allowed.

---

[24] The Probation and Welfare Service had formerly provided social inquiry reports but had ceased to undertake this work since 1995 and courts were therefore unable to acquire them.

Finally, in relation to the actual presentation of the reports to the courts, most social workers indicated that their work was appreciated and received positively, though there were a few exceptions to this. However, some suggested that the judiciary did not realise the extent of the resources required to produce reports, particularly in the context of other demands on social workers' time. The judges interviewed expressed satisfaction with all the reports that they had received.

On the basis of his findings, Edwards recommended that health boards should focus their reports more narrowly on the issue of whether or not care or supervision orders are appropriate, in order to discourage judges from misusing the procedure. He also suggested that the health boards should lobby the District Court Rules Committee to ensure that Form 32s are modified and used to ensure fast and effective communication of information. He advocated that health boards should negotiate with the President of the High Court in relation to practice guidelines, including guidelines on the format and length of a section 20 report. In the same vein, he recommended that the health board and judiciary should jointly decide on a protocol for the presentation of reports in court.

Finally, he advocated training for members of the judiciary in relation to the Child Care Act, 1991, particularly focusing on the correct use of section 20.

The *guardian ad litem* system

Section 26 of the Child Care Act, 1991 provides that under certain circumstances, the courts have the power to appoint a *guardian ad litem* (GAL) for a child who is the subject of care proceedings under the Act. The guardian's principal role, while not defined in the Republic of Ireland, is taken to mean safeguarding the interests of the child and ensuring that all information relevant to the child's case is presented to the court. While the provision has been welcome, there has been criticism of the paucity of statutory detail regarding the operation of this legal measure and little research on its actual operation. A GAL 'system' has been operating for some time in Ireland, but in the absence of regulation, certain informal arrangements have determined the way that it functions and concerns have been expressed about the inconsistent manner in which the role is operated (Walsh, 1997; Shatter, 1997; Martin, 2000). Two projects to be discussed in this section were undertaken to examine the system, firstly as it functions in the republic under the Child Care Act, 1991, and secondly, as it operates in Northern Ireland under the Children Order 1996.

Firstly, a study was undertaken in 1998 by Grace Kelly, a manager in the ISPCC which is one of the agencies who have taken on a role in providing guardians for the courts. She sought to explore the perceptions held by two professional groups, social workers and guardians, in relation to the GAL service as it was currently operating in Ireland. Kelly initially intended to include all the country's health boards in her study. However, her initial survey of child care managers yielded a response from less than half of the boards and she was forced to confine her research to only three health board regions. Additionally, she found that it was not possible to interview both social workers and guardians involved in the same cases. Ultimately, she carried out in-depth interviews with five guardians and three social workers who had been involved in different cases where guardians had been appointed. Four of the guardians had been employed by voluntary organisations and one was a solicitor with a legal aid board. Four had acted once as guardians and one had acted twice. Four had been appointed by the court, and in another case, the child's solicitor had been appointed as guardian during court proceedings.

Kelly found variations in the manner of appointment and the number of visits carried out by guardians. This did not surprise her, given the absence of guidelines for the operation of the service. However, she did find a degree of consistency between the professional groups with regard to their support for and understanding of the role of the guardian and the positive effect on the outcome for the child. While most guardians found that communication with health boards was relatively smooth, some difficulties had been observed. For example, one of the social workers interviewed indicated that pressure of time prevented the exchange of 'quality' information. In general, social workers had found working with guardians to be a positive experience, though one respondent expressed anxiety about the independence of the guardian she had encountered in one particular case who, she believed, had accepted the health board's point of view 'too readily'. Similarly, some social workers felt that not only did judges have a poor understanding of the role of the guardians, but that they tended to treat them as expert witnesses while 'dismissing the professionalism' of health board social workers. Another reservation expressed by social workers concerned the ad hoc manner in which specific named guardians were selected by courts rather than appointed from a national panel.

Kelly's interview data also raised some issues about resources. Social workers were wary that GALs would make unrealistic or unattainable recommendations for the children they represented. Conversely, guardians felt that their independence from the health boards allowed them to make recommendations in the child's best interest rather than in line with the availability of resources.

Other reservations raised by both social workers and GALs included the lack of training and supervision for guardians as well as the lack of protocols and clarity concerning their role, a point already highlighted in Irish research. On the basis of her own findings, Kelly expressed concern about the informal manner in which decisions were made on whether or not to appoint guardians and the choice, in certain cases, of solicitors to act as guardians. She argued that knowledge and training in child welfare related areas as well as specific skills in working with children were essential attributes for the task. In conclusion, Kelly offered the following recommendations for the future development of the service:

- the development of practice guidelines for GALs
- the development of a manual for panel managers
- the availability to the courts of a list of panel members
- the development of appointments and complaints procedure
- the development of an appraisal system
- the maintenance of national statistics on the use of the service
- the mandatory appointment of guardians in child care cases, except where it is not deemed to be in the child's best interests
- the provision of training and supervision
- the production of annual reports
- the automatic entitlement of a guardian to legal representation in court.

The second study on this area was carried out in 2000 by Carol Anne Coolican, a legal aid board solicitor. Bearing in mind the reservations that had been expressed regarding the operation of the GAL system in Ireland, her research aimed to examine the Northern Ireland experience. Her ultimate aim was to make recommendations for a more streamlined system in the Republic. Coolican began her study by examining the legislation operating in N. Ireland including the Order establishing NIGALA (The Northern Ireland Guardian ad Litem Agency). She then compared the 1995 Children Order operating in N. Ireland with the Child Care Act, 1991. She later conducted interviews with a manager and assistant manager from NIGALA and presented her findings to her legal colleagues in order to ascertain their views on how to improve the system.

The most immediate and obvious finding in relation to the legislation was the difference between what Coolican termed the 'legislative imperative' to appoint a GAL under the 1995 Children Order and its 'discretionary corollary' under the Child Care Act, 1991. As she pointed out, the child's welfare in the Republic is legally constructed in terms of parental rights, duties or failures, and there is no automatic procedure whereby a child's wishes are taken into account by a court. She cited recommendations for constitutional change in order to balance the rights of children with those of their parents (Department of Health, 1993).

The choice in N. Ireland to establish a specialist agency for the delivery of the GAL service was, in Coolican's view, designed to give a degree of independence from Health and Social Services. It had succeeded in this endeavour by establishing, on a regional but uniform basis, a panel of professionals with experience in child care or adoption work. Under the agency's norms, in compliance with the legislation, a solicitor is always appointed for a child on the basis that his or her legal expertise and advocacy skills complement the particular skills of the GAL. As Coolican points out, while the guardian's role is investigative and advisory, the solicitor will advocate the view of the child and provide independent and impartial advice, acting on behalf of the child and in accordance with his or her legal interests and rights. GALs in NIGALA receive monthly supervision as well as individual and group consultation. Its independence is illustrated by the manner in which the agency, rather than the individual, is appointed by the court, thus avoiding the possibility of 'cosy relationships' developing between magistrates and GALs. Good practice norms are supported by a secondment scheme that operates between NIGALA and child care agencies which allows staff the opportunity to stay in touch with mainstream social work.

One of the concerns raised by Coolican's legal colleagues in relation to the GAL system was the comparative exclusion of parents from the legal process and the risk that guardians may prioritise the view of the health board social worker over that of the family when conducting their investigation, leaving parents 'locked into combat' with those who took their children. They also expressed concern about the way in which the child's views are presented to the court and the assumption that the child is always happy with his or her opinion being made so public.

While Coolican was unable, due to time constraints, to produce an actual model of practice, she was satisfied that her study represented the beginning of a process that may ultimately lead to the formation of effective policy in this area. She considered the N. Ireland scheme to be forward thinking and progressive, and made the following recommendations which are very similar to Kelly's:

- a legislative imperative to establish panels of GALs, together with an amendment to the Constitution to equalise children's rights in line with those of parents
- the establishment of an independent agency similar to that operating in Northern Ireland to ensure independence
- the establishment of a 'tandem' system of appointment of a GAL and a solicitor
- the development of policy and procedure, the identification of training needs and the appointment of a chief executive of the GAL agency prior to the commencement of the service
- the use of consultation by already existing agencies such as NIGALA.

Conclusion

While the studies discussed in this chapter apply to only a small number of the sections contained in the Child Care Act, 1991, they offer interesting insights into the way the law is being operated in the short time since its implementation. In keeping with many of the studies reported in this volume, the project undertaken to explore how far the welfare of children is being promoted in a multi-disciplinary fashion under the legislation indicates that a broadening of focus is required. Attention to the areas of child development and attachment are shown to be essential elements of a comprehensive assessment but appear to take a lower priority in the context of more urgent responses to child abuse. This is despite the requirement imposed on the health board by the Act to be pro-active in its efforts to promote child welfare.

With regard to section 19, which provides for the making of supervision orders, the research studies discussed here raise a number of important issues. While the orders are considered to be empowering and facilitative of maintaining children in their family homes, the research indicates that the orders themselves do not and cannot either protect children or necessarily bring about change. It was concerning to see that such orders can be used to compensate for the absence of satisfactory out-of-home placements for children. Once again, the need for family support at an early stage is stressed and it is notable that in some of the cases examined, social support of the families concerned had been very low prior to the imposition of the order. The difficulty of applying a technical approach to the definition of thresholds of good enough care is again stressed.

The studies on assessment orders and the *guardian ad litem* system both highlight the need for clear protocols regarding the use of the orders, and the potential for their misuse in the absence of guidance and surveillance. The potential for abuse by the judiciary of the section 20 order which can be invoked to compensate for the lack of a court welfare service is clearly highlighted. The requirement for a *guardian ad litem* to have expertise in child welfare is emphasised, a point which receives support in the literature from Shannon (2000, p.132) who describes the guardian's role as 'a great idea, short on detail'.

What these studies show, more than anything else, is that while the implementation of the Child Care Act, 1991 has been a major milestone in terms of a movement towards promoting the rights of children and creating a more child-centred and pro-active child protection and welfare system, it may take many years and considerable refinement before both the courts and the health boards get to grips with the various complexities made visible in practice and are facilitated and trained to use the legislation effectively. None the less, the studies indicate its potential and highlight considerable support for its positive orientation.

=15=

Messages from the Research

The different sections in this volume represent a substantial body of research carried out in different parts of Ireland during the first few years in which the Child Care Act, 1991 was operative and at a time when the child protection and welfare system was undergoing considerable development. While the individual studies are small in scale, the exploration of common themes in different areas means that their outcomes can be considered both cumulatively and comparatively. In addition, their generalisability and validity is enhanced by the fact that they have been conducted within similar legislative and procedural frameworks.

Each of the chapters in this volume has highlighted the scale of the child protection network and illustrated the wide range of professionals who carry responsibilities in relation to the protection of children from harm. The outcomes, therefore, have relevance for all agencies providing services for children even if their remit is not primarily child protection and welfare. In this final chapter, the key findings from the research will be reviewed in relation to their implications for Irish child protection and welfare practice and policy in the foreseeable future. The aim is to highlight the achievements of the past ten years and consider the challenges to be met in the next phase of development.

The projects were considered in terms of the primary, secondary and tertiary functions of the services and programmes under study. Starting at a primary level, an important argument that has been emphasised repeatedly in these studies and in international research concerns the need to create and maintain preventive services that will support families and children in their own communities, thus pre-empting or minimising the crises that invoke more complex and difficult interventions for all concerned. While the studies showed that service provision in this area has been progressing steadily, some shortcomings were inevitably highlighted. In relation to early years and pre-school services it was shown that, despite the fact that Part VII of the Child Care Act, 1991 has been in place for several years, the more qualitative aspects of child care have been less amenable to regulation than others and still require improvement. The studies in this area also emphasised the importance of providing specific services for adolescent parents and the need for adequate standards, provision of staff training and implementation of procedures in the area of early childhood service provision. Equally, they highlighted the need for staff to be sensitive to children's individual developmental needs and the importance of tapping into already existing resources and supports in the community.

The projects on direct provision of family support services to vulnerable groups illustrated the key role of the relationship between family support workers and clients of the service. They identified, as one of the key challenges for practitioners, the need to sensitively and empathetically engage family members who may be resistant to intervention. Similarly, they highlighted the necessity for workers and families to work together within firm contractual agreements focusing on specific and realistic goals. The studies that explored social support networks confirmed the view that community based interventions are more likely to endure than those with a more clinical base. Other important elements identified included commitment to long-term work and the provision of support, supervision and decent employment conditions for family support workers in order to sustain consistency and quality of services to families over the longer term. The positive outcomes from those programmes already up and running included reduced concerns about child neglect, improved parental self-esteem, competence, confidence and problem-solving abilities, enhanced parent-child bonding, interaction and expanded social networks. These findings are encouraging and lend weight to the important role played by social support in terms of empowering families and thereby reducing risk and promoting child welfare.

Moving on to child protection at a secondary level, the research reported here indicates that considerable progress has been made by professionals and agencies in terms of their potential for identifying and addressing risk and harm, particularly when training programmes have been specifically targeted at this area. Multi-agency and inter-professional responsibility is strongly emphasised in *Children First* in its assertion that any organisation providing services to children must have in place a set of procedures to help them identify risk and vulnerability and deal with any suspicions of child abuse. However, as the studies reported in this volume have shown, the ability of professionals to fulfil these obligations cannot be taken for granted. While professional awareness of child abuse has risen over the past decade, the research discussed here has shown how confusion can still exist about the boundaries between acceptable care, vulnerability and risk. To address this, they have offered useful guidance on the sort of information that can inform decision making in relation to thresholds of significant harm and have proposed models for recording and utilising relevant information.

Notwithstanding the increasing use of procedures and guidelines, the studies raised some points of a worrying nature in relation to the implementation of regulations and protocols intended to protect children. It was concerning to observe from one project that recruitment practices in pre-school settings are not being operated safely, yet are not breaching regulations attaching to Part VII of the Child Care Act, 1991. Most of the recently implemented referral systems have undoubtedly made a positive difference to the ability of staff, families and children to make their concerns known. However, it is clear from the studies that the implementation of guidelines and complaints procedures in both community and residential services does not necessarily guarantee that they will be used with confidence. While *Children First* has advocated the appointment of designated officers to deal with suspected child abuse, some of the research reported here has challenged 'line management' approaches to making complaints and referrals on the basis that an extra 'filtering tool' may be added to the process, thus creating a weak link.

Some of the projects replicated a trend already visible in Irish and British literature (Buckley, Skehill and O'Sullivan, 1997; Gibbons, Conroy and Bell, 1995; Farmer and Owen, 1995) whereby child care services were shown to be dominated by concerns about risk and dangerousness at the cost of attention to the wider welfare needs of children and families. In addition, interesting and important issues have been raised in relation to the type of response made by health board workers to reports of child neglect. Although neglect is the most commonly reported and the most detrimental form of child maltreatment (Stevenson, 1998; Dubowitz, 1999; Buckley, 1999) it appears from some of the projects to be the category that elicits the most ambivalent and least efficient response from professionals in child protection. Part of the difficulty relates to the fact that the framework for assessment most commonly employed apparently fails to consider the full range of families' needs and capacities. While not minimising the challenges and dilemmas inherent in assessment of families experiencing a range of stresses, the studies discussed here offer useful guidance to enable practitioners to respond to families in a holistic manner, emphasising the need to utilise developmental and structural theories and employ specificity in relation to the effect of social and familial problems on parenting capacity. They also highlight the importance of early intervention by showing how, in a number of instances where either supervision orders were secured or children were separated from their parents, support services had not been offered prior to the crisis that precipitated the legal action.

Problems associated with inter-agency co-operation were visible throughout all the chapters in this volume, affirming that it is one of the most trenchant difficulties experienced in child protection work. Yet, as the various studies showed, it is one where major improvements can be effected by both training and the implementation of specific strategies. The question of joint interviewing and joint Garda/ health board investigative teams was explored in different areas and some of the studies challenged the view that such arrangements are necessarily optimal. The pros and cons of specialisation were debated, and the outcomes of these studies indicated that much work and development will need to take place before multi-disciplinary teams can function effectively. Projects focusing on co-operation between health board social work teams and other professional groups and agencies highlighted the importance of basic communication of information. A point that was raised on numerous occasions concerned lack of feedback from health boards to referring agencies, a matter that is undoubtedly linked, in practice, with concerns about confidentiality. This appears to cause immense frustration to certain professional groups, particularly teachers. However, it is not beyond amelioration and underscores the principle that respect for the contributions of others is a fundamental element of good inter-agency relationships. The issue of child and family centredness emerged in these studies as crucial to the formation of good working relationships and an important recommendation concerned the potential for agencies to work together to identify and address needs rather than rigidly adhere to their own professional norms and limits.

The importance of culturally competent child protection intervention, an issue that is becoming more and more pertinent as Irish society becomes more diverse, was illustrated in the studies that focused on the Traveller community. The research on direct work with children in care offered good examples of how adapting perspectives to fit individual attitudes, values and world views can enhance a child's self-esteem and confidence.

The tertiary level of child protection and welfare work is where organisations and professionals intervene with children and families to help them deal with the effects of past abuse and try to reduce the risk of re-occurrence. The studies dealing with family violence affirmed a view already put forward in the literature about the need for social workers in particular but also other professionals in the child protection network to take domestic violence seriously in terms of its destructive effect on children. They also urge professionals to attempt as far as possible to create trusting relationships with victims and their children whilst connecting them with appropriate services. The positive shift in the practices of An Garda Síochána under the Protocol for Dealing with Domestic Violence (1994) and the Domestic Violence Act, 1996 were illustrated by the projects carried out both prior to and following these policy and legislative changes, indicating a fairly radical change over the past decade but leaving no room for complacency as yet. Reflecting further progress, different models of intervention with families who have experienced domestic violence and sexual abuse as well as evaluations of assessment and treatment services illustrate the diverse range of child protection activities that have been ongoing in different areas. They also offer a number of options for use by professionals and agencies engaged in this type of work.

One of the areas where much positive development appears to have taken place is the system that provides out-of-home care for children who have been separated from their families. The projects on access, reviews and after-care illustrate a distinct shift towards child-centred practice and commitment to enabling children to develop and maintain a positive sense of identity. The voices of children in care were reflected in many of the projects, bringing strong reminders in relation to the factors that hindered or facilitated a successful trajectory through the care system. A strong argument was made for legal reform in relation to the health board's obligation to provide after-care services and useful frameworks for policy and practice were provided.

Whilst many of the areas of child protection and welfare discussed in this document are already the focus of practice and policy developments, a number of issues were highlighted that, up to now, have been less visible and are worth some consideration. One of these concerns the role of public health nurses in child protection and welfare work. The projects have illustrated the challenges presented to and accepted by public health nurses with the implementation of the Child Care Act, 1991. While social workers have been traditionally considered the most appropriate key workers in child protection cases, it has become clear from the research carried out by public health nurses that they play an increasingly significant role with vulnerable families, often as the sole workers. The need to expand and sharpen their assessment skills, their ability to communicate and negotiate with other professionals, particularly at child protection conferences, and their requirement for training in relation to court work have all been clearly articulated through the projects. One of the most crucial challenges for the profession concerns supervision and support. The studies show that while supervision has traditionally had negative associations for nurses, it has now become a necessary element of their daily work, particularly in the current climate.

Another important area highlighted in the research is that of parental involvement in the child protection process. It arose principally in relation to two areas, the involvement of parents whose children are in out-of-home care, and parental participation at child protection conferences. The studies show that a lot of progress has been made in relation to the former and several individual projects have demonstrated very successful methods of actively engaging parents in the care process. Ways of improving the consistency and quality of access between parents and children in care have also been explored. Less movement, however, appears to have taken place in relation to the involvement of parents at child protection conferences. While there seems to be general support for the concept, there was also a sense that partial involvement was the more desirable option. It is possible that practices within agencies have changed since these studies were conducted, but the findings raise an important challenge to the assumption that full participation is always the preferred practice. *Children First* stipulates that parents should be invited to attend full child protection conferences unless specific reasons exist for their exclusion. Virtually no research has been carried out in Ireland to evaluate child protection conferences where parents or children have attended full meetings, so the data to date are largely speculative. However, research findings in the UK where parental participation has been the norm for some time cautions against assumptions that it is always an empowering and inclusive process for families. The message from recent British studies is that while full attendance by parents generally precipitates improved communication at conferences and better outcomes in terms of agreement around plans and interventions, parents often feel they have little influence over the proceedings (Thoburn, Lewis and Shemmings, 1995; Farmer and Owen, 1995; Corby, Millar and Young, 1996; Bell, 2000). These findings, together with the outcomes of the projects reported here, indicate that practices of parental involvement should not be implemented lightly or without full consideration of the necessary preparation and infrastructure. An important point made by some of the projects was that parental involvement in child protection conferences is only one way in which inclusiveness can be extended to families and children, and that other options can and should be explored for the future.

While all the studies discussed here advocate provision of services of one type or another, a recurring theme has been not simply the lack of resources, but the lack of their attractiveness at times. In particular, the studies related to primary preventive work have highlighted the low uptake of ante-natal classes, parenting courses and services offered to young parents by family centres. Most of the studies drew attention to the need to make these resources more user-friendly, but also to engender a sense of ownership by the community by including service users in planning and running them.

Though none of the studies dealt specifically with the issue of gender, it was spectacularly present at each level of child protection and welfare under study and manifested itself in different ways. One of the more obvious examples was the low interest and participation of young men in health promotion activities to do with sexuality and teenage pregnancy. There was a marked lack of involvement by teenage fathers with their children and many instances where they were not in any contact at all. Access between children in the care system and their fathers appeared to be markedly low. While this issue was not actively explored, it may be speculated that the exclusion of fathers is supported by the collusion of child protection and welfare practitioners who tend to focus on women's involvement with their children and hold low expectations of men. Gender issues amongst staff were highlighted by the studies carried out by members of An Garda Síochána, in terms of the expectation that female officers would carry a disproportionate number of child protection cases. It was illustrated in another interesting way by one of the projects dealing with stress, where it appeared that male Gardaí were less willing than their female colleagues to discuss the emotional effects of dealing with traumatic incidents. Throughout all the studies, one of the most consistent trends was the high prevalence of single, mainly female, parent families in the child protection system. This issue presents certain dilemmas to practitioners and policy makers who are anxious not to marginalise individual groups of clients. However, the unique vulnerabilities and needs of this group were so clearly articulated in these studies that they appeared without doubt to be in need of specific policies and services.

The stresses associated with child protection work were clearly demonstrated in a number of studies, illustrating that it is an issue for a number of disciplines. The research clearly showed that while professionals like An Garda Síochána are often assumed to be impervious to the effects of dealing with sexual abuse or any other kind of child protection case, they are, just like other professionals, often deeply traumatised and require the same level of support. Likewise, public health nurses experience difficulty with the pressure of trying to provide a service to the community as well as fulfil their child protection and welfare obligations under the Child Care Act, 1991. The research illustrated their requirement for a supervisory and support structure at least equivalent to that operating in social work. Whilst acknowledging the inevitability of stress in child protection work, several of the studies offered models of supervision and techniques for improving case management with the objective of relieving burnout and facilitating practitioners to regain a sense of control over their professional tasks and responsibilities.

The high turnover of child protection staff, particularly in social work, is obviously related to the stress inherent in the work. As one project demonstrated, some of the underlying reasons for practitioners' loss of motivation to remain in the area included experiences of unmanageable case loads, lack of resources and feelings of worthlessness. Another study highlighted the frequency with which fear of violence is experienced by workers and linked it with withdrawal of services in certain cases. These are crucial issues for health boards who are trying to maintain adequate staffing levels in order to offer an effective service and the studies reported here offer valuable insight into the nature of the difficulties as well as recommending methods for addressing them.

Though the Child Care Act, 1991 has provided a constructive and positive basis for child protection and welfare work and has made available useful tools for its conduct, some of the studies discussed here have illustrated two very important points in relation to specific sections of the law. One is the need for regulations and protocols and training around the use of the *guardian ad litem* system, supervision orders and access orders; the other, related, point is the risk that courts will misuse these sections in the absence of guidance.

In line with its international counterparts, the Irish child protection and welfare system is becoming more reflexive and, enabled by the currently buoyant economy, is developing rapidly. As the research indicates, caution must be exercised in relation to achieving the correct balance. Work aimed at safeguarding and meeting the needs of children will always be challenging and complex, and high-profile cases continuously remind us of the weaknesses and inadequacies of the system. One of the important functions of research in child protection and welfare is to challenge complacency and continuously question the status quo. Its most important role, however, is to constantly feed into the policy and practice loop in a constructive fashion and reflect what is significant and effective. It is fair to assume that many of the projects reported here have informed policy in individual areas. It is also likely that they have in different ways both influenced and been reflected in the new national child protection and welfare guidance. Dissemination of the studies in this form will, it is hoped, ensure that the larger child protection network will benefit from the contribution that each of the researchers and their organisations have made to knowledge on this important subject.

Bibliography

Ainsworth, M.D.S. (1991) 'Attachment and Other Affectional Bonds Across the Life Cycle' in C. Murray Parkes, J. Stevenson-Hinde and P. Marris (eds), *Attachment Across the Life Cycle*, London: Routledge/Tavistock, pp 33-51

Aldridge, M. and Wood, J. (1998) *Interviewing Children: A Guide for Child Care and Forensic Practitioners*, Chichester: Wiley

Axline, V. (1969) *Play Therapy*, New York: Ballantine Books

Barth, R.P. and Schinke, R.P. (1983) 'Coping with daily strain among pregnant and parenting adolescents', *Journal of Social Science Research*, 7:51-63

Bebbington A. and Miles, J. (1990) 'The Supply of Foster Families for Children in Care', *British Journal of Social Work*, 20: 283-302

Bell, M. (2000) *Child Protection: Families and the Conference Process*, Aldershot: Ashgate

Bene, E. and Anthony, J. (1985) *Family Relations Test – Children's Version. Rev. Manual* (NFER-Nelson, Windsor, Berks.)

Berridge, D. and Cleaver, H. (1987) *Foster Home Breakdown*, Oxford: Blackwell

Berridge, D. (1996) *Foster Care: A research review*, London: HMSO

Biddy, P. (1994) *Personal Safety for Social Workers*, Aldershot, Arena

Birchall, E. and Hallett, C. (1995) *Working Together in Child Protection*, London: HMSO

Blyth, E. and Milner, J. (1990) 'The process of inter-agency work' in The Violence Against Children Study Group *Taking Child Abuse Seriously*, London: Routledge, pp 194-211

Boushel, M., Fawcett, M. and Selwyn J. (2000) *Focus on Early Childhood: Principles and Realities*, London: Blackwell

Bowlby, J. (1979) *The making and breaking of affectional bonds*, London: Routledge

Bowlby, J. (1982) *Attachment and Loss*, London: Hogarth Press

The Bridge Consultancy (1996) *Paul: Death Through Neglect*, London: The Bridge Consultancy Service

Bronfenbrenner, U. (1979) *The Ecology of Human Development*, Cambridge MA: Harvard University Press

Buckley, H. (1996) 'Child abuse guidelines in Ireland: for whose protection?' in H. Ferguson and T. McNamara (eds) *Protecting Irish Children: Investigation, Protection and Welfare*, Dublin: Institute of Public Administration, pp 37-56

Buckley, H. (1997) 'Child Protection in Ireland', M. Harder and K. Pringle (eds) *Protecting Children in Europe: Towards a New Millineum*, Aalborg: University Press, pp 101-126

Buckley, H., Skehill, C. and O'Sullivan, E. (1997) *Child Protection Practices in Ireland: A Case Study*, Dublin: Oak Tree Press

Buckley, H. (1998a) 'Conflicting Paradigms: General Practitioners and the Child Protection System', *Irish Journal of Social Work Research*, 1: 29-42

Buckley, H. (1998b) 'Filtering out fathers: the gendered nature of social work in child protection', *Irish Social Worker*, Vol.16, No. 3, pp 7-11

Buckley, H. (1999) 'Child protection: an ungovernable enterprise', *Economic and Social Review*, 30:21-40

Buckley, H. (2000a) 'Inter-agency Co-operation in Irish Child Protection Work', *Journal of Child Centred Practice*, 6: 9-17

Buckley, H. (2000b) 'Working Together to Protect Children: Evaluation of and Inter-Agency Training Programme', *Administration*, 48: 24-42

Burgoyne, J., Ormonde, R. and Richards, M. (1987) *Divorce Matters*, Penguin: Harmondsworth

Burman, M. and Lloyd, S. (1993) 'Inter-agency responses to childhoood adversity; the experiences of two Scottish police forces', in H. Ferguson, R. Gilligan and R. Torode (eds) *Surviving Childhood Adversity: Issues for Policy and Practice*, Dublin: Social Studies Press

Butler, N.R., Ineichen, B., Taylor, B. and Wadsworth, J. (1981) *Teenage Mothering*. Report to the UK Department of Health and Social Security

Butler, S. (1996) 'Child Protection or Professional Self-Preservation by the Baby Nurses? Public Health Nurses and Child Protection in Ireland', *Social Science and Medicine* 43: 303-314

Butler-Sloss, E. (1988) *Report of the Inquiry into Child Abuse in Cleveland 1987*, London: HMSO

Byrne, C. (1994) 'Devising a Model: Health Visitor Supervision Process'. *Health Visitor*, Vol. 67 No. 6

Casey, M. (1987) *Domestic Violence Against Women*, Dublin: UCD

Cawson, P. and Martell, M. (1979) *Children Referred to Closed Units*, Report No. 5, London: HMSO

Children's Legal Centre (1997a) *Secure Accommodation in Child Care*, Papers from a seminar organised by the Children's Legal Centre, Dublin: Children's Legal Centre

Children's Legal Centre (1997b) *The Children Bill, 1996*, Dublin: Children's Legal Centre

Christie, A. (2001) 'Gendered Discourse of Welfare, Men and Social Work' in *Men and Social Work: theories and practices*, Basingstoke, Palgrave, 7-34

Clarke, M. (1998) *Lives in Care: Issues for Policy and Practice in Children's Homes*. Dublin: Mercy Congregation and The Children's Research Centre, TCD

Cleaver, H. and Freeman, P. (1995), *Parental Perspectives in Cases of Suspected Child Abuse*, London: HMSO

Cleaver, H., Unell, I. and Aldgate, J. (1999) *Children's Needs – Parenting Capacity. The impact of parental mental illness, problem alcohol and drug use, and domestic violence on children's development*, London: Stationery Office

Cloke, C. and Naish, J. (1992) 'The Politics of Child Protection Work in Nursing Practice' in C. Cloke and J. Naish, *Key Issues in Child Protection for Health Visitors and Nurses*. Chichester: Wiley

Connolly, S. (1997) 'A Review of Placements within the Eastern Health Board Centralised Emergency Carer's Project: October 1992 – January 1994', *Irish Journal of Social Work Research*, 1: 36-52

Cooney, T. and Torode, R. (eds) (1989), *Report of the Irish Council for Civil Liberties Working Party on Child Sexual Abuse*. Dublin: ICCL

Corby, B. (1987), *Working with Child Abuse*, Milton Keynes: Open University Press

Corby, B. (1993; 2nd edition 2000) *Child abuse: towards a knowledge base*, Buckingham, Open University Press

Corby, B., Millar, M., and Young, L. (1996) 'Parental Participation in Child Protection Work: Rethinking the Rhetoric', *British Journal of Social Work*, 26, pp 475-492.

Crawford, A. and Jones, M. (1995) 'Inter-agency Based Co-operation and Community-Based Crime Prevention', *British Journal of Criminology*, 35: 17-33

Dale, P., Davies, M., Morrison, T. and Waters, J. (1986) *Dangerous Families: Assessment and Treatment of Child Abuse*, London: Tavistock/Routledge

Daniel, B., Wassell, S. and Gilligan R. (2000) *Child Development for Child Care and Protection Workers*, London: Jessica Kingsley

Department of Education (1991) Procedures for Dealing with Allegations or Suspicions of Child Abuse. Dublin: Department of Education

Department of Education & Science (2001) *Child Protection Guidelines and Procedures*. Dublin: Department of Education and Science

Department of Health (1980) Task Force on Child Care Services, *Final Report*, Dublin: Stationery Office

Department of Health (1985) *Committee on Social Work Report*, Dublin: Department of Health

Department of Health (1987) *Child Abuse Guidelines: Guidelines on Procedures for The Identification, Investigation and Management of Child Abuse*, Dublin: Department of Health

Department of Health (1993) *Report of the Kilkenny Incest Investigation*, Dublin: Government Publications

Department of Health (1994) *Shaping a Healthier Future*, Dublin: Government Publications

Department of Health (1995) *Notification of Suspected Cases of Child Abuse between Health Boards and Gardaí*. Dublin: Department of Health

Department of Health (1995a) Child Care Statistics, Dublin: Department of Health

Department of Health (1995b) *Child Care (Placement of Children in Foster Care) Regulations 1995*, Dublin: Stationery Office

Department of Health (1996a) *Report of the inquiry into the operation of Madonna House*. Dublin: Government Publications

Department of Health (1996b) *Putting Children First: Discussion Document on Mandatory Reporting*. Dublin: Department of Health

Department of Health (1997a) *Putting Children First: Promoting and Protecting the Rights of Children*. Dublin: Government Publications

Department of Health (1997b) *Child Care (Standards in Children's Residential Centres) Regulations, 1996* and Guide to Good Practice in Children's Residential Centres. Dublin: Stationery Office

Department of Health and Children (1999) *Children First: National Guidelines for the Protection and Welfare of Children*, Dublin: Government Publications

Department of Health and Children (2001) Child Care Statistics

Department of Health [UK] (1991) *Working Together – a Guide to Inter-Agency Co-operation for the Protection of Children from Abuse*, London: HMSO

Department of Health [UK] (1995) *Messages from Research*, London: HMSO

Department of Health, Home Office, Department for Education and Employment [UK](1999) *Working Together to Safeguard Children*, London: Stationery Office

Department of Health, Home Office, Department for Education and Employment (2000) *Framework for the Assessment of Children in Need and Their Families*, London: Stationery Office

Department of Social Studies, TCD (1993) Research on child protection practices in the WHB area. Unpublished research

De Shazer, S., Berg, I.K., Lipchik, E., Nunnally, E., Molnar, A., Gingerich, W. and Weiner Davis, M. (1986) 'Brief Therapy: Focused solution development', *Family Process*, 25: 207-221

Dingwall, R. (1979) 'Problems of Teamwork in Primary Care' in Briggs, T. Webb, A. and Londsdale, F. (eds) *Teamwork in Health and Social Services*, London: Croom Helm, pp 111-37

Dingwall, R., Eekelaar, J. and Murray, T. (1983), *The Protection of Children: State Intervention and Family Life*, Oxford: Blackwell

Dobash, R.E. and Dobash, R.P. (1984) 'The nature and antecedent of violent events' in *British Journal of Criminology*, 24: 269-288

Doherty, D. (1996) 'Child Care and Protection: Protecting the Children – Supporting Their Service Providers' in H. Ferguson and T. McNamara (eds.) *Protecting Irish Children: investigation, protection and welfare*. Dublin: Institute of Public Administration, pp 102-113

Dubowitz, H. (1994) 'Neglecting the neglect of neglect', *Journal of Interpersonal Violence*, Vol 10: 556-560

Dubowitz, H. (1999) (ed.) *Neglected Children: Research, Practice and Policy*, Thousand Oaks, Sage

Dullea and Mullender (1999) 'Evaluation and Empowerment' in I. Shaw, and J. Lishman (eds) *Evaluation and Social Work Practice*, London: Sage

Eastern Health Board (1996) *Review of Adequacy of Child Care and Family Support Services 1995*, Dublin: EHB

Eastern Health Board / Impact Review Group (1997) *Report of the Eastern Health Board/Impact Review Group on Child Care and Family Support Services*, Dublin: Eastern Health Board

Eastern Health Board (1998) *Child Care and Family Support Services: Review of Adequacy*, Dublin: Eastern Health Board

English, R. (2000) *Professional Fostering: A Model of Care for the Future?* M.Sc. thesis, University of Dublin, Trinity College

Everitt, A and Hardiker, P. (1996) *Evaluating for Good Practice*, Basingstoke: Macmillan

Fahlberg, V. (1992) *Fitting the Pieces Together*, London: BAAF

Farmer, E. and Owen, M. (1995), *Child Protection Practice: Private Risks and Public Remedies*, London: HMSO

Ferguson, H. (1993), 'Surviving Irish Childhood: Child Protection and the Death of Children in Child Abuse Cases in Ireland since 1884', H. Ferguson, R. Gilligan and R. Torode (eds) *Surviving Childhood Adversity: Issues for Policy and Practice*, Dublin: Social Studies Press

Ferguson, H. (1994) 'Child abuse inquiries and the Report of the Kilkenny Incest Investigation: A Critical Analysis', *Administration* 41:385-410

Ferguson, H. (1995) 'Child Welfare, Child Protection and the Child Care Act 1991: Key Issues for Policy and Practice' in H. Ferguson and P. Kenny (eds.) *On Behalf of the Child: Child Welfare, Child Protection and the Child Care Act, 1991*. Dublin: A & A Farmar, pp 17-41

Ferguson, H. and Sinnott, P. (1995) 'Intervention into Domestic Violence in Ireland: Developing Policy and Practice with Men who Batter' in *Administration*, Vol. 43 No. 3 (Autumn 1995) pp 57-81

Ferguson, H. (1998) 'Working with men and masculinities', *Feedback: The Magazine of the Family Therapy Institute of Ireland*, pp 33-36 Vol. 8

Ferguson, H. and O'Reilly, M. (2001) *Keeping Children Safe: Child Abuse, Child Protection and the Promotion of Welfare*, Dublin: A & A Farmar

Finkelhor, D. et al (1988) *Nursery Crimes: Sexual Abuse in Day Care*, California: Sage

Fitzgerald, J. (1983) *Understanding Disruption*, London: BAAF

Forum on Homelessness (2000) *Report of the Forum on Homelessness*, Dublin: Eastern Regional Health Authority

Fry, P.S. (1985) 'Relations Between Teenagers' Age, Knowledge, Expectations and Maternal Behaviour', *British Journal of Developmental Psychology*, 3

Gadsby Waters, J. (1992) *The Supervision of Child Protection Work*, Aldershot: Avebury

Gagan, R., Cupoli, J. and Watkins, A. (1984) 'The families of children who fail to thrive: preliminary investigation of parental deprivation among organic and non-organic cases', *Child Abuse & Neglect*, Vol. 8: 93-103

Gallagher, B., Hughes, B and Parker H. (1996) The nature and extent of known cases of organised abuse in England and Wales, in P. Bibby (ed.) *Organised Abuse – The Current Debate*, Aldershot: Arena/Ashgate

Gibbons, J., Conroy, S. and Bell, C. (1995), *Operating the Child Protection System*, London: HMSO

Gilligan, R. (1991) *Irish Child Care Services: Policy, Practice and Provision*. Dublin, Institute of Public Administration

Gilligan, R. (1996) 'Children Adrift in Care? – Can the Child Care Act 1991 rescue the 50% who are in care five years and more?' *Irish Social Worker*, Vol. 14, No. 1, pp 17-19, 1996

Gilligan, R. and Chapman, R. (1997) Developing Good Practice in the Conduct of Child Protection Case Conferences: An Action Research Project. Cork: Southern Health Board

Gilligan, R. (1999a) 'Child Welfare Review 1998' *Irish Social Policy Review* eds. A. McCashin and E. O'Sullivan *Administration* (special issue) 47, 2, (Summer), 232-256, 1999

Gilligan, R. (1999b) 'The Importance of Schools and Teachers in Child Welfare', *Child and Family Social Work*, Vol.3, pp 13-25

Gilligan, R. (2000a) 'Family Support in Disadvantaged Communities' in J. Canavan, P. Dolan and J. Pinkerton (eds) *Family Support: Direction from Diversity*', London: Jessica Kingsley

Gilligan, R. (2000b) Men as Foster Carers – a Neglected Resource? *Adoption & Fostering* 24, 2, 63-69

Gordon, L. (1989), *Heroes of their own Lives: The Politics and History of Family Violence, Boston 1880-1960*, London: Virago

Government Information Services (1982) *Press Release Issued on Behalf of Department of Health*, 26 July, 1982

Grimshaw, R. and Sinclair R. (1997) 'Planning for Children in Care in Northern Ireland', London: National Children's Bureau

Hallett, C. and Stevenson, O. (1980) *Child Abuse: Aspects of Interprofessional Co-operation*, London: George Allen & Unwin

Hallett, C. and Birchall, E. (1992) *Co-ordination and Child Protection: A review of the literature*, London: HMSO

Hallett, C. (1993) 'Working Together in Child Protection' in L. Waterhouse (ed) *Child Abuse and Child Abusers: Protection and Prevention*. London: Jessica Kingsley, pp 139-153

Hallett, C. (1995), *Interagency Coordination in Child Protection*, London: HMSO

Harris, R. and Timms, N. (1993) *Secure Accommodation in Child Care*, London: Routledge

Hayes, N. (1999) *Early Childhood: An introductory text*, Dublin: Gill & MacMillan

Hester, M. (1994) 'Violence against Social Services Staff: a Gendered Issue' in C. Lupton and T. Gillespie, *Working with Violence*

Hester, M., Pearson, C. and Harwin, N. (2000) *Making an Impact: Children and Domestic Violence: A reader*, London, Jessica Kingsley

Holmes, J. (1993) *John Bowlby and Attachment Theory*, London: Routledge

Holt, S. (2000) *Social Workers and Domestic Violence: A local evaluation*, M.Sc Thesis, Department of Social Studies. Trinity College Dublin

Home Office [UK] and Department of Health (1992) *Memorandum of Good Practice on Video Recorded Interviews with Child Witnesses for Criminal Proceedings*. London: HMSO

Hooper, C.A. (1992), *Mothers surviving child sexual abuse*, London: Routledge

Horgan, D. (1996) 'Inter-agency co-operation: Team Work and Child Protection', *Irish Social Worker*, Vol. 14 pp 4- 6

Horgan, G. (1996) 'You're Not There! Young people's views on Review Meetings', *Child Care in Practice*, 3:60-67

Horwath, J. (2000) 'Assessing the World of the Child in Need: Background and Context' in J. Horwath (ed) *A Child's World: Assessing Children in Need*, Department of Health, NSPCC and the University of Sheffield

Horwath, J. and Morrison, T. (1999) *Effective Training in Social Care*, London: Routledge

Howe, D. (1992) 'Child Abuse and the Bureaucratisation of Social Work', *Sociological Review* 40: 490-508

Hudson, F. and Inchiechen, B. (1991) *Taking it all lying down: Sexuality and Teenage Motherhood*, Hong Kong: Macmillan

Hughes, B., Parker, H. and Gallagher, B. (1996) *Policing Child Sexual Abuse: the view from police practitioners*, Home Office Police Research Group, February 1996. London: Home Office

Hughes L. and Pengelly, P. (1996) *Staff supervision in a turbulent environment: managing process and task in front line services*, London: Jessica Kingsley

Hugman, R. (1991) *Power in Caring Professions*, London: Macmillan

Hunt, P. (1994) *Report of the Independent Inquiry into Multiple Abuse in Nursery Classes in Newcastle upon Tyne*, Newcastle upon Tyne: Newcastle City Council

Inbucon Management Consultants (1982) *Community Care Review Report, Commissioned by Community Care Review Steering Group, Department of Health*, Dublin: Stationery Office

Irish Social Services Inspectorate (2001a) *Irish Social Services Inspectorate Annual Report 2001*, Dublin: ISSI

Irish Social Services Inspectorate (2001b) *Newtown House High Support Unit Inspection Report*. Dublin: ISSI

Iwaniec, D. Herbert, M. & McNeish, A.S. (1985) 'Social Work with failure to thrive children and their families – Part I: Psycho-Social Factors, *British Journal of Social Work*, Vol. 15, 243-259

Iwaniec, D. (1995) *The Emotionally Abused and Neglected Child*, Chichester: Wiley

Jack, G. (2000) 'Ecological Perspectives in Assessing Children & Families' in J. Horwath (ed.) *The Child's World: Assessing Children in Need*, Leicester, NSPCC, University of Sheffield, Department of Health

Jackson, S. (1988) 'Education and Children in Care' *Adoption & Fostering*, 12

Johnson, C. Loxterkamp, D, and Albanses, M. (1982) 'Effect of high school students' knowledge of child development and child health on approaches to child discipline', *Paediatrics*, 69:558-562

Johnson, D.E. (1999) 'Medical and developmental sequalae of early childhood institutionalisation in international adoptees from Romania and the Russian Federation' in C. Nelson (ed.) *The effects of early adversity on neurobehavioural development*, Mahwah, N.J. Lawrence Erlbaum Associates Inc.

Johnson, Z., Howell, F. and Molloy, B. (1993) 'Community mothers' programme: randomised controlled trial of non-professional intervention in parenting, *British Medical Journal*, 306: 1449-1452

Kahan, B. (1979) *Growing up in Care*, Oxford: Blackwell

Keats, D. (1997) *Culture and the Child: A Guide for Professionals in Child Care and Development*, Sussex: Wiley

Kelleher and Associates and O'Connor (1995) *Making the Links: Towards an integrated strategy for the elimination of violence against women in intimate relationships with men*, Dublin: Women's Aid

Kelleher and Associates (1998) *Out on their own: young people leaving care in Ireland*, Dublin: Focus Point

Kelleher, P. and O'Connor, M. (1999) *Safety and Sanctions: Domestic violence and the enforcement of law in Ireland*, Dublin: Women's Aid

Kelly, J. (1997) 'What do Teachers do with Child Protection and Child Welfare Concerns which they Encounter in their Classrooms?' *Irish Journal of Social Work Research*, 1:23-35

Kelly, L. (1996) 'When Woman Protection is the Best Kind of Child Protection', *Administration*, Vol. 44 pp 118-135

Kennedy, M. (1992) 'Not the Only Way to Communicate: A Challenge to Voice in Child Protection Work, *Child Abuse Review*, 1: 169-177

Kenny, B. (2000) *Responding to the Needs of Troubled Children: A Critique of High Support and Secure Special Care Provision in Ireland* (Policy Briefing 3) Dublin: Barnardo's

Kinnibrugh, A.D. (1984) *Social Work Case Recording and the Client's Right of Privacy*, Bristol: School for Advanced Urban Studies, University of Bristol

Kolb, D. (1988) 'The process of experiential learning' in D. Kolb (ed.) *Experience as the Source of Learning and Development*, London: Prentice Hall

Landy, S. Cleland, J. and Schubert, J. (1984) The individuality of teenage mothers and its implication for intervention strategies, *Journal of Adolescence*, 10:7-23

Lea-Cox, C and Hall A. (1991) 'Attendance of general practitioners at child protection case conferences', *British Medical Journal*, Vol. 302: 1378-1379

Levy, A. and Kahan, B. (1991) *The Pindown Experience and the Protection of Children: The Report of the Staffordshire Child Care Inquiry*, Stafford: Staffordshire County Council

Lewisham Social Services Department (1989) 'The Doreen Aston Report', London: Lewisham Social Services Department

London Borough of Brent (1985) *A Child in Trust: Report of the Panel of Inquiry Investigating the Circumstances Surrounding the Death of Jasmine Beckford*, London: London Borough of Brent

London Borough of Greenwich (1987) *A Child in Mind: Protection of Children in a Responsible Society, The Report of the Commission of Inquiry into the Circumstances Surrounding the Death of Kimberley Carlile*, London: London Borough of Greenwich

McGrath, K. (1996) 'Intervening in Child Sexual Abuse in Ireland: Towards Victim-Centred Policies and Practices' *Administration*, Vol. 44, pp 57-72

McGuire, J. and Richman, N. (1986) 'Screening for Behaviour Problems in nurseries: The reliability and validity of the pre-school behaviour checklist' in *Junior Child Psychiatry*, 27:7-32

McIntyre, D. and Carr, A (1999) 'Helping Children to the Other Side of Silence: A Study of the Impact of the Stay Safe Programme on Irish Children's Disclosures of Sexual Victimization', *Child Abuse & Neglect*, Vol. 23 pp 1327-1340

McKeown, K. and Gilligan, R. (1991) 'Child Sexual Abuse in the Eastern Health Board Region of Ireland in 1988: An Analysis of 512 Confirmed Cases', *Economic and Social Review* 22: 101-134

McKeown, K. (2000) *A guide to what works in family support services for vulnerable families*, Dublin: Government Information Services

McKinsey and Co. Inc. (1970) *Towards Better Health Care: Management in Health Services*, Dublin: Department of Health

Maluccio, A. N. Kreiger and Pine (1990) *Preparing Adolescents for Life After Foster Care*, Child Welfare League of America, Washington DC

Marchant, R. and Page, M. (1992) *Child Protection Work with Children with Multiple Disabilities*, Leicester: NSPCC

Marchant, R. (2000) 'The Assessment of Children with Complex Needs' in J. Horwath (ed) *The Child's World: Assessing Children in Need*, Department of Health, NSPCC and the University of Sheffield.

Martin, F. (2000) *The Politics of Children's Rights*, Cork: Cork University Press

Menzies, I. (1961) *The Functioning of Social Systems as a Defence against Anxiety*, London: Tavistock

Metropolitan Police and Bexley London Borough (1987) *Child Sexual Abuse – Joint Investigative Project*, London: Her Majesty's Stationery Office

Mid-Western Health Board (1997) *Safe Care in Foster Care: Guidelines on the Promotion of Safety and the Management of Complaints in Foster Care*, Limerick: Mid-Western Health Board

Mid-Western Health Board (1998) *Review of Child Care & Family Support Services*, Limerick: Mid-Western Health Board

Millham, S., Bullock, R., Hosie, K and Haak, M. (1986) *Lost in Care*, Aldershot: Gower

Milner, J. (1996) 'Men's Resistance to Social Workers' in B. Fawcett, B. Featherstone, J. Hearn, C. Toft (eds), *Violence and Gender Relations: Theories and Interventions*, London: Sage, pp 115-129

Morgan, M. and Fitzgerald, M. (1992) 'Gardaí and Domestic Violence Incidents: A Profile Based on a National Sample of Investigations', Paper presented to the Conference on Safety for Women, Dublin, 3rd October 1992

Morrison, T. (1996) 'Partnership and Collaboration: Rhetoric and Reality, *Child Abuse and Neglect*, Vol. 20, pp 127-140

Morrison, T. (1997) 'Emotionally competent child protection organisations: Fallacy, fiction or necessity?' in J. Bates, R. Pugh, and N. Thompson (eds) *Protecting Children: Challenges and Change*, Aldershot: Arena pp 193-211

Mullender, A. (1996) *Rethinking Domestic Violence: The social work and probation response*, London: Routledge

Murphy, M. (1997) 'Delivering staff care in a multidisciplinary context' in J. Bates, R. Pugh, and N. Thompson (eds) *Protecting Children: Challenges and Changes*, Aldershot: Arena

Murphy, R. (1998) *Report of the Independent Inquiry into Matters Relating to Child Sexual Abuse in Swimming*, Dublin: Government Publications

National Childcare Strategy (1999) *Report of the Partnership 2000 Expert Group on Childcare*, Dublin: Government Publications

National Children's Strategy (2000) *Report of the Public Consultation*, Dublin: National Children's Office

NAYPIC (1989) *Report on Violations of the Basic Human Rights of Young People in the Care of London Borough of Greenwich and other Local Authorities*, London: NAYPIC

Nixon, S. (2000) 'Safe care, abuse and allegations of abuse in foster care' in G. Kelly and R. Gilligan (eds) *Issues in Foster*, London: Jessica Kingsley Publishers

Nunno, M.A. and Motz J.K. (1988) 'The Development of an Effective Response to the Abuse of Children in Out-of-Home Care, *Child Abuse & Neglect*, 12: 521-528

North Western Health Board (1998) *West of Ireland Farmer Case: Report of the Panel of Inquiry*, Manorhamilton: North Western Health Board

Oaklander, V. (1978) *Windows to our Children*, Real People Press, Utah

O'Brien, V. (2000) *Family Group Conference Pilot Report: Evaluation Report*, Dublin: ERHA

O'Connor, M. (1996) 'Protecting Abused Women and Their Children: The Irish Context' in H. Ferguson and T. McNamara (eds.) *Protecting Irish Children: investigation, protection and welfare*, Dublin: Institute of Public Administration, 44:114-117

O'Hagan, K. (1993) *Emotional and Psychological Abuse of Children*, Buckingham: Open University Press

O'Hara, G. and Dewar, C. (1988) 'Fostering teenagers – what works for whom and why' *Adoption & Fostering*, Vol. 12, 38-42

O'Higgins, K. (1993) 'Surviving Separation: Traveller Children in Substitute Care', H. Ferguson, R. Gilligan, and R. Torode (eds) *Surviving Childhood Adversity: Issues for Policy and Practice'*, Dublin: Social Studies Press, pp 146-156

O'Higgins, K. and Boyle, M. (1988) *State Care – Some Children's Alternative: Analysis of Data from Returns to the Department of Health*, Dublin: Department of Health

O'Higgins, K. (1996) *Disruption, Displacement, Discontinuity? Children in Care and their Families in Ireland*, Aldershot: Avebury

O'Mahony, A. (1985) *Social Need and the Provision of Social Services in Rural Areas: A case Study from the Community Care Services*, Dublin: An Foras Talúntais.

O'Sullivan, E. (1993) 'Irish Child Care Law: The Origins, Aims and Development of the 1991 Child Care Act' *Childright*, (June) No. 97, pp 8-9

O'Sullivan, E. (1996) 'Adolescents Leaving Care or Leaving Home and Child Care Provision in Ireland and the UK: A Critical View' in M. Hill and J. Aldgate (eds) *Child Welfare Services: Developments in Law, Policy, Practice and Research*, London: Jessica Kingsley pp 212-224

O'Sullivan, E. (2000) 'A review of the Children Bill, 1999' *Irish Social Worker*, 18: 10-13

Parker, R. (1991) *Looking After Children: Assessing Outcomes in Child Care*, London: HMSO

Parton, C. (1990) 'Women, gender oppression and child abuse', in The Violence Against Children Study Group, *Taking Child Abuse Seriously*, London: Unwin Hyman, pp 41-62

Parton, N. (1997) 'Child protection and family support: current debates and future prospects' in N. Parton (ed) *Child Protection and Family Support:Tensions, Contradictions and Possibilities*, London: Routledge, pp 1-24

Parton, N. (1998) 'Risk, Advanced Liberalism and Child Welfare: The Need to Rediscover Uncertainty and Ambiguity', *British Journal of Social Work*, 28: 5-27

Pence, D. and Wilson, C. (1994) *Team Investigation of Child Sexual Abuse: The Uneasy Alliance*, London: Sage

Pinkerton, J. (1998) 'The Impact of Research on Policy and Practice: A Systematic Perspective' in D. Iwaniec and J. Pinkerton (1998) *Making Research Work: Promoting Child Care Policy and Practice*, London: Wiley pp 25-45

Pinkerton, J. (2000) 'Emerging Agendas for Family Support' in J. Canavan, P. Dolan and J. Pinkerton (eds) *Family Support: Direction from Diversity'*, London: Jessica Kingsley

Pithouse, A. (1987), *Social Work: The Social Organisation of an Invisible Trade*, Aldershot: Gower

Polnay, J. (2000) 'General Practitioners and Child Protection Case Conference Participation: Reasons for Non-Attendance and Proposals for a Way Forward. *Child Abuse Review*, Vol. 9: 108-123

Pringle, K. (2001) 'Men in Social Work: The Double-edge' in A. Christie (ed.) *Men and Social Work*, Basingstoke: Palgrave, 35-48

Prior, V., Lynch, M. and Glaser, D. (1999) 'Responding to child sexual abuse: an evaluation of social work by children and their carers' *Child and Family Social Work*, 4:131-144

Quinton, D. and Rutter, M. (1988) *Parenting Breakdown: The Making and Breaking of Inter-Generational Links*, Aldershot: Avebury

Raftery, M. and O'Sullivan, E. (1999) *Suffer the Little Children*, Dublin: New Island Books

Reder, P., Duncan, S. and Gray, M. (1993), *Beyond Blame: Child Abuse Tragedies Revisited*, London: Routledge

Reder, P. and Lucey, C. (1995) *Assessment of Parenting: psychiatric and psychological contributions*, London: Routledge

Reformatory and Industrial Schools Systems Report (1970) (The Kennedy Report). Dublin: Stationery Office

Report of the Review Group on Mental Handicap Services. *Needs and Abilities – A Policy for the Intellectually Disabled* (1990) Stationery Office

Richardson, V. (1985) *Whose Children?*, Dublin, Family Studies Unit, University College Dublin

Rindfleisch, N. and Bean, G.J. (1988) 'Willingness to Report Abuse and Neglect in Residential Facilities'. *Child Abuse & Neglect*, 9: 285-295

Roberts, B. and Endres, J. (1988) Nutrition Management of Teenage Pregnancy, *Journal of the American Dietetic Association*, 89: 105-109

Rose, W. (2000) 'Assessing Children in Need and their Families: an Overview of the Framework' in J. Horwath (ed) *The Child's World: Assessing children in need*, London: Department of Health, NSPCC and University of Sheffield

Rothenberg, P.B. & Varga, P.E. (1981) 'The Relationship Between Age of Mother and Child Health and Development' *American Journal of Public Health*, 71, No. 8

Rowe, J. Cain, H., Hundleby, M. and Keane, A. (1984) *Long Term Foster Care*, London: Batsford/BAAF

Royal Ulster Constabulary (1992) *Protocol for the joint investigation, by social workers and police officers, of alleged and suspected cases of child abuse*, Belfast: RUC

Rutter, M. (1981) *Maternal Deprivation Reassessed*, London: Penguin

Rutter, M. (1985) 'Family and School Influence on Behavioural Development' *Journal of Child Psychology and Psychiatry*, 26

Rutter, M. (1991) 'A fresh look at maternal deprivation' in P. Bateson (ed) *The Development and Integration of Behaviour*, Cambridge: University Press

Rutter, M. and the English and Romanian Adoptees study team (1998) 'Developmental catch-up and deficit following adoption and after severe global early privation', *Journal of Child Psychology and Psychiatry*, Vol. 39, No. 4, pp 465-476

Rutter, M. and the English and Romanian Adoptees study team (1999) 'Quasi-autistic patterns following severe early global privation', *Journal of Child Psychology and Psychiatry*. Vol. 40, pp 537-549

Sanders, R., Jackson, S. and Thomas, N. (1996) 'The Balance of Prevention, Investigation and Treatment in the Management of Child Protection Services', *Child Abuse and Neglect*, Vol. 20, pp 899-906

Sanders, R. Jackson, S. and Thomas, N. (1997) 'Degrees of Involvement: The Interaction of Focus and Commitment in Area Child Protection Committees', *British Journal of Social Work*, 27:871-892

Scott, D. (1997) 'Inter-agency conflict: an ethnographic study', *Child and Family Social Work*, 2:73-80

Scottish Police College (1991) *Child abuse: the 'Fife' experiment*, Scottish Police College, Tulliallan

Shannon, G. (2000) 'Giving a Voice to the Child: the Irish Experience', *Irish Journal of Law, Policy and the Family*, 14: 131-147

Sharland, E., Seal, H., Croucher, M. Aldgate, J., and Jones, D. (1996) *Professional Intervention in Child Sexual Abuse*, London: HMSO

Shatter, A. (1997) *Family Law*, Dublin: Butterworth

Shaw, I. (2000) 'Evidence for Practice' in I. Shaw, and J. Lishman (eds) *Evaluation and Social Work Practice*, London: Sage

Shine, J. (1998) 'Culturally Sensitive Child Protection Practice: A Comparison Between the Travelling Community in Ireland and the Native Community in Canada, *Irish Social Worker*, Vol. 16 no. 4

Simms, M. and Smith, C. (1986) *Teenage Mothers and Their Partners*, London: HMSO

Singleton, R. (1983) 'How satisfied are we' *Community care*, 461: 22-23

Skehill, C. (1999) *The Nature of Social Work in Ireland*, Lampeter: Edwin Mellon Press

Stark, E. and Flitcraft, A. (1996), *Women at Risk: domestic violence & women's health*, London: Sage

Stein, M. (1993) 'The Abuses and Uses of Residential Child Care' in H. Ferguson, R. Gilligan, and R. Torode (eds) *Surviving Childhood Adversity, Issues for Policy and Practice*, Dublin: Social Studies Press

Stevenson, O. (1995) 'Case Conferencs in Child Protection' in K. Wilson and A. James (eds) *The Child Protection Handbook*, London: Balliere Tindall, 227-241

Stevenson, O. (1998) *Neglected Children: Issues and Dilemmas*, London: Blackwell

Stevenson, O. (1999) Children in Need and Abused: inter-professional and inter-agency responses' in O. Stevenson (ed.) *Child Welfare in the UK*, London: Blackwell

Streetwise National Coalition (1991) *At What Cost? A Research Study on Residential Care for Children and Adolescents in Ireland*, Dublin: Focus Point

Summit, R. (1983) 'The Child Sexual Abuse Accommodation Syndrome', *Child Abuse & Neglect*, Vol. 7: 177-93

Task Force on the Travelling Community (1995) *Report of the Task Force on the Travelling Community*, Dublin: Government Publications

Taylor, C., Roberts, J., and Dempster, H. (1993) 'Child Sexual Abuse: the Child's Perspective' in H. Ferguson et al (eds) *Surviving Childhood Adversity: Issues for Policy and Practice*, Dublin: Social Studies Press

Taylor, S. and James, D. (1987), 'Children at Risk: The changing role of the Health Visitor' *Health Visitor*, Vol. 60, pp 329 – 330

Thoburn, J., Lewis, A. and Shemmings, D. (1995) *Paternalism or Partnership? Family Involvement in the Child Protection Process*, London: HMSO

Thorpe, D. (1994), *Evaluating Child Protection*, Milton Keynes: Open University Press

Thorpe, D. (1996) 'Categorising referrals about children: child protection or child welfare? in D. Platt and D. Shemmings (eds) *Making enquiries into alleged child abuse and neglect*, Brighton: Pennant

Tracy, E.M. and Whittaker, J.I (1990) 'The Social Network Map: Assessing Social Support in Clinical Practice', *Families in Society: The Journal of Contemporary Human Services*, Oct, 461-470

Trinder, L. (1996) 'Social work research: the state of the art (or science)', *Child and Family Social Work* 1: 233-242

Triseliotis, J. (1993) 'Social Work Decisions About Separated Children' in H. Ferguson, R. Gilligan and R. Torode (eds) *Surviving Childhood Adversity: Issues for Policy and Practice*, Dublin: Social Studies Press

Triseliotis, J. Sellick, C. and Short R. (1995) *Foster Care: Theory and Practice*, London: B.T. Batsford in Association with BAAF

Triseliotis, J., Borland, M. and Hill, M. (2000) *Delivering Foster Care*, London: BAAF.

Tunstill, J. and Aldgate J. (2000) *Services for Children in Need*, London: Stationery Office

Wagner, P.J. (1995) 'Schools and Pupils, Developing their Responses to Bereavement' in Best et al (1995) *Pastoral Care and Personal – Social Education*, Cassell: London

Wallerstein, J.S. and Kelly, J.B. (1980) *Surviving the Break-Up: How Children and Parents Cope with Divorce*, Grant McIntyre: London

Walsh, T. (1997) 'The Child's Right to Independent Representation: Developments Arising from the Child Care Act 1991, *Medico Legal Journal of Ireland*

Ward, P. (1997) *The Child Care Act 1999*, Dublin: Round Hall Sweet & Maxwell

Wardhaugh, J. and Wilding, P. (1993) 'Towards an explanation of the corruption of care' *Critical Social Policy*, 13:4-31

Warner, N. (1992) *Choosing with Care: Report of the Committee of Inquiry into the Selection, Development and Management of Staff in Children's Homes*, London: HMSO

Waterhouse L. and Carnie, J. (1990) Investigating child sexual abuse – towards inter-agency co-operation *Adoption and Fostering*, Vol 14, No. 4

Waterhouse Report (2000) Lost in Care – Report of the Tribunal of Inquiry into the Abuse of Children in Care in the Former County Council Areas of Gwynedd and Clwyd since 1974. London: The Stationery Office

Westcott, H. and Clement, M. (1992) *Experience of Child Abuse in Residential Care and Educational Placements*, London: NSPCC

Westcott, H. and Cross, M. (1996) *This far and no further*, Birmingham: Venture Press

Westcott, H. and Davies, G. (1996) 'Sexually abused children's and young people's perspectives on investigative interviews' *British Journal of Social Work*, 26:451-474

Westcott, H. and Jones, D.P.H. (1999) 'Annotation: the abuse of disabled children' *J.Child Psychol.Psychiat*, 40:497-506

Western Health Board (1996) *Kelly – a child is dead*. Interim Report of the Joint Committee on the Family, Dublin: Government Publications

Weston, J. and Colloton, M. (1993) 'A legacy of violence in non-organic failure to thrive' *Child Abuse and Neglect*, Vol.17: 709-714

Whittington, C. (1983) 'Social Work in the welfare network', *British Journal of Social Work* 13: 265-86

Winnicot, C. (1984) 'Face to Face with Children', in D. Batty (ed) *Working with Children* London: BAAF

Wolfe, D.A. and McGee, R. H. (1991) 'Psychological Maltreatment: Towards an operational definition' in *Development and Psychopathology*, Vol. 3 pp 3-18

Authors of Projects

Postgraduate Diploma in Child Protection and Welfare
Department of Social Studies, Trinity College, Dublin

Ahern, Maria (1996)
Development of a format to assist public health nurses in reporting to case conference

Acton, Margaret (1992)
Sex, pregnancy and the teenager

Barry, Clare (1996)
Whither pre-natal care for teenage women in Dublin's north inner city?

Beechinor, Anne (1997)
A qualitative study of the provision of a support service to families in the Southern Health Board

Blake, William (2000)
Child protection – raising awareness

Blake, Margaret (2000)
'I wanted orange ...' how do we listen to children in the provision of child abuse assessment services?

Bradshaw, Teresa (1998)
The school's approach to bereavement and loss in students – needs and responses

Buckley, Karen (2000)
Allegations of child abuse in foster care: incidence, intervention, support and outcomes in one community care area

Campion, Valerie (1999)
A study of knowledge base and experiences of Gardaí in a rural setting in their dealings with child sexual abusers

Canny, Phil (1993)
Schools and residential child care: a co-operative exploration of policy and practice between one residential child care agency and local schools

Carty, Catherine (1996)
The client is given the opportunity to speak

Churchill, Marie (1994)
A study of supervision orders under Section 19 of the Child Care Act, 1991 from the perspective of field social workers

Coen, Mary (1997)
The involvement of parents at child protection case conferences

Coggins, Bernadette (1999)
Public health nurses and child protection case conferences

Comerford, Regina (1993)
The shared rearing project with survey of Traveller children as reported in care in 1992

Connolly, Siobhán (1995)
A review of placements within the EHB centralised emergency carer's project October 1992-January 1994

Conway, Brenda (2000)
A pre-school initiative in a rural community

Coolican, Carol Anne (2000)
What lessons can we learn from the Northern Ireland experience of establishing a Guardian ad Litem service?

Coughlan, Joe (1993)
To identify the role of the staff of the Kerry Diocesan Youth Services in relation to child protection and welfare

Culhane, Helen (1992)
Running a support group for professionals engaged in 'direct work' with children in care

Deegan, Gerry (2000)
Child pornography on the internet. A police response

Delmar, Mary (1997)
The 1995 guidelines on the notification of suspected cases of child abuse between the health boards and Gardaí

Devlin, Rachel (1993)
Review of vulnerable/ at risk families and their management on public health nurses' caseload in Tallaght

Doherty, Mary (1998)
An exploration into how individual Gardaí cope with psychologically/emotionally demanding investigations

Dolan, Pat (1993)
The challenge of family life in the Westside – a six weeks course for parents of young people attending the Neighbourhood Youth Project

Donohoe, Elizabeth (1997)
Discussion document on the future development of Kildare family support service based on an evaluation of key elements of current service

Durkin Boyle, Agnes (1995)
Are public health nurses satisfied with case conferences? Discussion and recommendation from public health nurses in the Donegal area of the North Western Health Board

Dunne, Breda (1996)
Supplementary supervision of social workers in child protection work

Dyas, Margy (1998)
Kids speak about access: ascertaining children's views about contact with their families

Edwards, John (1997)
The Section 20 direction – useful tool or useless toil?

English, Renee (1998)
Children received into care in one community care area: a study of their career paths

Fagan, Andrew (1995)
Strategies for preventing violence by the young people in a residential unit for adolescents with emotional and behavioural problems

Faughey, Marie (1996)
A case study of a special intervention in non-organic failure to thrive

Fegan, P.J. (1993)
Residential child care and parent participation: study of a group in an aftercare centre

Fitzpatrick, Margaret (1997)
Towards a model of group supervision for public health nurse practice in child welfare and protection

Flynn, Patricia (1997)
A study of staff's willingness to report incidents of abuse within a custodial care setting

Fulham, Enda (1997)
Staff retention problems in community care social work: the causes and the cure

Gallagher, Emer (1992)
A profile of the junior chalet population at St Augustine's School

Gannon, Patrick (1994)
Developing a multi-disciplinary training process in child protection

Gordon, Gildas (1998)
Family support workers: do they make a difference?

Graham, Brian (1998)
Overwhelmed or underwhelmed? The response of an area social work team to neglect

Grant-Murphy, Martina (1995)
A study of the process involved in preparing a care plan for adolescent boys in care

Grossman, Barbara (1994)
A study of the process of emergency reception into care for children

Hally, Seamus (1999)
A study of the perspectives of former service users and their carers

Heller, Karl (1997)
Inter-agency co-ordination – a study of the development of child protection practices

Holt, Stephanie (1999)
The role of the lay family support worker in preventing domestic violence

Holten, Mairéad (1993)
Recording in social work: introducing a service user access and shared recording practice in a community care department

Hughes, Deirdre (1994)
The identification of the training needs of Gardaí and health board social workers in relation to the shared aspects of their respective roles in the investigation and management of child abuse

Johnson, Eileen (1998)
Promoting parental involvement in the protection and welfare of deaf boys in a residential centre

Joyce, Mary (2000)
Staff recruitment methods in pre-school day care centres

Kane, Sue (1998)
Staff recruitment methods in pre-school day care centres

Keegan, Teresa (1994)
A study of the factors influencing low rates of breast-feeding among women in the lower socio-economic groups

Kelly, Grace (1998)
The Guardian ad Litem service in Ireland: a service or disservice?

Kelly, John (1998)
Teachers' perceptions of their caring and health promotion roles: possibilities for co-operation between the school and health systems

Kelly, Tara (2000)
The importance of maintaining the cultural identity of Traveller children in settled family foster care

Kennedy, Elizabeth (1999)
Attachment theory: an explanation of its use in social work practice

Kennedy, Mary (2000)
An exploration of the role of male staff working in residential child care

Kenny, Brian (1995)
Day nursery services in Barnardos. An assessment of existing provision and consideration of their further development

Kenny, Hilary (1998)
An evaluation of the child protection policies of IPPA, the early childhood organisation

Kenny, Pat (1991)
Clinical supervision of social work in child protection practice

Keogh, Liam (1999)
Responding to allegations of abuse within a voluntary organisation for people with learning disabilities

Kiernan, Donal (1999)
Conducting research with a view to devising a training programme for members of An Garda Síochána in interviewing people with communication and comprehension disabilities

Killion, Mary (1992)
A study of battered/abused women's perceptions of the justice system, Gardaí and social work service

Kingston, Mary (2000)
The trials of the public health nurse in child protection and welfare – an assessment of legal training and support needs

Lally, Vera (1991)
A study of fostering breakdown with a procedures manual for handling fostering breakdown

Lernihan, Maura (1998)
Towards developing a best practice approach between the Gardaí and health board in the investigation of child abuse in one Garda District

Leyden, Triona (1992)
Stress among public health nurses: a survey and recommendation undertaken in County Donegal

Liberman, Monique (1998)
Assessment of child welfare under the Child Care Act, 1991 Part II, Section 3

Logan, Anne (1997)
Reporting child abuse – some ideas for improvement

Logue, Andrew (1991)
The improvement of methods of recording in Roselawn Day Nursery, Blanchardstown

Lowry, Gerard (1995)
Evaluation of child protection and social work

Lynam, Michael (2000)
A critical analysis of the current child protection policies in the National Care and Education Unit formally known as Finglas Children's Centre

Lynch, Danny (1996)
The involvement of parents/families in the assessment process

Madden, Anna (1997)
How public health nurses make decisions about vulnerable families

Maguire, Annette (1999)
From care to high-support – the decision-making process

Maguire, Róisín (1992)
A study of foster placement decisions made by the Fostering Case Committee, Mayo Committee Care, Western Health Board

Mangan, Breege (1998)
An examination of the necessity for the development of supported lodgings schemes

Meehan, Ann (1991)
Special project on fostering services for adolescents

Meehan Dorothy (1994)
A training day on the identification and management of children at risk

Minogue, Valerie (1995)
Aftercare – the identification of the optimum aftercare service for a residential childcare centre

Monaghan, Gus (1993)
The management of sexual issues in a secure unit: preparation for dealing with child sexual abuse

Montgomery, Kevin (1994)
The training needs of foster parents: the views of foster parents in County Donegal

Murphy, Josephine (1999)
Review of reviews

McAuley, Terry (1991)
Development of case review worksheet

McCormack, Ann (1999)
Exploratory study of supervision orders

McDaid, Manus (1991)
A project in the use of caseweighting

McEvoy, Raymond (1996)
Establishment of a group therapy project for male adolescent sex offenders in the Dundalk area of the North-Eastern Health Board

McLoughlin, Colette (2000)
An analysis of the working relationship between residential care workers and community care social workers

Nee, Laura (1999)
'Where do I go from here?' the young person's experience of aftercare

Neylon, Ger (1993)
An exploratory study of children and their playgroups in Co. Clare

Opgengafen, Ria (1995)
An evaluation of a family support service in the Midland Health Board Area

Ormond, Paddy (1992)
'The Quiet Room': towards establishing the systematic use of a special room at the St Vincent de Paul Child Care Centre

O'Connell, Pat (1996)
What the young people think

O'Doherty, Colm (1991)
Improving access arrangements in a community care social work department

O'Kelly, Val (1993)
Recommendations for the development of child abuse case conferences in a health board community care setting. Based on survey of professionals involved in case conferences at management and field level

O'Neill, Eileen (1997)
A study of access/contact arrangements of children in long-term foster care from the Offaly region with (a) their parents and (b) their siblings in care in a different placement

O'Neill, Sr Anne (1991)
'Safe Place'. A qualitative survey of the use and impact of a 'special room' in a children's home

O'Neill, Marguerite (2000)
Child neglect: a family affair

O'Regan, Nuala (1994)
Evaluating the implications for practice of access under Section 37, Child Care Act, 1991

O'Rourke-Higgins, Deirdre (1992)
A training workshop on child protection and welfare for public health nurses

O'Sullivan, Ann (1994)
Adolescent mothers: a study of the first year

O'Sullivan, John (1993)
The completion of preparatory work with children and parents in advance of child sexual abuse assessments

Pritchard, Anne (1998)
An exploration of working practices and working relationships between a child guidance team and their local community

Reddy, Agnes (1994)
A review of the response of the Gardaí in Kilkenny to domestic violence, and a discussion of the feasibility of setting up a specialist unit within the Gardaí at Kilkenny to deal with domestic and sexual crime

Ritchie, Heather (1999)
Leaving care and after: meeting the needs of young people

Rogers, Antoinette (1996)
The perspectives and practices of general practitioners in relation to the management of child abuse

Ronan, Samantha (1997)
Parents' perspectives of the child sexual abuse investigative assessment service offered by the Child and Family Centre, Limerick

Ryan, Breda (1996)
Key issues for public health nurse in child protection and welfare examined in a pilot project using professional support and supervision

Ryan, Sheila (1994)
Review of foster carers in Kerry

Ryan, Una (1992)
Focus on case conferences

Ryan, Gillian (1996)
Caring for the carers – stress and how it affects the Gardaí when investigating sexual crimes

Stack, Lorraine (1993)
Violent crimes against women and children: an evaluation of the Gardaí's response

Symonds, Marie (2000)
The adoption of institutionalised children: implications for post-adoption services

Tierney, Rosemary (1992)
Implementing a care planning model of practice in a residential care setting

Tighe, Ann
The views of ten young people in the care of the Western Health Board

Underwood, Pauline (1999)
Violence against child protection and welfare staff in the health board and its implications for practice

Valentine, Anne (1993)
Report on a group for mothers whose children were victims of extrafamilial sexual abuse

Walsh, Denise (2000)
An exploration of four professionals perceptions' of 'liaison management teams'

Ward, Fiona (2000)
'There's good in every child' – learning from success

Wogan, Lorna (1992)
The practice of including families in residential work at Mount St Vincent's Children's Centre; professional and parental perspectives